Resources, Regimes,
World Order

Pergamon Titles of Related Interest

Dolman GLOBAL PLANNING AND RESOURCE MANAGEMENT: Toward
International Decision Making in a Divided World
Haq DIALOGUE FOR A NEW ORDER: New Strategies for North South
Negotiations
Laszlo RCDC (REGIONAL COOPERATION AMONG DEVELOPING COUNTRIES)
Meagher AN INTERNATIONAL REDISTRIBUTION OF WEALTH AND POWER:
A Study of the Charter of Economic Rights and Duties of State
Rothko/Chapel TOWARD A NEW STRATEGY FOR DEVELOPMENT

Related Journals*

BULLETIN OF SCIENCE, TECHNOLOGY & SOCIETY
GEOFORUM
INTERNATIONAL JOURNAL OF INTERCULTURAL RELATIONS
LONG RANGE PLANNING
REGIONAL STUDIES
SOCIO-ECONOMIC PLANNING SCIENCES
TECHNOLOGY IN SOCIETY
WORLD DEVELOPMENT
PROGRESS IN PLANNING
*Free specimen copies available upon request.

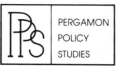

PERGAMON
POLICY
STUDIES ON INTERNATIONAL DEVELOPMENT

Resources, Regimes, World Order

Antony J. Dolman

With a Foreword by
Jan Tinbergen

Published in cooperation with
Foundation Reshaping the
International Order (RIO)

Pergamon Press
NEW YORK • OXFORD • TORONTO • SYDNEY • PARIS • FRANKFURT

Pergamon Press Offices:

U.S.A.	Pergamon Press Inc., Maxwell House, Fairview Park, Elmsford, New York 10523, U.S.A.
U.K.	Pergamon Press Ltd., Headington Hill Hall, Oxford OX3 0BW, England
CANADA	Pergamon Press Canada Ltd., Suite 104, 150 Consumers Road, Willowdale, Ontario M2J 1P9, Canada
AUSTRALIA	Pergamon Press (Aust.) Pty. Ltd., P.O. Box 544, Potts Point, NSW 2011, Australia
FRANCE	Pergamon Press SARL, 24 rue des Ecoles, 75240 Paris, Cedex 05, France
FEDERAL REPUBLIC OF GERMANY	Pergamon Press GmbH, Hammerweg 6, Postfach 1305, 6242 Kronberg/Taunus, Federal Republic of Germany

Library of Congress Cataloging in Publication Data

Dolman, Antony J.
    Resources, regimes, and world order.

    (Pergamon policy studies on international develop-
ment)
    Report resulting from a project of the RIO
Foundation.
    Bibliography: p.
    Includes indexes.
    1. International organization. 2. International
cooperation. I. Title. II. Series.
JX1954.D59   1981   327.1'7   81-11874
ISBN 0-08-028080-3   AACR2
ISBN 0-08-028079-X (pbk.)

Printed in the United States of America

To Elisabeth, Inga and Jan
and the causes to which they
have devoted their lives.

There is nothing more difficult to carry out,
nor more doubtful of success, nor more dangerous
to handle, than to initiate a new order of things.
For the reformer has enemies in all who profit by
the old order, and only luke-warm defenders in all
those who would profit by the new order. The luke-
warmness arises partly from fear of their adversar-
ies who have the law in their favor; and partly from
the incredulity of mankind, who do not truly believe
in anything new until they have had actual experience
of it.

Machiavelli
The Prince, 1513

Contents

CHAPTER 3 - TOWARD STRATEGIES FOR
GLOBAL REFORM: ISSUES, ELEMENTS
AND IMPLICATIONS

CHAPTER 4 - INTERNATIONAL INSTITUTIONS
AND GLOBAL REFORM

Acknowledgments

This volume is the main result of a project entitled RIO - A 'Second Round' undertaken by the RIO Foundation in the period mid-1978 to April 1981. It was a project in which a large number of people have been involved and it is both my pleasure and my duty to record the help and guidance which I have received.

A number of steps were taken in the early days of the project which were to prove very significant. Firstly, a small Steering Committee was formed to guide the investigation. Jim Grant, Roger Hansen and Mahbub ul Haq agreed to serve as its members and, despite their impossible work loads, found time to give valuable advice on how the project could best be undertaken. That advice is gratefully acknowledged. Secondly, a group of distinguished specialists were invited to prepare position papers on some of the key issues to be addressed by the project. These papers were subsequently to serve as important building blocks and to their authors - Silviu Brucan, Harlan Cleveland, Richard Falk, Johan Galtung, Johan Kaufmann, Stel Kefalas, Elisabeth Mann Borgese, Arvid Pardo, Christopher Pinto and Bert Röling - I extend my thanks and appreciation.

The project's interim results, contained in a progress report and background papers, became available in the summer of 1979. Sartaj Aziz, Göran Bäckstrand, Archie J.Bahm, Jan Czarkowski, Elliot Eisenberg, J.King Gordon, Ryan McCarthy, Brian Oliver, Arvid Pardo, John G.Ruggie, Rein and Geraldine Skinner, Jan Tinbergen and P.Verloren van Themaat all found time to comment on them. I acknowledge their contribution and hope that they will find that their comments, some of which were highly critical, have been put to good use. The interim results were discussed at a two-day seminar held in Rotterdam attended by Wim Burger, Al Francis, Elisabeth Mann Borgese and Bert Röling. I greatly benefitted from the comments which they then made.

To my friends at the RIO Foundation who worked under conditions
which were sometimes far from ideal to produce the manuscript I
convey my sincere thanks. Maria Derwort Lievaart, Peet Gerritsma
and Anneke Mohr together typed the manuscript in what must have
been close to record time. Robbert Elshout and Jan van Ettinger
together supervised its production. My debt to Jan is far more
than an organizational one for I recall the many substantive
discussions we have had on the problems addressed by the book.
I owe a similar debt to Peter O'Brien with whom I spent hours
discussing all kinds of questions during the rewarding time
we spent together in Tanzania.

On behalf of the RIO Foundation I gratefully acknowledge the
support received from the Ministry for Foreign Affairs, Sweden
for funding the RIO - A 'Second Round' project. Without this
support the volume could not have been written.

Special thanks are due to my wife Arda and to my daughter Sarah
Rosanne. To my wife for the encouragement she gave me to complete the book; to my daughter for providing the motivation to
do so.

Finally, I dedicate the book to Elisabeth Mann Borgese, Inga
Thorsson and Jan Tinbergen who have set examples of courage
and commitment that most of us can only aspire to. To Elisabeth
especially I acknowledge a deep and lasting debt, a debt which
is in evidence in every chapter of the book.

Foreword

In *Reshaping the International Order*, a report to The Club of
Rome, published in 1976, an attempt was made by a group of
twenty-one personalities from all continents with a good deal
of experience in international cooperation to chart a course
in the direction of a New International Economic Order. The
group examined problems and formulated proposals in ten different fields judged vital to the future management of our
planet. It chose to recommend, as one of the ways to attain
a more equitable international order, a number of 'packages
for comprehensive negotiation'. One of these focused on the
question, considered of central importance by the group, of
finding ways to strengthen capacities for global planning
and resource management.

As a follow-up to this suggestion, the RIO Foundation embarked
upon a project, known as RIO - A 'Second Round', which set out
to elaborate some of the elements of the package. The first
results of the project appeared in 1980 with the publication
of the book *Global Planning and Resource Management*, edited by
Tony Dolman, in which eleven specialists presented their views
on questions related to the development of a planning and management capability at the world level.

The present book is the result of Tony Dolman's attempt to integrate a coherent set of ideas derived from his continued
penetration into this challenging subject. Since the publication of the RIO Report it has become even more challenging.
New storm clouds have darkened the sky of our future. The help-
lessness of politicians to come to grips with stagflation and
the conflicting short-term interests of the many parties involved have added new problems to the unsolved ones of the
past.

1

Our world has become demonstrably more complex in the past
decade. New issues have emerged which, like the environment,
energy and the desperate need for arms control, demand an
urgent response. Fortunately, efforts are being made to integrate into planning techniques the many aspects which confront
us. Building blocks for constructing the needed response are
to be found in a number of places, including the U.N. Secretariat, the World Bank, UNCTAD and UNIDO (in the shape of the
UNITAD model) and a variety of non-governmental research institutes.

Tony Dolman, following a careful but provocative analysis of
the world political situation, comes to reject deterministic
blueprints for change which presuppose the existence of a commanding or shared vision of what our world is and what it
should become. Rather, he advocates the need for a step-by-
step approach to the development of a planning and management
capability, an approach which could contribute to the much
needed process of confidence building.

In the present book he maps out courses of action in four areas
which would help get our world under some form of rational and
equitable control: the strengthening of international institutions; the application of the concept of the common heritage
of mankind - presented as a concept which has the potential to
transform the relations between rich and poor countries - to
new domains; the progressive introduction of a system of international taxation as an eventual alternative to the present
'aid order'; and the international management and control of
so-called 'dual-purpose' technologies, or those which can be
used for both peaceful and destructive purposes. These are
challenging fields in which I share the hope that the international community may yet display the foresight and wisdom
required to make some progress, progress which will enhance
prospects for a more just and peaceful world.

Tony Dolman's book combines breadth of vision with attention to
detail. In it, the reader will find very useful and inspiring
ideas and suggestions for building paths to a better world.

                        Jan Tinbergen

1 Crisis Syndrome: The Passing of the Post-War Period

> In individuals insanity is rare,
> but in groups, parties, nations
> and epochs it is the rule.
>
> Friedrich Nietzsche
> *Beyond Good and Evil*, 1886

GENERAL INTRODUCTION

This book sets out to identify possible ways in which planning and management capabilities at the world level could be strengthened and to examine the various problems which could seriously frustrate attempts which might be made by the international community in this direction. It is the 'final product' of the RIO Foundation's project RIO - A 'Second Round' which started in 1978.

The essential background to the project is provided by the *RIO Report*. (1) First published in October 1976, it reflects the thinking of a distinguished group of 21 specialists with widely varying backgrounds who, under the leadership of Jan Tinbergen, set out "to translate into politically feasible first steps the courses of action which the existing international community might choose to take in the direction of a more human and equitable order". (2) So far published in eleven languages, the report has sold close to 200,000 copies.

Although the *RIO Report* has much to say about problems of national development, it is on the international order that the report obviously focuses. It suggests that there are at least ten areas in which effective and equitable international

3

responses need to be formulated if progress in the direction
of a fairer distribution of resources and opportunity is to be
ensured. (3) The Report contains medium- and long-range proposals
with varying degrees of specificity for each of these areas,
about 100 proposals in all.

Conscious of the fact that such an extensive 'agenda' might
serve to paralyse rather than to promote discussion of what
needs to be done, the RIO Group examined ways of combining many
of the proposals made into 'packages for comprehensive negotiation'. The Group felt that such packages, despite their Madison
Avenue overtones, possessed a number of important and distinct
advantages. (4) Firstly, packages can be usefully employed not
only to demonstrate but also to utilize the trans-sectoral link-
ages between proposals. Recognition of what the Report calls
"chain-reactions" and "ripple-effects" makes it possible to
present proposals in a more integrated fashion. Secondly, packages have a tactical usefulness in that they can serve as a
means for balancing the divergent interests of rich and poor
countries. They provide a framework for devising positive-sum
games. And thirdly, packages can facilitate the process of negotiation. Consideration of groups of proposals rather than isolated initiatives increases the chances of comprehensive outcomes
and the likelihood that results will have a wider degree of acceptance.

The *RIO Report* contains proposals for three 'packages for comprehensive negotiation'. The first of these seeks to redress
gross inequities in the distribution of wealth and opportunity
through a "global compact", aimed at eradicating the worst manifestations of poverty and satisfying the basic material needs
of the world's "poor majority" in the course of a single decade.
The second package groups together various proposals which would
help come to terms with the serious disruptions in the international economic system and ensure more harmonious global
growth. The third and final package aims at putting into place
some important elements of a system of global planning and resource management.

The RIO Group considered its proposals for 'packages' as being
one of the most important ideas contained in the *RIO Report*. (5)
It was only natural, therefore, that the RIO Foundation, when it
came to draw up its first work program in 1977, should choose to
focus part of its attention on trying to elaborate one of the
packages. But which one?

The idea of elaborating the first package - the "global compact"
on poverty - was soon rejected. It was felt that the basic problem it addressed would receive more than adequate attention
both within and outside the intergovernmental system as a result
of the efforts to fashion an international development strategy
for the 1980s. It was also feared that proposals aimed at the

eradication of poverty and the satisfaction of needs were in
danger of being coopted by entrenched and vested interests
which would present them as an alternative to the structural
changes being demanded by the developing countries as part of
their efforts to build a New International Economic Order. Our
assumptions and our fears, as it turned out, were not unrealistic.

The idea of elaborating the second package aimed at ensuring
the harmonious growth of the world economic system was also
rejected. At the time of drawing up the Foundation's work program there appeared every indication that this area of concern
would be adequately covered by the Brandt Commission, to say
nothing of an array of other studies then in the pipeline. (6)
Whether we were right in this assumption is a matter of interpretation and choice rather than of fact.

This left the third package: the strengthening of global planning and resource management capabilities. A subject of undoubted importance, it is of contextual significance to the
other packages and the building of a more rational and equitable
international order. Since the RIO Foundation was initially
established for the purpose of "promoting a widening and deepening dialogue on the creation of a more equitable international
order" it was both natural and appropriate for it to attempt to
elaborate the planning and management package. This became the
project which has resulted in this publication. Through it the
Foundation seeks to contribute to the 'second round' of debate
on the institutions and mechanisms required to increase the
degree of rationality and equity in international relations.
Hence the project's title, *RIO - A 'Second Round'*.

It was realized from the outset that the problems which would
beset the project would be formidable indeed. The field of investigation is littered with booby traps of every description.
There are problems resulting from the very size of the area.
The subject of global planning and resource management is so
broad that there are obvious dangers of falling into the emp-
tiest of generalizations and, on the other hand, of building
analytical walls around areas which are so small that contextual problems are completely lost sight of.

The subject is also one which easily lends itself to flights of
fancy and starry-eyed prescription. Indeed, the very terms
'global planning' and 'international resource management', with
their connotations of 'idealism', are enough to bring a twisted
smile to the faces of those who deify the market. Certainly,
analyses of global problems are bound to be colored by value
premises and ideological orientation. When made explicit there
is nothing wrong with that. But when the canvas is global planning, the analyst must withstand the almost irresistible temptation to paint pastoral utopias in shades of supranationalism
and brotherly love.

Then there are the problems of theory. He who sets out to
examine ways in which planning and management capabilities at
the global level can be strengthened will soon discover that
there is no formally constituted and internally consistent
theory upon which he can draw. No matter how he delineates the
boundaries of his investigation, his approach will need to blend
concepts and theories drawn from such areas as international
relations, international organization and international economics, all of which are themselves the subject of raging academic
controversies as to what is the 'right' and the 'wrong' theory.
The approach selected is thus almost bound to be eclectic,
choices being conditioned by ideological preferences and by
concepts of 'political feasibility'.

The analyst is usually the prisoner of his own background and
he carries the intellectual baggage of his own professional
discipline. However much he advocates the need for transdisciplinary approaches to the study of complex phenomena, he inevitably wears monodisciplinary spectacles which condition his
view, not only of how problems should be tackled, but also, and
more importantly, of which problems should be tackled. The analytical dilemma has been succinctly stated by Abraham Kaplan:
"I call it the Law of the Instrument and it can be formulated
as follows: Give a small boy a hammer and he will find that
everything he encounters needs pounding. It comes as no particular surprise to discover that a scientist formulates problems
in a way which requires for their solution just those techniques
in which he himself is skilled". (7)

Acutely conscious of these and allied problems, the Foundation
sought to expand and strengthen the theoretical and analytical
underpinnings of the project as well as its disciplinary scope
by soliciting the views of a group of distinguished specialists
on some of the questions which we knew would be central to the
investigation. What, for example, are the 'objective forces'
which divide the world's nations and continuously frustrate attempts to strengthen planning and management mechanisms? What
lessons can be learnt from past attempts to fashion planning
and management institutions and how relevant are these lessons
in today's world? How effective is the United Nations as a planning and management body and how, if at all, could it be made
more effective? Can transnational enterprises be afforded a
positive role in the reshaping of the international order or
are corporate structures and the transnationalization of production likely to prove immutable obstacles to the fairer
sharing of the world's resources? How can the legal basis of
attempts to build planning and management institutions be
strengthened? Are there new concepts which have a paradigmatic
significance or which could contribute to a political breakthrough? And what will be the role and influence of 'power' in
all of this?

Ten specialists - Silviu Brucan, Harlan Cleveland, Richard Falk, Johan Galtung, Johan Kaufmann, Stel Kefalas, Elisabeth Mann Borgese, Arvid Pardo, Christopher Pinto and Bert Röling - gave the Foundation the benefit of their thinking on these and related questions. The papers they prepared have been of great value to the project and have been reproduced elsewhere in the hope - and expectation - that others will find them of no less interest. (8)

SOME DEFINITIONS

In our discussion of global planning and resource management we will use a number of key concepts. Some of the more important are defined below.

Let us begin with *resources*. The Oxford English Dictionary defines a resource as "a means of supplying some want or defi- ciency; a stock or reserve upon which one can draw when neces- sary". (9) A resource is anything found by man in his natural or man-made environment that may in some way be used to satisfy his needs and to help achieve his objectives. Resources can be human or physical; physical resources are either natural or man- made. *Human resources* include such things as intelligence, leadership and personal qualities, all of which can be linked to processes of human endeavour. *Man-made resources* are the pro- duct of man's intelligence and his capacity to organize and to create. They include artefacts, techniques and technologies. *Natural resources*, those to be found within the natural environ- ment, can be conveniently divided into *renewable* and *non-renew- able resources*. Renewable resources may be termed *flow resources* for the reason that with judicious use they may last indefinite- ly. A forest, for example, managed on a sustained yield basis, can produce timber and other forest products year after year without the depletion of the resource. Non-renewable resources may be termed *stock resources* and are subject to depletion by use. Oil, other fossil fuels, and metalliferous resources, like ores, are examples of such resources.

Although subject to depletion through use, not all stock re- sources are consumed. Mercury, for example, can be mined, trans- ported, processed, used and subsequently discarded but as much mercury exists at the end of the process as at the beginning. In this context, pollution can be defined as 'resources out of place'. The notion of recycling thus becomes essential to the understanding of resources, especially natural resources. In- dustrial, agricultural and domestic wastes can, through re- cycling, be transformed into a valuable resource. Sewage, for example, long considered an obnoxious waste, is increasingly being viewed as an important natural resource in the industrial-

ized world, although it has long been considered as such in
many parts of the developing world.

The concept of resources is *subjective*, *relative* and *functional*.
(10) Neither the natural nor man-made environment are resources
per se. They become resources only if, when and in so far as
they are, or are considered to be, capable of meeting man's
needs, solving his problems and achieving the ends which he
has set. Because a resource is an expression of perception and
appraisal, it is in essence a subjective concept. It is a relative concept because it can only be discussed in terms of a
relationship to man. This relativity is twofold: the resource
aspects of the environment vary according to human needs and
desires and to the capacity of man to use his environment and
to shape it according to his designs. Finally, the concept is
a functional one since the resource environment must function
in the process of human needs satisfaction, resources thus becoming a function of human needs and of man's capacity to meet
them.

The concept of resources is highly dynamic. It changes with
time, change being determined by man's perception of his needs,
the evolution of his technology, and the choices he makes in
order to satisfy his needs and to achieve his aims. The physical
structure or chemical composition of oil, for example, does not
make oil a resource. It becomes one because man has needs which
can be satisfied by releasing its stored-up energy and turning
it into heat or work and because man possesses the technology
to utilize oil in that manner.

The process of resource creation is not strictly linear. Change
may create new resources but may also result in their destruction. Creating the new may destroy the old. Whereas creating
the new usually means creating the better it may also mean
creating the bad at the expense of the good.

Availability for human use, not mere physical presence, is thus
the chief criterion of resources. For all intents and purposes,
a universe without people is a world devoid of resources. The
point has been succinctly stated by Erich Zimmermann: "Resources
are not; they become". (11)

Availability - the process of becoming - is in large part a
question of *technology*, itself a resource. Any statement on the
future availability of resources, however defined, is an implicit
statement about the development of technology and man's capacity
to harness it in the pursuit of the goals he has set. (12) Technology creates resources. Copper ore is, for example, being
mined today that would have been discarded as waste just a few
decades ago. The technology required to mine seabed minerals,
a vast new source of minerals, is in the process of development,
as is the technology required to turn ocean currents into a
source of energy. Technology we will define in a broad sense

as a system of knowledge, skills, experience and organization
required to produce, utilize and control goods and services
and the tools which we can call techniques. It follows that
countries with an established technological infrastructure and
with the capacity for innovation have a greater capacity to
create and mobilize resources than do countries with limited
infrastructure and technological capacities.

Resources are characterized by specificity of occurrence and by
complexity of interaction with other components of the natural
and man-made environment. (13) They become subject to *management*.
By management we mean the organization of effort to achieve a
particular distribution of goods and services, costs and benefits over a certain period of time among a set of groups and
individuals. (14) Resources may be managed through a *regime*.
A regime is defined as a system of rules and administrative arrangements, together with a collection of institutions, formal
or informal, for the implementation and enforcement of the
rules and arrangements. (15) A regime change can be said to
occur when there is a change in the system of rules and arrangements. Regimes may be national or international. A *national
regime* consists of rules made by a single state to regulate
activities - such as the use of resources - within the area of
its jurisdiction. An *international regime* consists of rules
agreed between a number of states to regulate matters of common
concern. International regimes can take many forms: they may be
incorporated in formal interstate agreements or they may be
merely implicit; they may be highly centralized or decentralized;
stable or unstable.

International regimes are a part of as well as conditioned by
world order. World order we define as a pattern of power relations among international actors capable of ensuring the functioning of various activities according to a set of rules,
written and unwritten. (16) As such, the study of world order
is concerned with the structures of power, authority and influence, types of conflict and methods of settlement used by
international actors in the pursuit of their goals. (17) International actors include non-state actors as well as nation-
States. *Transnational relations* exist where one of the actors
involved is not a government or, more succinctly, where "con-
tacts, coalitions and interactions across state boundaries are
not controlled by the central foreign policy organs of government". (18)

STUDY CONTEXT

The essential context for this study is, we will argue, a world
in deep crisis. It is a multifaceted crisis in which political
social and economic problems form inextricable strands of the

same problematique. It is essentially a survival problematique.
Crisis, we will argue, is destined to become a permanent feature
of the years ahead and the development of a planning and management capability at the world level amounts to the capacity to
manage crises which threaten a catastrophe, be it war - conceivably nuclear war - or human misery on a massive scale. The
world's nations, weak and strong, big and small, old and new,
will be thrown together by the sheer force of circumstances.
The cooperative approaches they will need to find will not be
starry-eyed, shaped by utopian prescriptions and a common view
of what the world is and how it should become. The process will
be painful, messy and full of conflicts and tensions. It will
be nonetheless necessary for there is no alternative which
cannot be spelt out in apocalyptic terms.

Every generation is inclined to believe that it lives in a
period which is historically unique. In a certain sense of
course it does. There are very serious reasons for believing,
however, that the period we have just passed through and are
about to enter involves thresholds unknown in human history.
Never before have so many problems converged in a world so
small, so fragile and so vulnerable to the consequences of the
failure to find answers to those problems. The competitive armaments race, growing inequalities, the struggle for resources,
the disruption of global life-support systems, the structural
crisis of capitalism are all problems which carry their own
threats and dangers. As linked processes they conspire to form
a problematique which, having already surpassed our capacity
to manage it, threatens even to outrun our imagination.

Global problems are a new phenomenon. One hundred years ago
there were no such problems. There could be none for there was
no world system to give them global dimensions. Today we have
a world system which, shaped by the forces of modern science-
based technology, has given us world problems, problems which
demand global responses. In some cases, the demands for global
'solutions' emanates, not from individual or groups of nations,
but from the system as a whole. In such cases the world system
will have to go beyond confrontation in order to prevent a catastrophe which could engulf all the world's nations. A century
ago, British cavalry officers lowered their lances and headed
for annihilation on the battlefield of Balaclava. Today, the
whole world could become one giant battlefield and every man,
woman and child a potential victim.

When history is written the 1970s will undoubtedly be recorded
as a watershed decade. It was the decade that witnessed the
passing of the post-war period. It saw the end of an order
created in the aftermath of the Second World War and based
upon the supremacy and hegemony of the United States. It
brought to a close a period of relative stability and, for
a handful of nations, of unparalleled prosperity.

Was there a single event which heralded the passing of the
post-war period, the end of the Americo-centric world? Was it
the decision of Richard Nixon in 1971 to devalue the dollar and
to withdraw its gold convertibility, a decision which effectively pulled the rug from under the financial and monetary institutions created at Bretton Woods and from which the Western World
has so much benefitted? Was it the 1973 'oil crisis' when, for
the first time since the rise of Western capitalism, a decision
affecting the world economy was taken outside the West? Was it
the forced withdrawal of the U.S. from a country it had laid to
waste? Or was it earlier? Was it the Cuban missile crisis when
the superpowers learnt that their nuclear arsenals could not be
used and that from that point on, in the words of Robert McNamara,
"there is no longer any such thing as strategy, only crisis management"? Or was it perhaps the killing of John F.Kennedy in November 1963. Did the death of a President, a man who, in Alistair
Buchan's judgement, was more mourned than any other leader since
Pericles, also mark the demise of an order? (19) It was all of
these things and much more.

The 1970s were a traumatic decade for the United States, the
world's dominant power. It witnessed the end of the 'American
Century', a century that lasted barely three decades. (20) In
the space of just ten years supreme self-confidence and unshak-
able belief in the American dream gave way to doubt and uncertainty. As they entered the 1970s, Americans saw themselves as
the chosen people, the sole inhabitants of a Noah's Ark, free
from doubt, desolation and the afflictions which beset more
ordinary people. It was an armor-plated Noah's Ark, full of
richness, variety and vitality, symbolic of hope and progress.
In the 1970s the Noah's Ark ran aground and Americans are
still picking up the pieces of what was once their world.

Cherished beliefs were dashed on the jagged rocks of the decade:
the belief that the U.S. was invincible; that it was inherently
and intrinsically 'good'; that its leaders were men of wisdom
and unimpeachable integrity; that it was feared and respected
and revered as a 'model' of what others should seek to become.
Vietnam was to demonstrate that the country could be defeated
and that it was capable of monstrous crimes. Watergate showed
that its faith in its leaders was sadly misplaced. Iran was to
signal the sharpest rejection of the U.S. 'model' in a world
that has grown to distrust and resent the U.S. rather than to
respect and fear it.

The 1970s were, in the words of Richard Holbrooke, a "slum of a
decade for the United States". (21) It was a decade which left
traditional concepts of power and might in charred ruins in an
Iranian desert and which brought forth a library of books with
such evocative titles as *The Retreat of American Power* (22),
The Defeat of America (23), even *America as an Ordinary Country*
(24).

In the 1970s the world became immensely more complex both substantively and politically. Complexity is the enemy of power
politics. Whether the United States can adjust to these new
complexities is, we will argue, a very significant world order
question. Whether, in fact, the passing of the post-war period
marks the coming of age of the United States.

The world will become still more complex in the 1980s. Problems
will become bigger, more intractable, more urgent. As the need
for positive intervention becomes greater, so the scope for intervention threatens to become smaller. The signs are that
deepening crises will further blur the visions of nations.
Their concerns will become more parochial, their interests more
narrowly defined, their time-frames more short-term. Some nations,
the most privileged among them, may seek to escape the crises
which are piling up rather than to meet them head on. But in
turning away they will discover that there are no longer any
sanctuaries, not even for the rich.

As we enter the 1980s there are many rational causes for serious
concern. Many new ones will emerge. Where the deepening economic
crisis will take us, for example, is a matter of grave concern.
Already the most severe in half a century, the signs are that
it will worsen rather than improve. Consider briefly the situation. In the West, the 1970s witnessed a dramatic fall in real
output, a tripling of inflation rates, and the replacement of a
trading surplus with a staggering deficit. The outlook for the
1980s, in the words of the OECD, an organization mandated to
look on the bright side, does "not look particularly encouraging".
(25) Unemployment, around 3 per cent at the end of the '60s, now
tops 10 per cent in some Western nations and is expected to reach
15 per cent by the mid 1980s. Inflation, around 4 per cent a
decade ago, is currently running at 10 per cent and steadfastly
refusing to respond to treatment. Unemployment and inflation
have effectively subverted the traditional apparatus of Western
hope and self-improvement: hard work and saving. As prosperity
gives way to doubt and uncertainty, the economic malaise may be
the harbinger of political and social stresses and strains which
will follow in its wake.

Doubt and uncertainty have entered the daily perceptions of millions of people in the Western world. There is a gnawing feeling
that the good times are over. Polls are showing that, for perhaps
the first time in history, Westerners are no longer sure that the
future will be better than - or even as good as - the past. Politicians, businessmen and scientists of all kinds are telling them
that their standards of living can be expected to decline, that
their aspirations are unlikely to be fulfilled. In the space of
little more than a decade they have been forced, in historian
Geoffrey Barraclough's words into a "growing awareness of the
fragility and precariousness of civilization". (26)

The curtailment of the future is a traumatic experience and like all such experiences its consequences are incalculable. Will the new pessimism and cynicism, the rising tide of discontent and anxiety become a force which can be mobilized for change? Is disillusionment a first step in a process of learning? Will it give rise to questioning which is challenging as well as skeptical? Or will it give rise to apathy and defencism? To increased fragmentation, growing tensions, still further weakened institutions and, eventually, civil disorder? Must the 'new world' be built on the ruins of the old? (27)

Similar questions haunt the future of the centrally planned economies of Eastern Europe. Once believing themselves to be islands of socialist tranquility in a sea of economic turmoil, immune from the evils that bedevil capitalism, they have discovered that, in an integrating world economy, it is impossible to build protective walls.

Their growing trade with the West has inevitably brought debt to the West. The indebtedness of Eastern Europe was around $ 40 billion in 1976. It had increased to $ 60 billion by 1979 and, according to some estimates, could reach $ 200 billion by the end of the 1980s. (28) Poland and the Soviet Union have been responsible for two-thirds of the debt accumulated to date. Poland, an economic disaster by any standard, currently has to devote 60 per cent of its export earnings just to service its mushrooming debt.

Economic recession, rising prices combined with shortages of consumer goods, severe housing problems and, in some countries, energy deficiencies are much in evidence in Eastern Europe and are fuelling political and social unrest. Such problems, Edward Giereck once observed, "keep me awake at night". (29) They were also the cause of his downfall, just as they were the downfall of his predecessor. The same problems no doubt interfere with the sleep of Janos Kádár. He told the 12th Party Congress held in March 1980 that the fat years are over for good and that the future will be one of lean years. Hungarians, he said, must from now on expect slower rates of growth of income and standards of living. Similar messages have echoed around other Eastern European capitals.

If the economic and social situation is gloomy in the West and East, it is one of darkness in large parts of the Third World. The situation actually deteriorated in the 1970s and is now more critical than at any other time in the post-war period. In the words of Amir Jamal, Tanzania's highly respected Finance Minister, "the issue in many cases is one of survival... they could go over the precipice if they are not careful". (30)

According to the ILO, the standard of living of about one half of the population of the Third World actually declined in the period 1965-1975, a decline which is continuing. Even industrial

workers, the privileged few in many developing countries, saw
their real wages fall. (31)   Nationally, economies strained under the growing pressure of rising import bills and oil prices.
The combined deficits on current account of the developing countries increased from $ 31 billion in 1978 to around $ 75 billion
in 1980, largely as a result of increases in oil prices. To keep
afloat, the majority of Third World countries have been forced
to borrow, some of them very heavily. Total Third World debt
stood in 1980 at a staggering $ 325 billion and 60 per cent is
supposedly due for repayment in 1982. Overall debt service, at
present equivalent to 15 per cent of annual exports, is growing
rapidly. Some countries have already reached the impossible
stage where they must spend 90 per cent of their foreign exchange earnings just to satisfy their modest fuel needs and to
pay their creditors.

The prospects for many non-oil exporting developing countries
are grim. A further deterioration can only mean, in Jamal's
words, "political chaos. It means violence, it means turbulence,
upsetting of the order". (32)

Even the 'economic miracles' within the Third World - the so-
called newly industrializing countries (NICs) - are finding it
increasingly difficult to disguise acute economic and social
problems. Their industrialization has been indebted industrialization and much of the debt is owed to Western banks. The
figures are now so large that major defaults could throw the
Western banking system into chaos. (33) The City Bank, for
example, has lent Brazil an amount equivalent to its own capital. The consequence is that banks have to lend more money
under the threat of default and the NICs are forced to borrow
money just to service their ballooning debts. This is a process which has its inherent limits.

The style of their industrialization - offering Western transnationals a cheap and well-disciplined labor force and a high
rate of return on investments of capital and technology - is
also giving rise to growing internal inequalities and social
unrest. Whether the NICs will first crack under the weight of
their growing debts or under the pressure of internal social
tensions is a question which remains to be answered. In an
'economic miracle' even optimism can seem grim.

Economists, one suspects, no longer understand the problems let
alone have answers to them. Their analytical and prescriptive
cupboards have become embarrassingly bare. As one of the doyens
of neo-classical economics has whistfully observed: "I wish
there were some new 'supply-side economics' that could be relied
on to tame stagflation. There is not". (34) Politicians, driven
to acts of desperation, have resurrected monetarism for probably
no other reason than when you pull the monetary lever 'something'
happens. This, they seem to believe, has something to do with

dealing with the problems, even when the solution adds to unemployment and worsens the lot of the poor. It is indeed difficult to image how an economic philosophy which, in the words of its founder, Friedrich von Hayek, seeks to lead the world back to the nineteenth century days of limited Whig government can do anything more than cast us further into the hole. (35)

And the 1980s, we will argue, will be full of holes. Ways in which some of these could be circumnavigated is the subject of this book. It is not particularly optimistic about whether we shall succeed. It is nonetheless well-intended.

STRUCTURE OF THE BOOK

The book has seven chapters. The first of these you have almost read. In it we have been concerned with providing essential background, defining key concepts, sketching a context and setting a 'tone'.

Chapter 2 looks at the prescriptions of 'experts' as contained in a range of world order studies published in the past decade for 'escaping the crisis'. The prescriptions are used to develop a typology of world order thinking based upon the division systems-maintaining, systems-reforming, and systems-transforming. The majority of thinking reflected in the studies can be conveniently categorized as systems-maintaining thinking which argues that escaping the crisis does not necessitate fundamental changes in the institutions and mechanisms which govern the relations between the world's nations. We take issue with this conclusion and go on to question the validity of the theory upon which so much world order thinking has been based.

Chapter 3 is the most lengthy, setting the scene for the chapters that follow. It is concerned with finding ways to manage crises and with identifying the principles which should guide attempts to build a more rational and equitable international order. The chapter has three main sections. The first focuses on the New International Economic Order (NIEO), and its relevance as a global management strategy. The second section is concerned with global management strategies. The essential context for such strategies is first sketched and their key elements then discussed. The principles which should shape the development of resource management regimes are formulated. The third section focuses on the strategies of the rich countries, first toward the Third World, then for national development.

International institutions are the subject of chapter 4. The relationships between such institutions and the development of world order is first discussed. Guiding principles for the development of a strengthened institutional presence are formu-

lated, institutional strategies focusing upon the relationship
between national sovereignty and international institutions,
the development of Third World institutions, and the strengthening of the legal framework. The past, present and possible
future role of the United Nations as a crisis management organization receives a good deal of attention.

Chapters 5, 6 and 7 are devoted to three subjects identified as
key elements of global strategies in chapter 3. The first of
these, the common heritage of mankind, is the subject of chapter 5. The concept, it is argued, gives real expression to the
resource management principles formulated in chapter 3 and has
the potential to transform the relations between rich and poor
nations. The origins of the concept are described and its elaboration within the framework of the Third United Nations Conference on the Law of the Sea is reviewed. Lessons from the
Conference for the development of international resource
management regimes are formulated. Ways in which the concept
can be expanded to cover new domains - living resources of the
oceans, outer space and the results of space activities, and
the Antarctic continent - is the subject of the final section.

Chapter 6 is concerned with the design of regimes for international resource mobilization through taxation systems. The
growth of support for international taxation as an alternative
to the present 'aid order' is first documented and various proposals made for taxation systems are presented. The main requirements for an effective and equitable system of international
taxation are formulated and some of the main taxation alternatives are listed and discussed. The alternatives are compared
with evaluation criteria and conclusions drawn. It is suggested
that taxation systems based upon the concept of the common
heritage of mankind appear to possess special potential.

Chapter 7 is about technology. It argues that it will prove impossible to get the world under more rational control and to effectively manage resources without coming to grips with some of
the questions posed by the development of modern science-based
technology. The role of technology in the arms race and in the
process of development is discussed. It is argued that a promising management response would be one which seeks to regulate and
control the use of those technologies which have a strong dual-
purpose character: those which have a potential for massive destruction and for development through peaceful applications. Six
such technologies are reviewed - nuclear technologies, chemical
and biological technologies, space and satellite technologies,
marine technologies, laser technologies, and environmental modification technologies - and the efforts so far made by the international community to manage and control their use and development are discussed. The chapter concludes with some general
comments on the building of dual-purpose management regimes.

RENEWABLE VS. NON-RENEWABLE RESOURCES

A final note. The subsequent chapters focus upon non-renewable
resources rather than renewable resources. This is not because
the latter are found to be unimportant. Far from it. The question of renewable resources - of the global environment - has
a life and death bearing on mankind's capacity to survive the
next century. The essential point is that this is now widely
known and accepted. It has even been possible to build a large
measure of consensus on what the problems are and on what needs
to be done. In the areas of information, research, monitoring,
and policy important initiatives at the global level have been
taken:

• In the area of information, INFOTERRA has been established.
It collects and disseminates sources of information on the environment. As of 1978 it brought together 87 national focal
points and 6500 registered sources of information, the system
being used about 150 times a month. It is at present the most
advanced operational international information referral system.

• In the area of research, the Man and Biosphere programme (MAB)
has been established. MAB is organized around 14 themes which
are pursued through some 500 research projects in more than 50
countries. It can be considered the most successful attempt to
date at a global research effort.

• In the area of monitoring, the Global Environmental Monitoring
System (GEMS) has been established. GEMS includes climate related monitoring, monitoring of the long-range transport of pollutants, health-related monitoring, monitoring of terrestrial
renewable resources, and ocean monitoring. It is the most comprehensive non-military monitoring system in existence.

• In the crucial area of policy, the world's nations have embraced the World Conservation Strategy. The Strategy has three
main objectives: to maintain essential ecological processes
and life-support systems; to preserve genetic diversity; and to
ensure the sustainable utilization of species and ecosystems.
Launched simultaneously in 31 capitals, including Washington,
Moscow and Peking, the Strategy has so far been adopted by more
than 70 nations. Considering that the 1972 World Environment
Conference was characterized by disagreement and dissension
between the world's rich and poor nations, the wide consensus
given the World Conservation Strategy must be considered a
remarkable, and significant, achievement.

These are all life-signs. (36) Whereas they do not necessarily
mean that anything will be done, they do give expression to the
realization that something needs to be done. There are, by com-

parison, few life-signs in the highly politicized world of non-renewable resources. If the counterpoint to the World Conservation Strategy (for renewable resources) is the New International Economic Order (for non-renewable resources), then there is neither agreement on ends or means. It was this lack of agreement and the limited prospects for progress which led to the decision to focus upon non-renewable resources.

NOTES AND REFERENCES

(1) Jan Tinbergen (Coordinator), *Reshaping the International Order: A Report to the Club of Rome*, E.P.Dutton, New York, 1976.
(2) Ibid, p. 4.
(3) The ten areas are the international monetary order, development financing, food production and distribution, industrialization and trade, energy and raw materials, science and technology, transnational corporations, human environment, arms reduction, and ocean management. Working groups, usually made up of persons from both the 'North' and 'South, were formed to analyze problems and to formulate proposals in each of these areas.
(4) *RIO Report*, chapter 19, pp. 176-187.
(5) This view was generally shared by the 250 participants from nearly 60 countries who attended a meeting held in Algiers from 25-28 October 1976 at which the *RIO Report* was 'unveiled' to the international community. See the report of that meeting: *Towards a New International Order: An Appraisal of Prospects*, published by the governments of Algeria and the Netherlands in cooperation with the RIO Foundation, 1976.
(6) A number of these studies are reviewed in chapter 2.
(7) Abraham Kaplan, *The Conduct of Inquiry: Methodology of Behavioral Science*, Chandler, San Francisco, 1964, p. 28.
(8) The papers are reproduced in Antony J.Dolman (ed.), *Global Planning and Resource Management: Toward International Decision-Making in a Divided World*, Pergamon, New York, 1980.
(9) *Oxford English Dictionary*, vol. VIII, p. 533.
(10) See Erich W.Zimmermann, *World Resources and Industries*, Harper, New York, 1951, chapter 1 (first published 1933). Although written nearly 50 years ago, this remains one of the most complete and interesting discussions on the subject of resources.
(11) Ibid, p. 15.
(12) On the relationship between technology and resources, see Joseph S.Nye, 'Independence and Interdependence', *Foreign Affairs*, vol. 22, 1976, pp. 130-161, viz. pp. 159-160.
(13) See the paper prepared by UNESCO for the U.N. Conference

on Science and Technology for Development, summarized in
'The Management of Natural Resources', *Science and Public
Policy*, February 1980, pp. 43-49.

(14) Definition derived from C.M.Mason (ed.), *The Effective
Management of Resources*, Frances Pinter, London, 1979, p. 6.

(15) For a discussion of the concept of regime and the issues
underlying their design, see: Ernst Haas, 'On Systems and
International Regimes', *World Politics*, vol. 27, January
1975, pp. 147-174, and 'Is there a Hole in the Whole? Know-
ledge, Technology, Interdependence and the Construction of
International Regimes', *International Organization*, vol. 29,
Summer 1975, pp. 827-876; Robert O.Keohane and Joseph S.Nye,
Power and Interdependence: World Politics in Transition,
Little, Brown, Boston, 1977; Edward L. Morse, 'Managing In-
ternational Commons', *Journal of International Affairs*, vol.
31, no. 1, Spring/Summer 1977, pp. 1-21; and Oran Young,
Resource Management at the International Level, Frances
Pinter, London, 1977.

(16) Definition derived from Silviu Brucan, 'The World Authority: An Exercise in Political Forecasting' in A.J.Dolman,
op.cit., pp. 53-71, at p. 60.

(17) See Richard A.Falk, *This Endangered Planet*, Random House,
1971, p. 215.

(18) Joseph S.Nye and Robert O.Keohane quoted in Susan Strange,
'The Study of Transnational Relations', *International Affairs*, vol. 52, July 1976, pp. 333-345, at p. 344.

(19) See Alistair Buchan, *Change Without War*, Chatto and Windus,
London, 1974, p. 21.

(20) See Daniel Bell, 'The End of American Exceptionalism', *The
Public Interest*, no. 41, Fall 1975, pp. 193-224.

(21) See Richard Holbrooke, 'A Sense of Drift, A Time for Calm',
Foreign Policy, no. 23, Summer 1976, pp. 97-112, at p. 112.

(22) Bruce M.Russett and Henry Brandon, *The Retreat of American
Power*, New York, 1975.

(23) Henry Steele Commanger, *The Defeat of America*, Simon and
Schuster, New York, 1975.

(24) Richard Rosecrance (ed.), *America as an Ordinary Country*,
Cornell University Press, Ithaca, N.Y., 1976.

(25) See Sylvia Ostry, 'The World Economy in the 1970s and 1980s',
OECD Observer, no. 103, March 1980, pp. 13-15, at p. 13.

(26) Geoffrey Barraclough, *Turning Points in World History*,
Thames and Hudson, London, 1979, p. 87.

(27) For arguments to the effect that it must, see Robert L.
Heilbroner, *An Inquiry into the Human Prospect*, W.W.Norton,
New York, 1974; Harrison Brown, *The Human Future Revisited:
The World Predicament and Possible Solutions*, W.W.Norton,
New York, 1978; and Ronald Higgins, *The Seventh Enemy*, Hod-
der and Stoughton, London, 1978. For works of fiction which
share the same apocalyptic mood, see, for example, Doris
Lessing, *Briefing for a Descent into Hell*, Knopf, New York,

1971; and Walter Percy, *Love in the Ruins*, Farrar, Straus, New York, 1971. For the view that the present 'age of chaos' is an age of transition to something else which, if not paradise, promises to be much more acceptable than today's world, see William Irwin Thompson, *Darkness and Scattered Light*, Anchor Books, Garden City, New York, 1978.

(28) Estimates of the Vienna based Institute for Comparative Economic Studies reported in 'A World Deep in Debt', *Newsweek*, December 3, 1979, p. 50.

(29) Quoted in *The Observer*, January 6, 1980.

(30) Amir Jamal, interviewed in *D + C* (publication of the German Foundation for International Development), no. 1, 1981, pp. 28-29, at p. 28.

(31) See ILO, *Yearbook of Labour Statistics, 1979*, Geneva, 1980.

(32) As footnote 30, p. 29.

(33) On this see, for example, Patrik Engellau and Birgitta Nygren, *Lending Without Limits - On International Lending and Developing Countries*, Secretariat for Futures Studies, Sweden, 1979.

(34) Paul A.Samuelson, 'Where the Economy Stands', *Newsweek*, April 28, 1980, p. 61.

(35) See the interview with Friedrich von Hayek in *Newsweek*, November 5, 1979, p. 68.

(36) On international responses to problems of the global environment, see John G.Ruggie, 'On the Problem of 'Global Problematique': What Roles for International Organizations?', *Alternatives*, vol. V, no. 4, January 1980, pp. 517-550, viz. pp. 526-549.

2 Escaping the Crises: The Views of the Experts

The fact is that while there is a
great desire to know what the future
of world politics will bring, and
also to know how we should behave
in it, we have to grope about in the
dark with respect to the one as much
as with respect to the other. It is
better to recognize that we are in
darkness than to pretend that we can
see the light.

Hedley Bull,
The Anarchical Society, 1977,
p. 320.

INTRODUCTION

Is there an answer to the crises which increasingly threaten to
engulf the world's nations? For more than a decade this question
has been studied by distinguished groups of specialists around
the world and it is to the various views presented on 'strategies for survival' that we will now turn. We do so with the intention of pulling together the variegated strands of world
order thinking and the aim of weaving them into a richer understanding of the 'global problematique' and of the steps required
to come to terms with it. Given our terms of reference - the
management of the world's resources - we will focus our review
on prescriptions for the development of global institutions and
the role afforded the Third World in the management of the world
economy.

Let us be clear as to what this chapter is not. It does not set
out to review world models or to examine their usefulness as a
policy tool in the 'real world' of decision-making. There are a
number of excellent studies which already do exactly that. (1)
Nor does our review have any pretences as to completeness:
neither with respect to presenting all of the elements of the
strategies formulated in the different studies nor with respect
to the studies included in the review. The guiding principle
has been to include both quantitative and qualitative analyses
made of the global problematique over the course of the past
ten years: to cast the net widely with the aim of harvesting a
rich collection of views which could usefully serve as a basis
for constructing a typology of world order thinking.

The sixteen studies referred to have been grouped somewhat arbi-
trarily under three main headings: studies which fit within the
Malthusian *Limits to Growth* tradition; those which seek to explore the future of the North-South relationship; and a looser
collection of rich world thinking on the future of the world
economy and the place of the developing countries within it.
This division into three groups, it should be stressed, is motivated by reasons of convenience rather than more stringent considerations.

THE MALTHUSIAN TRADITION: THE CONTINUING
STORY OF LIMITS TO GROWTH

In 1971 Jay Forrester, building on his earlier work on industrial and urban dynamics, published *World Dynamics*. (2) In it Forrester uses a computer to examine the relationship between five
interlinked "global sub-systems": population, natural resources,
capital, agriculture and pollution. He reaches the important
conclusion that these sub-systems are so inextricably enmeshed
that attempts to solve one problem will almost inevitably exac-
erbate another. Attempts to come to terms with population
growth, for example, would be inherently self-defeating since
the consequent rise in living standards would serve to accelerate world industrialization and this, he argues, is ecologically
more destructive than population growth.

Forrester characterizes the anticipated decline as "overshoot
and collapse". Whether it can be avoided is seen to depend on
the attainment of a vaguely defined "equilibrium society" brought
about through the implementation of a package of population, resource, industrialization and environmental policies. A central
problem is seen to be impending resource scarcities which, Forrester suggests, could usher in "a new era of international conflict". (p. 70) Physical shortages, however, cannot be viewed
in isolation. Attempts to solve the problem of shortages inde-

pendently of measures aimed at curbing population increases
would, Forrester argues, merely "transfer the pressure to the
social area, resulting in such symptoms as loss of confidence
in government, kidnappings, aircraft hijackings, revolutions
and war". (p. 125) He concludes that emphasis on physical shortages without adequate attention for questions of population and
industrial growth means that "we essentially say we will accept
major atomic war as a solution to the growth problem; when put
this way", he observes, "I doubt that it is a good trade".(p.125)

Proposals for finding a better trade are conspicuous through
their absence. Forrester argues that mankind should seek to
equalize pressures" and be prepared to "tolerate some hunger,
some energy shortage and some revolutions". Only with "effective arbitration", presumably through international institutions,
can war over resources be avoided. (p.125) Evidently aware that
his prescriptions pale into insignificance when compared to his
diagnosis, Forrester notes that "Only broad aspects of the world
system are discussed here, not the difficulties of implementing
the changes that will be necessary if the present course of
human events is to be altered". (p. ix)

Where do the developing countries fit into this scheme of things?
Forrester is not very precise although he does suggest that it
might be unwise for them to industrialize. Elsewhere he anticipates collapse in those developing countries which are unable to
cope. This leads him to counsel the rich countries to dissociate
themselves economically and politically from the poor countries
so as to avoid being affected by the collapse. (3)

The much publicized *Limits to Growth* (4) followed quickly on the
heels of *World Dynamics*. The work of a group of scientists led
by Dennis L. Meadows, the study, like *World Dynamics*, sets out
to review prospects in five areas of global concern - rapid population growth, accelerating industrialization, wide-spread
malnutrition, the depletion of non-renewable resources and the
deterioration in environmental quality - and to examine their
interrelationship. The message of *Limits to Growth* was unequivocal and served to project the study's initiators, The Club of
Rome, into the living rooms of countless homes around the world:
"if present growth trends....continue unchanged, the limits to
growth on this planet will be reached sometime within the next
one hundred years. The most probable result will be a rather
sudden and uncontrollable decline in both population and industrial capacity". (p. 29) A dismal prospect. But one which, the
report notes, is essentially optimistic. Unlike Forrester, the
Meadows' team refuses to speculate on war and revolution. It
does, however, note that if "discontinuous events such as wars
and epidemics" had been included in the development of the model
then these would undoubtedly have brought an end to growth "even
sooner". The report thus concludes that the model used is "biased

to allow growth to continue longer than it can in the real
world". (p. 132)

Like *World Dynamics*, *Limits to Growth* has little to say on how
the impending catastrophe could be avoided. It refers to the urgent need for a "general strategy" aimed at achieving "global
equilibrium", a situation in which "population and capital are
essentially stable, with the forces tending to increase or decrease them in a carefully controlled balance". (p.177) The report does not define the main elements of the required "general
strategy" nor does it have much to say about "global equilibrium" although this appears to necessitate that world population
and capital be deliberately held constant at something less
than twice 1970 levels. It would also require acceptance of the
need to trade certain basic human freedoms such as "producing
unlimited numbers of children or consuming uncontrolled amounts
of resources, for other freedoms such as relief from pollution
and crowding and the threat of collapse of the world system".
(p. 189) (5)

Limits to Growth has virtually nothing to say on the possible
role of the developing countries in the world economy and does
not discuss the implications of no growth scenarios for the
poor world. It is strangely silent on the potential role of
global institutions. It accepts the international status quo as
given: questions of power and changes in the power structure
are not discussed. (6)

On the required transition from growth to global equilibrium,
the report somewhat blandly notes that "we can say little at
this point about the practical, day-by-day steps that might
be taken to reach a desirable, sustainable state of global equilibrium". (185) It makes a general call for a "controlled, orderly transition" (p.188) and notes the importance of "managing" the process of change. "More study and discussion", the
report contends, are required before strategies of transition
can be drawn up. (p. 187)

Given the cataclysmic nature of the message which emerges from
Limits to Growth, the study's parting words - "if we have stimulated each reader to begin pondering how (a) transition might
be carried out, we have accomplished our immediate goal". (p.185)
- can be considered something of an anticlimax and of little immediate value to those policy-makers struggling to formulate
some kind of response to increasingly pressing global problems.(7)

Just as the dust stirred up by *Limits to Growth* was settling,
the second report to The Club of Rome, *Mankind at the Turning
Point*, was published. (8) The product of an interdisciplinary
team led by Mihajlo Mesarovic and Eduard Pestel, its results
are derived from a global computer model which is presented
as a technical *tour de force*: it boasts no less than 100,000

equations compared with Meadows' 200 and Forrester's 40.

Mankind at the Turning Point supports the thesis of *Limits to Growth* that there are a "rapid succession of crises which are currently engulfing the entire globe" and that inactivity and "a passive course leads to disaster". (p. vii) These crises are not temporary phenomena but the manifestation of long-term and deeply rooted global problems. The solutions to them can only be developed in a global context, on a comprehensive basis, through a process of cooperation rather than confrontation. (pp. 143-4)

Although the report expresses considerable concern about possible long-term physical shortages and environmental damage as well as the dangers attached to a "Faustian bargain" involving nuclear energy, it is a good deal less pessimistic than Forrester and Meadows about the future availability of global resources. It does note, however, that "long-term availability cannot be taken for granted" and that the world may again be approaching "an era of scarcity". (p. 85)

The report also has more to say about the North-South relationship and questions of income redistribution on a global scale. It expects the gap between rich and poor countries to continue to widen. Some of the poorest countries in Asia will have great difficulties staying afloat and the report anticipates "collapses" at a regional level "possibly long before the middle of the next century". Growing disparities between the rich and poor nations are viewed as an important source of political tension which could threaten world stability. The widening gap is seen to carry the threat of nuclear war. This, the report argues, makes closing the gap a "question of the survival of the world as such". (p. 57) It notes that unless the gap is closed "there will be a thousand desperadoes terrorizing those who are now "rich" and eventually nuclear blackmail and terror will paralyze further orderly development". (p.69)

How can the gap be narrowed? The report looks at this question in terms of aid and investment flows. The total costs to the rich world of reducing the disparities to 5:1 in the poorest countries and 3:1 in the countries of Latin America by 2025 - the targets suggested by the Tinbergen Committee for the Second United Nations Development Decade - are estimated at $7,200 billion (deflated 1963 prices without interest) over the fifty year period 1975-2025. This could be reduced to $2,500 billion, the report concludes, if an increased amount of aid is provided in the period up to 2000 after which the developing countries "become fully self-sufficient". (pp. 58-63) Under this scenario, the maximal annual cost of coming to terms with the gap is estimated at "only $250 billion".This is still an enormous amount and, although the report notes that it "cannot help but have serious doubts" about the "political will power" of the rich

countries to make such funds available, it argues that it will
need to be found as a matter of urgency. "Ten or twenty years
from today it will probably be too late, and then even a hundred
Kissingers, constantly crisscrossing the globe on peace missions,
could not prevent the world from falling into the abyss of a nuclear holocaust". (p. 69)

In terms of a more general strategy, *Mankind at the Turning Point*
advocates a path of "organic growth". The report makes no effort
to define in general or specific terms what is meant by this
term. The closest it comes to a definition is "functional interdependence" between constituent parts of the world economic system in which regions and nations fulfill a role assigned them
by historical evolution. (p.5) Organic growth is differentiated
growth - growth which is "rich and varied" - and it would allow
all nations to make their own contribution "to the organic development of mankind". "If the world system could embark on the path
of organic growth", the report contends, "the organic interrela-
tionships would act as a check against undifferentiated growth
anywhere in the system". (p.5)

The imprecision with respect to the concept of organic growth is
not compensated for by the authors' thinking on transition strategies. "Now is the time", they argue, "to draw up a master plan
for organic sustainable growth and world development based upon
global allocation of all finite resources and a new global economic system". (p. 69) The main elements of the required master
plan are not defined. The report does argue that recognition of
the fact that we live in a world of interdependent part "demands
that all actions on major issues anywhere in the world be taken
in a global context and with full consideration of multidisci-
plinary aspects". (p.31) The role of international cooperation is
stressed. The solution of global problems, the report contends,
requires that international co-operation becomes a "question of
necessity" rather than a matter of goodwill or preference. (pp.
144-145) The report also calls for a "new global ethic" manifest
in a "world consciousness", the use of material resources, attitudes toward nature and solidarity with future generations.(p.
148) Above all, the report stresses the need for urgent action.
Delays in devising global strategies are seen as being much more
than detrimental or costly. "Mankind's options for avoiding catastrophe are decreasing ....delays in implementing the options
are, quite literally, deadly". (p. 129)

The computer model used in *Mankind at the Turning Point* was not
developed as an academic toy, but as a "comprehensive global
planning model" which can be used by "political and economic
decision-makers in various parts of the world to act in anticipation" of short and long-term crises. (p. ix) It has reportedly
been sold to and used by the governments of Egypt, Venezuela,
West Germany and pre-revolutionary Iran. (9)

Catastrophe or New Society (10) was published in 1976 and constitutes a Third World view on the future of the world economic
system. It was developed as a reaction to the school of thought
exemplified in *Limits to Growth* (11). It concerns itself with
current trends in the world economy and the widening gap between
the rich and poor nations. It argues that the common goal of
mankind in the face of these trends must be to reorient development toward a new society, "more humane than the present one",
and, at the same time, more compatible with the environment.
Unlike Forrester and Meadows, it argues that the major problems
which must be confronted are not physical but political and it
is political obstacles which obstruct the attainment of a new
society. The report emphasizes the scientific and technological
superiority of the rich countries and argues that this has become a new instrument of domination.

The new society the report calls an "egalitarian society". It
is one in which production is oriented toward the satisfaction
of basic human needs, and determined by societal requirements
rather than profit considerations. Ownership and the use of
property and means of production are afforded considerable importance, an emphasis which suggest "a shift toward a society
that is essentially socialist...."

The model describes a world in which consumption is divided
evenly within four regions: Latin America, Asia, Africa and the
rich world. The report seeks to demonstrate how each of these
regions could develop to a maximum, environmentally responsible
level. The importance of regional cooperation is stressed. The
report argues that the regions should seek to pursue their desired goals on the basis of their own resources only - an approach which the report calls "autarky" - and on "regional economic complementarity". Possibilities for trade are not excluded. Differences between socialist and capitalist countries in
the world economy are not made explicit in the model and, in
any event, all countries are assumed to "follow" the same policy after 1980", (p. 43) an important observation, which the report relegates to the place of a footnote.

The report examines an "international solidarity" scenario in
which the rich countries transfer 2 per cent of their income
to the regions of Africa and Asia, a scenario not too dissimilar
to the one advocated by Mesarovic and Pestel. Such a transfer
does not appear to affect the time period within which Africa
can attain the satisfaction of its people's basic needs, and
for Asia it makes very little difference. Much more important
is income redistribution and its relation to economic growth
within each of the regions.

Although developed as a Third World reaction to rich world
thinking on the global problematique, the assumptions in *Catastrophe or New Society* with respect to trade are formally and

quantitatively little different from those used in *Mankind at
the Turning Point*. (12) And although it is highly normative and
prescriptive, the report lacks policy proposals and fails to explore the mechanisms through which change is to be brought about.
Obstacles in the political field, viewed by the study as the
greatest impediment to the attainment of a new society, are nowhere discussed. It has indeed been suggested that *Catastrophe
or New Society*, despite all of its political noise, can in some
ways be considered one of the most naive world order studies
published in recent years. (13)

No doubt such criticisms would be rejected by the study's authors.
"History shows", they argue, that "it is very difficult to predict the process through which social change will take place".
Then, more diffidently, they note: "In any case this was not the
aim of the exercise....The main objective is to demonstrate that
it is possible to liberate society from underdevelopment, oppres-
sion and misery". Echoing the sentiments of *Limits to Growth*,
they conclude: "If the model contributes to mobilizing this will
in the proposed direction, it will have fulfilled the objective
of the authors". (p. 10) (14)

                     THE FUTURE OF THE NORTH-SOUTH
                           RELATIONSHIP

We will begin our review of studies on the future of the relationship between rich and poor countries with *The Planetary Bargain*, a report which emerged from a four week international workshop convened in 1975 by the Aspen Institute for Humanistic Studies. (15) Reportedly representing "the consensus view" of a core
group of workshop participants from France, Indonesia, Iran, Japan, Sri Lanka and the United States, (p. 3) the report's emphasis and orientation suggest that Harlan Cleveland was its principal architect.

The Planetary Bargain sets out to formulate proposals for a New
International Economic Order to meet basic human needs. It advocates the setting of "international floors" under human needs.
The "first floor" concerns those needs which, like food, health
and education, "each person should be entitled to by virtue of
being born into the world". (p. 17) Ensuring that these needs
are met is seen as the joint responsibility of each nation and
of the community of nations. The "second floor" concerns needs
defined by nations for their own people, "within the context of
the interdependence of all societies". The meeting of "second
floor" needs, the report argues, "is the purpose of political
and economic self-reliance and self-restraint, the criterion of
fairness and the basis for international cooperation". (p. 17)
It is a national responsibility to be exercised on the basis of

cooperation with other nations.

The report interprets the major challenge as being one of designing a dynamic international system which meets four requirements:
enables countries to meet the basic human needs of their populations; enables nations to choose different development strategies
yet work together to pursue them; is fair to both rich and poor
nations; and provides for a greater sense of security and predic-
tability in international economic relations. Meeting this challenge, the report argues, requires the establishment of a bargaining process from which it is possible for all nations to gain
more than they lose. "We think it is useful to see the "new order",
the report contends, "as a global bazar in which negotiators are
continuously engaged in parallel negotiations about strategically
related but tactically separable matters". (p.3)

Arguing that much needs to be done but not everything can be done
at once, *The Planetary Bargain* contends that governments should
seek to construct "positive sum bargains" in eight main areas:
food supply and agricultural production; the price and supply of
key commodities; the review and regulation of transnational enterprises; the shift in industrial geography; the protection of
the global environment and the conservation of scarce resources;
the management of the ocean commons; the design of a new system
for development financing; and the reform of the world's monetary
arrangements. (p.22)

The report laments that the world lacks effective mechanisms for
negotiating bargains and for monitoring trends in all of these
and other areas, a situation which is seen as "a sad but instruc-
tive commentary on the primitive state of the present international order". (p. 27) Institution-building must thus form an essential ingredient of attempts to shape a new order. Indeed, the
"planetary bargain", the report's name for "the sum of practical
arrangements for a new international economic order" (p.3), "will
require a period of creative institution-building comparable to
that which followed the Second World War". (p.5)

What would be the institutional priorities? *The Planetary Bargain*
stresses the need for a World Food Council, an umbrella Commodity
Institute, an International Information and Review Agency for
Transnational Corporations, an International Seabed Authority,
and an Environmental Monitoring System. It further argues that
importance should be afforded to the creation of a "capability
for global systems thinking" in the central offices of the United
Nations. This capability should be used to analyze global alternatives, "to catch problems before they become insoluble by peaceful means, to identify new technologies that will need to be controlled and channeled by new institutions to human rather than
anti-human purposes". (p.27) The report further argues that the
process of planetary bargaining would be greatly facilitated by
"extranational bodies" modelled along the lines of the European

Community where national sovereignty is "loaned" to the Commission.

The Planetary Bargain calls for "major surgery on the world's economic institutions" (p. 27) and for "new ideologies of reconciliation" to help overcome "the mood of malaise and mistrust" which characterizes North-South relations. (p.3) Whether this requires or will result in new configurations of power the report does not say. Given its acceptance of the international status quo as 'given' it is probably fair to say that implicit in *The Planetary Bargain* is the notion that neither "major surgery" nor "new ideologies" carry many implications for the present distribution of privilege and power.

Quite different is *What Now*, the 1975 Dag Hammarskjöld Report on Development and International Cooperation. (16) Published on the occasion of the Seventh Special Session of the United Nations General Assembly it represents the collective thinking of a distinguished group of politicians and development practitioners who, assisted by a small research secretariat, met on various occasions in the period January to June 1975. *What Now* is a more politicized examination of the future of rich world-poor world relationships. "The existing 'order' is coming apart, and rightly so", the report observes "since it has failed to meet the needs of the vast majority of peoples and reserved its benefits for a privileged minority. The task is to create another one. This will not be possible without a clear identification of the often divergent interests at stake, without struggle and without eventual transformation". (p.6)

The key to the process of struggle and transformation, the report contends, is "another development aided by a new system of international relations". (pp.7-8) "Another development" is defined as an integrated process built around human beings; it is endogenous and self-reliant and oriented toward the eradication of poverty and the satisfaction of needs. It is seen to depend upon the transformation of social, economic and, especially, political structures at the international and, often, the national level. "The development of each society and a readjustment of international relations", the report argues, "are organically linked: no strategy of change can ignore this". This link, rather than constituting an impediment to change, is actually viewed as a "reason for hope. For, whatever the conflicts in immediate interests, the fundamental and long-term interests of the majority of the world's peoples are not opposed; in fact", the report observes, "it is in the interests of all peoples to curb the existing power structure". (p.8)

Although it goes to great lengths to stress the need for change in the political plane, *What Now*'s power strategies are not always well articulated. It has trouble drawing lines between the need for confrontation and cooperation, between stridency and propitiation. It questions whether the poor countries can achieve much through the process of negotiation with the rich countries. It argues that the struggle of the Third World should be organized within the framework of collective self-reliance, "backed by a potential for confrontation damaging to the industrial economies". (p.70) It also argues that the "international community as a whole has the responsibility of guaranteeing the conditions for the self-reliant development of each society, for making available to all the fruits of other's experience and for helping those of its members who are in need". (p.7)

What Now is certainly right to stress the central importance of the question of power. Yet the concept it uses - "the power structure" - is monolithic and faceless. Whereas it can be used for kicking against, it is a poor basis from which to derive well articulated power strategies. (17) At the international level, *What Now* calls specifically for measures to improve Third World access to basic foodstuffs; the reorientation of science and technology toward "another development"; the redefinition of policies of international resource transfers; the creation of a world authority to manage mankind's common heritage; and the restructuring of the United Nations system to make it more responsive to changing needs and requirements. It goes on to draw up an agenda for negotiation between rich and poor countries in various areas "in which positive negotiations could yield tangible short- to medium-term results". This agenda includes the transfer of basic foreign owned assets to national control; changes in the pattern of production and trade involving a "transition towards a new industrial geography of the world"; technology development and transfer arrangements; financial transfer; and access to food.

Among the most important institutional proposals contained in *What Now* are the creation of an International Trade Organization, an International Resource Agency, an International Seabed Authority, and a World Authority for the global commons.

On the Creation of a Just World Order was another important study published in 1975. (18) One of a series of studies "Preferred Worlds for the 1990s", it is the product of a transnational research enterprise known as the World Order Models Project (WOMP). The WOMP study does not really fit under our heading of 'the future of the North-South relationship'. Its origins are firmly planted in 'war prevention' and it could thus perhaps be better listed under studies devoted to 'the future of the world'. We include it here for no other reason than it deserves to be included somewhere.

The WOMP project sets out to identify "relevant utopias" or world order systems, achievable by the 1990s, that make clear not only the main elements of alternative worlds but also the necessary transitional strategies toward them. The project has generated a number of book length studies which are characterized more by their diversity than similarities. Those involved in the project, however, are said to share five "fundamental values" - peace, economic well-being, social justice, ecological stability and positive identity - which should shape the relevant utopia and strategies for its realization. Commitment to these values leads the WOMP group to argue that mankind will face five major problems in the decades ahead: war, poverty, social injustice, environmental decay, and alienation.

Although interesting for their range and scope, few of the essays contained in On the Creation of a Just World Order are very prescriptive in terms of either 'preferred worlds' or strategies toward them. (19) Richard Falk's contribution is the most elaborated. (20) His "relevant utopia", considered possible around the year 2000, suggests a "dual emphasis on the trade-off between global managerial build-ups and partial dismantling of national bureaucracies". (p. 240) It anticipates a centralized administration of many realms of human activity - health, environmental protection, money, business operations, oceans and the use of space, disarmament, disaster relief, peace-keeping and dispute settlement, and resource conservation - the superagencies proposed exercising competence only in relation to their respective functional domains. Falk describes the main elements of the central guidance system which would be entrusted with general functions of coordination and oversight. In Falk's "preferred world", institutional mechanisms would mediate between concerns for efficiency and dignity, and authority is allocated between global and regional levels as the nation-state system is progressively dismantled.

In his contribution Johan Galtung discusses ways in which international organizations can serve to further the prospect of peace. (21) He affords importance to the development, over time, of a U.N. arms control and disarmament agency, a U.N. space agency, a U.N. space communication agency, a U.N. seabed authority, a U.N. food agency and a U.N. energy agency. The rationale of this institutional proliferation is to help ensure that space, space communication and the seabed are demilitarized, to help see that benefits from the use of the oceans and space accrue to all mankind, and to help secure independent sources of income which could be spent in accordance with agreed United Nations programs and procedures. "Above all", Galtung argues, the institutional build-up should "start globalizing what have so far been the monopoly of the big powers, particularly the superpowers, and what are two of the basic economic resources of all of us: food and energy". (p. 172) Galtung thus argues that future peace in the world is in part dependent upon the formulation of an international managerial response to the problems of food and energy.

A study which fits clearly within the 'future of the North-South relationship' category is the RIO Report, published in October

1976, and now available in eleven languages. (22) Coordinated by
Jan Tinbergen, the *RIO Report* represents the thinking of a distinguished group of 21 specialists from the North and South on
the type of international order required to meet, "to the extent
practically and realistically possible the urgent needs of today's population and the probable needs of future generations".
(p. 1) It defines its terms of reference as "to translate into
politically feasible first steps the courses of action which the
existing international community might choose to take in the
direction of a more human and equitable international order".
(p. 4) Because the original idea for the project reportedly comes
from Aurelio Peccei, the *RIO Report* is published as a Report
to The Club of Rome.

Given its multiple parentage, the *RIO Report* is somewhat inevitably eclectic. There is, for example, a basic tension in the report between the advocates of the 'free market' and of Third
World 'autonomy building' which occasionally comes to the surface. Jan Tinbergen's thinking on optimum levels of decision-
making is evidently one of the report's main integrating forces.
The report has a distinct value orientation - called "humanistic
socialism" - although it is clear that not all members of the
RIO group were equally enamored with this expression. (23)

The *RIO Report* documents the dynamics which are leading to ever
growing disparities between the world's rich and poor. Mankind's
future, the report contends, "depends upon it coming to terms
with these differences, with developing a new understanding and
awareness, based upon interdependence and mutual interest of
working and living together". (p. 23) The present crisis in the
international system is presented as an historic opportunity
for forging new structures from which all nations, but especially the poorest and most disadvantaged, can gain.

The *RIO Report* takes a detailed look at the 'widening gap' between the world's rich and poor. An individual living in the
richest part of the world in 1970 had, according to the report,
13 times the purchasing power of someone living in the poorest
part. This ratio of 13:1 and the trend toward greater inequality, the report contends, "must be deemed unacceptable for reasons of human decency and for the danger of political instability
which they imply". (p. 87) Coming to terms with the 'widening
gap' is seen not only as a precondition for a fairer world; it
will also, the report argues, have a "considerable bearing on
mankind's success in surviving the twentieth century". (p. 88)
Elsewhere the report notes there is "nothing new in the existence of rich and poor. History has known nothing else and has
in part been shaped by the struggles between them. But the rich
and poor have in the past mainly existed within individual societies. What *is* relatively new is the enormous differences
among societies.... these differences will, in a shrinking world,

exert growing stress on already frail international institutions".
(p. 23)

Future political stability, the report argues, is dependent upon
reducing the disparities between rich and poor from 13:1 to about
3:1, the present ratio, "considered barely acceptable, between
the rich and poor *regions* within the EEC". (p. 94) How could this
be achieved? The *RIO Report* contends that this requires a 5 per
cent growth rate in per capita incomes in the Third World, a
growth rate of "only" 1.7 per cent in the industrialized countries,
a maximum growth in world food production of 3.1 per cent a year
(compared with 2.7 per cent in the period around 1970), and a population growth of 0.1 per cent less than the most optimistic U.N.
forecasts. Taking the optimistic population forecasts as a starting point, the same ratio of about 3:1 could be achieved on the
basis of the same assumptions with the exception that per capita
income growth in the rich countries would need to fall to 1.2 per
cent instead of 1.7 per cent. On the basis of these - admittedly
rose-tinted - assumptions, the reduction of the gap from 13:1 to
about 3:1 would take more than forty years. "The question is, of
course", the report asks, "whether the poor are prepared to wait
half a century to attain what is now barely acceptable in the
industrialized world". (p. 94)

The *RIO Report* argues that the fundamental aim of the world community must be to come to terms with the forces which are driving
the rich and poor worlds ever further apart and "to achieve a
life of dignity and well-being for all world citizens".(p. 61)
Efforts to achieve this aim should be shaped by six guiding principles - equity, freedom, democracy and participation, solidarity,
cultural diversity, and environmental integrity - the building
blocks of "humanistic socialism". The report reviews the consequences resulting from acceptance of these principles for development strategies in both rich and poor countries.

It is on the international order, however, that the *RIO Report*
obviously focuses. It makes a clear distinction between strategies of short- and long-term change. In the short-term the creation of a more equitable international order is seen to be mainly dependent upon the attainment and exercise of full sovereignty by the developing countries so that the members of the international community are more able to deal among themselves as
equal partners. In the long-term the creation of a more equitable
international order is seen to depend upon the readiness of the
world's nations to accept a reinterpretation of the concept of
national sovereignty. The need for efficient decision-making,
participation and social control, the report argues, "suggest
a *functional* rather than a territorial interpretation....or
jurisdiction over determined uses rather than geographical space.
Conceptually, this interpretation will make possible the progressive internationalization and socialization of all world resourc-

es - material and non-material - based upon the 'common heritage
of mankind' principle. It also permits", the report goes on,
"the secure accommodation of inclusive and exclusive uses of
these resources, or, in other words, the interweaving of national
and international jurisdiction within the same territorial space".
(p. 83) (24)

The *RIO Report* is in many respects a supranationalist's delight.
It identifies ten areas in which supranational decision-making
is considered necessary - monetary matters, development financing, food, trade and industrialization, energy and raw materials,
science and technology, transnational enterprises, human environment, arms reduction, and the oceans - formulating medium- and
long-term proposals for each area, about 100 proposals in all.
Some of the proposals are subsequently grouped into "packages
for comprehensive negotiation" which have a threefold purpose:
to balance the divergent interests of rich and poor countries;
to demonstrate and utilize the interlinkages between sectoral
proposals; and to facilitate the process of negotiation. (pp.
177-178). The report presents three high priority packages: the
first designed to "redress gross inequalities" (a "global compact"
aimed at the eradication of the worst manifestations of poverty
and the satisfaction of the material needs of the world's population "over the course of the next decade"); the second aimed at
ensuring the "more harmonious growth of the global economic system"; and the third aimed at developing a global capability for
planning and resource management. (pp. 181-185) With respect to
the latter, the report argues that "it is only a question of
time" before the route followed at the national level of ensuring
"greater planning and coordination of diverse economic activities
within the framework of overall national objectives is repeated
at the international level". (p. 184)

The *RIO Report*'s supranationality and its commitment to the notion of functional sovereignty are strongly reflected in the importance it attaches to international institutions. At "the level
of world affairs", these are, the report argues, "the prime movers of planned change". (p. 100) The report's medium-term institutional proposals include the transformation of UNCTAD into a
World Trade and Development Organization, the creation of a World
Energy Research Authority, a World Agency for Mineral Resources
(within the framework of a transformed UNCTAD), a World Technological Development Authority backed by an International Bank for
Technological Development, an International Authority on Transnational Enterprises, a World Disarmament Agency, an international organization to define and implement a regime for the 'international commons', and the creation of an institutional regime
for the management of the world's oceans. In the long-term the
RIO Report calls for the establishment of a World Treasury (to
administer a growing system of international taxation) and, more
generally, the progressive transformation of the United Nations

into a World Development Authority vested with a mandate for "managing the socio-economic affairs of the international community".
(p. 185)

The *RIO Report* is noticeably self-conscious of its long list of
institutional proposals. "While we must be conscious of the multi-
plicity of organizations", it notes, "we must recognize that they
are essential to the "more effective planning and coordination of
the global economic system". (p. 185)

The *RIO Report* was officially unveiled to the international community at a special symposium hosted by the government of Algeria in October 1976. The deliberations of the 200 distinguished
persons who attended this meeting are summarized in *Towards a
New International Order*, a report published jointly by the governments of Algeria and the Netherlands in cooperation with the RIO
Foundation. (25) The report calls for a "global design" which extends "the same opportunities to all people" and provides for the
"rational management of the planet's resources in the interest
of all countries in order to promote the continuing and balanced
progress of all peoples..." (p. 25) The recommended "global design" should serve to institutionalize cooperation between both
North and South and East and West and to "strengthen the individual and collective autonomy of the countries of the Third World".

Although it argues that the long-term interests of the North and
South are fundamentally convergent, *Towards a New International
Order* dismisses planning at the world level as being "premature".
It argues that emphasis should be placed upon increasing the power position of the developing countries through their affirmation
of national sovereignty. It contends that "the harmonization of
international, interregional, regional and national planning could
be carried out more easily within the framework of respect for
national sovereignty while preparing actively the objective conditions for functional sovereignty in a growing number of sectors". (p. 28)

Two important reports on the future of rich-poor relations were
published in 1977: *Goals for Mankind* and *The Future of the World
Economy*. *Goals for Mankind*, published as a report to The Club
of Rome, is concerned with the longer-term strategies required
to come to terms with global problems and, more specifically,
with the goals which could shape such strategies. (26) In their
foreword to the volume, Aurelio Peccei and Alexander King argue
the importance of consensus on the need for and the direction of
change: "If our goals are unrealistic, narrow and shortsighted,
world problems will lead to catastrophes, while if they are realistic and farsighted, new horizons of need fulfillment and peace
can open for the world community". (p. xi)

An ambitious undertaking involving some 130 specialists who worked in regional, national and functional groups, *Goals for Mankind*

sets out to draw up a "world atlas of contemporary goals". It
seeks to identify "the goals of different regions, ideologies
and religions of the world" which could serve to define the
main elements of longer-term strategies of transformation. These
shared goals could "become the nuclei of solidarity for all
peoples" and contribute to a "world solidarity revolution" which
the report sees as "the great imperative of our time". (p. 415)

The report specifies goals which, it argues, are "shared by the
whole of humanity" in the areas of global security, food and nutrition, energy and natural resources, and development. In other
areas it refers to the "shockwaves of worldwide consciousness -
ecological consciousness, population consciousness, exhaustible
resource consciousness, all coming together in a new awareness of
our planet as a fragile spaceship". (p. 416) The report argues
that "these developments help prepare the way for a truly species-
level humanism which may prove to be the indispensable means of
achieving a sustainable, just, and humanely satisfying future".
This new consciousness, the report contends, will help "prompt
serious debates" and thus serve "to head off crises and .....
open new horizons". (p. 416)

Goals for Mankind has something to say on resource management
goals. The most appropriate resource goal of the world community,
the report argues, should be "not merely to make the most of
available natural resources, but to assure an adequate supply
without at the same time aggravating related problems in other
areas of the economy, the environment, public safety and health".
(p.295) It calls upon the governments of developed and developing countries to formulate resource conservation minded development strategies and points to the need for international agreements which effectively regulate access to natural resources outside national boundaries: the oceans, Arctic regions, and eventually space and the moon. This is seen to require a major institutional build-up. "Implementation of world resource management
goals poses the need for a coordinating agency to perform (certain) tasks....Uniform standards need to be specified, multilateral trade agreements concluded, and equitable access assured
to resources on national territories, as well as in the "global
commons". "The need", the report concludes, is for a World Non-
Renewable Resource Agency, "that can coherently perform all the
tasks currently attempted by scores of separate national, regional, and international bodies". (p. 299)

Any discussion of 'global goals' is bound to be characterized by
statements of a very general nature and there are many of these
in *Goals for Mankind*. Discussion of goals must also be deemed
incomplete without consideration of the obstacles to their attainment. The report is also deficient in this respect. Only one
of the report's nineteen chapters is devoted to "the current
goals gap", the "difference between today's goals and the global-

ly required alternatives..." (p. 365) The discussion of constraints and obstacles is highly descriptive and demonstrates
little sensitivity to questions of power and vested interest.

The Future of the World Economy is the title of an econometric
study undertaken for the United Nations by a team led by Wassily
Leontief. (27) It sets out to examine "the impact of prospective
economic issues and policies on the International Development
Strategy for the Second United Nations Development Decade". (p.
iii) Using an input-output model of the type pioneered by Leontief the study first depicts the world economy in 1970 and then
compares it with hypothetical projections for the years 1980,
1990, and 2000.

The 'income gap' between the world's rich and poor in 1970 is
estimated at 12:1. This ratio is comparable with that contained
in the *RIO Report*, although it is arrived at through a different
route. The Leontief study shows that the economic targets set
for the Second U.N. Development Decade - 6 per cent per annum for
gross product and 3.5 per cent for gross product per capita in
the developing regions as a whole assuming an average 2.5 per
cent annual growth of population - "are not sufficient to start
closing the income gap". (p. 10) It goes on to propose a policy of "accelerated development" in the developing countries with
the aim of reducing the 'gap' to about 7:1 by around the year
2000. "Accelerated development" requires "substantially higher"
per capita growth rates in the South combined with rates of
growth lower than those experienced in the 1960s in the North.
The attainment of these growth rates is seen to depend upon "far
reaching internal changes of a social, political and institutional character in the developing countries" combined with "significant changes in the world economic order". Taken separately,
the report argues, these measures will prove insufficient; only
when "developed hand in hand (will they) be able to produce the
desired outcome". (p. 11)

As in the case of other computer studies, the report is silent on
the kind of changes required in the international system and in
national orders "to produce the desired outcome". Such changes
are treated as economic prerequisites and are not given a political dimension. The report does contain a somewhat half-hearted
listing of 'predictable' economic measures required at the international level. These include a faster change in relative
prices of primary commodities vis-à-vis manufactured goods; a
decrease in the dependence of the developing countries on imports
of manufactured goods; an increase in the share of the developing
nations in world exports of manufactured goods; larger aid flows;
and changes in flows of capital investment.

The main policy recommendations can be considered both disap-
pointingly meagre and vague. It has been suggested that they did
not in fact emerge from the analyses undertaken but were append-

ed by the U.N. Secretariat in an attempt to summarize the report and to give it a policy relevance. (28) If this is the case
it is interesting to note that *The Future of the World Economy*
goes beyond arguing that the "economic prospects of the rich and
poor countries are mutually interdependent" (p. 69) to the implicit suggestion that the accelerated development of the Third
World is dependent upon its more effective and complete integration in the world capitalist economy.

Perhaps the greatest value of the study lies in its demonstration of the fact that approved U.N. growth targets and development strategies fail to come to terms with the 'income gap' and
that a 'if present trends continue' scenario will certainly ensure that the North and South are placed on an irreconcilable
collision course.

OTHER RICH WORLD THINKING ON GROWTH, GAINS AND GAPS

The Council on Foreign Relations, Inc.

The Council on Foreign Relations is a U.S. organization with a
membership of some 1700 persons "with special interest and experience in international affairs". A private body that receives
no funding from the U.S. government, its reports tend to be widely read, especially in 'establishment' circles. (29) In recent
years it has been devoting increasing attention to future relations between rich and poor countries. Given its audience it
would seem appropriate to include some of the views associated
with the organization in our review of world order thinking. We
will look at three reports published under the auspices of the
Council: one published in 1974 on the interdependence issue and
two more recent studies on the "politics and economics of relations between rich and poor countries" prepared as part of the
Council's ambitious 1980s Project.

Miriam Camps' study, *The Management of Interdependence*, published
in 1974, sets out to provide tentative answers to questions concerning "the kind of international system we should be seeking
to nudge things toward" during the next decade or so. (30) Her
prime concern is to find ways of managing increasing interdependence which, she believes, "is likely to be one of the central
problems of the next twenty years". (p. 10) Examining the most
appropriate kind of institutional response, she rejects the idea
of deterministic master plans which imply the existence of a
commanding or shared vision in favor of a more flexible and responsive approach which combines centralization with decentralization of decision-making competences. She argues the need for "institutionalized collective management" in four major areas: se-

curity; the management and conservation of natural resources;
the management of the international economy; and development.
"These are not the only areas requiring some form of international management", she notes, "but they seem to me to be the main
ones". (p. 19)

With respect to global economic management Mrs. Camps argues the
need for measures which reach "well down into the domestic area"
(p.90) and which recognize the primacy of the position in the
international economic order of the leading capitalist nations.
Concerning the problem of development, which, she contends, is
"in some ways the most difficult", she argues that the future
of the poor countries is inextricably linked to that of the
rich countries. The concept of 'delinking' she rejects as a
"prescription for stagnation in many parts of the developing
world". (p. 68) Instead, the underlying concept, she argues,
must be that of "one world" and the central task one of bringing
the nations of the Third World "into the global system and to
make them fully functioning parts of the world economy". (p. 77)

A similar conclusion is reached by Albert Fishlow, a former
Assistant Secretary of State for Latin American Affairs, in his
contribution to *Rich and Poor Nations in the World Economy*, published in 1978. (31) The challenge, he argues, is "to amend the
old economic order to make it more consistent with the realign-
ment of international political power that has occured since
1945". (p. 46) The new economic order must recognize the nature
and extent of growing North-South interdependencies. It must,
Fishlow argues, "incorporate seriously the claims of the developing world (for) it is no longer marginal to the interests of
the industrialized nations". (pp. 46-47)

Fishlow argues that the rich and poor nations should cooperate
in the building of what he terms a "moderate international order",
an order to be shaped by two "simple principles": the "joint commitment to extending and making markets more effective (and)
greater participation of developing nations in policing such
markets and in making specific rules". (p. 54) Pausing to reject
Marxist claims that the existing international order is exploitative, Fishlow argues that it is reform within a global system,
not autarky and collective self-reliance, which the developing
nations should pursue and advocate. He goes on to outline measures in three priority areas in which significant progress could
be made to improve the efficiency of market mechanisms: trade,
international capital flows, and direct private investment (including technology flows). Reforms in these areas, Fishlow argues,
would be mutually beneficial.

The effect of these measures? Of making the market work? The new
order, Fishlow conceeds, "does not represent a radical change".
The reforms proposed, however, would, he argues, "create an environment linking interdependence and development and facilitating

both". (p. 82) True, it would not result in a real redistribution of wealth and opportunity. But it would, Fishlow believes,
make possible a world in which the North-South dichotomy becomes
sufficiently blurred to allow cooperative solution of pressing
global problems that threaten the prospects for a just and orderly global community of nations. Many poor nations may not be
quite so certain.

The question of Third World strategies is discussed by W. Howard
Wriggins in his contribution to *Reducing Global Inequities*, published as part of the Council's 1980s Project. (32) After reviewing six Third World options in the area of coalition building - commodity coalitions, regional coalitions, universal coalitions, "association with a major power", and "irregular violence" - he concludes that "the world of the 1980s..... is not
likely to fit the convenient, tidy, and rather nostalgic model
of global bargains or nicely balanced quid pro quos. It is far
more likely that it will be disorderly, messy and punctuated by
periodic disorders and even occasional local conflicts". (p. 116)

The rich countries and international institutions which mediate
North-South relations can, Wriggins argues, be expected to "face
more complex problems than they have thus far faced". To deal
with the complicated and uncertain probabilities which will sur-
round North-South relations, Wriggins argues the need for "specific proposals designed for quite particular situations" in
preference to "generalized policy prescriptions". He concludes
that the rich countries, notably the U.S., will need to make a
much more serious effort to understand the problems which confront the developing world. The emphasis must be placed upon
constructive collaboration with Third World leaders in an effort
to "search out mutually advantageous patterns of interdependence
....laying a foundation of more obvious common interests between
North and South for the future". (p. 117)

And the Third World? Wriggins' thinking echoes that in other
Council on Foreign Relations studies. The more developed of the
developing nations should seek to further their effective integration in the capitalist world economy. The OPEC nations and
the newly industrializing countries will, Wriggins believes,
"continue to prosper. And as they do, they are more than likely
to draw away from the more hard-pressed and less productive of
the Third World states, perceiving their own interests to be more
closely linked to the prosperity and the economic order shaped
by the Northern states than to those who remain behind". (pp.
115-116) Some of those who do "remain behind" can, Wriggins conceeds, be expected to become a thorn in the side of the rich.
There will be nations, he argues, which will "mount irregular
violence against local opponents or neighbors who will dramatize
their grievances by selective action against Northern centers of
power". Given the militarization of the Third World, this drama-

tization of grievances "could well lead to more frequent conflict". (p. 116)

The Trilateral Commission

The Trilateral Commission was founded in 1973, the brain child
of David Rockefeller of Chase Manhattan Bank and Zbigniew Brzezinski. Rockefeller was reportedly "getting worried about the
deteriorating relations between the U.S., Europe and Japan"
(33) and saw in the Commission an opportunity to both patch up
the alliance and to create a high level forum for discussing what
was wrong with the world and what should be done to put it right.
(34) The Trilateral Commission has nearly 200 members including
representatives of the world's most powerful banks, business
corporations, communication conglomerates, international organizations, and research institutes. (35) Its membership reads like
a who's who of the industrialized world and has included Jimmy
Carter, Cyrus Vance, Walter Mondale, Michael Blumenthal and
Elliot Richardson as well as Zbigniew Brzezinski (36) Obviously,
when the Trilateral Commission speaks, the world would be fool-
ish not to listen.

The Commission has published several reports on the future of
the world economy and the place of the developing countries
within it. The main theme of many of these reports has been,
like that of the Council on Foreign Relations, the need to find
ways of 'managing interdependence'. Its first report, published
in October 1973, provides the perspective: "Interdependence is
nothing new... but its present scale certainly is". (37) In a
later report the challenge confronting the Trilateral Commission's partners is presented as follows:

"The overriding goal is to make the world safe for interdependence, by protecting the benefits which it provides for each
country against the external and internal threats which will
constantly emerge from those willing to pay a price for more
national autonomy. This may sometimes require slowing the pace
at which interdependence proceeds, and checking some aspects
of it. More frequently, however, it will call for checking the
intrusion of national governments into the international exchange
of both economic and noneconomic goods". (38)

The effective management of interdependence is thus intrinsically linked to the unimpeded growth of international business.

Towards a Renovated International System is a Trilateral Commission report published in 1977. (39) It looks at the longer-
term future of the Commission's partners and at their changing
relationship with the developing world. Unlike other of the
Commission's reports it focuses on technical questions and at-

tempts to present a "global vision" for the management of interdependence. Although it rejects "detailed plans of action on a
large scale" as being too ambitious and too prone to lead to inaction, it does call for a range of measures which demand much
higher levels of international cooperation than at present exist.
The report maintains that such cooperation is particularly required in the maintenance of peace, the management of the satisfaction of basic human needs, the promotion of human rights and
the safeguarding of the environment.

With respect to the management of the world economy the report
calls for strategies of "piecemeal functionalism" which aim at
keeping issues apart so as to facilitate decision-making. The
management of interdependence, the report contends, should aim
"to minimize the extent and complexity of cooperation required".
This will be far from easy. It is seen to require nothing less
than a "deliberate effort to design the international regime as
a framework of rules, standards, and procedures and to decentra-
lize decision-making and operational management".

The report calls for increased cooperation between small groups
of countries with group participation "guided by the nature of
the problem, the degree of interest in the solution, and the
prospect of success in reaching agreement on a solution". "It
would not make sense in today's world", the report argues, "to
freeze any institutional arrangements into a particular pattern
or membership. Collaboration among nations must allow for, and
even encourage, changes in institutional relationships.... so
that effective decision-making and management may continue". In
this process of "evolutionary change" there will be a prime felt
need for responsive international institutions. (p. viii)

On the question of world poverty *Towards a Renovated International System* contends that advances in communication and concomitant trends toward a global village have given rise to "psychological interdependence" shaped by the rising expectations and
aspirations of the poor and the guilt feelings of the rich. Aid
is seen as a powerful instrument for coming to terms with poverty and it calls upon the rich countries to contribute to progress
in nutrition, health and education through considerably increased flows of concessional resources. Aid should be "conditioned
in such a way as to fulfill (its) purpose" and be closely monitored to assure its efficacy. Noting that there are developing
countries that feel that aid and the conditions applied to it
interfere with their sovereign rights, the report notes that
these countries should simply refuse to accept aid. (p. 28)

The Thinking of the OECD

Following an initiative by the government of Japan, the OECD es-

tablished a research project in 1976 to study "the future development of advanced industrial societies in harmony with that of
the developing countries". The project, known as *Interfutures*,
was completed at the end of 1978 and resulted in the OECD publication *Facing the Future: Mastering the Probable and Managing
the Unpredictable.* (40)

Interfutures is a prospective analysis of mainly economic problems and its results are aimed at providing member governments
"with an assessment of alternative patterns of longer-term world
economic development in order to clarify implications for the
strategic policy choices open to them in the management of their
own economies, in relationships among them, and in relationships
with developing countries". (p. iii) In other words, the report
asks what can the rich countries expect of the future, what can
they do about it together and alone and where do the poor countries fit into the picture.

The *Interfutures* report is a solid piece of work and contains
much which is controversial to both rich and poor countries. As
a sophisticated rich world assessment of the future of the world
economy it warrants careful reading. It paints a dynamic picture
of the process of growth and change, arguing that the transformation which will take place in the rich countries in the next
25 years will be certainly no less than those which have taken
place in the past 25 years. Mankind is seen to be "involved in
an irreversible process of progressive and fundamental transformation which will go on for the next fifty years or so". (p. 278)
In this process of transformation, the issues of the energy transition, conditions for and constraints on economic growth, the
redeployment of industry, the emergence of new values within the
rich countries, and the need to achieve greater equity and the
better distribution of the world's goods both within and between
nations are judged as requiring special attention.

The world described by *Interfutures* is characterized by a global
interdependence "which fuses together the links within and between the North, the East and the South, especially within the
OECD area which", the report notes, "is at present the heart of
the world economy". (287) World-wide interdependence is seen to
transcend the purely economic, having political, military, cultural, social and institutional dimensions. *Interfutures* expects
global interdependence "to grow at an increasing rate". The economies of the rich countries will become increasingly interpenetrated and North-South interdependencies will grow in different
sectors. *Interfutures* does not anticipate any insurmountable
physical limits to growth in the next half century. The main limits to growth and constraints on the capacity to adjust will,
the report contends, be political, economic and social.

Interfutures discusses at great length the capacity of the rich
Western nations to adapt to changes in the world economy and the
international division of labor and expresses concern about various "structural rigidities" - in population growth, the labor
market, state intervention, and foreign trade - which can be expected to seriously impede the process of adjustment and adapta-
tion. Strategies aimed at attacking these rigidities, the report
argues, can be expected to run into various "troublespots" resulting from changes in value systems and the structure of social
organization. The report goes on to outline "general principles"
which should underpin strategies of change as well as various
"specific guidelines which should be used in the search for solutions to concrete problems. The combination of internal constraints and external uncertainties resulting from higher levels
of interdependence leads *Interfutures* to reject the idea that
the OECD area can return to the high rates of economic growth
characteristic of the post war period. The good old days are over
and seem destined never to return.

A piquant detail. Conscious of the trend toward population stabilization in the rich countries, *Interfutures* refers to "certain
demographers" who argue that the younger a nation's population
the greater its self-confidence and its "ability to meet challenges by proposing new responses". (p. 416) There follows a controlled exhortation for the rich to have more children. More
children, the report implies, could mean an eventual improvement
in rich world relations with the Third World. The report is silent on the possible resource use implications.

One of the main 'messages' of *Interfutures* is that national strategies will not be "sufficient to ensure a harmonious evolution
of the advanced industrial societies. It is also necessary to establish new forms of cooperation between developed countries and
between them and the developing countries, together with suitable
management of global interdependence in all its aspects". (p. 196)
In this context, the report observes, "it is in the interest of
the developed countries to devise active and global strategies
with respect to the developing world". (p. 198)

How exactly is interdependence to be managed and what form should
cooperation with the Third World take? First and foremost, the
management of interdependence is seen to call for increased cooperation between the seven rich countries which participate in
the annual 'summit' - the U.S., Canada, France, Italy, West Germany, United Kingdom and Japan - and, secondly, among all the member
states of the OECD. Cooperation is seen to be vital in a number of
sectors which cannot be treated in isolation: the management of
natural resources, the coordination of economic policies, the reform of the international monetary system, trade and industry issues, and North-South relations.

Concerning rich world strategies toward the developing nations,

Interfutures stresses that the heterogenity of the Third World
will be far greater by the year 2000 than is presently the case.
This requires that the rich countries "adopt a multilateral approach in order to take account of the differences in situations
between groups of countries, and a global approach in order to
participate in the gradual evolution of the international economic system as a whole". (p. 199)

The "multilateral approach" recommended by *Interfutures* requires
that priority be given to ensuring that the newly industrializing
countries (NICs) are effectively integrated in the world capitalist economy. The report expects that the NICs will have industrialized on a diversified basis by the end of the century and
that, by that time, some "will have caught up with the industrial nations" (p. 198), i.e. will have a GNP per capita of over
$2,500 at 1976 prices. The population of the NICs is expected to
grow from its present 470 million to 760 million by the year 2000.

The NICs are the central pillar upon which *Interfutures* constructs
its strategy toward the Third World. They are, the report argues,
the "middle class of an evolving world society" and of "fundamental importance for future equilibrium". (p. 400) The rich countries should thus "accept them gradually as economic partners,
on an equal footing" and be prepared to afford them "a share in
the management of the world economy". (p. 281) The OECD Secretariat could, *Interfutures* suggests, "gradually bring (them) into
its joint activities". (p. 401) China will also need to be given
special attention. *Interfutures* expects it to have become "an important part of the world economy" (p. 198) and "a great power
by the end of the century". (p. 233)

The primary aim of this widened cooperation should be to make international market mechanisms function properly. The market is
viewed as "an excellent resource allocation mechanism" and it is
argued that "the only possible solution....seems to be to take
the present system and progressively improve it until it is significantly transformed". (p. 414)

As far as the remainder of the Third World is concerned, *Interfutures* distinguishes between the OPEC group, the "intermediate"
countries and the poorest. The OPEC countries are expected to
stay in line. "These countries", the report notes, "have gradually come to realize that their own development depends upon the
prosperity of the OECD countries". (p. 281) The "intermediate"
countries should be given support for their efforts to develop
agriculture, to get industrialization started, and to develop
their energy and mineral resources.

That leaves the poorest countries. *Interfutures* expects some
1,650 million people to be living in countries with a per capita
GNP of $300 or less by the end of the century. These countries,
the report notes, should be helped "to ensure some degree of dig-

nity for their populations". (p. 282) According to *Interfutures'*
estimates, poverty in the year 2000 will be concentrated in two
regions: sub-Sahara Africa and South Asia. These two areas, the
report argues, should receive almost the entire increase in aid
(an ODA target of 0.5 per cent of GNP is recommended) and "special assistance plans", along the lines of a Marshall Plan,
might be drawn up for them. In *Interfutures'* world, the poor
countries have little role to play in the management of the world
economy: their future is seen to reside in their own hands and
in the strategies they choose to adopt for their own development.
The report does not speculate on whether the two regions of concentrated poverty could ever develop into breeding grounds for
the 'wars of redistribution' anticipated in other world order
studies. It simply notes that while it is impossible to assess
the political consequences of the existence of two large areas
of mass poverty, it seems reasonable to assume that, in the long
run, it "can only be a factor leading to tension". (p. 303)

The cooperation advocated by *Interfutures* is seen to require a
major institutional build up. International institutions, if
they can be kept free from what the report calls "institutional
sclerosis", are deemed "the ideal framework in which to devise
a way of managing world-wide interdependence". (p. 402) The report observes:

"What is asked is not to increase the number of organizations
but to define their functions more specifically in relation to
one another, to adapt government membership to trends in the
world economy and to improve the way these organizations operate,
notably by establishing clearer assignment distinctions as between collecting information, evaluating policies, serving as a
forum for negotiations, managing programmes and restoring to the
executive bodies a real power of initiative". (p. 402)

Interfutures observes that its view of how the world should develop could be invalidated by "breakdowns". Principal among
these could be: failure to make the energy transition (conservation, nuclear energy and coal are the keys); socio-political
instability in the Third World; the decline of democracy or a
weakening of the state in the industrialized countries; and the
spread of protectionism. The risk of a major crisis may not derive solely from the difficulties encountered in a specific
field but is more likely, the report believes, to result "first
and foremost from a conjunction of problems". (p. 96) Faced with
this situation, the report contends, "it is for all governments,
and not only those of Western developed countries, to create conditions in which the most favourable developments can occur, and
to reduce the risk of breakdowns and procure the means of coping
with them if they should occur". In other words, the report concludes, governments should seek to "improve the probable and manage the unforeseeable". (p. 398) Several computer-based scenarios

were developed as part of the *Interfutures* study. Of considerable interest, they can be summarized as follows: (i) sustained
high rates of economic growth in the rich countries; (ii) several
moderate growth scenarios defined by various sets of growth constraints; (iii) a North-South confrontation scenario involving
Third World disengagement from the world economic system; and
(iv) a fragmentation scenario involving the breakup of the rich
world combined with mounting protectionism and the emergence of
regional groupings centered around three poles: the U.S. (with
a special relationship with Latin America); the EEC (with a special relationship with Africa and the Middle East); and Japan
(with a special relationship with the ASEAN group and other countries in East and South Asia).

Irrespective of the scenario, the OECD's share of the world product is expected to fall from around its 1975 level of 62 per
cent to somewhere around 50 per cent by the end of the century.
The Third World's share would increase from 22 per cent to around
one third in the same period, with Eastern Europe moving from
16 per cent to up to 20 per cent. In all scenarios the Third
World's share of world industrial output is around 25 per cent
by the year 2000, being highest in the 'confrontation' and 'fragmentation' scenarios.

Under the North-South confrontation scenario (which *Interfutures*
dismisses as having little "political plausibility" and only a
very slight "economic probability" (p. 314)), the magnitude of
the upheavals are found to be very significant. Although the
U.S. would be "relatively little affected", Japan's growth is
greatly curtailed due to its loss of markets and the difficulties it would have in securing supplies of essential raw materials. Hardest hit, however, would be the EEC. Most affected by
the confrontation scenario in the Third World are the NICs.
Lower rates of growth, however, would in part be compensated for
by improved income distribution. *Interfutures* also concludes
that there could be less malnutrition in the world as a direct
result of North-South confrontation.

In the fragmentation scenario the U.S. is again little affected
and the negative effects for Japan are estimated to be less than
in the confrontation scenario. Hardest hit is again the EEC since
its foreign trade would be greatly disrupted.

The logical conclusion from these scenarios is that the EEC and
Japan should be at the forefront of efforts aimed at developing
new structures of cooperation with the Third World. As far as
Western Europe is concerned the report concludes that "there
can be hardly any other strategy than to take the narrow path in
search of a consolidated internal market, keep open frontiers...,
develop relations with the Third World, and improve decision-making procedures within the present or enlarged community". (p. 400)

The *Interfutures'* scenarios demonstrate that a slow down of growth
in the OECD countries is accompanied by a slow down in the Third
World. The reduction, however, varies considerably between countries and regions. If the rate of growth in the rich countries
falls by 0.5 per cent, so will the growth in the middle income
developing countries, with Latin America being less affected
than the Middle East and the NICs in South East Asia. The effect
on the world's low-income developing countries, however, is very
much less. *Interfutures* suggests that a 0.5 per cent reduction
in rich world growth would probably slow the growth of the poorest countries by no more than one fifth of a percentage point.
The conclusion derived from this by *Interfutures* that both "North
and South can lose by failing in the long-term to find ways of
cooperating" (p. 320) thus seems too general and categorical. It
should be modified to read that the rich world and the NICs stand
to lose most, the world's poorest countries - and conceivably the
U.S. - the least.

WORLDVIEWS COMPARED

In this final section we will compare the studies reviewed above
with three different approaches to world order thinking in an attempt to identify the main directions in which 'specialist opinion' is taking us. We will call the different approaches 'systems-
maintaining', 'systems-reforming' and 'systems-transforming'.
Before setting out to describe these approaches to world order
thinking or to group worldviews according to them, however, a
few general observations on the studies reviewed appear to be in
order.

The world order studies keep alive the tradition of scholastic
speculation on the future of international relations, a tradition
which dates back certainly to Dante, perhaps even to the Greeks
with their concern for the political, social and economic relations between autonomous communities. (41) Although the tradition
is long and honorable it is only in the past decade that such
studies have begun to be taken seriously and their acceptance has
been fitful and controversial. In many respects they are themselves the product of an age of uncertainty and it is the need to
search out new directions which has promoted their acceptance.

Acceptance does not necessarily imply utility. While it has no
doubt contributed to a better understanding of the 'global problematique', world order thinking has yet to prove that it has a
direct policy relevance. (42) Much of the thinking has certainly
been characterized by naive rationalism. 'Relevance' in policy-
making is, however, notoriously difficult to define and it would
be absurd to believe that world order studies could ever contain
the 'golden key' required to unlock the door to a brave new fu-

ture. (43) The world, of course, does not work like that. Solutions to today's problems will not be found in the combination
of intellectual analysis and 'goodwill'. (44)

There are many similarities in the studies reviewed. They all
share a common concern about the state of the international order. There are concerns with respect to growing inequities (in
income, in opportunity, in power, in access to resources, etc.),
to the structures which define and govern the behavior of the
system, and to the substantive problems which must be confronted
(energy, food, science and technology, environment, and so on).
(45) Many studies also express a deep dissatisfaction with present concepts of development in both the North and South and
call, in the words of *What Now*, for "another development". Although the development models proposed vary in many important
respects, there is a general consensus that new models of development should have a strong basic needs orientation. Some studies, notably *The Planetary Bargain*, argue that the basic rationale of international reform is to make it possible for the poor
nations to satisfy the basic needs of their populations.

There is also considerable agreement that the solution of world
problems, however defined, will require a major institutional
build up at the global level. In some cases recognition of the
need for stronger institutions is grudging, in others in verges
on the ecstatic.

All studies express concern - some a very grave concern - about
the consequences of failure to formulate appropriate national
and international responses to global problems. Apocalyptic visions are painted in vivid colors and words like 'catastrophe',
'collapse', 'chaos', 'disaster' and 'despair' are *de rigeur*.
Indeed the Four Horsemen of the Apocalypse seem permanently to
ride over large areas of world order thinking. Some studies save
their most declamatory language to describe the consequences of
failing to come to terms with the 'widening gap' between the
rich and poor worlds. A number of studies contend that the two
worlds are locked into a collision course. And the calculations
in the *RIO Report, the Future of the World Economy* and *Mankind
at the Turning Point* provide incontrovertible evidence that even
with the best will in the world, which there isn't, a 'more of
the same' strategy will be powerless to prevent such a collision.

The studies document changes in thinking with respect to 'limits
to change'. Whereas early world order studies, especially computer models in the Malthusian tradition, saw physical scarcities
as the source of political conflicts and major obstacles to the
formulation of required policy responses, more recent studies
convey the clear message that the big problems are political, social and institutional and not physical. Did we really need ten
years of world order modelling to reach this conclusion, one
wonders?

As a general rule we can conclude that computer studies, especially the early ones, sometimes display a lamentable degree of
naiveté about the nature of politics and the process of change.
(46) Later studies, especially those with a pronounced value
orientation, are much more sensitive to political issues and to
the extreme complexities associated with strategies of change.
Generally speaking, the more simplistic the world view, and
there is a clear link here with quantitative thinking, the more
ambitious is the recommended strategy. Systems analysts have the
tendency to believe that figures and computer print outs speak
their own language. If they do, it is not one which is generally
understood by decision-makers. Certainly, 'decision-makers' have
problems in identifying with and in advocating a vaguely defined
"general strategy" (*Limits to Growth*) or "master plan" (*Mankind
at the Turning Point*), nor are they normally very sensitive to
messianic exhortations for "global cooperation".

Quantitative models much more than qualitative models can easily
become the victims of their own assumptions. There is little
space for nuance or sublety. If it assumed, for example, that
pollution cannot be controlled technologically, as it is in *Limits to Growth*, then you get doomsday results. If you assume it
can be controlled, at manageable costs, as it is in *The Future
of the World Economy*, you get optimistic results. There is an
irresistable temptation to quantify the quantifiable and to conveniently forget the unquantified and unquantifiable.

At face value, many of the studies reviewed are guided by common
value premises. Few would disagree, for example, with WOMP's
"world order values" or RIO's "guiding principles". These common
value premises translate into general world order goals which
could be expected to and indeed do command wide support. Who
would argue with RIO's "life of dignity and well-being for all
the world's population" or with those tabulated in *Goals for
Mankind*. This surface level consensus conceals fundamental disagreements on the problems which must be addressed in strategies,
how they are to be tackled and why. Shared goals do not translate
into common objectives for reshaping the international order nor
into criteria required for evaluating its performance. And even
if broad agreement could be reached, it is characteristic of
strategies that they are unable to simultaneously achieve all
the objectives which are set. There are always basic conflicts
and tensions in a set of norms which govern prescription. In
such cases, the 'right course of action' is never a matter of
fact but always of choice. And choice, as we know, is always a
matter of politics and ideology. Common goals and starting points
can thus easily conceal fundamentally different interpretations
of what is wrong and what needs to be done.

Let us now try to classify the studies reviewed according to the
tripartite distinction 'systems-maintaining', 'systems-reforming'

and 'systems-transforming' in an attempt to discover some of
the basic disagreements concerning diagnosis and prescription.
(47) The classification is not nor can it be watertight. It is
at best an approximation predicated on the belief that each of
the three approaches draws upon the theoretical, analytical and
normative apparatus of different traditions. This leads the approaches to different interpretations of the 'problematique'
and thus to different strategies for coming to grips with it.

The Systems-Maintaining Approach

This approach to world order thinking is concerned with identifying the means for sustaining a system and maintaining its stability under changing conditions. It acquaints order with established patterns of privilege and power and the institutions
which serve and service the status quo. The theoretical and analytical apparatus is derived from such sources as neoclassical
economics, structural functionalism in sociology and functiona-
list approaches to the study of international relations. Its
spiritual fathers include Adam Smith, Durkheim, Pareto, Milton
Friedman, Talcott Parsons, R.A. Dahl and Daniel Bell. It is
inherently conservative.

Characteristic of the systems-maintaining approach is an image
of society based upon consensus, order and the forces that maintain the integrated functioning of its different components.
The ideal order is traditionally portrayed as an equilibrium.
The approach castigates attempts which might be made by the
state or international bodies to regulate 'natural' processes
and contends that such interference, despite the goodness of
the underlying intentions, will upset the desired equilibrium
and its balance of functions in unpredictable ways. Intervention can only result in a reduction of overall levels of welfare and serves to impede rather than enhance the adaptive evolution of the system. The market mechanism is deified. It is uncritically accepted as the only possible resource allocation
mechanism.

In terms of international relations, different breeds of systems maintainers can be identified:

● *Isolationists*: Isolationists seek to restore the tradition of
rich world detachment from geopolitical concerns. Although it
was an Englishman, Lord Salisbury, who declared nearly 100 years
ago that it was Britain's duty to pursue its policies in "splen-
did isolation", isolationists, as a breed, are mainly found today in the United States. The policy recommendations which emerge
from world order thinking are, however, sometimes addressed to
them: remember Forrester advises the rich countries to keep away
from the Third World because it could pull them under when it

goes down.

● *Imperialists*: Imperialists are those who, in the words of
Richard Falk, "identify various categories of barbarians at the
gates and seek to bar their entry". (48) They are attracted to
such concepts as 'lifeboats' and 'triage'. They stress the importance of military power and tend to confuse 'might' with
'right'. Imperialists are critical of attempts to appease the
developing countries, the leaders of which are seen to be abus-
ing the rich countries in their desparate efforts to find an
external scapegoat for their miserable failures on the home
front. The imperialists attitude to the Third World has been
neatly summarized in an editorial in the *Wall Street Journal*,
the voice of Western capitalism. Addressing itself to the Third
World it warned: "Don't expect (us) to serve you up prosperity
and don't think you can get it through extortion". And along the
same lines: "If the Third World countries want to be rich like
us, they might try doing a few things our way". (49)

● *Managers*: Systems-maintaining managers are those who recognize
that the world does not stand still and that the future of the
rich countries is dependent upon them striking a series of bargains around those issues which challenge the system by disturb-
ing the status quo or by threatening to throw it into chaos. The
key expression is 'the management of interdependence' and it has
been much in evidence in our review of world order thinking.

The managers believe that the post-war economic order has "served the world well" but recognize that it has in some respects
become deficient and is in need of repair. The main cause of the
disruption is viewed in terms of difficulties within the rich
world - mainly between the Trilateral partners - and not, or
very much less so, between the rich countries and the Third World.
Since the solution to some of the problems is seen to reside in
higher levels of cooperation, such cooperation is first sought
among the dominant Western powers, especially the 'locomotives
of growth', and then the rich world as a whole, thinking exemplified by *Interfutures*.

The manager's ideal is a fully integrated world economy. This
vision requires that the Third World, especially the few nations
with a capacity for disruption, be 'fitted in'. The developing
countries are seen to have no other future than one which organically links them to the capitalist world economy. Even the interests of the poorest of the poor, the managers argue, will be better served by such an association. (50) Managers go so far as to
argue that it is the duty of the poor countries to seek more effective integration, to eschew disruptive action, to contribute
to the growth and expansion of the world economic system for, in
the words of Fishlow, "there can be no basis for repayment of accumulated debt, no assurance of efficient industrialization, no
guarantee of greater production of foodstuffs and raw materials

unless an expanding and competitive market in the industrialized
nations is assured". (51)

Interdependence managers are keen to stress the diversity within
the Third World. They advocate policies toward it based upon 'differentiation', policies geared to worlds within the Third World.
The prime concern of this differentiated approach has been to
find a basis for accommodation with the OPEC group. Most managers
now seem to subscribe to the view that the group has come to learn
which side its bread is buttered and no longer constitutes a
threat. As *Interfutures* noted, the OPEC countries "have gradually
come to realize that their own development depends upon the prosperity of the OECD countries". The main emphasis today is on integrating a handful of NICs into the world economy. These countries are seen, again to quote from *Interfutures*, as the "middle
class of an evolving world society" and of being of "fundamental
importance for future equilibrium".

In the manager's scheme of thinking, the NICs are allowed to develop into regional hegemonic powers and function as citadels of
Western capitalism in their own universe of want and deprivation.

Transnational corporations are regarded as the embodiment of an
interdependent world economy dominated by the rich capitalist nations. Not surprisingly, the attitude of systems-maintainers to
international business ranges from congeniality to idolatry, the
latter characterized by Moynihan's observation that transnational
corporations are "arguably the most creative international institutions of the twentieth century". (52)

Systems-maintaining managers search for 'efficient' technical and
functional solutions to world problems. They worship at the altar
of economic growth and measure success in GNP increases. They disregard or downplay political issues. These only become relevant
when and to the extent that they pose managerial challenges. And
when they become too intractable, when they refuse to succomb to
technical and functional logic, the manager readily discovers that
his imperialist bretheren are only too prepared to take up the matter further.

The management of interdependence is seen to call for new arrangements around those problems in which the 'hidden hand' remains
permanently invisible and which threaten the status quo. The challenge, in the worlds of Daniel Bell, is "to design effective international instruments - in the monetary, commodity, trade, and
technology areas - to effect the necessary transition to a new
international division of labor that can provide for economic and,
perhaps, political stability". (53) Innate conservatism and the
strong mercantilist tradition in the systems-maintaining approach
which insists that greater emphasis be placed on national political and economic objectives than on considerations of global economic efficiency mean that this challenge cannot easily be met.

The insistence of the NICs that comparative advantage should also
be allowed to apply to them also does not help much.

The search for solutions is kept alive by the fear that the world
economic system, a system which has been so bountiful, could unravel, producing grave domestic crises and international conflicts
which could get so out of hand that they plunge the whole system
into chaos. In a world which is armed to the teeth, a plunge into
chaos could easily mean a plunge over the nuclear precipice. As
we have seen, a large number of world order studies have found it
necessary to speculate on this eventuality.

The Systems-Reforming Approach

This approach reflects the realization that structural modifications over a broad number of issues will be required in response to new problems and changing geopolitical realities. These
modifications, however, are not seen to be so fundamental as to
require or to result in a basic reordering of established power
configurations. Unlike systems-maintainers, reformers characteristically stress the problems rather than the advantages resulting from established patterns of privilege and power. Instead of
beating the drum for free trade and *laissez-faire*, for example,
they argue the need to 'correct' and 'augment' market mechanisms.

The approach is sustained by and can draw upon a long tradition
of reformist thinking from religious and secular fields. Humani-
tarianism, christianity and socialism are all tributaries which
have fed the flow of reformism. The sources are so diverse that
attempts to list the spiritual fathers of the tradition can easily degenerate into a pointless exercise. The social sciences
alone have contributed so many stars to the reformist firmament
that it is difficult to list the names of those who have most il-
luminated the tradition. If restricted to the recent past, however, such a list would certainly include John Kenneth Galbraith,
Gunnar Myrdal, Jan Tinbergen, Celso Furtado and Ralf Dahrendorf.

The ideal world of the systems reformer is a mixed economy with
regulating agencies (the state or 'democratic' international institutions) playing the role of arbiter in social and economic
conflicts. Whereas systems-maintainers tend to regard conflict
as "deviant behavior" or an illness to be treated, (54) reformists
recognize it as a basic consequence of pluralistic systems and
divergent interests and seek to provide dispute settlement procedures in an effort to ensure that such conflicts are contained.

At the level of international relations, reformists are much more
sensitive to the grievances of the Third World, grievances which
are perceived to be just and which need to be taken seriously.
The tone of the reformer is accommodating and propitiatory, his
goal one of seeking to effect a reconciliation between the 'legi-

timate' interests of the rich and poor countries and the collective needs of the planet as a whole. The reformer is the guardian of the interests of the unborn. He has many constituencies and talks in terms of 'mutual interest', 'positive sum games' and the exercise of 'enlightened self-interest', the need to sacrifice today in order to safeguard tomorrow. The frame of reference is long enough to fall beyond current contexts of choice and expedient definitions of political feasibility but short enough to engage the normative receptivities of outward looking policymakers.

While firmly predicated on the primacy of the nation-state, reformist thinking has firm global aspirations. As in the case of some systems-maintaining thinking, the emphasis is managerial, only more so. More so leads to a greater stress on the potential role of international institutions - the "prime movers of change" as the *RIO Report* calls them - in the complex process of reform. Systems-reformers seek to use existing institutional mechanisms - although when in doubt they do not hesitate to suggest the creation of new ones - for directing change in deliberate ways with the intention of institutionalizing fundamental values and of maximizing welfare. The reformers faith in the ability of mankind to make something of the United Nations borders on the demonic.

Systems reformers are critical yet basically friendly toward such phenomena as the transnational corporation. They acknowledge that some activities of big business in the developing world have been injurious and disruptive, guided by motives which are too narrowly defined, but nurture the belief that transnationals, with judicious encouragement and a little coercion, "can play a positive role in improving the living conditions of the poor masses in the Third World". (55)

For all their good intentions, reformers traditionally underestimate the influence of power on the probability of positive outcomes as well as the depths of antagonisms between the world's nations and the durability and robustness of the structures - cognitive and social - which maintain them. They are also prone to exaggerate the negotiability of the 'planetary agenda' and they presuppose the efficacy of moderation and the spirit of compromise. They are prevented from seeing the dark corners of world order by the stars in their eyes. They cling to hope that justice must prevail over injustice and have confidence in the exercise of reason and in the spirit of reasonableness. When their confidence is shaken, as indeed it often is, they resort to stressing the 'power of ideas' and the need to 'educate public opinion'.

The Systems-Transforming Approach

This approach is predicated upon the belief that the cause of the

world's predicament is deeply rooted in the structures which determine and legitimize the operation of the social and economic
system and that the only hope for the future lies in the transformation of these structures.

There are two main types of systems-transformers. The most important are those of the 'radical left', the representatives of
the Marxist and neo-Marxist traditions. These - for want of a
better word we will call them the radicals - stress the dialectical interplay between ideology and social relations. They do not
view change as an evolutionary or natural process but rather as
being conditioned by the interests of dominant and powerful
classes. Peoples' consciousness is conditioned by their milieu
and position in society. The social system, however, is seen to
be characterized by basic contradictions without which the system could not exist. These contradictions offer potential for
the development of a revolutionary consciousness which is the
motive force for the process of transformation. The radical tradition draws heavily upon the Marxist paradigm and is represented by such social scientists as Ernest Mandel, Samir Amin, Andre
Gunder Frank, Herbert Marcuse and Perry Anderson.

The second school of systems-transformers can be termed the
'supranationalists' or 'superreformers'. (56) They see today's
predicament as being rooted in an archaic system of antagonistic
nation-states, the prerogatives of which are being increasingly
eroded by powerful economic and technological forces. Mankind
is viewed as a whole rather than as a collection of autonomous
political units and although cultural and political differences
are recognized, increasing social interdependence is seen to have
virtually eliminated the ability of one government to live and
act in isolation from others. More than any other tradition, they
invoke the analogy of 'spaceship earth' and 'global village' to
illustrate the dangers to which a shrinking and highly vulnerable
planet is exposed. (57)

Supranationalists stress that the economic and technological forces
are irresistible and are pressing for world integration. These
forces, they believe, will eventually predominate over the political and make essential some form of world governments or, at
least a world institution which, in the words of Marxist Silviu
Brucan, is "vested with the authority to plan, to make decisions,
and to enforce them". (59) Supranationalists argue that the main
contours of a global community are already clearly discernable
and that global governance cannot be far behind. Global governance
is not a choice but rather an objective necessity which will be
forced upon mankind by the pressure of events. It will come whether
we like it or not. In the words of Saul Mendlovitz, director of
the World Order Models Project: "It is my considered judgement
that there is no longer a question of whether or not there will
be world government by the year 2000. As I see it the questions

we should be addressing at ourselves are: how it will come into
being - by cataclysm, drift, more or less rational design - and
whether it will be totalitarian, benignly elitist, or partici-
patory (the probabilities being in that order)". (59)

In terms of rich-poor relations whereas the radicals emphasize
the need for Third World autonomy-building, the supranationalists
argue that the North-South distinction has become or is rapidly
becoming obsolete and that the only framework - theoretical, analytical, normative - is 'one-worldism'.

Both radicals and supranationalists are highly sceptical about
mankind's ability to shape the kinds of international institutions which can help steer the world out of crisis. The radicals
contend that there is little or nothing which the poor can gain
from negotiations with the rich and they view the United Nations
as deeply conservative, Western dominated, and unresponsive to
the needs of the poor. The supranationalists despair of a world
committed to the nation-state and, at a time when super-strong
international institutions are desparately required, see the
United Nations as so ineffective and powerless that the only
sensible thing to do is to 'start again' with a fresh sheet of
paper. Gloom prevails in the worlds of both radicals and supranationalists. The radicals are sustained by a deep sense of outrage, the supranationalists by an optimism born out of the belief
that when it has exhausted all other possibilities, mankind must
surely resort to the rational.

The greatest weakness of the systems-transformers is their inability to mobilize widespread support partly because they are unable to depict a credible transition process - how do you go
about overthrowing capitalism or building world government - and
partly because those with vested interests in the status quo are
able to shape, or at least confuse, public opinion on prospects
for and the effects of a transition. Both groups are left to
preach to the converted. Moreover, their insistence on structural
change alienates them from public opinion and the policy-making
mainstream, both of which are inherently conservative, overwhelm-
ingly gradualist and intolerant and fearful of things which smack
of 'extremism'.

Classification of Studies; Conclusions

Let us now compare the world order studies reviewed with the three
approaches to world order thinking outlined above. Such a comparison is attempted in the illustration. Here studies are plotted
along two axes: the three approaches together represented as a
continuum running from systems-maintenace through systems-reform
to systems-transformation; and a time scale for indicating the
year in which the studies were published. Studies are indicated

with the letter C to denote computer studies and the letter N
to indicate more normative, non-mathematical thinking. It is
recognized that the continuum presentation of world order approaches is deficient in one important respect: there is a dis-
crete difference between approaches which call for the maintenance or reform of a system and one which demands the creation
of something 'new'. It should also be stressed that the location of individual studies along the continuum is an approximation. It is the overall picture in which we are interested
rather than the precise classification of world order thinking.

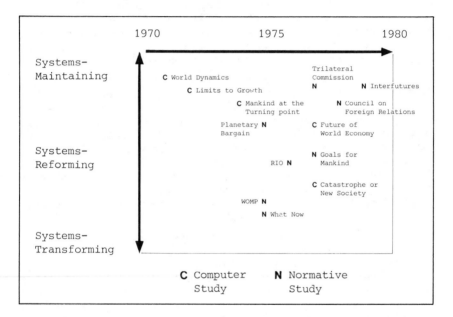

It comes as no great surprise to discover that the majority of
studies reviewed must be located at the systems-maintaining end
of the continuum. All these studies can in many respects be considered the product of a system in deep crisis. Although they
display significant differences with respect to emphasis, orientation and methodology, they share an important characteristic:
the problems discussed and the proposals for change advocated
are subordinated to the strategic aim of saving the system.

Two studies, *RIO* and *Goals for Mankind* can, despite their obvious differences, be conveniently located half way along the continuum. Both can be characterized as systems-reforming approaches to world order thinking, an approach based upon the explicit
recognition that the system will need to change if it is to be
saved. *RIO* epitomizes the reformist approach.

Three studies have been located at the systems-transforming end of the continuum: *What Now*, *WOMP* and *Catastrophe or New Society*, studies which either have their roots firmly planted in the Third World or which have strong Third World participation. There would no doubt be those who would disagree with the placing of these studies. *WOMP*, for example, does not represent a single worldview but is rather an umbrella under which various world-views, some considerably more radical than others, have been enunciated. In the case of *Catastrophe or New Society* we have already drawn attention to the fact that some of the assumptions used in the model, for example those relating to trade, do not differ much from those used in studies which clearly 'belong' to the systems-maintaining tradition. And in the case of *What Now* close inspection of the report suggests that, its dialectical approach notwhithstanding, it is as much reformist as transform-ing, a judgement dependent upon the pages read.

At the beginning of this chapter we asked the question: what does expert opinion tell us that mankind should do to escape the crises which now confront it? We are now in a position to answer this question. The mainstream of thinking, which has its origins in the rich world and in the system itself, tells us that the way out resides in judicious attempts to adjust the international system to substantive complexities, especially those resulting from increasing interdependence, and changing geopolitical reali-ties. According to the mainstream, escaping the crises does not necessitate fundamental changes in the structures which govern the relations between the world's nations.

There is some thinking which tells us that more than remedial tinkering is required and still more which tells us that the only way out is the transformation of the structures which deter-mine the behavior of the capitalist world economy. We can also legitimately conclude that studies which call for the transforma-tion of the international order have a tendency to work with con-cepts which do not readily translate into operational strategies.

THE RELEVANCE OF THEORY

Our examination of world order thinking certainly raises ques-tions concerning the relevance of the theory which experts seem committed to applying to global problems. Many of the instruments used for understanding and solving problems appear crude and blunt, their inherent limitations matched only by the faith which specialists appear to have in their efficacy.

Nowhere is this more in evidence than in the "dismal science" of economics, especially neo-classical economics - the theory of the systems-maintainer and systems-reformer. It has been characteris-tic of neo-classical economic theory to stress the separation of

efficiency in production from equity in distribution. Welfare
economists have generally failed to formulate an objective and
universally valid principle of distribution. Failing in this,
they have tended to conclude that questions of welfare are preeminently political questions and thus the business of politicians. Economists have traditionally advised on how a given distribution could best be achieved but as a group they have, with
a few exceptions, been strangely silent on the desirability of
the distribution itself. (60)

One can go further. If one looks at the evolution of the mainstream of economic thought over the past 200 years one can, with
only slight exaggeration, conclude that it has basically sought
to show how those who are already rich, through their control
of capital and land, can act to further increase their wealth.
In doing so it has given little attention to the question of
whether those who have nothing or little and who are restricted
to the sale of their labor will become worse or better off in
the process. Mainstream economic theory is in other words a
theory of accumulation for those who have accumulated. That the
'working classes' of the North are now better off than they have
ever been can be explained, not by the efficacy of the economic
policies followed and the theory underlying them, but by the
exploitation of colonial peoples and by the overexploitation of
nature everywhere. (61)

The idea that the 'development' of capitalism could be a corol-
lary to - perhaps the prime cause of - the underdevelopment of
the poor countries is traditionally regarded by Western politicians and economists as subjective, value-loaded, unscientific
and ideologically motivated. Even worse, it runs counter to 'economic logic' but, in doing so, is able, in Schumpeter's words,
to arouse "the dark powers of the subconscious".(62) What, however, is the prevailing and dominant logic? It can be argued
that the logic so strongly defended by the majority of economists
has changed little since its birth in the seventeenth century.
(63) Neither the advent of marginalism that distinguishes classical from neo-classical economics, nor recognition of the possibility of involuntary unemployment that distinguishes Keynesian
from neo-classical economics, resulted in real revolutions in
mainstream economic thought with its origins in Adam Smith, David
Ricardo and J.S. Mill. On the contrary, they served as the means
by which the survival of the existing paradigm was ensured. (64)

The 'economic logic' evolved over several centuries does not
seem to be taking anyone - rich or poor - anywhere when applied
to many of today's problems. As John Kenneth Galbraith, a thorn
in the side of many an economist but hardly a radical, recently
observed: "Not many will think that government economists and
economic advisers have much distinguished themselves of late,
but they have succeeded, quite remarkably, in making themselves

and their principles ridiculous. This they have accomplished by
a combination of innocent hope, repetitive banality, and uncom-
plicated fraud". (65)

Viewed from the perspective of the Third World, the words hope,
banality and fraud seem appropriate for describing some of the
notions so treasured by mainstream economists. The notion of
'free trade' is an example. So often presented as a precision
instrument for the engineering of a more equitable international
order, it is as much a capitalist blunt instrument for pounding
the poor. (66) Economic theory teaches us that the conditions
required for the effective working of the market are so exact
and stringent that it must be considered surprising that any
market works at all. Certainly, many of the markets of interest
to the developing countries are 'imperfect' markets: the market
principle does not operate freely, for example, in agricultural
trade, the movement of labor, manufactured goods in so-called
sunset industries and in financial markets, nor, of course, where
monopoly or oligopoly power exists. Moreover, as Helleiner has
shown, even the perfect competition described in economic text-
books are insufficient to guarantee equitable outcomes in international transactions. (67)

Consider the case of agricultural trade. The rich nations currently spend more than $20 billion - more than they give in aid
to the developing countries - in protecting and supporting their
agriculture. Bob Bergland, Secretary for Agriculture in the
Carter administration, has described the idea of a free market
in agricultural commodities as a "dream world". (68) He has supported the idea of an Organization of Wheat Exporting Countries,
modelled on OPEC lines, which would "shave off the peaks and val-
leys" of fluctuating wheat prices. (69) It would, in other words,
do exactly for a U.S. commodity what the Third World wants to
do for its commodities in the face of cries of 'unacceptable intervention'.

The world wonders at U.S. agriculture - a miracle of 'private
enterprise' - where one farmer feeds 75 persons (compared with
10 persons in the Soviet Union). U.S. law, however, provides
farmers with considerable protection against the vicissitudes
of the market place. Ever since the depression farmers have been
protected from drops in grain prices. Washington makes cash payments to farmers when prices fall below government-set 'target
prices' and encourages farmers to store on their own land, partly at taxpayers' expense, any crops which they cannot sell immediately. Until the early 1970s the Department of Agriculture
bought grain surpluses and stored them temporarily in huge and
expensive granaries. The Department also paid farmers to take
their land out of production. Costing about $1 billion, this was
perhaps the most expensive support program ever initiated by the
U.S. government, although its support of Chrysler, another ex-

ample where the market is not working and cannot be allowed to
work, may eventually surpass it.

The results of this 'economic logic' is that our world is one
in which perhaps 50 million people died of hunger in 1979 while
the U.S. holds stocks of grain which are three years old.

The situation in Western Europe is comparable if not worse. The
European Economic Community is essentially an agricultural com-
unity. The Common Agricultural Policy - the foundation upon
which the Community is built - takes up 75 per cent of the Community's budget, or some $16 billion. Remove intervention in
agricultural markets from the EEC and there is no EEC. In Western European nations the story is much the same. British farmers,
for example, whose political and social charisma is eclipsed only by that of motherhood, are featherbedded to the tune of more
than $20,000 each a year, a subsidy more than five times that
of the British steelworker. (70)

The notion of the 'free market' is a cornerstone of liberal ideology and has become inseparably linked to the values of liberty and democracy. Yet market systems foster neither. They can
in fact be as coercive as the most stringent government intervention. (71) Certainly, the 'market', like 'capitalism', means
different things in and translates differently into the contexts
of developed and developing countries. Viewed from the perspective of the Third World, the only thing 'free' about the 'free
market' is that it is free of any effective mechanism for sharing wealth more equitably. When uncorrected by institutions of
justice, the market enriches the rich and pauperizes the poor.

The principle of comparative advantage is another example of
theory which has damaged the interests of the poor. The foundation of neoclassical theories of international trade, comparative advantage alleges that it is in the interests of all countries to specialize in the production of the goods in which they
have the greatest relevant efficiency, and to trade in the goods
in which they have disadvantages. Specialization, the theory
suggests, will raise the level of total income in terms of use
values in the different countries. Since restrictions on trade
limit the degree to which all nations can enjoy mutual benefits,
it can be assumed that free trade must be the best course for
all nations.

There is no denying the attraction of the theory. As Paul Samuelson has written: "If theories could win beauty contests, comparative advantage would certainly rate high in that it is an
elegantly logical structure". It offers, he suggests, "a most
important glimpse of the truth" and argues that "a nation that
neglects comparative advantage may pay a heavy price in terms
of living standards and potential growth". (72)

This piece of 'economic logic', however, assumes such things as perfect competition, full employment, immobility of capital and labor between countries (and perfect mobility within countries) imports and exports balanced by price movements, and static conditions of resources, technical knowledge, population and capital stock. These assumptions, enough to relegate the theory from its lofty position of a whole truth to at most a partial truth, make comparative advantage insensitive to such phenomena as inflation, balance-of-payments problems and structural unemployment, all of which appear resistent to the blandishments and tools of the economists. Most important from the viewpoint of the developing countries is that the theory takes no account of power configurations and of 'levels' of development. (73) It ignores the mechanisms endemic in the international system which effectively channel the benefits of increased productivity in the poor exporting developing countries to the rich importing countries. When applied to unequal situations, comparative advantage tends to aggravate inequalities rather than to reduce them. (74) Economists like Myrdal, Lewis, Singer and Prebish as well as the 'radical' school have all pointed to this phenomenon (75), being forced to conclude, as Myrdal did, that the classical theory of international trade exists for no other purpose than "explaining away the international equity problem". (76)

Most developing countries have every right to be suspicious of the purveyors of comparative advantage (77). In this context, they may, as Cole and Miles have suggested, be in some respects in a similar position to that of revolutionary Russia. (78) When it became clear that communist revolution would not follow in other countries in Western Europe and thus the possibilities for developing a socialist international division of labor had failed to materialize, the Soviet Union was confronted with the question of the development of its trade and industry and with the need to develop a modern economy. Bukharin argued that the Soviet Union should trade with the capitalist West, exporting agricultural goods and importing industrial equipment - as the theory of comparative advantage suggested it should 'logically' do. Preobrazhensky along with Trotsky and his followers disagreed. They called for rapid industrialization and for the extraction of a surplus from agriculture, involving the severe restriction of peasants' consumption, so as to increase investment in industry. (79) By the mid 1920s the Soviet Union was firmly set on its course of planned industrialization, the speed of which was to be dramatically increased under Stalin.

The strategy of rapid industrialization constituted a deliberate rejection of the then existing international division of labor which would have assigned the Soviet Union to agricultural labor to the benefit of the West. Only gradually was foreign trade, which Preobrazhensky had viewed as a drain on surplus and as a vehicle for generating undesirable political links, accepted as a means of acquiring the commodities which could not be produced domestically.

Certainly, the social costs and the human suffering associated
with the Soviet strategy of forced 'superindustrialization' were
enormous. (80) It resulted in the virtual extermination of a
class - the Kulaks - and the death, according to Solzhenitsyn,
of six million peasants in the Ukraine and Kuban River basin.
(81) The fact remains, however, that had the Soviet Union accepted Ricardian logic sixty years ago, it would not today be a
superpower. It would be a backward supplier of the agricultural
commodities required to sustain capitalist growth. (82)

Today it is a superpower and it has no quarms about comparative
advantage. It believes that "foreign trade is mutually advantageous for countries that are on different levels of economic
and technological development" (83), a change in position which
says more about the Soviet Union than about theories of international trade.

These criticisms of neo-classical theory are not to suggest that
all is well in the world of 'radical' economics. Far from it.
Many Marxists argue that the Marxist paradigm has in many respects reached a stage of crisis. (84) The difference between
observed reality and expectations generated by theory are increasing and undermining the analytical and conceptual apparatus. This has given rise to intense debates between Marxists
about the most appropriate lines to follow and the most relevant theory. Nowhere is this debate more intense than the labor
theory of value, the key to the understanding of Marxist economics. Whereas some Marxists continue to defend it, others argue
that this can no longer be used to explain the workings of a
modern capitalist economy. (85) And if you take the labor theory
of value away from Marxist economists they are left rather empty-
handed. (86)

Moreover, it should be recognized that 'radical' economics has
not developed independently of the neo-classical and Keynesian
tradition. Both of course have their 'core' theories which their
advocates defend, theories which have developed over the past
100 years. But this development did not nor could it take place
in a vacuum. The different streams of thought have influenced
each other, sometimes to the extent that dividing lines can only be drawn by the serious student of economics. The consequence
is that each school of thought can only really be understood in
relation to the others. In other words, the development of mainstream economics has influenced in different ways the development of 'radical' economics, just as the radical tradition has
influenced the mainstream. A stage is reached where the radical
tradition becomes part of the mainstream, deradicalizing it in
the process. (87)

Similar situations apply in other of the social sciences. Atkin-

son has argued, for example, that in sociology the dominant
schools of thought - as represented by Parsons, Weber and Marx
- together constitute a consensus. (88) Most would place Parsons
and Marx at opposite ends of the sociological spectrum - two uneven camps grouped under the banners of cohesion (Parsonian)
theory and conflict (Marxist) theory. The structures and contents of the concepts current in each camp, their use, even
their views of man, however, can be shown to contain striking
and lasting similarities. The work of contemporary scholars,
such as Marcuse, Rex and Dahrendorf, has served, Atkinson argues, to reinforce this consensus. The result is that the mainstream of modern sociological thought, like economic thought,
contains an established orthodox view of society whose implications are in fact deeply conservative.

What can we conclude from all of this? That there is something
rotten in the state of theory. If it had been as relevant as
some of its protagonists continue to suggest, then the world
would not be engulfed in crisis, the disparities between rich
and poor would not be growing, and there would be no call for
a more rational and equitable international order. We must also
conclude that orthodox consensus, so strongly reflected in the
thinking and proposals of systems-maintainers, offers little
promise for discerning new directions in human endeavour which
are genuinely worthwhile. Orthodox consensus, with its roots
firmly planted in a different age, tells us that to escape the
crisis we need more of the same that led us into crisis.

The need is thus for new analytical paradigms and conceptual
apparatus. The new paradigms - especially those used by economists - will need to be much more sensitive to questions of
power and the distribution of wealth and opportunity. Commenting
on the relationship between politics and economics, Fred Hirsch
has observed that "Economics is when I have it; politics is when
you want it", implying that economic advantage can be derived
from political ascendancy and transformed back into political
power. (89) From the viewpoint of the developing countries, economics - a set of theories of accumulation for those who have
accumulated - must go beyond 'having' and give greater articulation to questions of 'wanting'. If it is to do this, then economics must again become political economy. And political economy must be built on the values of equity and justice, values
which the 'free' market does not and cannot recognize.

The new analytical paradigms must, however, go beyond the de-
ification of the market. As such, economic analysis will need to
be subordinated. Preoccupation with economic questions and with
the economic aspects of complex problems to the exclusion of
others, a situation which fairly characterizes much thinking in
the post-war period, has contributed toward the exacerbation of
many of today's problems. The world is too complex and indeed

too valuable to be viewed in exclusively economic terms, and
economic theory, irrespective of its ideological plumage, is an
inadequate basis for coming to terms with the complex array of
problems which must be faced. This is surely what Pierre Trudeau,
a leader who by Western standards has more than his fair share
of headaches, meant when he suggested that the answer to problems "that we cannot easily solve" is not be found in the prognostications and prescriptions of economists but in the teachings of a "political, philosophical or moral leader" who can
convince people that there are new directions which the future
says we should follow. (90)

If the new analytical paradigms and conceptual apparatus are to
tender such hope, then they must transcend orthodox Western concepts of rationality and science - including those derived from
Marx - which have traditionally attended to the problems of empirical truths to the general exclusion of the realms of ethics
and morality. 'Rightness' and 'oughtness' must shine through our
analytical and conceptual prisms. And if they are to do this,
theory will need to go beyond questions of having and of wanting
to essential questions of being. (91)

NOTES AND REFERENCES

(1) For a comprehensive review of global models, see Sam Cole,
    'The Global Futures Debate 1965-1976', in Christopher Free-
    man and Marie Jahoda, *World Futures: The Great Debate*,
    Martin Robertson, Oxford, 1978, pp. 9-49. See also John M.
    Richardson, 'Global Modelling: A Survey and Appraisal',
    paper prepared for the Seminar on Natural Resource Policies,
    University of Wisconsin, Madison, Wisconsin, December 1977
    (mimeo); Don Munton, 'Global Models, Politics and the
    Future', paper presented to the Annual Meeting of the
    Canadian Political Science Association, London, Ontario,
    May 1978 (mimeo); Guy Poquet, 'The Limits to Global Model-
    ling', *International Social Science Journal*, vol. 30, no. 2,
    1978; Dick A.Leurdijk, *World Order Studies: World Order
    Studies, Policy-Making and the New International Order*,
    Foundation Reshaping the International Order, Rotterdam,
    February 1979; and Jorge Lozoya, Jaime Estevez and Rosario
    Green, *Alternative Views of the New International Economic
    Order:A Survey and Analysis of Major Academic Research
    Reports*, Pergamon Press, New York, 1979.
(2) Jay W.Forrester, *World Dynamics*, Wright-Allen, Cambridge,
    Mass., 1971.
(3) Quoted in Cole, op.cit., pp. 27-28.
(4) Donella H.Meadows et al., *The Limits to Growth*, Signet
    Books, New York 1972.
(5) The report lists a number of "practical discoveries that
    would enhance the workings of a steady state society": new

methods of waste collection, more efficient techniques for
recycling, improved product design to increase product life-
times and reduce maintenance, advances in solar energy technology, methods of natural pest control, reductions in death
rates through medical advances, and contraceptive advances
to promote population stabilization. (pp. 181-182)

(6) On the lack of political analysis in *Limits to Growth*, see
Johan Galtung, 'The Limits to Growth and Class Politics',
Journal of Peace Research, vol. 10, 1973, pp. 101-114. He
argues that global modelling efforts not only lack class
consciousness but also run counter to the interests of the
poor.

(7) For an extensive criticism of *Limits to Growth*, see Sam Cole
et al., *Models of Doom*, Universe Books, New York, 1973. For
a Third World criticism see Mahbub ul Haq, *The Poverty Curtain: Choices for the Third World*, Columbia University
Press, New York, 1976, chapter 5.

(8) Mihajlo Mesarovic and Eduard Pestel, *Mankind at the Turning
Point: The Second Report to The Club of Rome*, Signet Books,
New York, 1974.

(9) See Leurdijk, op.cit., p. 62.

(10) Amílcar O.Herrera et al., *Catastrophe or New Society? A
Latin American World Model,* International Development
Research Centre, Ottawa, 1976.

(11) See Graciela Chichilnisky, 'Development Patterns and the
International Order', *Journal of International Affairs,*
vol. 31, no. 2, Fall/Winter 1977, pp. 175-204. Ms. Chichilnisky was one of the members of the project team.

(12) See Cole, op.cit., p. 40.

(13) This is implied by Munton, op.cit., in his analysis of
global modelling efforts.

(14) It is worth recording the statement made by Amílcar Herrera, director of the project team, at an IIASA global modelling symposium held some two years prior to the publication
of the report. Asked about the policy relevance of the project's likely findings he agreed "that it should be a means
for helping (the) policy planner" although, he went on, "we
do not intend to create an instrument for practical policy".
He chose to call the model a utopian model and an ideological contribution aimed at influencing public opinion rather
than policy-making. See Gerhart Bruckmann (ed.), *Latin
American World Model: Proceedings of the Second IIASA Symposium on Global Modelling*, document CP-76-8, Laxenburg,
October 1974.

(15) Aspen Institute for Humanistic Studies, *The Planetary Bargain: Proposals for a New International Economic Order to
Meet Human Needs*, Princeton, New Jersey, 1975.

(16) Marc Nerfin (ed.), *What Now: The 1975 Dag Hammarskjöld
Report on Development and International Cooperation*, published as a double edition of *Development Dialogue*,

nos. 1/2, 1975.

(17) On the question of Third World power strategies, see Johan Galtung, 'Power and Global Planning and Resource Management', in A.J.Dolman (ed.), *Global Planning and Resource Management: Toward International Decision-Making in a Divided World*, Pergamon, New York, 1980, pp. 119-145.

(18) Saul H.Mendlovitz (ed.), *On the Creation of a Just World Order: Preferred Worlds for the 1990s*, Free Press, New York, 1975.

(19) Some of WOMP's participants have presented their views on the future in other volumes of the 'Preferred Worlds for the 1990s' series. See: Rajni Kothari, *Footsteps into the Future: Diagnosis of the Present World and a Design for an Alternative*, Free Press. New York, 1974; Ali A.Mazrui, *A World Federation of Cultures: An African Perspective*, Free Press. New York, 1976; Richard A.Falk, *A Study of Future Worlds*, Free Press, New York, 1975: Gustavo Lagos and Horacio Godoy, *Revolutions of Being:A Latin American View of the Future*, Free Press, New York, 1977; and Johan Galtung, *The True Worlds:A Transnational Perspective*, Free Press, New York, 1980.

(20) Richard Falk, 'Towards a New World Order: Modest Methods and Drastic Visions', in Mendlovitz, op.cit., pp. 211-258.

(21) Johan Galtung, 'Nonterritorial Actors and the Problem of Peace', in Mendlovitz, op.cit., pp. 151-188.

(22) Jan Tinbergen (coordinator), *Reshaping the International Order:A Report to The Club of Rome*, E.P.Dutton, New York, 1976.

(23) An international order characterized by "humanistic socialism" is one in which the emphasis is on the equalization of opportunities both within and among nations within a framework of universal human values". The report notes that "Many in the RIO Group" subscribe to the use and definition of the term "humanistic socialism", implying that there were some who were against its introduction. (p. 63)

(24) We will take up some of these issues as well as the concept of the 'common heritage of mankind' in chapter 5.

(25) *Towards a New International Order: An Appraisal of Prospects*; Government Printing Office, The Hague, 1977.

(26) Ervin Laszlo et al., *Goals for Mankind:A Report to The Club of Rome on the New Horizons of Global Community*, E.P.Dutton, New York, 1977.

(27) Wassily Leontief et al., *The Future of the World Economy: A United Nations Study*, Oxford University Press, New York, 1977.

(28) See Leurdijk, op.cit., p. 73.

(29) Officially, the studies published under the auspices of the Council are the responsibility of individual authors rather than the Council as such. Before publication, however, a manuscript is reviewed by the Council's Committee

on Studies which decides whether it constitutes "a responsible treatment of a significant topic worthy of presentation to the public".

(30) Miriam Camps, *The Management of Interdependence: A Preliminary View*, Council on Foreign Relations, Inc., New York, 1974.

(31) Albert Fishlow, 'A New International Economic Order: What
Kind?',in Roger D.Hansen (ed.), *Rich and Poor Nations in the
World Economy*, McGraw-Hill, New York, 1978, pp. 9-83. There
are three other essays in the volume: Carlos Díaz-Alejandro
sets out to present and anlyze the case for collective self-
reliance and selective 'delinking'; Richard R.Fagin reflects
upon the potential of a "reformed" international economic
system to enhance the development goals of the Third World,
especially the capacity to eliminate absolute poverty; and
Roger Hansen provides an overview of the three essays, considering in more detail some of the issues raised.

(32) The 1980s project is a series of studies "concerning issues
of potentially great importance in the next decade (1980)
and beyond, such as resource management, human rights,
population studies, and relations between the developing
and developed societies". It will give rise to some 30
volumes.

(33) The words are those of the Commission's Executive Secretary
George Franklin, quoted in Robert Manning, 'A World Safe for
Business', *Far Eastern Economic Review*, March 25, 1977, p. 39.

(34) Manning, op.cit., has another quote from Franklin: "Mike
Blumenthal (another founder member) said he thought things
were in a very serious condition in the world and couldn't
some kind of private group do more about it?... So then
David again made his proposal...." Manning notes that
Brzezinski,a close friend of Rockefeller, (then) carried
the Rockefeller-funded ball and organized the Commission".
(p. 39)

(35) Jeff Frieden in 'The Trilateral Commission: Economics and
Politics in the 1970s', *Monthly Review*, vol. 29, no. 7,
December 1977, pp. 1-18, lists some of the members of the
Trilateral Commission. They include editors and directors
of *Time, The Los Angeles Times, The Economist, La Stampa,
Die Zeit,* the *Japan Times,* Kyodo News Service, *Foreign
Policy,* the *Financial Times,* the *Washington Post,* and the
Columbia Broadcasting System. Banking and investment in-
terests are represented by Chase Manhattan, Lehman Bros.,
Bank of America, Banque de Paris et des Pays-Bas, Belgium
National Bank, German Banking Federation, Lloyds of London,
Bank of Tokyo, Sumitomo Bank, Dai-Ichi Kangyo Bank, Mitsu-
bishi Bank, Compagnie Financière Holding (Rothschild), Bar-
clays Bank International, Fédération Française des Sociétés
d'Assurances, Teh Sanwa Bank, Fuji Bank and Nikko Securities.
'Big business' corporations represented include Coca-Cola,
Bendix, Pan Am, IBM, Texas Instruments, Caterpillar Tractor,

Hewlett-Packard, Fiat, Tyssen Vermögensverwaltung, La Rinas-
cente, Dunlop, Royal Dutch Shell, Unilever, The Federal Union
of German Industry, Mitsubishi Nippon Steel, Nissan Motor,
Matsushita Electric, Sony, Toyota, Mobil, Merck and Co.,
Exxon, Cie Saint-Gobain-Pont-à-Mousson, and Japan Air Lines.
National and international organizations and think-tanks are
represented by the Brookings Institution, the Commission of
the European Community, the Italian Institute for International Affairs, the Asian Development Bank, the RAND Corporation, the Foreign Policy Association, the World Bank,
the International Monetary Fund, North Atlantic Treaty Organization, the Organization for Economic Cooperation and
Development, the Royal Institute of International Affairs
(London), and GATT.

(36) Frieden, op.cit., p. 13 lists the Trilateralists who have
served in the Carter administration: Cyrus Vance, Michael
Blumenthal, Zbigniew Brzezinski,C.Fred Bergsten, Richard
Holbrooke, Leonard Woodcock, Warren Christopher, Richard
Gardner, Harold Brown, Richard Cooper, Andrew Young, Lucy
Benson, Sol Linowitz, Paul Warnke, Anthony Solomon, Elliot
Richardson and Henry Owen. He notes that "Trilateralists oc-
cupy virtually every major post in the Departments of State,
Defense, and the Treasury, and include one federal judge,
the head of and a consultant to the National Security Coun-
cil, three ambassadors (Japan, Italy, and at-large), a
"personal representative", the U.S. delegate to the United
Nations, and of course the president himself and his vice
president". (p. 13)

(37) See François Duchene, Kinhide Mushakoji and Henry D.Owen,
The Crisis of International Cooperation, A Report of the
Trilateral Political Task Force to the Executive Committee
of the Trilateral Commission, Tokyo, October 22-23, 1973,
The Trilateral Commission, New York, 1974, p. 14.

(38) C.Fred Bergsten, Georges Berthoin and Kinhide Mushakoji,
The Reform of International Institutions, A Report of the
Trilateral Task Force on International Institutions to the
Trilateral Commission, New York, 1976, p. 2.

(39) Richard Cooper, Karl Kaiser and Masataka Kosaka, *Towards
a Renovated International System*, Trilateral Commission,
New York, 1977.

(40) Organization for Economic Cooperation and Development,
*Facing the Future: Mastering the Probable and Managing the
Unpredictable*, Paris, 1979.

(41) For a review of world order thinking from the twelfth century onwards, see F.H.Hinsley's admirable *Power and the
Pursuit of Peace*, Cambridge University Press, Cambridge,
1963.

(42) For an assessment of the policy relevance of world order
thinking see the references listed under footnote 1. A
useful discussion can also be found in OECD, *A Comparative*

Evaluation of World Models, chapter 11 of the 'Intermediate
Results' of the Interfutures Project, Paris, 7 April 1977.

(43) Richardson, op.cit., p. 41, argues that a world order model
can be considered implemented "when the perspective of the
model becomes part of the perspective of one or more decision-
makers". It could also be argued that the main purpose of a
model is simply to reveal the limitations of another model.

(44) This is argued by William Irwin Thompson in *Evil and World
Order*, Harper and Row, New York, 1976. The evil is systems
analysis and its main cousins.

(45) According to Leurdijk, op.cit., the questions of aid, industrialization and trade, food, and energy and raw materials
have received the greatest attention in the world order
studies published in the past decade. The questions of science
and technology and human environment have received somewhat
less attention and treatment of such matters as disarmament
and ocean management has been conspicuous through its absence.

(46) This is not to suggest that computer models are apolitical.
As Munton, op.cit., p. 49, observes "each of (these) models
is based implicitly, or less often, explicitly on a plethora
of political assumptions". Indeed, it could be argued, as it
is in *Catastrophe or New Society* (p. 7), that because every
model has an inbuilt ideological position and preference it
is not justifiable to distinguish between quantitative and
qualitative models. The point, however, is the degree of
sophistication surrounding the treatment of political issues,
not whether certain types of world order thinking could conceivably be considered 'value free'.

(47) In defining the characteristics of the three approaches to
world order thinking considerable use has been made of the
following sources: Richard A.Falk, 'Contending Approaches
to World Order', *Journal of International Affairs*, vol. 31,
no. 2, Fall/Winter 1977, pp. 171-198; Richard A.Falk,'Beyond
Internationalism', *Foreign Affairs*, vol. 23, 1976, pp. 65-
113; Ian Miles, 'Worldviews and Scenarios', in Freeman and
Jahoda, op.cit., chapter 8.

(48) 'Beyond Internationalism', p. 84.

(49) 'A Word to the Third World', *Wall Street Journal*, July 17,
1975, p. 18.

(50) For another lengthy study which reaches this conclusion,
see William R.Cline, 'A Qualitative Assessment of the Policy
Alternatives in the NIEO Negotiations', in W.R.Cline (ed.),
Policy Alternatives for a New International Economic Order,
Praeger Publishers, New York, 1979.

(51) Fishlow, op.cit., p. 56.

(52) Daniel P.Moynihan, 'The United States in Opposition',
Commentary, March 1975, pp. 31-44, at p. 41.

(53) Daniel Bell, 'The Future of World Disorder', *Foreign Policy*,
vol. 27, Summer 1977, pp. 109-136, at p. 134.

(54) This is the conclusion reached by Bart van Steenbergen in his review of Talcott Parsons' thinking on the subject of conflict. See *Orde of Conflict: Tegengestelde Maatschappij-visies Binnen de Futurologie*, Euroboekje, Wolters-Noordhoff, Groningen, 1969, p. 12.

(55) The *RIO Report*, p. 157.

(56) For an extensive profile of the supranationalist, see Robert Gilpin, 'Three Models of the Future', in C.Fred Bergsten and Lawrence B.Krause (eds.), *World Politics and International Economics*, The Brookings Institution, Washington, D.C., 1975, pp. 37-60, viz. pp. 39-42.

(57) For a description of the characteristic elements of the 'spaceship earth' world order paradigm, see Alan D.Buckley's 'Foreward' to the Fall/Winter 1977 edition of the *Journal of International Affairs*.

(58) See Silviu Brucan, 'The World Authority: An Exercise in Political Forecasting', in Antony J.Dolman (ed.), *Global Planning and Resource Management: International Decision-Making in a Divided World*, Pergamon Press, New York, pp. 49-66, at p. 50.

(59) Saul Mendlovitz in his introduction to *On the Creation of a Just World Order*, p. xvi.

(60) This argument is developed in John Friedmann, 'The Crisis of Transition: A Critique of Strategies of Crisis Management', *Development and Change*, vol. 10, 1979, pp. 125-153.

(61) There is a school of radical thought that argues that although the 'working classes' of the West may be oppressed and alienated, they have been among the main beneficiaries of the exploitation of the Third World. Even that the determination of Western workers to continually raise their standards of living has contributed more to the impoverishment of the developing countries than have the activities of commercial enterprises. For the presentation of such a view, see K.Buchanan, 'The Third World - Its Emergence and Contours', *New Left Review*, vol. 18, 1963, pp. 5-23.

(62) J.A.Schumpeter, *Sociology of Imperialism*, Meridian Books, London, 1955, p. 11. (First published 1919).

(63) The thesis of B.Ward, *What's Wrong with Economics*, Basic Books, New York, 1972.

(64) This argument is developed in Guy Routh, *The Origins of Economic Ideas*, Vintage Books, New York, 1977.

(65) John Kenneth Galbraith, 'The No-WIN Society', *The New York Review of Books*, June 12, 1980, pp. 3-4, at p. 3.

(66) For a spirited defense of the liberal faith in the free, if imperfect, market, see Harry G.Johnson, *Economic Nationalism in Old and New States*, Allen and Unwin, London, 1968; and P.T.Bauer, *Dissent on Development*, Weidenfeld and Nicholson, London, 1972. For a presentation of the defects of the market mechanism as an instrument for promoting human welfare, see, for example, Fred Hirsch, *The Social Limits to*

Growth, Routledge and Kegan Paul, London, 1978.

(67) G.K.Helleiner, *World Market Imperfections and the Developing Countries*, Occasional Paper No. 11, Overseas Development Council, Washington, D.C., May 1978. Elsewhere he has suggested that a truly equitable distribution of the gains from international trade - indeed from world economic activity in general - would be possible through world government, a likelihood he is quick to reject. See his Introduction to *A World Divided: The Less Developed Countries in the International Economy*, Cambridge University Press, Cambridge, 1976, pp. 1-28.

(68) Bergland is quoted in Michael Harrington, *The Vast Majority: A Journey to the World's Poor*, Simon and Schuster, New York, 1977, p. 131.

(69) Ibid.

(70) See Marion Shoad, *The Theft of the Countryside*, Maurice Temple Smith, London, 1980.

(71) For a discussion of the relationships between political systems and markets, see Charles E.Lindblom, *Politics and Markets: The World's Political Economic Systems*, Basic Books, New York, 1978.

(72) Paul A.Samuelson, *Economics*, McGraw-Hill Kogakusha, New York and Tokyo, 1973 (ninth edition), p. 680.

(73) For a general discussion of the limitations of the theory, see M.K.Pedersen, 'The Rise of an Issue: Adjustment Assistance Measures: The Trade Context and its Theoretical Framework', in K.Worm (ed.), *Industrialization, Development and the Demands for a New International Economic Order*, Samfundsvidenskabeligt Forlag, Copenhagen, 1978, pp. 41-63. Marxists of course content that the ideas of Ricardo have been completely transcended by Marx. Some, like Samir Amin, regard comparative advantage as 'vulgar economics' and put continued interest in the theory in the Angelo-Saxon world down to the fact that Marxism is not well understood, a consequence of the "philosophical impoverishment" of Britain and the U.S. See Samir Amin, *Imperialism and Underdevelopment*, Monthly Review Press, New York/London, 1977, p. 125 ff. His criticism of comparative advantage can be found in *Unequal Development*, Monthly Review Press, New York/London, 1976, chapter 3.

(74) 'Radical' economics has developed the theory of unequal specialization and exchange to describe this process. Based upon a Marxist interpretation of price formations, this theory holds that because of the existence of a very considerable wage differential, overpriced goods from the rich countries are exchanged for underpriced goods from the poor countries on the world market. Unequal specialization and exchange means that the international division of labor requires the poor countries to produce for and to adapt to the needs of the rich countries. For an exposition of the

theory, see Samir Amin, op.cit., 1976; and Arghiri Emmanuel,
Unequal Exchange: A Study of the Imperialism of Trade,
Monthly Review Press, New York/London, 1972.

(75) Myrdal, Lewis, Singer and Prebisch were among the first to
examine the external factors which constrain the development
process and identified specific and automatic mechanisms in
the system of international trade which consistently work to
the benefit of the rich countries. Gunnar Myrdal concentrated
on the effects of colonization and, especially, the relationship between the mother countries and colonies. He examined
the unequalizing effects that manifest themselves in this
relationship. Hans Singer, focused his analysis on the secular deterioration in the terms of trade of the poor countries.
Arthur Lewis related the mechanism of the transfer of gains
resulting from the increase in productivity to the unlimited
supply of labor of the traditional rural sector of the poor
countries. Raul Prebisch substituted the concept of an integrated and hierarchical world system based upon the capitalist mode of production for the world of international trade
based upon comparative advantage. The affluence of the rich
countries, he concluded from his analysis, was based upon,
and a result of, the continuing poverty of the poor countries. The center-periphery model developed by Prebisch was
later developed by Johan Galtung to construct a structural
theory of imperialism based upon dominance relations between
collectivities, especially countries, although his work has
been criticized by some Marxists for failing to adequately
deal with economic relations. The center-periphery model
was further developed by Immanuel Wallerstein and used to
examine accumulation processes at the world level and the
integrating forces in the world system. For Myrdal's views,
see *Economic Theory and Underdeveloped Regions*, Duckworth,
London, 1954; *An International Economy*, Harper, New York,
1956; and *The Challenge of World Poverty*, Pantheon, New
York, 1970. For the views of Hans Singer, see his *International Development: Growth and Change*, McGraw Hill, New
York, 1964; and 'The Distribution of Gains Between Investing
and Borrowing Countries', *American Economic Review*, May 1950.
For the views of Arthur Lewis, see 'World Production Prices
and Trade, 1870 - 1960', *The Manchester School of Economic
and Social Studies*, vol. 20, 1950; 'Economic Development
with Unlimited Supplies of Labour', *Manchester School of
Economic and Social Studies*, vol. 24, May 1954; and *Theory
of Economic Growth*, Allen and Unwin, London, 1955. Raul
Prebisch first published his views on underdevelopment in
*The Economic Development of Latin America and its Principal
Problems*, U.N. Commission for Latin America (CEPAL), Santiago, 1950; see also his *Towards a New Trade Policy for Development*, UNCTAD, Geneva, 1964 for an articulation of center-
periphery thinking. For an interesting comparison of the

views of Myrdal, Singer, Lewis and Prebisch from a radical
perspective, see Tamás Szentes, *The Political Economy of
Underdevelopment*, Akadémiai Kiadó, Budapest, 1976, viz.
pp. 101-110. Johan Galtung's exposition of center-periphery
relations was published as 'A Structural Theory of Imperialism', *Journal of Peace Research*, vol. 5, 1971, pp. 375-395.
Immanuel Wallerstein's views are to be found in *The Modern
World System*, Academic Press, New York, 1974; and *The Capitalist World Economy*, Cambridge University Press, Cambridge/
New York, 1979.

(76) Myrdal, *The Challenge of World Poverty*, p. 277.

(77) As Hans Singer and J.Ansari report they are in *Rich and
Poor Countries*, George Allen and Unwin, London, 1977,
section 6.4

(78) See Sam Cole and Ian Miles, 'Assumptions and Methods:
Population, Economic Development, Modelling and Technical
Change', in C.Freeman and M.Jahoda (eds.), *World Futures:
The Great Debate*, Martin Robertson, Oxford, 1978, pp. 51-
75, viz. pp. 66-67.

(79) For a summary of Preobrazhensky's theory of socialist accumulation, see I.Deutscher, *The Prophet Unarmed*, Oxford University Press, New York, 1959, pp. 415-426. Preobrazhensky's
work was published in 1926 and is widely regarded as the
best work on the economic problems of the Soviet Union then
produced. For such a view, see M.Lewin, *Russian Peasants
and Soviet Power*, George Allen and Unwin, London, 1968,
viz. pp. 148-154.

(80) As Lewin, op.cit., p. 515 observes: "seldom was any government to wreak such havoc in its own country". For an analysis of development of Soviet agriculture and the social
costs incurred, see R.W.Davies, *The Industrialization of
Soviet Russia*, vol. 1, *The Socialist Offensive: The Collectivisation of Soviet Agriculture 1929-30*, Macmillan, 1979.

(81) See 'Solshenitsyn on Communism', *Time*, February 19, 1980,
pp. 12-13.

(82) As Cole and Miles, op.cit., note this does not mean to say
that all developing countries could or should follow the
Soviet example. There are international and domestic political constraints and problems resulting from the small
size and resource deficiencies of the majority of developing countries. It is also now recognized that while industrialization should form part of the development process,
it is by no means the only part. Experience has shown that
investment in industry does not necessarily bring prosperity,
nor does it necessarily create employment.

(83) V.Solodnikov and V.Bogoslovsky, *Non-Capitalist Development*,
Progress Publishers, Moscow, 1975, p. 199.

(84) See Paul M.Sweezy, 'A Crisis in Marxian Theory', *Monthly
Review*, vol. 31, no. 2, June 1979, pp. 20-24.

(85) This is argued in B.Hindress, P.Kirst, A.Hussain, A.Cutler,

Marx's Capital and Capitalism Today, Routledge and Kegan Paul, London, 1977.

(86) For a review of the role of value theory in Marxist economic theory, see, for example, S.Amin, op.cit., 1977; M.Desai, *Marxian Economic Theory*, Gray-Mills, London, 1974; and E. Mandel, *Marxist Economic Theory*, Monthly Review Press, New York, 1968.

(87) It might be noted here that economists like Samuelson, op. cit., and Morishima (*Marx's Economics*, Cambridge University Press, London, 1973) have sought to absorb Marxist theories into the mainstream of economic thinking.

(88) Dick Atkinson, *Orthodox Consensus and the Radical Alternative: A Study in Sociological Theory*, Heinemann, London, 1971.

(89) Fred Hirsch, 'Is there a New International Economic Order?', *International Organization*, vol. 30, no. 3, Summer 1976, pp. 521-531, at p. 528.

(90) Interviewed by Joseph Kraft in the *Washington Post*, May 17, 1977.

(91) On this, see Erich Fromm, *To Have or To Be?*, Jonathan Cape, London, 1978.

3 Toward Strategies for Global Reform: Issues, Elements and Implications

> The complexity, in many ways praiseworthy, with which the history of an age now has to be composed, naturally causes everyone to worry as to how our later descendants are going to cope with the burden of history which, after some centuries, we are going to leave them. Without doubt they will care for the history of the distant past, for which the documents will long since have perished, only from the standpoint which interests them, namely, what nations and governments have contributed to a world order or how they have damaged it.
>
> Immanuel Kant, *Idea for a Universal History,* 1784

INTRODUCTION

In the previous two chapters we have sought to sketch the main contours of a deepening global predicament and have looked at some of the prescriptions of expert opinion for coming to terms with it. We have argued that the global crisis is one which, to varying extents and for different reasons, affects all the world's nations. We have also been forced to conclude that much specialist opinion, especially that of the more-of-the-same variety, appears to hold out little hope for escaping the crisis. This led us to question the relevancy and efficacy of the theoretical apparatus and analytical tools used by specialists, especially economists, to comprehend the set of crises and to discern directions equal to the challenge which confronts us.

We will now turn our attention to strategies. In this chapter we will attempt to identify some of the main elements of approaches to global reform. We will go on to take a closer look at rich world strategies, toward the Third World and for national development, and their relationship to attempts to shape a more rational and equitable international order. In outlining some of the issues and alternatives involved, we will attempt to provide a context for the remaining chapters of this volume, each of which will address key aspects of the 'problematique'.

We will begin our discussion of strategies, however, by taking a closer look at a 'strategy' to which we have already made repeated reference: the Declaration and Program of Action on the Establishment of a New International Economic Order (NIEO). The NIEO is in many respects a world strategy for non-renewable resources. It seeks to establish a basis for pursuing the goal of economic justice through more equitable access to and distribution of the world's riches and resources. The questions of how these resources are to be managed and who is to manage them are central to the NIEO program as well as to the negotiations on it. As formulated and presented by the Third World, the route to a NIEO passes through more rational and equitable resource management and this passes through structural change. We can thus conclude that failure to implement NIEO proposals does not augur well for attempts to strenghten global planning and resource management capabilities. By the same token, lessons which can be derived from the failure to implement the NIEO package may help us craft global management strategies which have a better chance of success.

THE NEW INTERNATIONAL ECONOMIC ORDER
AS A GLOBAL MANAGEMENT STRATEGY

The New International Economic Order (NIEO) is a program of proposals launched by the Third World which sets out to redress some of the inequities endemic in the prevailing international economic order. This order is far from 'new'. Its origins can be traced to the sixteenth century and the emergence of modern capitalism in Europe. Historians continue to debate the specific conjunction of factors which led to the emergence of modern capitalism at that time. (1) They refer to the proselytizing zeal and militancy of the Christian, especially Protestant, faith, so different from the other worldliness of the Buddhism and Hinduism and the equipoise of Confucianism. Max Weber has shown how Calvinism taught the bourgeoisie and parvenus that the pur-

suit of wealth was not merely desirable, but a duty; that labor
was not merely an economic means, but a spiritual end. (2) The
pursuit of riches, once feared as an enemy of religion, was welcomed as its natural ally. In the sixteenth century, capitalism
became the counterpart of theology.

Historians also stress the importance of the 'New Instauration',
the new learning based upon mathematics, mechanics and inductive
method with its aim of finding out about 'things'. (3) They
refer too to the impact of Cartesian philosophy and to the idea
that through science, as Descartes believed, men could become
"the masters and possessors of nature". The new learning gave
man the tools to conquer nature and the new 'faith' the inclination to do so. Scientific discovery was linked to processes
of capital accumulation and to the readiness to seek domination
over others and to impose cultural values.

These and other factors gave Europe, to use Wallerstein's term,
a "slight edge". It was turned to enormous advantage. For once
the process of self-generating growth was established, it was
reinforced in many different ways. In the early period of growth
and consolidation, these included slavery, murder and plunder.
The arms of capitalism took hold of the world; continents were
enchained; peoples subjugated. Western civilization gave birth
to capitalism and capitalism spawned barbarism. (4)

The historical process of capitalist expansion created a world
assimilated to capitalism and to the needs of the colonizing
powers. Trading relationships were established in the colonial
period. Based upon extreme inequality, they bestowed upon the
poor countries the role of reservoirs of raw materials which
were exchanged for the higer priced industrial goods produced
in the center of capitalism. These unequal exchange relationships persist today and work to the continuous disadvantage of
the poor countries.(5) For once a pattern of inequality has been
established, the simple operation of market forces will maintain and accentuate it. In this context, the working of an ostensibly 'fair' system of free trade can be almost as damaging
to the developing countries as processes of imperial extraction
from tributary territories. (6)

The wave of political liberation that swept across the Third
World in the post war period did not bring emancipation from the
forces which maintain economic dependence. The poor nations soon
discovered that with fewer resources, less know-how and severely
limited opportunities to utilize that which they had, they were
in fact less 'free' than the rich countries. They discovered
that political liberation does not necessarily expand economic
independence and that without economic power a nation's political independence is incomplete and insecure.

When the poor countries questioned the basic premises of an in-

national system which leads to ever widening disparities between
rich and poor and the persistent denial of equality of opportunity, they were informed that this was merely the workings of
market mechanisms. Through hard work and the astute exploitation
of their 'comparative advantages' they could, over time, take
their place in the international system, even though they might
never 'catch up' with the industrialized nations. To help pla-
cate them, the rich assured the poor that there would be a true
partnership in development and a genuine transfer of real resources. It did not take long before the poor countries discovered that there can be no partnership between unequals and that
the resource flows, when they came, locked them into new patterns
of dependence. (7)

Through a string of conferences stretching over two decades, the
developing countries sought modest reforms to the international
economic order. They failed to get any. (8) The unending debate
did not bring increased economic independence but a lot of talk
about economic interdependence. (9) This at least gave rise to
the hope that, through its connotations of 'common interests'
and 'we need each other' and its image of 'spaceship earth',
the discussions between rich and poor had entered a new phase
based upon, in Barbara Ward's term, a new "bedrock reality".(10)

This hope was unfounded. Many in the Third World have been forced
to conclude that the term interdependence has been used to ra-
tionalize relationships of dependence and domination and to limit the independence of the poor countries. (11) They have discovered that in today's world the verb to interdepend conjugates
as 'I depend, you rule'. They realize, too, that spaceship earth
is a very inadequate metaphor. Most of the world's population
does not inhabit a spaceship; it exists in a universe of hope-
lessness, squalor and despair. Spaceships have captains with
awesome powers. If the earth has a captain it is Kurt Waldheim.
And as its captain, he enjoys about as much authority as the
pilot of the most flimsy contraption of paper, glue and string
about to enter the eye of a hurricane. (12)

The rich nations talk of the web of interdependence. The poor
nations know that every web has its spider which feeds on the
blood of those that trespass the web. And it is no exaggeration
to say that the rich countries extract the very lifeblood and
bones of the poor of the Third World: Western companies have
grown rich on the profits they have made from selling the blood
of the poor; and Western children, in their centrally heated bi-
ology classrooms, can play with the skeletons of the corpses drag-
ged from the rivers and picked from the gutters of Calcutta. (13)

This situation is not the product of an evil conspiracy; a deliberate plot spawned in the citadels of capitalism aimed at
exploiting the poor and at maintaining them in servitude. It is
the product of a historical process with its roots planted in

a different age. Domination and dependence are built into the
institutions and mechanisms which govern the relationships between rich and poor countries. The international system has
evolved with self-propelling forces which must ensure that, unless corrected by positive intervention, the rich get richer
while the poor, if they don't get poorer, at least stay poor.

Inevitably and rightly, the Third World is insisting that the
time has come for change. Not remedial tinkering with international institutions, but the establishment of a New International Economic Order which will make it possible for the developing
countries to achieve their "full and complete economic emancipation". (14)

To the developing countries the NIEO has great historical significance. It is a reaction to colonialism and neo-colonialism
and to mounting frustration and alienation with two decades of
development efforts and of debates on the need for economic reforms. Through their proposals for a NIEO, the developing countries seek to redress institutional distortions in international economic relations which may cost them $ 100 billion a year.
(15)

THE MAIN ELEMENTS OF THE NIEO PACKAGE

The Declaration and Program of Action on the Establishment of
a New International Economic Order was adopted without a vote
at the Sixth Special Session of the U.N. General Assembly held
in the Spring of 1974. (16) The Special Session was the first
ever convened at the initiative of the Third World and the first
ever devoted to economic issues.

The Declaration sets out "to correct inequalities and redress
existing injustices and ensure steadily accelerating economic
development, peace and justice for present and future generations". It states that the Declaration "shall be one of the most
important bases of economic relations between all people of all
nations".

The Declaration emphasizes the right of every nation to full
permanent sovereignty over its natural resources. It holds that
each state is entitled to exercise effective control over its
resources and their exploitation, using means appropriate to
its own situation, including the right of nationalization or
transfer of ownership to its nationals. It also sets out the
principles that all states, territories and peoples under foreign domination have the right to restitution and compensation
for the exploitation of and damage to their natural resources.
The Declaration affirms the sovereign equality of states, the
self-determination of all peoples, the inadmissibility of the

acquisition of territories by force, and territorial integrity and non-interference in the internal affairs of states.

The Declaration notes that the benefits of technological progress are not shared equitably by all countries and that the developing countries, with 70 per cent of the world's population, account for only 30 per cent of the world's income. It calls for the regulation and supervision of the activities of transnational corporations through measures in the interest of the host countries.

On trade, the Declaration calls for a "just and equitable relationship between the prices of raw materials, primary products, manufactured and semi-manufactured goods exported by developing countries and the prices of raw materials, primary commodities, manufactures, capital goods and equipment imported by them". The aim must be, the Declaration states, to achieve sustained improvement in the unsatisfactory terms of trade of the developing countries and the expansion of the world economy. Other principles on trade deal with the need to improve the competitiveness of natural materials facing competition from synthetics, and preferential and non-reciprocal treatment for developing countries.

The Declaration stresses the need for the reform of the international monetary order and states that one of the main aims of such reform should be to increase and improve the flow of real resources to developing countries. The importance of technology in the process of development is also stressed and the Declaration calls for the creation of mechanisms to promote the transfer of technology to developing countries and for the development of indigenous technologies suitable to their economies.

The need for all nations to put an end to the waste of national resources, including food products, is stressed in a separate principle.

The Declaration is supported by a Program of Action of "urgent and effective measures" which need to be taken by the international community to assist the developing countries. The Program is of "unprecedented scope" and seeks to "bring about maximum economic cooperation and understanding among all States... based on the principles of dignity and sovereign equality". There are sets of measures covering problems of trade in raw materials and primary commodities, the international monetary system and development financing, industrialization, technology transfer, and the regulation and control of the activities of transnational corporations. The Program also contains measures with respect to the promotion of cooperation among developing countries, assistance in the exercise of permanent sovereignty of nations over their natural resources, the strengthening of the role of the United Nations system in the field of international

economic cooperation, and the special needs of the developing
countries most seriously affected by economic crises.

The adoption by the General Assembly of the Declaration and Program amounted to anything but agreement on the nature of the reforms required in the international economic order. The U.S.,
Japan and some of the larger members of the European Economic
Community expressed strong reservations. John Scali, the U.S.
representative, felt compelled to observe that the resolution
"does not represent unanimity of opinion in this Assembly. To
label some of these highly controversial conclusions as agreed
it not only idle, it is self-deceiving". (17)

Some issues were controversial. At the Seventh Special Session,
held just fifteen months after the Sixth Special Session, the
developing countries engineered success by omitting three of the
most controversial - permanent sovereignty over natural resources,
producer's associations, and control over transnational corporations - from their working paper. These tactical concessions
facilitated 'dialogue', and the then much heralded shift from
'confrontation' to 'cooperation'. (18) It enabled the European
Community to present a common front even though this was frequently achieved through extremely uneasy compromises. It even
helped Henry Kissinger, in a speech read by the U.S. Ambassador
to the U.N., to tell the poor countries: "We have heard your
voices. We embrace your hopes. We will join your efforts". (19)

Since then the NIEO has gone nowhere fast. The stage has been
reached where, following the Eleventh Special Session held in
August 1980, there is not only disagreement on the main elements
of the NIEO package but also on the very process to be used to
negotiate those elements. After five years of more or less continuous negotiations, the NIEO is, in a very real sense, now
further away than ever. (20)

THE NIEO PACKAGE RECONSIDERED

The NIEO package is not a carefully formulated and internally
consistent strategy for the reordering of the world economy. It
is rather a catalogue of longstanding Third World grievances.
Although presented as a revolutionary set of measures, it is in
fact nothing of the kind. It contains little that is 'new'. Its
novelty lies in its comprehensiveness and in the way in which
it was brought to the attention of the international community.
It was the context that was new, not the proposals for change.

In looking at the proposals in the areas of trade, commodities,
aid, technology, industrialization, there is an overriding sense
of *déjà-vu*. The Third World's concern for trade goes back to the
Havana Charter and the very early days of the United Nations

(cf chapter 4). The demand for more concessional assistance is similarly as old as the debate between the developed and developing countries: as early as 1961, the rich nations agreed in principle to target 0.7 per cent of their GNP to the poor nations in the form of 'official development assistance' (concessional transfers from or guaranteed by governments). Some two decades later, only four nations - Denmark, the Netherlands, Norway and Sweden - have achieved the target.

Particularly interesting is the commodity issue. The Common Fund and UNCTAD's Integrated Program on Commodities have become centerpieces of the NIEO package and the developing countries have put a good deal of effort into their negotiation. The commodity issue is, however, far from new. Like those of trade and aid, it is as old as the United Nations. Consider the record. In March 1947 ECOSOC established an Interim Coordinating Committee for International Commodity Arrangements which had the task of making recommendations to the Secretary General on the convening of commodity conferences. Some three years later, in August 1950, ECOSOC authorized the convening of intergovernmental conferences on specific commodity problems - conferences which resulted in the negotiation of three or five year agreements for four commodities (tin, sugar, olive oil and wheat) by the end of the 1950s. In 1954, ECOSOC established a subsidiary organ called the Commission on International Commodity Trade. Consisting of 18 members, its terms of reference were to examine measures designed to avoid large fluctuations in the prices and volume of trade in primary commodities. In 1958, the Commission's terms of reference were expanded to include studies on the terms of trade, focusing on the problems of the developing countries. In 1962, ECOSOC, after endorsing the Commission's work program, called upon the developed and developing countries to cooperate in solving commodity problems. It established a working group to make detailed studies of systems of compensatory financing to offset fluctuations in the export earnings of primary producing countries. The work of the group found its way into UNCTAD I, held in Geneva in 1964, a conference which goes down in history as the first major conceptual debate between North and South on global economic structures. (21)

The commodity debate continues today along the lines set two decades ago. But with one important difference. In the early days of debate, it was the Western nations which figured among the most ardent supporters of commodity agreements. The British Labor Government, for example, strongly advocated the conclusion of agreements whereby governments would commit themselves to buying or selling quantities of particular products at stated prices over periods as long as five years. Anticipating the logic of UNCTAD's proposals, it argued that the arrangements would benefit both buyer (assurances of supply) and the supplier (guaranteed outlets). The present British government is of course today one of the biggest critics of the very same logic.

It is a similar story with industrialization and technology. Nearly 30 years ago, on 12 January 1952, the General Assembly requested ECOSOC to investigate ways of promoting the rapid industrialization of the developing countries and to define the role which the industrialized countries could play in the process. It also called for an investigation into the ways in which science and technology could be applied to raise the productivity of people everywhere. These questions are still being asked.

Even the expression New International Economic Order is hardly new. Raul Prebisch, when Director of ECLA, called for a new economic order at UNCTAD I in 1964. So did the Afro-Asia Economic Seminar held in Algiers in the same year.

Albert Tévoédjrè has observed that the NIEO package bears a striking resemblance to the proposals formulated in his book *L'Afrique Révoltée*, which was published in 1958. (22) Mahbub ul Haq has even suggested that, in important respects, the NIEO package attempts to build the world which John Maynard Keynes tried to build at Bretton Woods. (23) Keynes advanced several proposals, such as automaticity in liquidity creation, the setting up of a commodity bank for primary commodity price stabilization, and the strengthening of the supranational element of financial institutions, which, in modified form, are today advanced by the Third World under the NIEO banner. (24) Then as today, these proposals met with fierce U.S. opposition. (cf chapter 4).

Many of the proposals which now make up the NIEO package are thus far from new. Some are as old as the United Nations and the debate on development. And if it has proved impossible to implement them in the past 30 years, we should not be unduly surprised if the same fate has befallen them in the past five years.

The proposals cannot be termed revolutionary, neither can their underlying logic. The NIEO's foundation's are firmly anchored in Western theory and value premises. Their rationale has been described by Gamani Corea who, as Secretary-General of UNCTAD, has been instrumental in drawing up the package in the following words: "I am of the opinion that the underlying desire, indeed demand, of all is that the countries of the Third World be incorporated into the system of world-wide trade. They do not any longer want to remain at the margin or outside of this system. They want to belong to it and to participate in the decisions and events that influence its development". (25)

In other words, the underlying ideology of the NIEO is impeccably capitalist. Using the terminology of chapter 2, we can safely call it a systems-reforming package. Inevitably, it has come in for strong criticism from radical circles and we will turn to these later.

In attempting to sum up the NIEO package one is, as Fred Hirsch
has noted, irresistibly drawn to Voltaire's famous dismissal of
the Holy Roman Empire - neither holy, nor Roman, nor Empire.
(26) And so with the NIEO. The program is far from new; some of
the proposals run counter to the development of an international
institutional presence; they are political and social as well as
economic; and the change which is to take place will be far from
orderly. But change will occur nonetheless. It is to perceptions
of the NIEO and to the processes of change which have been set
in motion that we will now turn.

ATTITUDES TO THE NIEO PACKAGE

Let us look briefly at the attitudes and reactions to the NIEO
package of the main negotiating parties. In doing so, we do not
set out to review the negotiations as such. A number of excellent reviews have already been published. (27) Nor do we aim at
a comprehensive appraisal, our review being deliberately selective.

The Western Industrialized
Nations and the NIEO

The West's participation in the North-South debate has been
based upon a grudging acceptance of the need to talk to the developing countries. Western negotiators have generally been
driven to the world's NIEO negotiating tables, not by the grievances of the Third World and the plight of the poor, but by the
plight of their own economies and by the serious dislocations in
the international economic system, the source of much of their
wealth. Hence their preoccupation with the need to safeguard
essential supplies of raw materials, especially oil.

The readiness of the West to discuss the NIEO package reached
its peak in the mid 1970s. Since then it has progressively declined. There are several reasons for this. First and foremost,
the West no longer fears OPEC. As the Interfutures report observes: "These countries have gradually come to realize that
their own development depends upon the prosperity of the OECD
countries". (28) Petrodollars have been recycled, arms and modern technology exported, links of dependency have been strengthened. The first strategic objective of the NIEO negotiations
- safeguarding supplies of oil - has been effectively achieved.

Secondly, the economic power of the Third World and, more importantly, its determination to use it collectively, was a threat
which never materialized. Internal difficulties within the Group
of 77 and the deterioration in the international political cli-

mate have resulted in a noticeable decline in developing country
support for some elements of the NIEO package. The West has seen
that the 'Third Worldism' of the mid 70s is increasingly giving
way to so-called 'pragmatic approaches' designed to maximize
national gains from participation in the international system.
(29) The economic problems of many developing countries are becoming ever more acute. The NIEO package, as it now stands, offers no way out and the very force of circumstances compels
them to wheel and deal with who they can with what they have.
As a Mexican banking magazine has pointedly observed: "the capitalist system is in crisis and everybody is trying to save what
he can". (30)

Thirdly, as the North-South negotiations progressed, the developing countries increasingly stressed the need for structural
changes in the international economic system. Structural change
is about the redistribution of privilege and power. Such change
cannot be brought about through a process of negotiation. It is
this simple but obvious fact which more than anything else ex-
plains the real lack of progress in the direction of the NIEO.
At a certain point in time all that negotiating parties can do
is, as the Chairman of UNCTAD V, Carlos P.Romulo, observed in
his closing address, "agree to disagree".

The change in the West's position to the NIEO package is well
reflected in the results of the 'summit' meetings held by the
leading seven economic powers in the second half of the 70s.
The Rambouillet Declaration, drawn up in the fall of 1975, the
good old days of the NIEO, emphasizes the importance of continued
economic growth and the need for harmony and cooperation among
all countries of the world. The Declaration of the Downing Street
summit, produced prior to the final meeting of CIEC, contains a
special section on North-South relations. It refers to the need
for "structural changes in the world economy" and observes that
"the world economy can only grow on a sustained and equitable
basis if developing countries share in that growth". The Western
leaders commit themselves "to a continued constructive dialogue
with developing countries" and to various measures designed to
help the poor nations. The Bonn summit of 1978 was widely regarded as having yielded the most concrete results of all those
held in the previous few years. Reference to North-South relations is, however, almost completely absent in the Bonn Declaration. Instead, the developing countries are requested to create a "good climate" for foreign private investment and to take
whatever steps are necessary to protect such investment. According to reports on the Bonn summit, the leaders simply did not
have sufficient time to get round to North-South issues, a clear
comment on the importance they attached to such issues. At the
Venice summit, held in June 1980, the seven managed to remain
completely silent on the report of the Brandt Commission, a report which, in Willy Brandt's own words, argues that the indus-

trialized countries should "be modern enlightened capitalists
who recognize that improving conditions for the broad masses
is also good business". (31)

The inescapable conclusion from this round of summit meetings
must be that the leaders of the largest Western powers, despite
previous statements and declared good intentions, no longer see
the need to involve the developing countries in their strategies
for economic reform or attach much importance to the NIEO debate.
This gives expression to the fundamental problem of the NIEO
package in most Western capitals: it simply is not and cannot be
taken seriously. (32) The 'systems-maintainers' described in
chapter 2 dismiss it virtually out of hand. The isolationists
argue that the NIEO is not only bad economics but also, because
it would most likely result in a worsening of relations with the
Third World, even worse politics. (33) The 'imperialists' give
preference to speculating on possible military approaches to
deal with an uppity Third Word. (34) The 'managers' see the NIEO
package as an extremist challenge full of overkill proposals.
For the 'manager', the international economic system is basically sound and the rules of the international game are essentially
fair. All that is required is more coordinated decision-making
in the West, the selective streamlining of international economic and financial institutions, and the more effective and
complete integration of OPEC countries and the NICs into the international economic system.

There are others in the West who, as self-styled friends of the
Third World, argue that the NIEO 'won't work' for reasons which
are not economic but essentially social and cultural. They stress
the Western origins of the NIEO package and of its basic ingredients. These ingredients, they argue, cannot be found outside
the West. They include widely shared assumptions with respect to
accomplishment and mastery as central to the meaning of Western
life; assumptions about the exploration and exploitation of the
material universe, the desirability of material possessions, the
value of knowledge, the importance of work. In no other region,
the critics argue, do similar assumptions exist. In regions where
Hinduism flourishes, shared assumptions concern a natural order
and predestination, manifested in fixed castes. Buddha, they
point out, preached a devotion to the simple and ascetism. The
idea of domination and control is similarly alien to those who
follow the teachings of Confucius and Lao Tze. Even Islam, a
religion associated with hostage taking and embassy burning, is
a religion of surrender to the will of God and is basically more
passive than Christianity. Regions where the great mass of people
subscribes to these otherworldly religions, so the argument goes,
cannot be fertile ground for belief in economic progress, industrialization and technological development. (35)

This is subtle but dangerous thinking, forming as it does the taproot of ideologies of ethnic and racial superiority. As we noted

earlier, the Judeo-Christian tradition provided sanctity to Western man's exploitative view of man and of nature. (36) Under such
a view, the legitimate instrument for expansion, conquest and
control was the state rather than the mind, as it traditionally
was in India and China. (37) It was a small step from this arro-
gant and self-centered view to the belief that some men were more
civilized than others and to the division of the human species
into advanced and backward peoples, into masters and slaves, into the chosen and the subject race. The view gave rise, in V.G.
Kiernan's phrase, to "lords of human kind" (38), to those who
believed that "we must obey our blood and occupy new markets and
if necessary new lands" because "in the Almighty's infinite plan
... debased civilization and decaying races" must disappear "before the higher civilization of the nobler and more virile types
of man". (39)

Ethnic superiority is intrinsic to the Western tradition and the
concept of *übermensch* and *untermensch* is inherent in the modern-
ist world view. Third World writers like Franz Fanon and Albert
Memmi have shown the terrible impact which the Western tradition
has had on the developing world (40); how colonialism became an
exercise in racial humiliation and was used to justify the most
brutal and brutalizing treatment. The poor were told that they
were inferior and, through the forced assimilation of an ideology of discrimination, came to believe they were. Colonialism
conquered souls as well as bodies and even when freed of tyranny,
the psychological scars are long in healing. As Franz Fanon observed, though the freed might have black skin, "they wear white
masks".

The NIEO is a historical attempt to redress some of the inequalities which have their roots in colonialism. It would be perverse
indeed if the very logic which underlied colonialism were to be
used to underpin a denial of reforms.

Does the NIEO package have a future in the West? Most of the
doors left ajar by the Seventh Special Session have now been
firmly closed and almost all the auguries are arrayed against
the NIEO being taken more seriously. The situation is worse than
it was five years ago. Central government in a number of Western
countries - notably the U.S. and U.K. - has been weakened by new
conservative administrations. In other countries there has been
a general movement toward the right which has eroded what support
there may have been for the NIEO. This together with a new interest in 'monetarism' and economic non-intervention makes it
more difficult than ever for the industrialized West to deal
with Third World demands. (41) Almost inevitably, there has been
some reneging on agreements reached earlier. At UNIDO III held
in early 1980 several Western nations backtracked on agreements
reached on trade, aid and technology transfer at UNCTAD V a year
earlier, and UNCTAD V was conspicuous for its lack of success.(42)

The cards are firmly stacked against the NIEO in the West. There
are those in the Third World who have been forced to the conclusion that the Western powers made concessions to the developing
countries out of fear. Those fears have now abated and it is
back to 'business as usual'. (43) If this is so, then the only
way of moving ahead may depend upon the Third World finding ways
of again making them nervous.

The Position of the United States. The RIO Report argued that
"the size and power of the United States impose special responsibilities both in continuing the operations of the international
organizations of which it is a member and in efforts to secure
agreements on means of making cooperation more effective. It especially must take the initiative in stimulating a constructive
North-South dialogue". (44)

As things turned out, the U.S. was at the forefront of attempts
to block international economic reforms. In this it has followed its historical role, a role which extends over half a century.
Franklin D.Roosevelt, for example, managed to sabotage the very
World Economic Conference he called in London in 1933. In doing
so, he managed to prevent the salvaging of the then world monetary system, an act which helped plunge Germany and Japan into
bankruptcy and everyone into the Second World War. At Bretton
Woods the U.S. successfully opposed Keynes' proposals for monetary reforms which, as we noted earlier, approximate those in
the NIEO package. And in turn, it was a U.S. President, Richard
Nixon, who scuttled the world monetary order created by the
U.S. at Bretton Woods.

The developing countries have traditionally been seen by U.S.
administrations as little more than pawns in the strategic chess
game with the U.S.S.R. (45) All world problems and processes are
reduced to this overwhelming concern with superpower politics.
It is a concern which prevents the U.S. from seeing the world as
it is, or has become. According to Stanley Hoffmann, the U.S.
began to lose its credibility in the conduct of its foreign policy once it lost touch with the increasing complexities of the
geopolitical system and when it failed to understand the games -
economic, political and military - which the world's nations
play. (46) With the Vietnam war it not only lost an ideological
struggle, but the very capacity to understand ideology. (47) Today, it simply does not understand why other peoples and their
leaders refuse to conform to its strategic blueprints, or to
bow to its narrowly defined interests.

The behavior of the U.S. has not only been disruptive to attempts
to forge new international economic relations. Its very pursuit
of its own strategic interests to the exclusion of much else,
including demands for more justice in economic relations, has
been a principal factor underlying demands for a more equitable
international order. Paradoxically and perversely, those very

demands have led the U.S. to become even more self-centered and
self-righteous than is its historical wont. (48)

There were hopes that things might have been different under the
Carter administration. But they were not. What happened to that
administration is a sobering lesson to the champions of the NIEO.
When Carter came to office he appeared to bring with him the
possibility of a new, more constructive response to the Third
World. The Nixon and Ford administrations, in which foreign policy was dictated by Henry Kissinger and thus a derivative of
his overwhelming preoccupation with superpower politics, had no
answer to the demands of the developing countries. (49) Carter
came to office with the promise of doubling U.S. aid to the
Third World by 1982. In his inaugural address, he promised to
"fight... against poverty, ignorance and injustice, for these
are enemies against which", he stated, U.S. "forces can be hon-
orably marshalled". He promised a "search for humility, mercy and
justice" and "equal treatment under the law, for the weak and
the powerful, for the rich and the poor". His presidency, he
decreed, marked the "day of a new beginning... to help shape a
just and peaceful world that is truly humane". In the early days
of the Carter administration, the talk may not have been of a
new world order but it was of a "new world system".

This new purpose was visible everywhere. It was evident in the
statement made by Cyrus Vance to CIEC 120 days into the new administration. Vance was a man who according to informed observers
brought to state as his most "cherished goal" the desire for the
U.S. to formulate a response to the Third World on the basis of
an understanding of the needs of the Third World. (50) He told
the delegates assembled in Paris that "There should be a new
economic system. In that system there must be equity; there must
be growth; but, above all, there must be justice. We are prepared
to help build that new system". A week earlier, Carter told the
graduating class of Notre Dame that the U.S. needed a "new American foreign policy... In this world", he observed, "our policy
must shape a new international system". In similar vein, Zbigniew Brzezinski, in an interview with US News and World Report
(51), referred to a new era of creativity in international affairs. "In our view", he argued, "we are now at a stage in history in which the United States again has to undertake a creative process of building a new world system". A few months
later he told the Trilateral Commission when it met in Bonn that
there was a "return to American idealism". In these early statements by Brzezinski, the views and values contained in a widely
read article written by him on foreign policy just prior to
taking office were clearly in evidence. (52)

All rhetoric? There were grounds for believing that this was not
so. Economists were brought into the administration who, although
firmly moulded in classical traditions, had proven that they

possesses an international outlook. Prime responsibility for the
fashioning of cooperative international economic relations fell
to Richard Cooper (Under-Secretary of State for International
Economic Affairs) and to C.Fred Bergsten (Under-Secretary of the
Treasury). Their writings as staff members of the Brookings Institution had commanded a good deal of attention.

Cooper had argued the case for a "New International Economic
Order for mutual gain" and stressed the need to reconcile national prerogatives with growing global interdependencies. (53)
Bergsten argued forcibly that U.S. administrations had consistently failed to formulate an adequate response "to the legitimate aspirations of the developing countries". A future administration, he contended, must develop a package of measures which
"includes more positive support... for primary policy objectives
of the Third World". The formulation of this new response should
not, he argued, be made dependent upon the cooperation of other
countries. "It is in the national interest of the U.S.", he contended, "to pursue such programs whether other potential donors
do so or not". Devising and implementing an adequate response,
he concluded, "is a worthy challenge for the economic and foreign
policy-maker of the United States, and indeed could provide its
primary focus for the rest of the 1970s".(54)

This is about as good a set of starting points as one could
reasonably hope for in the U.S. There was to be a new foreign
policy aimed at creating a new world system and there was to be
space for the legitimate interests of the Third World. It was a
policy founded on the desire to give Americans more confidence
in the aftermath of the Vietnam tragedy and more self-respect
following Kissinger's morally ambiguous realpolitik. Carter
sought to replace secrecy and intrigue with open diplomacy, to
make new friends in the Third World and to take up such 'survival' issues as the 'development gap' and the nuclear arms race.
Viewed from the perspective of the Third World, the omens were
good.

It soon started to go terribly wrong. On 15 February 1978, a
little more than a year after Carter's coming to power, the
Christian Science Monitor in an editorial felt compelled to ask
"Whatever happened to the great American concern about the Third
World". It has become clear, the editorial observed, that "the
Carter administration is postponing the building work". (55)

The administration soon became the prisoner of the U.S. political system, a system which is able to torpedo Presidential policy
initiatives and which is designed to erode policy discretion. (56)
Carter soon discovered that not only is there little scope for
'idealism' and 'creative thinking' but also that such things are
held in deep suspicion and even made subject to ridicule. As he
was forced to throw out of the window all of the values which
underpinned his acceptance speech, the U.S. bemoaned his failure

to reform the system while emasculating every attempt he made
to do so. It decried his lack of leadership while making it impossible. The U.S. political system transforms, deforms, and
cripples its executives: at the end of the Carter administration,
Cooper, for example, had become an arch conservative and Brzezinski's description of Kissinger's foreign policy - "covert,
manipulative, and deceptive in style, it seemed committed to a
largely static view of the world, based on a traditional balance
of power, seeking accommodation among the major powers on the
basis of spheres of influence, and more generally oriented toward preserving the status quo than reforming it" (57) - could
just as easily have been applied to his own style.

The strength and narrow-mindedness of U.S. conservatism is illustrated in the case of the Trilateral Commission. As we noted
in chapter 2, many of the most prominent figures in the Carter
administration, including Mondale, Vance, Brzezinski and Carter
himself (58), had been members of the Commission. The main concern of the Commission is to ' manage interdependence'. The
radical left sees the Commission as an imperial forum, one motivated by the desire to build "a capitalist world dominated by
the industrial capitalist nations (themselves dominated by transnational financial interests), cooperating in a concerted offensive against Third World revolutionism (and) in presenting a
common front to the socialist world on economic, political, and
eventually military matters". (59) A not particularly flattering
but hardly inaccurate description of the Trilateral Commission.
Hardly the description of a 'subversive' organization. Yet that
is exactly how it was presented by conservative and some labor
groups in the 1980 Presidential campaign. Bush and Anderson both
had to convince Republican conservatives that their association
with the Commission did not make them potentially dangerous sub-
versives, enemies of U.S. interests abroad. (60)

History will almost certainly judge the U.S. more harshly than
it will judge Jimmy Carter. As far as the NIEO is concerned, the
Carter administration may well signal the 'good old days'. Today
it is Ronald Reagan. When the U.S. requires a statesman who can
emancipate the nation from the misguided assumptions of the past,
who can expand national horizons and the sense of purpose, and
who can guide the country into new modes of thought, it has
elected a President who promises a vision of the world as it was,
not as it is, and certainly not as it must become.

Reagan has not been slow to implement his 1950s vision of the
world. It took him just two months to announce the biggest increase in arms spending in history. He has decided to put the
neutron bomb into production, a weapon which kills people and
leaves buildings standing. He has thrown the SALT II agreement
out of the window and refuses to talk to Soviet leaders who he
has accused of "international terrorism". He has sent military

advisers to prop up the non-representative regime in El Salvador, expressed the readiness to resume the sale of weapons to Argentina and Chile, and to generally strengthen links with authoritarian regimes in Latin America. With respect to the Third World, he has slashed U.S. aid programs and his country's support to the World Bank, the world's most important development agency. He has stalled on the Kreisky-Lopez Portillo backed North-South summit and threatens to sabotage the Convention on the Law of the Sea which has been eight years in the making. And on the home front he has rewritten Carter's energy policy in favor of the nuclear option and moved to soften air pollution standards. All in just sixty days. A record which hardly augurs well for the future.

It certainly holds out little hope for the Third World. No wonder Fidel Castro felt obliged to observe on the eve of the U.S. election when asked about Reagan that the developing countries "sometimes have the feeling that (they) are living in the time preceding the election of Adolf Hitler as chancellor of Germany". (61)

Not only are the developing countries threatened. The U.S. is itself threatened by a hubris that assumes that God, nature and history decree that the country always be number one in military and political power throughout the globe, and which regards competitors as enemies, allies as instruments and as 'cards' to be played by U.S. hands. (62) While this situation prevails, there can be little hope for the NIEO, and perhaps even little hope for mankind as a whole.

Henry Kissinger once observed that "Where the world is going depends importantly on the United States". (63) And this is true. It is a tragedy that the U.S. is unable to discern directions which are genuinely worthwhile. The question is not whether U.S. 'leadership' will become more receptive to the aspirations of the Third World. It is whether it is at all able to, even if it wanted to. While the U.S. continues to believe that its only duty to the world is to be rich and strong, it will not participate in the shaping of a more rational and equitable international order. (64) And if it will not or cannot participate, then ways will surely have to be found of doing it without it.

The Position of Western Europe. Western Europe's response to the demands for a NIEO have, with few exceptions, been similarly disappointing. The larger nations especially have demonstrated a lamentable inability to engage in a dialogue with the Third World at the global level. Even worse, when discussions have gone beyond posturing to serious negotiation, they have shown a readiness to take refuge behind the stone wall positions of the U.S.

The stake of Western Europe in the present international order

is very large, much greater than that of the U.S. It is the
biggest trading block and it has historical links - colonial
links - with the Third World, links which have, in the case of
the EEC, been institutionalized under the Lomé Convention. The
stake is such that Western Europe must be at the forefront of attempts to fashion new global strategies based upon a constructive
response to the aspirations and legitimate interests of the developing world. There is no alternative to such a role. (65)

Western Europe must learn to act more independently of the U.S.
and with more conviction. There is more to life and more at stake
than simply reacting to U.S. policy. A more independent line
would make it possible for Western Europe to 'take over' some
of the areas in which the U.S. is either inactive, ineffective, or
even disruptive. These areas include the NIEO and relations with
the Third World. This a task of historical dimensions. The fear
must be, however, as Michel Robert, the former French foreign
minister, has observed that "Europe is neither worthy of its
destiny nor equal to the moderating role it claims to be playing
in the present crisis... It was the day before yesterday that
Europe narrowly missed history. Now, alas, history is more than
ever beyond its reach". (66)

The Soviet Union and the NIEO

The Soviet Union has consistently supported Third World demands
for a NIEO. Given its growing role in international trade and
the intensification of its economic relations with the developing world, the Soviet Union sees the NIEO as being compatible
with its own interests. "The socialist nations", it argues,
"have nothing to gain from word economic chaos. Their collective
as well as national interests will best be met by a stable world
economic system based upon the principles of equality, justice,
mutual benefit and international cooperation". (67)

It has not, however, played a very active role in the North-South
debate on the NIEO. There appears to be three main reasons for
this. Firstly, Soviet spokesmen have persistently argued that
the new economic order represents indemnification for former
colonial exploitation. Since the centrally planned nations have
not participated in this exploitation, so they insist, it cannot be expected that they should share in the compensation.
Secondly, the Soviet Union recognizes capitalist reform proposals
when it sees them. Virtually all major international economic
and financial organizations are perceived by the Soviets as institutions created by the rich capitalist nations in order to
serve their own interests. Improvements in the efficiency of
these institutions, an essential ingredient of the NIEO, will
enhance the capacity for accumulation in the capitalist center.
Why should the Soviet Union participate in such an operation?

The third reservation is the most interesting. It stems from
the well-known Marxist thesis that a change of significant dimensions in international economic relations must necessarily
effect political relations, namely the international power structure, which is not exclusively set on ideological lines. The
Soviet Union is suspicious of the NIEO program. With its emphasis on interdependence it fails to recognize class antagonisms
and the importance and role of economic imperialism and neo-
colonialism, problems which need to be met head on in open
political confrontation. (68)

Interestingly, the Soviet Union has linked the notion of a NIEO
to the need for superpower cooperation in combatting the arms
race. As Alexei Gromyko told the Sixth Special Session, "the
economic upheavals which many states have been going through
have (of late) increased in intensity, and they are increasingly affecting the people's material situation. Statesmen and economists are racking their brains over the causes behind all this.
But the conclusion that is borne out every day and every hour is
beyond question: the aggravation of economic problems is largely
connected with the rising scale of the arms race and with soar-
ing military expenditure". (69) In the Soviet view, superpower
cooperation in arms reduction and political detente "constitutes
an indispensable condition for the establishement of a new international order". (70)

Soviet support for the NIEO has thus been largely rhetorical.
Words have not generally been translated into deeds. The developing countries are finding it difficult to mask their growing
impatience with Eastern Europe and Soviet condemnations of economic imperialism no longer receive the warm applause in international fora that they once enjoyed. Some five years ago Mexico's President Echeverría was forced to observe that "the richest socialist countries are not helping the developing nations
as much as they sometimes say they are". (71) Third World criticism is today even less modulated.

Sensitivity to the growing chorus of criticism no doubt played
a role in the recent decision of the Eastern European nations
to make concessions in the case of the Common Fund. To help demonstrate to the Third World that they are not totally motivated
by self-interest, they agreed to put up 17 per cent of the Fund's
capital in return for only 8 per cent of the vote.

The Third World and the NIEO

The collective objectives of the Third World in the North-South
debate have been, as in the past, to extract the maximum economic and political gains, especially from trade and resource flows,
at a minimum of costs to themselves. In this they have until

comparatively recently displayed a remarkable degree of unity,
even though the fruits of their labors have inevitably been
modest indeed. A much diluted Common Fund, the International
Fund for Agricultural Development, and the shrinking Interim
Fund for Science and Technology for Development is about all
they have to show as the tangible results of their efforts.

In an attempt to engineer progress, Third World negotiators have
resorted to what André Gunder Frank has called "salami tactics".
(72) They have sliced off their demands little by little in an
attempt to make their wares more appetizing for the rich. There
is a limit to such tactics, for a point is reached where there
is so little salami left that you cut your own fingers. Perhaps
salami is the wrong analogy. Perhaps the tactics have more
strongly resembled the peeling of an onion. Layers have been re-
moved, one after the other, in the hope of finding the NIEO inside. The danger here is that the Third World will end up with
nothing left to peel and with tears in its eyes.

The Third World has approached its negotiations with the rich
on the basis of an undifferentiated and unstructured list of
demands and without seriously attempting to clarify and elaborate its own objectives and negotiating tactics. It has been
prevented from doing this by internal differences and by the
lack of adequate institutional backstopping. (73) In this it has
failed to serve its own cause. There can also be little doubt
that some Third World leaders have used calls for more equity in
international economic relations to enhance their position and
status at home and abroad. (74) On the home front, some Third
World politicians have thrown much of the blame for the worsening conditions of the poor masses on external factors alone,
providing themselves with an excuse for ineffective policies,
lack of action, even the maintenance of structures of inequality.
(75) At the same time, they have resolutely, but not unreason-
ably, refused to discuss the linking of the reform of the international order to the transformation of their own national orders.

The main question, however, is whether the implementation of the
NIEO package will change much in the Third World. There are many
who argue that it will not. Johan Galtung is among those who
have asked what the world would look like if the NIEO reforms
were to become reality. "We are afraid the answer will have to
be relatively simple", he concludes. "It will look about the
same as before, but with two very important differences - there
will be more accumulation of capital in the center of the periphery, and there will be more independent capitalist activity
carried out by the centers in today's periphery". (76) Others
have argued that the NIEO reforms will serve as a means to advance the possibilities for accumulation for peripheral capitalism and for elitist groups, the servants of Western capitalism.
The reforms have little to offer the poor in the poor countries;
they may even work against rather than for their interests. (77)

This view is predicated on a perception of Western capitalism and its imperialist and neo-colonialist tendencies. The debate on capitalism and imperialism has been long and frequently bitter. Whereas we cannot hope to do justice to it here, a few observations on contending views would, given their relationship to perceptions of the NIEO package, appear to be in order.

Imperialism can be said to exist when a nation seeks to establish control beyond its borders over people unwilling to accept or unable to resist such control. Because of this unwillingness, imperialism always involves the use of various forms of power - military, economic, ideological - against its victims. Stated in these general terms, imperialism is obviously as old as history. (78)

The debate on capitalist imperialism has focused upon economic processes. (79) Virtually all the theories formulated share a common starting point which is economic: the doctrine of the declining tendency of the rate of profit and capital. Both liberals, such as Adam Smith, Thomas Malthus, J.S. Mill, Sismondi, David Ricardo and Hobson and radicals, like Karl Marx, Rosa Luxemburg and Lenin all built theories on explanations of this phenomenon. The central theme in all their theories is that colonial territories were acquired primarily because they were required for reasons of national economic development.

The liberals, notably Robertson, Hobson and Brailsford (80), argued that the main force was 'underconsumption', a principle derived from the Swiss economist Sismondi. The unequal distribution of wealth in capitalist societies, they argued, so deprived the mass of workers of buying power that the capitalist classes could not profitably invest their surplus capital in industry at home. Colonies were alternative fields for profitable investment. Many liberals, including Smith and Ricardo, rejected imperialism as a deliberate policy, arguing that whereas it might benefit a small privileged group, it can never serve the best interests of the nation as a whole.

Marxists sought other explanations and theories of capitalist imperialism have come to occupy a special place in the Marxist tradition. (81) Rosa Luxemburg reformulated Marx's analysis and sought to demonstrate the existence of a total world economy assimilated to capitalism. (82) Relating the accumulation of industrial capital to imperialism, she argued that capitalist countries were dependent upon trade with non-capitalist territories at all stages of their development and that the acquisition of colonies was primarily the result of a shortage of such extra-European 'commercial balancers'. By contrast, Hilferding, Bukharin and Lenin argued that imperialism was the product of the special economic problems of capitalism in its last, monopolistic, phase when 'finance capital' has absorbed competitive capital. In this last phase, monopolist economies are forced to

compete in the conquest of outlets for their overproduction and
surplus capital. (83)

In basically all these views, liberal and Marxist, the essence
of the argument is that capitalist imperialism was the product
of factors within European nations and that colonial territories
were acquired in order to save capitalism from a moribund condition in which the further accumulation of capital within Europe
was becoming impossible. The views are, however, sharply divided
on the question of whether imperialism was an irrevocable part
of capitalism. To the liberals it was not or need not be. Most
Marxists argued that a capitalist society is imperialist because
it has to be. In *Imperialism, The Highest Stage of Capitalism*,
Lenin sets out to show that imperialism is a "direct continuation
of the fundamental properties of capitalism in general". In this
respect, "imperialism is not a matter of choice for a capitalist
society; it is the way of life". (84) Not all Marxists agreed.
Some moderate Marxists like Karl Kautsky and Rudolf Hilferding
argued that imperialism need not be synonymous with capitalism;
that imperialism is a possible but not necessarily an inevitable
policy of the capitalist state. Their view thus approximates
that of the liberals.

These early writers established the ideological, theoretical and
analytical foundations upon which subsequent generations of ana-
lists have built. Most of the early writers were Europeans who
approached the problem of capitalist imperialism from the viewpoint of the imperialist power. In the post war period, a whole
school of critical thought has emerged - the so-called dependency school - which has as its starting point the situation of
the poor country.

The dependency theorists have continued the line of reasoning
pioneered by Lenin. For them, dependence is imperialism viewed
from the perspective of underdevelopment. (85)

To dependency theorists the world is best interpreted as an integrated and hierarchical system assimilated to capitalism. It
has a center comprising a handful of industrialized capitalist
powers and a periphery of dependent poor countries. The development of the center is seen to be intimately linked to the colonial and neo-colonial exploitation of the periphery. Underdevelopment is explained as a historical phenomenon which must be
understood, not in terms of the 'vicious circles' or 'stages'
of economic growth so dear to the liberals, but in the context
of the integration of the periphery into the international capitalist system. Dependence cannot thus be attributed exclusively to 'external factors' which can be addressed through 'appropriate' policy decisions, but as a conditioning situation in
which the specific histories of development and underdevelopment
transpire in different regions and countries. Underdevelopment,
a consequence of the dialectical process of the international-

ization of the world capitalist system, can thus occur in a
number of forms and in various stages.

The international capitalist system is not seen as being exclusively 'economic'. Rather, it comprises a structure of institutions, classes and power relations which underlie the functioning of the world economy. This hierarchical structure is characterized by a complex set of exploitative relations. As Baran
and Sweezy put it: "Those at the top exploit in varying degrees
all the lower layers, and similarly those at any given level exploit those below them until we reach the very lowest layer which
has no one to exploit". (86) The lowest layer is the poor in the
poor countries. The essential point, however, is that domination
and dependence is only possible when it finds support among local
groups which profit by it, and that the internationalization of
Western capitalism has shaped dependent national class and power
structures in the periphery; classes which have developed as the
weak servant of Western capitalism and reaped considerable rewards in the process. (87)

The relationships underlying the operation of the international
system are seen as the decisive force in the disruption of indigenous systems and cultural values. Few areas and peoples have
been left untouched by the expansion and consolidation of the
system. It has, in Frank's words, "effectively and entirely pen-
etrated even the apparently most isolated sectors of the underdeveloped world". (88) Laclau has sought to show how in Latin
America even the most backward peasant regions are bound by fine
threads to the 'dynamic' sector of the national economy and
through it to the world market. (89) Because the industries of
the periphery have developed to meet the requirements of the
center rather than the poor masses, it has meant that many developing countries are now less able to satisfy the basic needs
of their own populations than they were before the colonial
period. The structural imbalance between capital goods and consumption goods industries created in the colonial period has
been maintained and reproduced within the overall framework of
domination and dependence. Dependency has meant that developing
countries are national spaces rather than national economies,
having developed as internally incoherent systems. (90)

Dependency theory has greatly enriched the social sciences. (91)
It has given rise to a school of thought (92) in which some of
the streams have become antithetical to the Marxist tradition.
(93) Most dependency theorists would, however, contend that capitalism requires international inequity as a precondition for
its contradictory existence and thus cannot be the angel of salvation for the vast majority of poor countries. As Marx warned,
capitalism creates for itself a world in its own image. But rather than developing all the areas it touches, as Marx suggested,
it can positively lead to their underdevelopment. (94)

So far, dependency theory has been mainly used for purposes of critique: it has focused upon 'problems' rather than 'solutions'. (95) Inevitably, the dependency paradigm leads to the conclusion that, short of "bursting the imperialist snare" (96), there is little that can be done by the developing countries to advance their development. (97) And imperial snare bursting is neither the penchant of Third World elites nor the predilection of Third World negotiators. (98)

That the radical left is unable to take the NIEO package seriously should be obvious. Its critique has three essential components. (99) Firstly, it consists of an historical refutation of the notion that capitalism can be tamed; rather, capitalism is seen as an expansive system dedicated to reproducing a world in its own image. Secondly, it suggests that, as reform is impossible, disengagement from the system, however difficult this will prove in practice, is an essential prerequisite for both the internal and international change necessary to advance the interests of the great mass of poor people. And thirdly, it recognizes that the reformist option is crucial for the retention of power by incumbent, dependent leaders; the myth of reform is essential for those who are caught between the pressures of the poor and the intransigence of the rich. In the radical view, "the greatest illusion permeating the argument for the NIEO is that a new division of income between the rich and poor nations in the capitalist world system can be achieved through diplomatic negotiations". (100)

There is, of course, nothing new in dependence and domination: international society has long been stratified in many different ways. (101) Whether the radical view of capitalist imperialism is 'right' is a matter of debate, not of fact. (102) The question of whether the Third World is 'right' in its interpretation of its own backwardness, whether the processes of dependence and domination exactly correspond to the analyses presented by radical scholars is, however, a secondary consideration. The struggle for economic liberation is no less a political struggle than the fight for political independence. And in a political struggle, success is not determined by scientific truths or scholarly prognostications but by the ability to mobilize and catalyze. The argument of dependence and domination can be endorsed for political reasons, even at the level of diplomatic posturing. And when it is endorsed, it becomes a pragmatic truth and serves as a driving force.

At one level, there is nowhere to go, short of the bomb factory, with the radical alternative. At another, it is a catalyzing and legitimizing force and as such a crucial ingredient of the dialectics of change.

China and the NIEO

In discussing China's attitude to the NIEO a clear distinction
has to be made between the Maoist and post-Maoist period. Mao
interpreted the problem of world order as a struggle between the
defenders of the status quo and its revolutionary challengers.
(103) It is an image deeply imbued with justice rather than order, with change rather than stability. The moral and strategic
imperative of the interpretation was unequivocal: the international order is unjust and thus has to be destroyed before a new
and equitable order can be established.

The image of world order is antihierarchical. Basic to Mao's
view was the problem of the underdog struggling to survive in a
hostile environment. In this situation, 'great disorder' is an
objective fact. All basic contradictions in the world are seen
to be sharpening, particularly the contradictions between the
two superpowers and the peoples of all other countries on the
one hand and, on the other, between the two superpowers themselves. These contradictions and the disorder to which they give
rise are, however, seen as positive since they only hasten the
demise of the old order which is founded on colonialism, imperialism and hegemony. "In this turbulent world", the Chinese have
metaphorically stated, "the people in their fight are, like sea-
gulls flying high in the sky, harbingers of a rising storm. In
this great disorder they have nothing to lose but their chains;
they have a new world to win". (104)

The Maoist view of world order prevented the Chinese from taking
the NIEO enterprise very seriously. Since the death of Mao, however, economic and social policy has changed fundamentally. The
new leaders talk openly of "ten lost years" and of the duty of
the Chinese "to make money". (105) In the space of a few years,
China has moved from passivity on the NIEO stage to an active
participant. According to Kim, the People's Daily has begun to
report and analyze global economic issues, page 5 or 6 usually
being devoted to reporting on and analysis of problems or activities related to the NIEO. (106)

The new attitude is reflected in many ways. China is now actively exploring the possibilities of cooperative endeavors with the
citadels of capitalism. It recently announced its first batch of
joint ventures with foreign companies and new ones are limited
more by foreign exchange limitations than ideological considerations. (107) Between 1977 and 1979, China imported 71,000 scientific and technical study books, notably from the U.S., although
at present few can read them. But the situation is to change. As
Li Foe Ning, director of China's television university, recently
observed: "English is the first foreign language. We must learn
English like we drink water". (108) The opening of the doors to
foreign tourists - 800,000 in 1979 - and to Western films and
even television broadcasts are all part of the same process.

China has inevitably been criticized for betraying the revolution. Many radical scholars have bemoaned its *embourgoisiement*
and pointed to the importance of the shifts involved. (109) Most
in the West, however, welcome its newly acquired desire to more
fully and actively participate in international economic decision-making. It can only be 'good for business'. Like the Interfutures Study (cf.chapter 2), many now expect it to become "an
important part of the world economy" by the end of the century.
(110) It certainly seems destined to become a more active participant in new global negotiations on the creation of a NIEO.

                    THE NIEO AS A POINT OF DEPARTURE

What can we conclude from the above? There can be little doubt
that the international economic order, as it has evolved, is
fundamentally inequitable and the root cause of many of the afflictions which beset large parts of the Third World. There is
much that is wrong. There is much that needs to be put right.
It is right that we should try to put things right. The problem
is how. For when one moves from what is wrong to what needs to
be done the difficulties are enormous.

The international economic system is a juggernaut and, like a
juggernaut, it is an inexorable force that obeys its own laws.
True, it is an aging juggernaut, caught in a process of decline.
But it is no less powerful. It remains the guardian of the interests of the rich and, as such, it is insensitive to the needs
and aspirations of the poor.

The NIEO reforms will not tame the juggernaut, nor will they
hasten its demise. Themselves the product of the system they
seek to reform, they cannot lead to its transformation. They
will result in modest redistribution, enhancing the possibilities for accumulation in parts of the periphery. They will not
lead to significant improvements in the world into which hundreds
of millions of poor and desperate people are born and die.

There is, however, no radical alternative to the NIEO package
just as there is no alternative to the prevailing international
order which has any relevance outside academic debate. Existing
power arrangements do not permit plausible alternatives. We can
conceive them, but we cannot realize them. For while power structures are far from static, they will remain, at least for the
forseeable future, the coral reef upon which the radical ship
will run aground.

The NIEO reforms thus have inherent limitations. But they are
not without a historical significance. It is our duty to support
them. Not as a solution, but as a point of departure. Historically, they may serve as a fragile foundation upon which the

poor of the world may one day be able to build. The route to a
more rational and equitable international order passes through
the New International Economic Order.

GLOBAL STRATEGIES FOR GLOBAL REFORM

Let us now turn our attention to the aims and scope of strategies which will bring closer a more rational and equitable international order. In this section we will attempt to identify
some of the principles which should shape strategies and some
of the main elements of global reform. Prior to discussing these,
however, we will sketch the context for strategies, a context
which provides the essential perspective for the proposals contained in this as well as subsequent chapters.

Context for Strategies

That changes in the international order and in the forces which
shape it are necessary is no longer a matter of serious debate.
The question is what kind of change is required, who are to be
the main beneficiaries and, ultimately, whether the changes
will be brought about in a reasonably orderly fashion or whether
they will be born out of turmoil and violent conflict. The in-
dications are that violence will dominate international relations
in the 1980s and if, as Comte suggested, progress is the development of order, then it seems reasonable to assume that progress
in the direction of a more rational and equitable international
order will be slow and painful indeed.

History teaches us that fundamental change is born out of one
of two conditions: chaos and confusion or strength and confidence. In contemporary history it has been the former which has
dominated. Change has had its birth in the trauma following disaster and in the fear for a common enemy. New orders have been
created and imposed by one or a group of dominant powers following a period of turmoil and crisis, and often military adventures and war. (111) New orders have not emerged through the
joint exercise of enlightened self-interest. If history has
taught us one thing, it is that mankind only seeks a rational
solution to a problem when it has exhausted all other possibilities.

Experience of the past also points to the enormous difference
between knowing and experiencing. Knowledge of impending disaster
is not in itself sufficient to prompt preventative action. If
it were, our world would be free of nuclear weapons. Knowledge
of the horror which they can inflict has not halted their development and deployment and, tragic as it is, it will not pre-

vent their use. Pain, suffering and sorrow need to be experienced in bone and marrow before steps are taken to come to terms with a problem, by which time it is invariably too late. It is in this sense that Toynbee describes history as a continuous drama of failure to meet fundamental challenge. (112) It is surely one of the perversities of our time that the mentality required to meet the challenge of the nuclear arms race may only emerge from the rubble of a nuclear holocaust.

History's lessons are thus ominous. Survival may literally depend upon us refusing to accept them. For if we have to await a catastrophe of awesome proportions before attempting to build new institutions, we may have nothing left to build with but charred hands in a landscape of tragic desolation. (113)

There seems little doubt that the 1980s will go down in history as a period of unprecedented chaos and confusion. For, as Silviu Brucan has observed, "never before have so many social and political contradictions requiring structural changes converged in a world so small and so susceptible to destroying itself". (114) Prophets of all kinds have warned that the sea will be rough, the straights narrow, weather conditions poor, and navigation perilous. Even astrologers, drawing upon cosmic inspiration, have warned us that the 1980s will be stormy indeed.

Let us take a brief look at some of the main 'conflict formations' which will exist in the 1980s.

East-West Relations: Four Minutes to Midnight. The fires of superpower rivalries, fanned by Washington, have recently flared to new heights and may yet incinerate the world. The nuclear arms race, long devoid of logic and clearly out of control, threatens to lead us all, like lemmings, over the nuclear abyss, making the 1980s the execution block of history. (115) Distinguished scholars of all types continue to warn us of the desperate dangers we refuse to face. Von Weizsäcker, for example, believes an atomic war this century to be "highly probable". (116) Bernard Feld of Pugwash argues that there is one chance in three that a thermonuclear bomb will be used before 1984 and a fifty-fifty chance of nuclear war by the end of the century. He sets the nuclear clock at four minutes to midnight. "As the year 1980 drew to a close", he recently observed, "the world seemed to be moving unevenly but inexorably closer to nuclear disaster". (117) The trends support his conclusion: the abandonment of SALT II, the decision to manufacture the neutron bomb, the modernization of Euro-strategic weapons, the determination to increase 'defense' expenditures, official declarations that nuclear war is 'thinkable', all combine to push the world closer to the nuclear brink.

Superpower rivalries and the arms race have created a climate of suspicion and mistrust and poisoned the well of international cooperation. They have spilt over into the Third World and led to the militarization of world politics. According to the Soviet Union, the U.S. has built 2,500 military bases and projects throughout the world, ostensibly to defend its strategic interests. (118) Where the world is going will greatly depend upon where the superpowers take us. There may be nothing inevitable about convergence theory. (119)

North-South Conflicts: The Revolt of the South. The 1980s will witness the continuation and intensification of the global fairness revolution. Developing countries will continue their struggle for equality of opportunity in international economic relations and for a greater say in economic decision-making. This struggle will be combined with growing resentment of Western economic dominance and distrust of Western 'deals', 'principles' and 'models'.

Conflicts within the West: Transition to What? There is every reason to believe that the prevailing crisis of Western capitalism is much more than an unfortunate conjunction of negative cycles, as McCracken suggested it was (120), or the result of failure of 'appropriate' government policies, as many establishment economists in universities, business and government thought it might be. Today, economists of different political persuasions are asserting that the crisis of capitalism marks a crucial historical turning point and nothing short of very basic changes will suffice.

Radical economists have long predicted the crisis and regard it as inevitable. The problems besetting capitalist societies - inflation, unemployment, declining productivity, monetary instability, growing indebtedness, alienation, the resurgence of protectionism - they regard as symptoms. The roots of the crisis are, they argue, to be found in the very structures that have in the past guaranteed economic growth and in the contradictions which capitalism requires to maintain itself. The crisis of capitalism is a crisis of capitalist structures. (121)

Many conservative economists, though they dispute the diagnosis, share the sense of urgency. They point in increasing numbers to the seriousness and enormity of the 'challenge' facing the West. Rostow, for example, having examined so-called long cycles, has been forced to conclude that "The greatest challenge to industrial civilization, since it began to take shape two centuries ago, is upon us now and in the generation ahead". (122)

Whereas it is too much to suggest that the 1980s will witness the death throws of capitalism, it will witness an acceleration of the process of decline, a process which is irreversible. How long the process of decline will last and what will replace it are matters of conjecture. (123) It seems certain, however, that the process will give rise to anxieties, recriminations and tensions. The decline will be far from peaceful. Anxiety and uncertainty have already entered the daily experiences and perceptions

of millions of people. There is a gnawing fear that the good
times may be over, that even modest expectations may not be fulfilled. This is and will increasingly be a traumatic experience
and, like all traumatic experiences, its consequences are incalculable. The consequences will, however, reverberate throughout
the 1980s.

Conflicts Within the East: The Dissolution of Empire. If the
West has to supervise the demise of capitalism, the East has to
deal creatively with the dissolution of empire. The Soviet Union
presides uneasily over the last remaining colonial empire. Itself the product of sixty republics and 100 different ethnic
groups, it maintains a firm grip on Eastern European satellites
which are in search of new freedoms.

The Soviet Union is a political monolith. The monolith is crack-
ing under the pressure of internal tensions and economic stresses.
The pressures will build as demands for autonomy and self-determination increase. Not the least of the pressures will be exerted
by the Soviet Union's Moslem population. The Soviet Union is the
third largest Islamic power. Its 60 million Moslems make up a
third of its population. By the year 2000 they will account for
40 per cent. The new combination of Islam and nationalism, forged
in the crucible of the Middle East, is a major threat to the
Soviet monolith. (124)

Whether the Soviet Union can develop the flexibility required
to creatively preside over the dissolution of its empire is a
very significant world order question. Experience tells us that
countries which are unable to deal with growing internal pressures frequently seek outside targets to which the pressures can
be diverted. There will be no shortage of outside targets in the
1980s. Related to this is the important question of whether the
West - notably the United States - will give the Soviet Union
room for maneuver. Should it maintain its determination to en-
circle the Soviet Union with ever more virulent weapon systems,
it is effectively denying the Soviet Union the opportunity to
formulate the required response. And in doing so, it is strengthening its prime position as an 'outside target'.

Conflicts Within the South: The Second Wave of Revolution. Tidal
waves of change will sweep across the Third World during the
remainder of this century. The capitalist middle classes and
ruling elites, linked to Western capitalism, will be subjected
to mounting pressure under the combined weight of rising expectations and persistent, crushing poverty. Men rebel when subjected by governments to supression in conditions of deprivation
(125), a situation which describes large parts of the Third
World. Some leaders will respond to the mounting pressures because their survival depends upon them doing so. Jahangir
Amuzegar, a moderate, has referred to "the growing impatience
of the masses in the Third World... Long suppressed aspirations

and genuine frustrations", he observes, "have made the public
in the developing countries highly disillusioned. They want action. And their persistent demands are becoming increasingly
difficult for their leaders to resist". (126)

Leaders that do resist will be swept aside. One wave of revolution has already swept across the Third World: the liberation
of nations from foreign rule and political domination. The second wave, a tidal wave compared with the first, is building.(127)
It will reach its peak when, in Julius Nyerere's words, "the
poor refuse to stay poor". (128) When they do, national orders
which maintain privilege and poverty will be transformed. And
because they will, violent change will become a permanent feature of the Third World. In a very real sense, the future of the
Third World still has to be invented. (129)

There will be no single ideology of revolution, although most
will find their inspiration in Marxism and be nurtured by re-
pression, internal and external. There will be Leninist groups
that build worker-peasant alliances, Maoist groups that mobilize
the peasantry, Castroite groups that wage guerilla warfare, and
Trotskyist groups that raise the political consciousness of the
urban proletariat. (130) The ideology will most likely be articulated by the intelligensia. The national bourgeoisie will be the
victims not the architects of change.

Certainly, societies will find it difficult to maintain revolutionary fervor in a world which distrusts revolution, seeks to
coopt and divert it, and which demands that homage be paid at
the alter of international trade. Today, international capitalism devours revolutionary children. But when real structural
transformations take place in the Third World, revolutionary
children may have no alternative but to take the knife to international capitalism, thereby hastening its inevitable demise.

All these processes - processes within and between worlds - are
inextricably interlinked. The development of superpower rivalries will in part be determined by changes within the Third
World. The decline of capitalism will have a cause-effect relationship with the changes that take place in the East and South.
There will be no major world order problem in the 1980s that
does not interact with other problems.

There will also be any number of flashpoints which can ignite
world politics. Some of these we can anticipate: South Africa,
the Persian Gulf, the Middle East are problems which have so far
defied solution. Others will no doubt take us by surprise. It is
worth noting that 'future studies' conducted in the 1950s did
not forecast Vietnam, and those made in the 1960s 'missed' the
oil crisis and Iran.

If there are keys to the future world order then they are probably the developing continents, notably Africa and Asia.

Asia is littered with world order questions: the Arab-Israeli
conflict, the Gulf and the future of Saudi Arabia, the destiny
of India, the unique experiment in democracy, and the historical
role of China, a superpower in the making. As far as Africa, especially Sub-Sahara Africa, is concerned, there is no future
which is not cast in grim and desperate terms. The people of
this continent will refuse to die quietly; to allow themselves
to be cast onto the scrapheap of history. Transformations will
take place in Asia and Africa. They will significantly alter the
balance of power. It is not reasonable to assume that the changes
that will and must take place can be accomplished peacefully.

What can we conclude from all this? Firstly, the world of the
1980s will be even more complex and explosive than it is today.
There will be more conflicts, more tensions, more flashpoints,
more weapons, more nuclear buttons. It will have enormous potential for large-scale violence and, by the end of the 1980s,
a political confrontation virtually anywhere in the world could
easily involve nuclear arms. Already, the complexity of the
global problematique defies the accumulated stock of analytical
and policy instruments. There are limits to human capacity to
design and manage, by political processes, large complex systems.
(131) We may already have gone beyond those limits. We will certainly transgress them during the 1980s. The problematique has
outrun our tools. It threatens to outrun our imagination.

Secondly, there will be no clear hierarchy of powers. The world
of the 1980s will increasingly become a multipolar world. (132)
It will be more than a collection of giants and dwarfs. There
will be an increasing number of middle-sized powers in the developed and developing worlds. Regional hegemonic powers will
emerge in the Third World; centers will develop in the periphery.
The situation will be further complicated by the growing importance of non-state actors in the world economy. Corporate activity will continue to spill over into arenas larger than any political entity can effectively control, taking large business
enterprises even further beyond the reach of governments.

Thirdly, there will be no clear hierarchy of issues and no hierarchy of purpose. Governments will attach different importance
to different issues, their scale of priorities derived from
their interpretation of self-interest. For this reason there
will be no natural, simple and shared vision of the world and
no 'obvious' solutions to world order problems. In a world already very complex it is interesting that so many answers are
categorical, one-dimensional and undifferentiated. The 1980s
will be the final resting place for such answers. (133)

Fourthly, the quest for peace entails conflict. The building of
a more just international order requires - is in some respects
equivalent to - changes in the distribution of power. The inter-

national power structure will undergo significant change in the
decades ahead. It is not static. The ability of a state to remain on top is never without challenge. As Wallerstein has observed: "The hounds are ever to the hares for the position of
top dog". (134)

Military powers will continue to have trouble in adjusting to
the new realities. They will continue to equate power with military strength, order with the status quo. They will increasingly need to distinguish power over others and power over outcomes.
(135) As the system becomes more complex, issues become less
hierarchical, and actors multiply, the power to control outcomes
will be progressively eroded. The loss of leverage over the system as a whole they will seek to compensate for by increasing
their leverage over client states and subservient allies. Even
here, however, they will increasingly discover that some of the
traditional instruments of leverage are no longer very effective.
Recent U.S. experiences in trying to implement trade embargoes
is a case in point. (136)

The dominant nations, in the East and West, will also need to
distinguish between the short- and long-term effects of the
exercise of power. In the longer-term, the use of force and recourse to manipulation breed enmity in friends as well as foes
and destroys legitimacy, whereas influence and authority, judi-
ciously exercised, may actually generate trust and enhance legitimacy. (137)

Leadership based upon hegemony is no longer a feasible alternative even for superpowers. (138) There can be no other role than
one based upon persuasion and compromise. These are roles which
superpower military establishments are eminently unsuited to
play. It is like asking tigers to become vegetarians. (139)

From a Third World perspective, there can be no reordering of
international power relations - short, that is, of a catastrophe
of one kind or another - without concerted action. Tomorrow's
power is group power. (140) Strength is born out of alliances
and the determination to use the alliance. Power does not, in
William Safire's words, "come out of the end of a mouth". (141)

Power no longer automatically translates into influence. But it
always impinges on weakness. (142) In its struggle to wrest power from the dominant nations, the Third World will no doubt discover that conflict and dissensus, while disfunctional to the
power holders, is functional to those who challenge for power.
There is an instrumental relationship between solidarity and
conflict. (143) Conflict can help build solidarity through the
articulation of needs and the elaboration of instruments. Despite the widespread fear of conflict and confrontation, and
hence the desire to mask it under a veneer of consensus and harmony, history amply demonstrates that conflict is invariably a
stepping-stone in directions which are worthwhile. The dynamism

of conflict is a luminous principle of institution-building and,
indeed, of development itself.

Crisis of Confidence. The processes sketched above will surely
give rise to a gigantic crisis of confidence. It will be a multifaceted crisis. People will lose faith in the capacities of
their elected officials. Governments will lose faith in their
capacities to govern; their horizons will become blurred, their
interests more parochial; 'strategy' will give way to ad hocism,
tinkering and drift. Institutions, be they formal, like organizations and agreements, or informal, like legal precedent or the
market mechanism, will look and become frail and inadequate; the
United Nations especially will appear increasingly ineffective
and vulnerable. The tools used to understand and cope with complex realities will look hopelessly blunt.

Alliances will be subjected to unprecedented strains. The logic
underlying their formation will be called into question. The
Western alliance, for example, will be subjected to increasing
pressures as Western Europe develops interests which are at
variance with those of the U.S. Most Western European nations,
as well as Japan, are much more dependent than the U.S. on trade
with the Third World, and hence friendly relations with it. Because they are dependent upon the Persian Gulf for their economic lives, they view adventurism in the Middle East with considerable alarm. And because they are closer to the Soviet Union,
they are more aware of the attractions of detente. (144) For
its part, the U.S. can be expected to attach growing importance
to the forging of strong economic links with the economic center
forming around the South and East China Seas. Already U.S.trans-
Pacific trade is greater than its trans-Atlantic trade.

The biggest strains, however, will be within the alliances of
the Third World, frustrating efforts to give concrete shape to
Third World solidarity. The Non-Aligned forum is already split,
possibly irreparably so. A handful of developing countries –
the so-called NICs – will interpret their future as being inextricably linked to the centers of Western capitalism. The
poorest countries will be on their own. Whether they will have
a friend in OPEC remains to be seen. (145) It would seem wise
for them to count on little support. For although the declared
policy of OPEC is the provision of aid to the poorest countries
and the reactivation of the stalemated North-South dialogue
(rather than further substantial increases in the price of oil),
OPEC action has in fact done more to erode the position of the
poorest countries than to improve it. Poor countries like Tanzania now have to spend some 60 per cent of their foreign exchange earnings to pay their modest oil import bills compared
with 5-10 per cent prior to 1973. (146) The bill would be even
greater if allowance is made for the servicing of debts accumulated in response to balance of payments dislocations where the

price of oil has been the most disruptive factor. OPEC has talk-
ed about the creation of a giant fund for the development of the
poorest countries - a fund in which every extra dollar paid for
oil is returned as a dollar for development (147) - but the actual trend in OPEC aid to the Third World is downwards not upwards. (148) And the aid that has been given has been far from
'soft': political strings and profit considerations have been
much in evidence.

Calderon Berti, Chairman of OPEC, has stated that OPEC could not
exist without the support of the Third World. (149) In terms of
the dialetics of struggle, it is important that such support be
extended. The poorest countries, forced to stand on the sidelines and watch OPEC grow fatter, may, however, find it increasingly difficult to give the support which OPEC evidently needs.

OPEC will have its hands full keeping its own show on the road.
The successes which it has achieved have, in retrospect, been
something of Pyrrhic victories. Its actions have caused a good
deal of gnashing of teeth but have not resulted in a reordering
of basic power relationships. Indeed, OPEC is probably now more
depedent upon the West than ever before. Even friends of the
Third World have been forced to admit that the oil cartel may
well have been rendered inocuous well before the end of the century. (150) Some OPEC countries may use a historical opportunity
to restructure their economies. But even if they do, the core of
Third World poverty will remain untouched.

There is nothing inevitable about the perpetuation of OPEC power, and certainly about its determination to wield it in ways
which will benefit the world's poor. Indeed, it has recently
been suggested that OPEC power is an illusion: that oil prices
and production decisions "probably would have evolved as they
did even if OPEC had never existed". (151)

The crisis of confidence will thus be deeply rooted and multifaceted. It will be reflected in many fields of human endeavor
and in international relations and it will be one of the principal obstacles to efforts aimed at building a more rational and
equitable world order. Nicola Chiaromonte has found the right
words to describe the problem. "Ours is not an age of faith, nor
is it an age of disbelief. It is an age of bad faith, of beliefs
which are clung to in order to oppose other beliefs which are
maintained in the absence of genuine convictions". (152)

The Moral Imperative. If this is the context for strategies, why
attempt anything at all? Is there anything that can penetrate
the dark jungle of suspicions, mistrust and resentment; traverse
the minefield of conflict and complexity. The guiding light must
surely be the very "genuine convictions" which are today so
little in evidence. The world problematique is above all a moral
and ethical problematique. It is the principles of 'rightness'

and 'oughtness' which must be used to find ways through the laby-
rinth, to steer away from the abyss. Within the overwhelming
complexity certain truths stand out, certain inequities are
self-evident, certain wrongs cannot be deemed right. They are
clear and they are simple. They are truths which illuminate the
darkness; they are the beacons to be used for chartering courses.

The main guiding force must be moral indignation with the state
of the world, a world built on injustices and which coldly con-
demns countless millions of people to lives of desolation and
despair. It is moral outrage with the trends and processes which
threaten human tragedy on an ever greater scale which must underpin attempts to build a new world order. The quest for a new
order is a quest for new values through the articulation of a
moral imperative. (153)

There is no law in history which requires that just causes tri-
umph over unjust ones. But what is history if it is not the story of human efforts to correct injustices? The story of the
world's religions and great reformist movements is the story of
these efforts.

There is an obvious link between the exercise of a moral preference and political ideology. Capitalism is morally ambivalent.
It could not exist on the scale it does today without the unjust
bargain and the unjust bargain is the taproot of imperialism,
itself the antithesis of morality. (154) Capitalism ignores,
even ridicules, notions of rightness; it is a coarse blanket for
smothering moral outrage.

By comparison, socialism is, or should be, to use Durkheim's
phrase, "a cry of pain" and it has been the duty of the left to
preserve the sense of horror, suffering and pain which characterizes so much of the world. (155) This socialism has little
in common with the cynicism and internecine squabbling which is
found in parties which bear the socialist banner. It is also
more than 'methodology'. Socialism is a morality play in the
drama of human suffering. It is through socialism that the moral
preference will be exercised.

To exercise the preference is not to suggest that guilt can constitute a basis for action. It is part of classic conservative
strategy to admit the last generation's guilt in order to justify this generation's reformed status quo. Guilt can easily serve,
not as an instrument of change, but as a device for the legitimization of things as they are or have become. (156)

Morality has its roots in the behavior of individuals. But it is
also in evidence in the behavior of states. Superpowers can be
superimmoral. By comparison, small nations can exercise a moral
strength well in excess of their military or economic size.

TOWARD GLOBAL STRATEGIES

The context we have sketched for global strategies is undeniably
gloomy. It is one which leaves little space for deterministic
blueprints and utopian visions of a brave new world. It would be
comforting to believe that it might be possible to draw up a
world resource strategy - covering renewable and non-renewable
resources - which, shaped by principles of justice and equity,
establishes a basis for sustainable development in the North and
South, and makes it possible to meet the basic needs of the
world's people and to alleviate human suffering and misery. However much such a strategy is required, it will not see the light
of day in the 1980s.

The 1980s, we have suggested, will be characterized by turmoil,
struggle and change - conceivably violent change - with farreach-
ing consequences for political, social and economic systems.
The rich nations will continue to associate order with established patterns of privilege and power and fight for the maintenance
of the institutions which have helped make them prosperous, even
though they no longer guarantee their prosperity. Key elements
of the rich world's strategy will, we have suggested, be determined but probably confused attempts to revive capitalist structures, and the more effective and complete integration of Eastern Europe and the Third World - or more particularly the handful of NICs - into the capitalist world economy.

Such a strategy, because it would maintain and consolidate present unequal relationships and result in increased fragmentation
and marginalization of the periphery, has little to offer the
majority of developing countries, especially the poorest among
them. Their only real choice is to pursue, however difficult
this will prove in practice, strategies of self-reliance aimed
at getting some kind of grip on their own future and at overcoming some of the worst forms of domination and dependence.
(157) Stated in these terms, self-reliance is more than an economic strategy. It is a power strategy and, as such, the essential starting point is power over oneself as a precondition for
power over others. And translated into the politics of today,
it would have dissociation, delinking and disruption as major
components. (158)

In this atmosphere of struggle and change, international cooperation and international institutions will be subjected to unprecedented stresses and strains. This is not to suggest, however,
that international relations are in or will enter a state of war
and that there is nothing short of war for bringing cooperation
about. Nations will not get together to paint pictures of pastoral utopias. But they will be thrown together by the sheer
force of circumstances. They will be compelled to jointly find
ways to manage inevitable conflicts so as to avoid catastrophes,

be they wars or extreme human misery.

At one level - the level of survival - there *are* common interests. There are also common problems. All nations, for example,
have an interest in security, in establishing a basis for sustainable development, in generating employment. No nation stands
to gain from disruptions in the oxygen cycle, from the spread of
contagious diseases and from chaos in the world's airways and
airwaves. Few nations benefit from persistant inflation and from
monetary instability.

All these problems defy solution by individual nations. They are
part and parcel of the global problematique and all aspects of
a single larger problem: that of introducing rationality into
human endeavor and of getting the world under some form of rational and equitable control. That is the challenge that confronts us. It is a challenge which we may be too late in meeting.

The 1970s have shown us that the processes required are not automatic processes. There are no autonomous stabilizers - no imposed order, no Pax Americana - and no mechanisms - like the
free market - which dispense answers. The free market cannot
solve the problems of the nuclear arms race, inflation, unemployment, hunger and poverty, nor can it respond to growing
demands for equality of opportunity and economic justice. To
suggest that it can is to surrender human sovereignty and this
is to surrender any hope we may have for salvation.

The challenge of introducing rationality and equity into international relations has to be met together. The nation-State is
and must be the starting point for strategies, but this is not
the same as saying that the nation-State is or ever can be an
autonomous unit for decision-making, especially in the field of
economics. Sovereign states pursuing interests with no restraints
other than those which are self-imposed is a precondition for
turmoil, injustice and, eventually, war. Certainly, power competition will be decisive in determining the future that awaits
us. But power competition does not exclude the possibility of
cooperation.

There can be no definition of a human future which does not include cooperation, cooperation which gives expression to human
solidarity and which is shaped by moral forces. In the absence
of such cooperation nations will, in Denis Goulet's words, "display and redefine their own worst qualities as they strike at
each other's throat". (159) Without cooperation, be it halting
and imperfect, the prospects for the human race are bleak indeed.
(160)

If greater rationality and equity are to be introduced into international relations it is essential to recognize that responses
to international crises will and must frequently differ from
responses to national problems. Marx clearly showed that deci-

sions which are rational from an individual's point of view may
not be rational from the viewpoint of society as a whole: individual rationality may easily mean collective irrationality.
In formulating joint responses to global problems it will be
necessary to go beyond the aggregation of individual national
requirements (161), a process which must inevitably mean that
some nations will lose while others gain. It follows from this
that international cooperation may not be in the immediate interests of all nations.

If there is a 'stabilizer' it is cooperation and it is through
cooperation that inevitable crises will need to be managed and
answers to global problems found. The stabilizer is not an automatic one, however, and the formulation of management responses
and the search for answers will be highly politicized and frequently messy. Neo-Keynesians would argue that one of the root
causes of the Great Depression was that no one was 'in charge'
of the world economy in the inter-war period: the role of 'un-
derwriter' was played by Britain in the period up to the First
World War and by the U.S. in the quarter century following the
Second World War. But there was no one in the driving seat between the wars. There is no one in the driving seat today. The
difference is that to day no one has a driving license: they
could not occupy the seat even if they felt it was their historical duty to do so. Today the vehicle for planning and management is international cooperation and thus the institutions
which make this possible.

International cooperation implies consensus on what needs to be
done. This consensus may well be shallow, masking fundamental
differences as to whether action is required for purposes of
systems-maintenance, reform or transformation. In the case of
North-South issues, for example, there will be little point in
trying to agree on the paradigms and politics which dominate the
debate. The differences are too fundamental for that. A more
fruitful approach will be to focus on specific issues and to
work backwards only to the parts of the paradigms and politics
that it is strictly necessary to agree upon in order to engineer
progress. It is a truism that scholars reach agreement by sharpening distinctions while politicians reach agreement by blurring
them. Progress in a number of areas may depend upon the tactical
obfuscation of issues, obscurantism becoming a principle of progress. (162)

In seeking to establish a basis for cooperative approaches it
will be necessary to move outside the structures which guarantee
failure. There will be very considerable scope, for example, for
selective action by limited groups of countries and for the formation of new coalitions, built around specific problems, aimed
at establishing new combinations of influence and power. (163)

A particularly significant coalition would be that forged between small- and middle-sized powers in the North and South against the two superpowers. It has become increasingly evident that superpower involvement in any problem of major importance - certainly the crucial issues of disarmament and development - virtually eliminates the possibility of progress. If progress cannot be engineered with the superpowers it is imperative that ways be found of moving ahead without them.

The framework for use in this search is provided by the Chinese version of the three world model: the first world comprises the two superpowers; the second world the industrialized countries; and the third world the developing countries. In the Chinese view, the second world exploits the third world but is itself exploited by the superpowers. Because of this, it is in the interest of both the second and third worlds to forge alliances which can resist and counter the hegemony of the superpowers.

Both the U.S. and the Soviet Union appear unable and unwilling to relinquish the imperial mission they assigned themselves at the end of the Second World War. They will not give up trying to run the world, scattering, as Michel Robert has observed, "the bloody harvest of their tragic cooperation". (164) They have few objectives higher than their own narrowly defined interests and doubt-ridden parities. Their attempts to come to terms with each other may well be at the expense of everyone else.

Friends and allies of the superpowers, be they in the East, West or South, can in some cases best serve their own interests as well as the interests of mankind as a whole by politely yet resolutely refusing to cooperate with the superpowers in adventures and processes which lead us further down the slippery slope. Survival may depend upon a *strategy of superpower desertion*. (165)

The apparent determination of the superpowers to turn Europe into a nuclear battlefield should provide sufficient motivation for the nations of Western and Eastern Europe to at least explore the possibility of opening a dialogue on European security. Countries like Austria, Finland and Sweden, with a tradition of neutrality, may have special responsibilities to discharge in this area. Similarly, Western Europe could by-pass the United States in the dialogue on development with the Third World. The so-called 'like-minded' forum - the group of small industrialized countries with a 'progressive' reputation - may have special responsibilities here. (166) France, a larger power, has also strongly advocated a Euro-Africa-Arab dialogue on development, a dialogue which would exclude U.S. participation. (167)

Guiding Principles for International Resource Management. The struggle for control of resources is and will increasingly become a source of international conflict. Throughout history wars

have been fought to gain such control: the Algerian War of Independence, the Congo Civil War, the Third Arab Israeli War,
the Nigerian Civil War, the El Salvador-Honduran War, the U.K.-
Iceland 'cod war', the Paracel Islands dispute, and the Western
Sahara revolt, for example, are all cases of post World War II
conflicts in which the question of access to resources, whether
hard minerals, oil or fish, was an important if not the primary
consideration. (168) In a resource hungry world such conflicts
seem destined to multiply. (169)

Attempts to manage resources are thus an essential ingredient
of attempts to manage crisis. The international management of
resources will need to be undertaken for a variety of reasons,
serve a variety of purposes, and therefore take a number of forms.
There are different groups of resources which carry their own
opportunities and threats and which will require their own management responses.

● There are resources whose uneven distribution threatens grave
imbalances and explosive world tensions. Food and energy are obvious examples. It will be impossible to establish a more rational and equitable world order without some degree of international management of such resources.

● There are resources, such as nuclear resources, whose development and peaceful applications entail concomitant dangers of
large-scale environmental degradation or diversion for military
purposes. Neither peace nor development can be safeguarded without attempts to manage these 'dual-purpose' resources.

● There are resources which fall beyond the limits of present
national jurisdiction. Such resources include those of the oceans
and the deep seabed, of Antarctica, outer space, the moon and
other celestial bodies. Such resources should be explored and
exploited for the benefit of mankind as a whole rather than the
handful of nations with the technology required for their exploitation.

Different types of management regimes will need to be developed
for these different types of resources. The need to introduce
more rationality and equity into international relations, however, suggests that all regimes should be shaped by the following three principles.

● *Allocation of resources*. At any given point in time the earth's
resources are finite and the ultimate survival of the human race
depends upon their fair allocation. (170) Resources change because society changes. The definition of a resource today will
be different from the one used tomorrow. But at any given time
nothing is successive; everything is contemporaneous.

● *Access to resources*. More important than the distribution of
resources is access to them. The poor must gain access to re-

sources early in decision-making processes and not merely as a
corrective measure to distribution systems which are fundamentally inequitable. (171)

● *Ownership of resources*. The world's resources belong to all
the world's inhabitants on the basis of priority needs, not on
the basis of geographical accident or the capacity to exploit
and to consume them. This requires that traditional concepts of
ownership eventually make way for new concepts of entitlement,
use and management.

Ways in which these principles can be progressively incorporated
into international management regimes is the main focus of subsequent chapters. Given the need for a step-by-step approach to
the development of a planning and management capability at the
world level, we will argue that action in three areas could
yield very substantial results in the short- as well as the
longer-term: the development of management regimes for domains
beyond the limits of national jurisdiction on the basis of the
concept of the common heritage of mankind (the subject of chapter 5); the development of a system of automatic resource mobilization through international taxation (the subject of chapter
6); and the development of management regimes for technologies
with a dual-purpose character (the subject of chapter 7).

Common Heritage Regimes. The common heritage of mankind is, we
will argue, an example of a systems-tranforming concept, carrying as it does the potential to transform the relationships between rich and poor countries. Through the Third U.N. Conference
on the Law of the Sea, the concept has become an accepted norm
of international law: it has been embraced by the community of
nations. (172)

As we saw in chapter 2, there is a wide measure of agreement on
the need for institutional regimes for what are sometimes termed
the 'global commons': the oceans, outer space and Antarctica.
(173) This agreement is to be found in the North and South. Establishment economists like Richard Cooper and Fred Bergsten
have argued their case. For Cooper, the design of ocean regimes
provides opportunities for "positive-sum thinking" and for the
development of regional as well as global management systems.
(174) Bergsten goes further. He has called for regimes, not only
for the oceans, but also for Antarctica, outer space and the
world's weather and climate. (175) As far as the Third World
is concerned, Mahbub ul Haq sees the "commercial exploitation of
international commons as one of seven key elements of a "long-
term negotiating strategy". (176) It might also be noted that
the desirability of a regime for Antarctica was the subject of
a chapter in the *World Conservation Strategy*, a document 'adopted' by some 50 nations.

There is thus agreement that something could and should be done.

The concept which can do the work is already on the legal statute books. No time should be lost in applying it to 'common
property' domains.

Automatic Resource Mobilization. Systems of international taxation based upon the principle of automaticity make it possible
to take the vexed question of aid out of the realm of charity
and into the realm of entitlement, substituting the principles
of justice and equity for the vagaries of philantropy and pater-
nalism.

Many types of direct and indirect taxation can be envisaged,
each with their own specific constellation of advantages and
disadvantages. From the viewpoint of institutionalizing the
three guiding principles specified above, the most attractive
types are those where it is possible to modulate the tax according to the nature and use of resources and according to the
principle 'each contributing according to his means and receiving according to his needs'.

There is, as we shall see, widespread agreement on the need to
progressively replace the present 'aid order', an order with
which neither the donors nor recipients are very happy, with a
system of automatic resource mobilization.

Managing Dual-Purpose Technologies. It will prove impossible to
get the world under some form of rational control without coming
to grips with the problem of modern science-based technology.
Technology and resources are intimately linked: any statement
about the future availability of resources implies statements
about the future development of technology. It follows that there
can be no real resource management without concomitant attempts
to manage technology.

Much modern technology is a double-edged sword. It combines vast
potential for improving the quality of life with enormous potential for developing new weapons of massive destruction. If technologies with a dual-purpose character can be identified in time
and made the subject of deliberate control and management, it
should prove possible to simultaneously advance the causes of
peace through development and disarmament through the prohibition
of certain weapons and weapon systems.

Progress in these three areas would help institutionalize the
guiding principles. It would help get our world under some form
of rational control and establish a basis for the more equitable sharing of resources. It would give real expression to the
idea of solidarity with existing and future generations and
introduce the notion of conscious planning and management practices for the benefit of all rather than a privileged few. It
would give a new expression to international cooperation. But it
would do more. Because the required institutional regimes would

need to be designed and implemented through the United Nations, it would add to the legitimacy of the organization. And if it were to do all of this, it would add to the much needed process of confidence-building.

Progress in these three areas would be very significant but hardly sufficient. It would need to be supplemented by agreements in other fields. An agreement in the area of energy policy would be particularly important since the 'oil question' has implications for other problems and is likely to remain of central significance in the North-South conflict. (177) Whether the threat of a serious oil shortage is real or imaginary remains to be seen. Because many do interpret it as a threat and a potential source of conflict, an agreement between the main producers and consumers could constitute an important confidence-building measure. An agreement could also incorporate principles of resource management. Such were evident in the 'world energy plan' proposed by Mexico's President Lopez Portillo at the 34th Session of the U.N. General Assembly. The plan, he suggested, should be based upon the recognition that "energy sources are the shared responsibility of all mankind" and give serious expression to the desire "to bridge the gap between extremes by making present day petroleum supply, demand and price structures compatible with the alternatives we seek for the future". Control over our energy future, Lopez Portillo argued, would "reconcile conscience and national values with the interests of fertile and harmonious internationalism". (178) It would, in other words, build confidence in international cooperation. The costs of this would be the cooptation of OPEC and the loss of its potential power for disruption.

A step-by-step approach to the building of management regimes could result in a system of cooperation which creates the confidence required to move on to more thorny and intractable problems, such as the progressive transformation of corporate structures, world hunger and the competitive armaments race. The essential task is to gain time for wise counsel to be voiced and heard, for the seriousness of the problems to sink in, and for the concepts which, like those of the common heritage of mankind and dual-purpose agents, promise a revolution in the relations between rich and poor nations. To gain time for, as Tennyson wrote, "tomorrow yet would reap today". (179)

RICH WORLD STRATEGIES
AND GLOBAL REFORMS

This book is concerned with global problems. The solution to such problems is dependent upon the creation of strong international institutions vested with the power to act. But this will be far from enough. It also requires the emergence of enlightened national bureaucracies, especially in the industrialized countries. Although there are problems which are genuinely global in their scale and implications, a large part of the global 'problematique' originates within states, remains within states, and some of the most powerful tools of corrective action are internal instruments. It follows that improved domestic policy leadership, especially leadership sensitive to the interpenetration of 'internal' and 'external' issues, is an essential prerequisite for effective global planning and resource management.

Since the response to any problem, global or otherwise, must be rooted in national action, inadequate domestic policies - those which, for example, perpetuate injustice and tolerate waste - can be legitimately considered a greater obstacle to the development of a real management capability at the world level than can weak international institutions. (180)

In this section we will look briefly at some of the issues confronting the industrialized countries in the formulation of national strategies. We will look first at strategies toward the Third World and then at strategies for national development.

Strategies Toward the Third World

What the Western nations must surely learn is that the biggest threat they face is not a classically military one, not even one of the escalation of superpower killing capacities, however dire that may be. The biggest threat is to be found on a more complex stage. It arises from the conjunction of superpower rivalries with an increasingly unstable and anarchical world of rising nationalisms, increasing inequalities, mounting tensions and antagonisms, and growing substantive complexities. The world is already armed to the teeth; it also has, as Karl Deutsch has observed, "more than enough social and psychological dynamite... to match its ample stock of TNT, uranium and plutonium". (181)

Just as there can be no alternative for the West than détente with the East, so there can be none but dialogue with the South. Tomorrow's world is either the world of the poor and the new nations or it is nothing. To make it something, tomorrow's world must be one in which the dreams and aspirations of others are included rather than excluded. This is an overriding precondition for survival. Not only of the West, but for the world as a whole.

In recent years a good deal has been made of the potential 'threat' of the Third World, a threat which is perceived to derive from the West's growing economic stake in the developing world and its dependence on certain strategic raw materials.

At first sight, the 'statistics' are impressive. In the case of
such raw materials as chromium, cobalt, manganese, natural rub-
ber and tin, the dependence on imports from Third World producers is virtually complete. With respect to trade, the U.S. and
EEC made a net profit of nearly $ 60 billion on their trade with
the Third World in 1977. The U.S. now exports more to the developing countries than it does to Western Europe and the Soviet
Union combined. The poor countries thus play an important part
in keeping Western factories running; about 10 million jobs in
industry are dependent upon exports to the Third World. There
can be little doubt that had the poor countries cut their imports by the amount needed to pay their recently increased oil
bills, there would now be many more - perhaps several million
more - people flooding the unemployment exchanges in the OECD
countries. But the developing countries did not cut their imports. Instead, they tripled their debt with loans from Western
banks.

The growing economic interest in the Third World has been behind
a number of the 'massive transfer of resources' proposals made
in recent years. These proposals - often referred to as 'Marshall
Plans for the Third World' - have been formulated by governments,
research groups and private business and are designed to stimulate global economic activity while accelerating the economic
and industrial development of the developing countries. (182)
The proposals assume that the Third World can help pull the West
out of recession. Their underlying logic has been described by
Claude Cheysson, the European Community's Commissioner for Development Cooperation, in the following words: "If we inject
(some) tens of billions of dollars into the economies of the
developing nations, all these billions will come back to us as
orders for industrial equipment... The access to industrial development and to higher living standards for hundreds of millions
of people in the Third World will turn into a gigantic impulse
to global non-inflationary growth". (183) Some estimates suggest
that a 3 per cent growth rate in the non-oil exporting developing
countries would be worth an extra $ 45 billion a year to the in-
dustrialized West in new export orders.

Although this 'Marshall Plan' logic is inherently faulty, it is
an interesting reflection on the way in which the economic importance of the Third World to the industrialized countries is
perceived to be growing. (184)

Despite the growing stake, the economic power of the Third World
and, more importantly, its capacity to use the power it has
against the West, is modest. The economic 'threat', with a few
obvious exceptions, can thus easily be exaggerated. (185) The
most real threat, however, is not economic, but political. The
developing countries may not possess the power to challenge the
West for the control of the international economic system, but
they will have the capacity to throw the entire system into chaos.

The Third World's importance is geopolicital. (186)

The idea that the poor countries are important to global balance is far from new: it was certainly recognized more than a century ago. (187) Similarly, the notion that the West has a strategic interest in the developing world is an old idea, not a post OPEC insight. Before the Second World War 'realists' were arguing that the division between 'have' and 'have-not' nations could constitute a serious source of conflicts: that growing disparities carry the seeds of strife and war. (188)

And the disparities between rich and poor countries are growing, setting the rich and poor worlds on a colliston course. There is, of course, nothing new in the existence of rich and poor. Indeed, history has known nothing else and has been largely shaped by the struggles between them. But the rich and poor have in the past mainly existed within individual societies. What *is* relatively new is the enormous differences which now exist between societies. At the beginning of the nineteenth century, the difference in per capita income may have been as little as 1:2 (189) Today the difference is between 1:13 and 1:60 depending upon how the ratio is measured. (190) It is moreover a visible difference for the rich cannot conceal their wealth in a 'global village'. The glaring differences are perceived by the poor thanks, perhaps paradoxically, to the rich world's technological dexterity. And their perception of these differences will, in a shrinking world, exert growing stress on already frail institutions. (191)

Islands of rich, old and frightened peopled will find it difficult to conduct their affairs in seething seas of young, poor and increasingly desperate people. Even Henry Kissinger, never very sensitive to nor interested in the North-South equation, did not fail to notice this contradiction. "A world in which a few nations constitute islands of wealth in a sea of despair is fundamentally insecure and morally intolerable", he has observed. "Those who consider themselves dispossessed will become a seedbed of upheaval". (192) The seedbed will indeed be fertile ground for the birth of forces which seek to challenge the status quo and the institutions which maintain countries in backwardness.

There can be little question that there is a relationship between violence and economic backwardness and that the trend for such violence is up, not down. (193) There can also be little doubt that ten years from now, a time in which perhaps 30-40 nations will be in a position to manufacture nuclear weapons, our world, torn apart by the struggles between the rich and poor and for resources, will have a nightmare potential for large-scale violence. A political confrontation virtually anywhere could plunge the world into the nuclear abyss. (194)

A growing number of scholars find themselves forced to speculate on the possibility of what Robert Heilbroner has called "nuclear

wars of redistribution". (195) "The possibility must be faced",
he reluctantly argues, "that the underdeveloped nations which
have "nothing" to lose will point their nuclear pistols at the
heads of the passengers in the first class coaches who have
everything to lose". (196) Wars of redistribution may not necessarily involve nations, however. They would more likely result from acts of terrorism and political extremism. Such possibilities evoke powerful images. As Joseph Nye, another of the
doyens of the study of international relations and one not prone
to flights of fancy, has asked: "Is it unrealistic to imagine a
small group of MIT-trained sons and daughters of Indian, Japanese, and American middle-class parents threatening to detonate
a crude plutonium bomb in Boston unless American aid to Asia is
immediately increased? Rather than the pacific image of a global
village, the growth of transnational communication in a world of
enormous inequality may merely bring us Patty Hearst with a global dimension". (197) As we saw in chapter 2, similar thinking is
evident in many types of world order studies conducted in recent
years. It has also found its way into recent fiction. (198)

Measured in terms of economic threats, the U.S. is least vulnerable to the Third World. When it comes to political threats,
however, it is probably right at the top of the list. It is
likely to prove a favorite target of those who, whatever the
background, are driven to acts of desperation. The U.S. is seen
as the most reactionary force, the defender of the status quo,
the enemy of the oppressed masses, the biggest obstacle to a
more equitable international order. Moreover, acts of violence
and terrorism against U.S. citizens will guarantee maximum pub-
licity. More envied and resented than respected or feared in
large parts of the Third World, the U.S. may discover that 'Iran'
is not an anti-American aberration, but a forerunner of a world
which is fiercely anti-American. (199)

And should it come to discover it, it will almost certainly fail
to understand the reasons for it. For the challenge of the Third
World, whether it comes from desperate leaders of desperate nations or militant leaders of extremist groups, will defy Western
concepts of 'rationality'. Challenges to injustices and inequalities in power and wealth cannot be confrontations of points of
view. Their logic and rationality are determined by the dialectics of struggle. Already the West is puzzled by such occurrences
as Third World support for OPEC action, Cuba's involvement in
African wars of independence, Yasar Arafat's triumphant reception
at the U.N. and the continuing rejoicing of the U.S. defeat in
Vietnam. Because they are indicative of the power of the periphery and the vulnerability of the center, they are all, in the
context of struggle, perfectly 'rational'.

The context was vividly sketched by Franz Fanon some 20 years
ago. "Diplomacy, as inaugurated by the newly independent peoples",

he wrote, "is no longer an affair of nuances, of implications, and of hypnotic passes... When Mr. Krushchev brandishes his shoe at the United Nations, or thumps the table with it, there's not a single ex-native, nor any representative of an underdeveloped country, who laughs. For what Mr. Krushchev shows the colonized countries which are looking on is that he , the moujik, who more-over is the possessor of space-rockets, treats these miserable capitalists in the way that they deserve. In the same way", Fanon continues, "Castro sitting in military uniform in the United Nations Organization does not scandalize the underdevel-oped countries. What Castro demonstrates is the consciousness he has of the continuing existence of the rule of violence. The astonishing thing is that he did not come into the U.N.O. with a machine gun; but if he had would anyone have minded?" (200)

In the stormy years ahead, the West will no doubt continue to associate 'order' with the international status quo. And they will almost certainly discover that the more they try to hang on to their riches and resources, the more likely they are of losing them.

Strategies for National Development

New globally responsible strategies toward the Third World must be combined with the determined search for new directions in national development. This search must find ways of dealing with the problem of 'overdevelopment', a relatively new phenomenon which has given rise to per capita resource demands which are so high that they not only place exhorbitant demands on global re-sources and ecosystems but also severely constrain the opportu-nities of the world's poor to satisfy their survival needs. 'Overdevelopment', the prerogative of the rich, is incompatible with the quest for a more rational and equitable international order and with the notion of sustainable development in the North as well as the South. It is thus an enemy of attempts to strengthen global planning and resource management capabilities. It is moreover an enemy that must be squarely faced at the na-tional level.

The problem of overdevelopment can best be understood in terms of consumption patterns and lifestyles and it is to these that we will briefly turn. (201) We will do so by attempting to sketch a crude 'profile' of the Western consumer. For the sake of con-venience (and no other reason) we will make our consumer a male and, given available information sources, a citizen of the United States. (202) Viewed in terms of Western European consumption patterns, the 'profile' is thus somewhat exaggerated. It should be noted, however, that in many areas Western Europeans either approximate North American consumption levels or apparently as-pire to them. We should also note that 'averages' can disguise ugly realities. Our 'model' consumer' is a citizen of a country in which 25 million people live on or below the poverty line. 'Overdevelopment' may thus be the prerogative of the rich but in the world of the rich some are clearly more 'overdeveloped' than others.

Let us start with the eating habits of our 'model' consumer for they are prodigious indeed. Every year he consumes nearly one tonne of cereals. Of this he eats only 90 kg directly in the form of bread, breakfast cereals and pastry. The remainder - by far the largest part - goes to feed meat and milk producing animals; he thus consumes the cereals indirectly. Not surprisingly, his appetite for meat and meat products is awesome and growing. His annual consumption of beef increased from 25 kg in 1940 to more than 50 kg today; his consumption of poultry increased from 9 kg to more than 20 kg in the same period. In the past decade, increased meat consumption has added 160 kg of cereals to his diet, an amount very nearly equivalent to an Indian's entire diet for a whole year. Whether this increased meat consumption has done him anything but harm he does not know. Heart specialists have warned that he now eats three times more meat than is good for him. In the past few years he has come to discover and then to fear cholesterol, a situation successfully exploited by advertising.

That his food requirements are excessive is demonstrated, not only by his waistline, but also by the fact that 20 per cent of the food which he buys is thrown away, as is 10 per cent of the beef which he regards as expensive. (203) Over half of the food he is served in restaurants he is unable to eat and finds its way into garbage cans.

Not surprisingly, the agricultural resources required to support our model consumer - land, water, fertilizers - are prodigious, amounting to about five times those required by an average Indian, Nigerian or Columbian.

Our consumer has grown up with gadgets. He carries nearly 10 tonnes of steel around with him in cars and household equipment. He 'uses' another 150 kg of both copper and lead and 100 kg of aluminium and zinc in his various appliances and artefacts. To keep him supplied with all the things he needs, his country's roads, railways and planes transport every year about 15,000 tons of materials per kilometer, and to his door they bring the TV sets, the washing machine and the refrigerator owned by 70 per cent of his countrymen.

Every year he uses nearly 300 kg of materials for wrapping, bottling and canning. Much of this, including 250 metal cans and 130 bottles, he subsequently throws away. His family produces between 2 and 3 kg of solid waste every day. If one adds industrial wastes - from mines and factories - the per capita figure is nearer 25 kg per day.

To sustain his prodigal life-style our consumer must have access
to enormous quantities of energy. Some thirty years ago, Buck-
minster Fuller estimated the amount of muscular energy required
to produce the then available supplies of power, and suggested
that each member of the affluent society had the equivalent of
153 slaves - 'energy slaves' - working for him. Today the figure
is closer to 400. These energy slaves have been captured by
burning fossil fuels, notably oil, at unprecedented rates.
There are grounds for believing that this 'energy explosion'
will affect the planet's heat balance, the relationship between
the amount of energy received from the sun and the amount reflected or radiated into space. The burning of fossil fuels results in an increase in the levels of atmospheric carbon dioxide
which, while not reducing incoming radiation, does absorb some
of the heat that is redirected. The resulting 'greenhouse effect'
could induce catastrophic changes in world climate. The concentration of CO_2 has increased by 12 per cent since 1860 and, of
that, 5 per cent was added in the last two decades. Climatologists are yet to fully agree on the consequences of these trends.
Some argue, however, that the atmospheric warming resulting from
prolonged 'greenhouse effects' could mean that average temperatures could increase by $1-1\frac{1}{2}$ $^\circ$C over the next 10-15 years. This
could cause the polar ice caps to start melting and eventually
result in a 15-20 metre rise in sea level. If this were to happen, the world would literally float into the twenty-first century. Coastal cities - perhaps including the one inhabited by
our model consumer - would be inundated.

It's the same story with water. Every day our consumer requires
6,000 litres to maintain him. Only 4 litres are required for his
liquid diet. Some 230 litres he uses for washing, cooking, bath-
ing and flushing. The vast majority of the remainder is used to
keep him supplied with food, goods and appliances. Many industrial processes require 1,000 tonnes of water to produce one
tonne of finished product: 40 litres of water are used to produce one can of vegetables, 10 litres to produce one litre of
petroleum; $3\frac{1}{2}$ cu.metres to manufacture one tonne of cement and
a staggering 200 cu.metres to produce one tonne of steel. Much
of this water is wasted and contaminated, the contaminated waste
water of industry polluting, on average, 25 times its own volume.

The city of one million inhabitants in which our consumer lives
requires 6 billion litres (over 6 million tonnes) of water each
day to meet its domestic and industrial needs. Such a level of
consumption has meant that, at a time in which 70 per cent of
the world's population has no dependable access to safe water
and in which water-borne diseases kill an estimated 25,000 people, mostly children, every day, some rich countries are now
using, and wasting, more water than can be supplied by natural
cycles.

The prodigious levels of consumption of our model consumer are
placing mounting stress on the natural environment. His rivers
are dirty, his air unfit to breathe. The soil is booby-trapped
with toxic substances and radio-active 'wastes' secreted by
those who came before him. He is exposed to half a million com-
pounds, some of them highly toxic, and he is able to 'consume'
about one tonne of air pollutants - coming in the overwhelming
majority of cases from cars and power stations - every year.
Acid rain has reached the stage where even slight increases in
its concentration may cause irreparable damage to his environment. His chances of contracting an environmentally induced illness are increasing. He may become one of the five million in
the rich world who are stricken each year with illness caused
by the micro-biological contamination of foodstuffs. Worse, he
has a one in four chance of contracting some form of cancer,
and, if he does, there is a 75 per cent chance that it will be
environmentally induced - the result of unsound diet, exposure
to air pollutants and industrial chemicals.

Two classes of man-made pollutants have recently been found to
react with the ozone layer which protects our consumer from the
sun's lethal ultraviolet radiation: nitrogen oxides (from super-
sonic aircraft, nitrogen fertilizers and the combustion of fossil fuels); and chlorofluorcarbons (used as refrigerants and
propellants for aerosol sprays). Both float up through the various layers of the atmosphere, react with the ozone, resulting in
its depletion. Although the seriousness of the problem has yet
to be finally established, there are grounds for considerable
concern. Even a 5 per cent decrease in the ozone concentration
involves a 10 per cent increase in the radiation reaching the
earth, and it has been estimated that such an increase could
result in an additional 20,000 to 60,000 cases of skin cancer a
year in the United States alone. If this is not bad enough, the
effect of increased radiation on soil microorganisms could violently effect the entire ecological balance in ways which are
very likely to be highly undesirable. Another example of how the
consumer places himself at risk by his own actions and procliv-
ities.

Nor is our consumer the only victim of his own indulgencies. The
spread of urbanization, the dissemination of toxic chemicals and
the callous exploitation of wildlife are resulting in the loss
of about one animal species or subspecies a year. According to
the International Union for the Conservation of Nature, some
1,000 birds, mammals, and fish are now thought to be in jeopardy.
The scale of plant extinctions is even more alarming and perhaps
even more significant since a disappearing plant can take with
it 10 to 30 dependent species, such as insects, higher animals,
and even other plants. The IUCN considers about 10 per cent of
the world's flowering plants - 20,000 to 30,000 species - to be
"dangerously rare or under threat". A great many of these are

in the industrialized world. (204)

His lack of respect for and concern with the natural environment
is evidenced by the careless and thoughtless way in which he has
disfigured the face of his nation with concrete and asphalt and
allowed the soil which grows his food to deteriorate. In the
past decade, 12,000 sq.km of agricultural land have been lost to
often indiscriminate urbanization and so much soil has been lost
to erosion that the country's potential to grow food - food required by the hungry of the world as well as himself - may have
been cut by perhaps as much as 35 per cent. He has attempted to
replace the nutrients lost to soil erosion with chemical fertilizers and is at present using 50 million barrels of fuel equivalent a year to offset past soil losses.

Despite undreamt of levels of material prosperity, our consumer
is subject to mounting stress. He walks twice as fast as his
country brother. His senses are assaulted by nearly 600 advertising messages every day, although he notices less than 80.
When he visits the doctor there is a 70 per cent chance that his
aches, pains and various complaints will be diagnosed as resulting from nervous disorders. Not surprisingly, perhaps, no less
than half of the hospital beds in the country in which he lives
are occupied by people suffering from mental disorders.

Fear has become an important element in his life. Like more than
one half of his fellow citizens, he owns a gun. In the country
in which he lives the number of firearms in private ownership
now outnumber those in the armed forces of NATO and the Warsaw
Pact combined. (205) Half of these weapons have been acquired in
the past five years or so in response to rising crime, outstrip-
ped only by the fear of it. More than one half of his fellow
citizens keep guns for self-protection and dress plainly to
avoid attracting the attention of attackers. Four out of ten admit that they live in constant fear of being assaulted. (206)
And as crime has followed him into the suburbs, he now locks,
like 70 per cent of his countrymen, his car door when driving
to and from home.

In search of much needed escape and relaxation, our consumer and
his family together spend 7 hours a day watching television. If
this doesn't work, he can, like millions of others, tame his
anxieties with Librium, Valium or a score of other psychic paci-
fiers. He can sleep chemically induced sleep. In his search for
relaxation, he might choose to dabble with yoga or transcenden-
tal meditation. More likely, he will prefer to blur his worries
in an alcoholic haze.

And in the summer months there is the annual vacation, the time
for the 'great escape'. Whereas some might seek a more simple
life as an alternative to the stress, pressure and boredom of
the daily routine, our model consumer will probably choose to

go mad; to rush around the world - the farther away the better - without any real aim or purpose other than in search of sensation in the most resource consuming conditions. The plane that takes him on his annual odyssey will alone use the energy required to feed 150,000 people for a day. When he reaches his destination he will be impervious to heat waves, mindless of the deepening gloom about inflation, recession or unemployment. He is prepared to suffer from dysanagnosia, diarrhea, dysentery and mysterious skin rashes. His flights will be overbooked, his food undercooked. He will be herded into jets and jeeps, cheated and laughed at, seduced and abandoned. But it is the great escape, and he will cry out for more.

He is in constant search of the exotic and unusual. What should he do this year? Take a pilgrimage to Mongolia and eat yak butter for breakfast? Paddle up mosquito ridden streams in Borneo to observe natives performing unspeakable rights? Spend a harrowing week with friendly Amazon headhunters, die of thirst on a three-week trip across the Sahara, or nearly freeze to death on a four-day dogsled trek across Greenland? Or simply roast in a vast cluster of simmering flesh across miles of palm fringed beaches? Wherever he goes and whatever he does he will be a missionary, anxious to spread the gospel of the good life in the Western world. Justifiably, he has been called the emissary of cultural imperialism and the agent of Western domination.

What can we conclude from this brief sketch of the archetypal Western consumer? We can safely conclude that his consumption pattern and life-style, characterized as they are by overconsumption and waste, carry some far-reaching implications:

● They have implications for others. Overconsumption and waste in a world of want and desperate poverty is not only morally objectionable; it is an act of criminal proportions, one which is directed against the interests and well-being of the majority of the world's people. Those who advocate the narrowing of the gap in wealth and opportunity between the rich and poor nations while at the same time envisaging a continuation of current consumption patterns in the rich countries, are supporting two irreconcilable streams of thought. If they advocate both and argue that they can be carried out simultaneously, then they can be considered either ignorant or mendacious. (207) Circles cannot be squared.

● They have implications for the natural environment and for ecological equilibrium. Overconsumption and waste do much more than give rise to local pollution; they have placed global life-support systems - those on which all living creatures are dependent - under unprecedented attack. There are good grounds for believing that, in certain areas, mankind might be closer to transgressing the outer limits imposed on its activities by the natural environment than it might care - or even dare - to think.

And to exceed the limits set by nature could conceivably result in a planet unable to support life.

• They have implications for the individual consumer and for the rich countries themselves. Overconsumption and waste have damaged rather than enhanced the quality of life. People in the rich world are three, five, even ten times richer than their grandparents. Yet few would argue that they are three, five or ten times more contented or self-fulfilled. Indeed, we are being forced to conclude that preoccupation with material well-being may be morally and ethically corrupting; that fundamental human values may be endangered by the philosophy and forces underlying the mania to consume. Man has only a limited capacity to consume material goods. For many in the rich countries that level has not only been reached, it has been passed. It has little sense to consume more of the same if the result is premature death, or an ever increasing need for tranquilizers and mental hospitals. (208)

Overdevelopment has brought overconsumption and enormous waste in a world of want, fragile ecological systems, and finite supplies of most raw materials. Every year the world's affluent minority 'throws away' some 11 million motor vehicles, 45 million tonnes of paper and board, 60 billion bottles and 100 billion metal cans and useless gadgets. Every child born into the rich world consumes, in the course of growing up, over one million calories and 13 tonnes of coal equivalent (over 10,000 litres) every year. This compares with the annual consumption of a child born into the poor world of half a million calories and almost no energy, save that which the child produces from those calories.

No sane person can seriously envisage a world in which the people of the Third World - 70 per cent of the world's total population - live like today's affluent minority, develop the same appetite for cereals, adopt the same standards of automobile use (96 per cent of all cars can at present be found in the countries of the OECD), consume 11 tonnes of natural resources, and each employ 400 'energy slaves'. In order for all the world's population to reach a standard of living equivalent to that of the United States in 1970, it would require the extraction of 75 times as much copper and zinc, 200 times as much lead, 250 times as much tin, and increases of similar orders of magnitude in the production of many other basic minerals. As for energy, such a standard of living would require the equivalent of 7 times as much oil, 8 times as much gas, and 9 times as much coal as are now produced annually. To believe that such general levels of consumption are possible is a dangerous illusion; to attempt to provide for them would be madness.

Whether someone born into the rich world is 50 or 500 times the ecological burden of someone born into the poor world is a sub-

ject of academic debate. That the difference in burden is significant is, however, obvious. Viewed in these terms and from
a global environmental and ecological perspective, population
control in the rich countries is as great a necessity as population control in the poor nations. (209)

A more rational and equitable international order cannot be
built on a foundation of national orders shaped by an exclusive
preoccupation with economic growth and the accumulation of material riches. The experiences of the rich countries shows that
even unparalleled economic growth does not necessarily lead to
increased social equalities and increased power sharing. Life
in the industrialized world has often been marked by the shortsighted use of technology and with disregard for the social
costs which have accompanied technical advance. (210) The growth
ideology has shown itself to be a constant stimulus to overconsumption of goods; the pursuit of quantity and the extravagent
and wasteful use of resources has often taken place at the expense of the fairer distribution of wealth, opportunity, and of
the quality of life. Is it any wonder that many in the Third
World, brought up on the belief that the 'West is best', have
come to reject the notions suggesting that the West must serve
as the model for development. (211)

Ultimately, the rich countries should seek to construct their
policies on a series of 'maxima' which define an appropriate
form of civilized living in a world of deprivation and which declare that all consumption beyond that fixed by the maxima is
not only waste but a conscious action against the welfare of
growing numbers of poor and disprivileged, their own children,
and the prospects for a peaceful world. (212)

Changes - fundamental changes - in the consumption patterns of
the rich must thus form an essential ingredient of attempts to
build a world which is more rational, more equitable and habitable. (213) There is increasing evidence for believing that such
changes are no longer a matter of choice. They are being forced
upon the rich world by changing resource relationships and problems of depletion, by a deteriorating natural environment, and
by a deepening economic crisis. The demands of affluence are,
for the first time in contemporary history, beginning to out-
strip life support systems. As pressures mount, so will scarcities. These could, in turn, give rise to intolerable strains
on social, economic and political systems. Some of these systems
will crack. (214) The pressures exerted by the developing countries will add to the stresses and strains.

NOTES AND REFERENCES

(1) On the formation of the world system, see Immanuel Waller-
    stein, *The Modern World System,* Academic Press, New York,
    1974, and *The Capitalist World Economy,* Cambridge Univer-
    sity Press, New York, 1979.
(2) See Max Weber, *The Protestant Ethic and the Spirit of Capi-
    talism,* Unwin University Books, London, 1965 (First publish-
    ed in 1904). Weber quotes (p.175) John Wesley, the founder
    of Methodism: "We ought not to prevent people from being
    diligent and frugal; we must exhort all Christians to gain
    all they can, and to save all they can; that is, in effect,
    to grow rich". For a discussion of the relationship between
    protestantism and the development of capitalism, see Waller-
    stein, op. cit., and S.N. Eisenstadt, (ed.), *The Protestant
    Ethic and Modernization,* New York, 1968.
(3) See chapter 7 for a discussion of the new learning on the
    development of science and technology.
(4) Geoffrey Barraclough quotes the Chinese writer Yen Fu who
    summed up "three centuries of progress" in the West under
    four headings: "to be selfish, to kill others, to have no
    integrity, and to lose the sense of shame". "That", as
    Barraclough observes, "is how the accomplishments of Western
    civilization appeared to an observer from the outside". See
    Turning Points in World History, Thames and Hudson, London,
    1979, p.79.
(5) Radical economics has developed the theory of unequal ex-
    change, a restatement in Marxist language of the analyses
    of Myrdal, Prebish, Singer and Lewis (cf. chapter 2, foot-
    note 75), to explain this phenomenon. Based upon an analysis
    of price formations, the theory shows how the surpluses re-
    sulting from trade are bound to accrue to Western capital
    rather than developing country labor. For presentations of
    the theory, see: Samir Amin, *Unequal Development,* Monthly
    Review Press, New York/London, 1976; Arghiri Emmanuel, *Un-
    equal Echange: A Study of the Imperialism of Trade,* Monthly
    Review Press, 1972; and Ranjit Sau, *Unequal Exchange: Impe-
    rialism and Underdevelopment,* Oxford University Press, India,
    1979. Unequal exchange relations between the EEC and the de-
    veloping countries are examined by Johan Galtung in *The
    European Community: A Superpower in the Making,* Allen and
    Unwin, London, 1973.
(6) For an argument to the effect that many of the 'benefits'
    associated with imperial policy can in fact be attributed to
    the workings of 'free trade' in unequal situations, see B.
    Semmel, *The Rise of Free Trade Imperialism,* Cambridge Uni-
    versity Press, London, 1970; and J. Gallagher and R. Robinson,
    'The Imperialism of Free Trade', *Economic History Review,*
    vol. 6, no. 1, 1953, pp. 1-15.

(7) For a presentation of changing Third World views on the North-South development debate, see Mahbub ul Haq, *The Poverty Curtain: Choices for the Third World,* Columbia University Press, New York, 1977.

(8) For a review of the negotiations between rich and poor countries during the '60s and '70s, see H.Santa Cruz, J.D.Valdovinos, G.Rojas, *Development, the United Nations and the North South Relationship,* Centre International pour le Développement, Paris, 1977.

(9) For a range of views on the interdependence debate, see: Denis Goulet, *World Interdependence: Verbal Smokescreen or New Ethic,* Development Paper 21, Overseas Development Council Washington, D.C., March, 1976; Roger Hansen, 'The Crisis of Interdependence: Where Do We Go from Here?', in Roger Hansen, (ed.), *The U.S. and World Development. Agenda for Action 1976,* Praeger, Washington/New York, 1976, pp. 41-66; Gerhard Malley, *Interdependence,* Heath, Lexington, 1976; Joseph S.Nye, 'Independence and Interdependence', *Foreign Affairs,* vol. 22, 1976, pp. 130-161; Richard Rosecrance, 'Wither Interdependence' *International Organization,* no. 3, 1977, pp. 425-475; A. Sergiyev, 'Bourgeois Theories of 'Interdependence' Serve Neo-Colonialism', *International Affairs,* Moscow, no. 11, 1976; Timothy M.Shaw, *Towards an International Political Economy for the 1980s: From Dependence to (Inter)dependence,* Centre for Foreign Policy Studies, Dalhousie University, Halifax, November 1980; Raimo Vayrynen, 'Interdependence vs. Self Reliance in Economic Relations', *Alternatives,* vol. 3, no. 4 May 1978, pp. 481-514.

(10) Barbara Ward, *Progress for a Small Planet,* Penguin, Harmondsworth, 1979, p. 244.

(11) See Sergiyev, op.cit., and Geoffrey Barraclough 'The Haves and the Have Nots', *New York Review of Books,* May 13, 1977.

(12) Interestingly, Kenneth Boulding, the father of the 'spaceship earth' analogy, has questioned the accuracy of the metaphor. In a more recent paper he substitutes the concept for that of a mesa surrounded by cliffs. See his 'Commons and Community: The Idea of a Public', in G.Hardin and J.Baden (eds.), *Managing the Commons,* Freeman, San Francisco, 1977.

(13) In 1975 the WHO uncovered a new international trade - in human blood. Western enterprises, it reported, were making immense profits by buying blood from poor people in Africa, Asia and Latin America and selling it for ten times the price in rich countries. One Filipino woman, the mother of eleven children, took to giving blood, sometimes several times a week, just to keep her family alive. She died, bled to death. Reported in Geoffrey Lean, *Rich World, Poor World,* George Allen and Unwin, London, 1979, p. 49. Calcutta is one of the world's largest centers for the export of human skeletons. A case of a developing country using its comparative advantage?

(14) Statement by the Third World Conference on Raw Materials, held in Dakar, Senegal, February 1975, as preparation for the Sixth Special Session.

(15) The costs of present institutional distortions are not known. The figure of $ 100 billion can be found in Mahbub ul Haq, op.cit., pp. 163-164, and has been used by the Third World in the presentation of its case. See Third World Forum, *Proposals for a New International Economic Order*, Report prepared by a Special Task Force of the Third World Forum, Mexico City, August 21-24, 1975, p. 3. Mahbub ul Haq has also suggested, op.cit., p. 159, that if developing countries were able to exercise the same degree of control over processing and distribution activities, their export earnings would be closer to $ 150 billion. For a general discussion of the 'costs' question, see Paul Harrison, *Inside the Third World*, Penguin, Harmondsworth, 1979, pp. 363-365.

(16) Resolutions 3201 (S-VI) and 3202 (S-VI), adopted at the 2229th plenary meeting. See U.N. document A/9556 (Part II), May 1, 1974.

(17) See U.N. document A/PV 2231.

(18) For reviews of the Seventh Special Session, see Branislav Gosovic and John G.Ruggie, 'On the Creation of a New International Economic Order: Issue Linkage and the Special Session of the U.N. General Assembly', *International Organization*, vol. 30, Spring 1976, pp. 309-345; Catherine B.Gwin, 'The Seventh Special Session: Toward a New Phase of Relations Between the Developed and Developing States?', in K.P.Sauvant and H.Hasenpflug, (eds.), *The New International Economic Order: Confrontation or Cooperation Between North and South*, Wilton House, London, 1977, pp. 20-35, Jyoti S.Singh, *A New International Economic Order: Toward a Fair Redistribution of the World's Resources*, Praeger, New York, 1977, chapter 2; and Orlando Letelier and Michael Moffit, *The International Economic Order (Part I)*, Transnational Institute, Washington, D.C. 1977, pp. 36-42.

(19) See U.N. document A/PV 2327.

(20) For a review of the North-South debate, see Geoffrey Barraclough, 'Waiting for the New Order', and 'The Struggle of the Third World', in *The New York Review of Books*, 26 October and 9 November 1978; Commonwealth Secretariat, *Review of Progress in the Implementation of Recommendations of the Report of the Commonwealth Experts' Group 'Towards a New International Economic Order'*, London, August 1978; the essays contained in Khadija Haq, (ed.), *Dialogue for a New Order*, Pergamon, New York, 1980; and André Gunder Frank, 'Rhetoric and Reality of the New International Economic Order', May 1978 (mimeo).

(21) See H.Santa Cruz, et.al., op.cit., for a review of UNCTAD I.

(22) See Albert Tévoédjrè, *Poverty: Wealth of Mankind*, Pergamon,

Oxford, 1978, p. 168.
(23) Mahbub ul Haq, op.cit., pp. 185-186.
(24) See Richard N.Gardner, *Sterling-Dollar Diplomacy*, New York, 1969, viz. pp. 112-128.
(25) Quoted in André Gunder Frank, op.cit., p. 14.
(26) See Fred Hirsch, 'Is there a New International Economic Order?', *International Organization*, vol. 30, no. 3, Summer 1976, pp. 521-531 at p. 531.
(27) See footnote 20 for references to reviews of North-South negotiations.
(28) OECD, *Facing the Future: Mastering the Probable and Managing the Unpredictable*, Paris, 1979, p. 281.
(29) See Miguel S.Wionczek, 'A Diagnosis of Failures and Prospects', in E.Laszlo and J.Kurtzman, (eds.), *The Structure of the World Economy and Prospects for a New International Economic Order'*, Pergamon, New York, 1980, pp. 46-47.
(30) *Commercio Exterior*, July 1977, p. 835, quoted in André Gunder Frank, op.cit., p. 43.
(31) Willy Brandt interviewed in *Newsweek,* March 24, 1980, p.56.
(32) For Western rejections of the NIEO package, see the following: M.Krenin, J.M.Finger, 'A New International Economic Order: A Critical Survey of Issues', *Journal of World Trade Law,* vol. 10, November-December 1976, pp. 3-22; Jurgen B. Donges, 'The Third World Demand for a New International Economic Order: Government Surveillance Versus Market Decision-making in Trade and Investment', *Kyklos,* vol. 30, 1977, pp. 235-258; H.G.Grubel, 'The Case Against the New International Economic Order', *Weltwirtschaftliches Archiv,* Band 113, Heft 2, 1977; P.T.Bauer and B.S.Yamey, 'Against the New Economic Order', *Commentary,* vol. 63, no. 3, April 1977, pp. 25-31; W.Laqueur, 'Third World Fantasies', *Commentary,* vol. 63, no. 2, February 1977, p. 43-48; P.T.Bauer and J.O'Sullivan, 'Ordering the World About: The NIEO', *Policy Review,* vol. 1, Summer 1977, pp. 55-69.
(33) See Nathaniel H.Leff, 'The New Economic Order: Bad Economics, Worse Politics', *Foreign Policies,* vol. 24, Fall 1976, pp. 202-217.
(34) Possible military approaches are discussed in G.J.Pauker, *Military Implications of a Possible World Order Crisis in the 1980s,* The Rand Corporation, Santa Monica, Ca., November 1977. This is presumably a 'sanitized' version of the report submitted to the U.S. Defense Department.
(35) For such a view, see William Pfaff, 'Reflections: Economic Development', *The New Yorker,* December 25, 1978, pp. 44-47.
(36) This is well documented in Lynn White, Jr., *Medieval Technology and Social Change*, Oxford University Press, London/New York, 1962.
(37) On this, see Rajni Kothari, *Footsteps into the Future,* Free Press, New York, 1974, viz. pp. 21-23.
(38) V.G.Kiernan, *Lords of Human Kind: European Attitudes to the*

Outside World in the Imperial Age, Weidenfeld and Nicolson, London, 1969.

(39) Albert Beveridge, quoted in J.William Fulbright, *The Arrogance of Power,* Random House, New York, 1966, p. 6.

(40) See Franz Fanon, *The Wretched of the Earth,* Grove Press, New York, 1966; and *Black Skin, White Masks,* Grove Press, New York, 1968; and Albert Memmi, *Colonizer and Colonized,* Beacon Press, Boston, 1967; and *Dominated Man,* Beacon Press, Boston, 1968.

(41) See F.van Dam, 'Noord-Zuid: De Werkelijkheid van 1980-1990', *Economische Statistische Berichten,* November 14, 1979, pp. 1188-1196, viz. pp. 1194-5.

(42) The declaration adopted by the foreign ministers of the 94 nations that attended the meeting of the Non-Aligned forum held in New Delhi in February 1981 refers to the "tendency" of the industrialized countries "to back out on commitments previously made by consensus". See 'Nonaligned States, Ending Conference, Accuse Rich Nations of Reneging on Aid', *International Herald Tribune,* February 16, 1981, p. 5.

(43) See Alain Vernay, 'Grand Designs Eclipsed - But Reality Remains', *Development Forum,* June 1978, pp. 1-2.

(44) Jan Tinbergen (coordinator), *Reshaping the International Order: A Report to The Club of Rome,* E.P.Dutton, New York, 1976, p. 53.

(45) This is the view of Henry Kissinger. See the interview with him in *Time,* May 12, 1980, pp. 19-20.

(46) Stanley Hoffmann, *Primacy or Word Order: American Foreign Policy Since the Cold War,* McGraw Hill, New York, 1978.

(47) The incapacity of the U.S. to understand ideology is one of the themes in Franz Schurmann's excellent *The Logic of World Power,* Pantheon, New York, 1974.

(48) This argument is developed by Michael Hudson in *Global Fracture: The New International Economic Order,* Harper and Row, New York, 1977, p. 165 ff.

(49) See Stanley Hoffmann, op.cit.

(50) According to *Time* correspondent Strobe Talbot. See 'Departure of a Good Soldier', *Time,* May 12, 1980, p. 18.

(51) *US News and World Report,* May 30, 1977.

(52) Zbigniew Brzezinski, 'America in a Hostile World', *Foreign Policy,* no. 23, Summer 1976, pp. 65-96.

(53) See Richard N.Cooper, 'A New International Economic Order for Mutual Gain', *Foreign Policy,* no. 26, Spring 1977, pp. 65-120.

(54) C. Fred Bergsten, 'The Response to the Third World, *Foreign Policy,* no. 17, Winter 1974-75, pp. 3-34. See also his earlier 'The Threat from the Third World', *Foreign Policy,* no. 11, Winter 1973, pp. 102-124.

(55) See 'Third World on Hold', *Christian Science Monitor,* February 15, 1978, p. 28.

(56) For an argument to this effect by a White House staffer,

see Lloyd Cutler, 'To Form a Government', *Foreign Affairs,*
vol. 59, no. 1, Fall 1980, pp. 126-143.

(57) See Brzezinski, op.cit., p. 73.

(58) See chapter 2, viz. footnote 36.

(59) Jeff Frieden, 'The Trilateral Commission: Economics and Politics in the 1970s', *Monthly Review,* vol. 29, no. 7, December 1977, pp. 1-18, at pp. 16-17.

(60) See 'The Trilateral Elite', *Newsweek,* March 24, 1980, p. 26.

(61) Quoted in 'Releases May be a Gift to Carter', *The Guardian,* October 5, 1980, p. 7.

(62) See Henry Steele Commager, 'In Search of American Statesmanship', *International Herald Tribune,* August 26, 1980.

(63) Henry Kissinger interviewed in *Time,* October 27, 1975.

(64) Herman Kahn is among those who has argued that it is a U.S. duty to be rich and 'independent'. If it is rich it can help the world. Or, as Kahn puts its, "If India, for example, goes under we want to be able to save her, not go down with her". See H. Kahn, W. Brown, L. Martel, *The Next 200 Years,* Morrow, New York, 1976, p. 216.

(65) This is the conclusion of the Interfutures Project. See OECD, op.cit., viz. p. 400.

(66) See Michel Robert, 'Indulgent with the East and Evasive Towards the U.S., Europe is Neither Worthy of its Supposed Destiny, Nor Equal to the Moderating Role it Claims to be Playing', *The Guardian,* May 13, 1980.

(67) B.S. Fromin, 'The New International Economic Order as Viewed in the CMEA countries', in E. Laszlo and J. Kurtzman (eds.) *Eastern Europe and the New International Economic Order,* Pergamon, New York, 1980, pp. 1-17, at. p.7.

(68) For a summary of official Soviet views of the world and of thinking on major issues in international relations, see N.I. Lebedev, *A New Stage in International Relations,* Pergamon, Oxford, 1978.

(69) See U.N. document A/PV 2210.

(70) B.S. Fromin, op.cit., p. 6.

(71) President Echeverría, interviewed in *Newsweek,* October 20, 1975.

(72) See André Gunder Frank, 'Rhetoric and Reality of the NIEO', May 1978 (mimeo).

(73) The question of Third World institutions is discussed in the next chapter.

(74) See Robert W.Tucker, *The Inequality of Nations,* Basic Books, New York, 1977.

(75) This is argued by Fawzy Mansour in 'Third World Revolt and Self-Reliant Auto-Centered Strategy of Development', Document 406, IDEP, Dakar 1977 (mimeo), viz. p. 83.

(76) Johan Galtung, 'Self-Reliance and Global Interdependence: Some Reflections on the 'New International Economic Order'', *Chair in Conflict and Peace Research, University of Oslo, Papers,* no. 55, 1977, p. 8.

(77) For such views, see, for example, Samir Amin, 'Self-Reliance
and the New International Economic Order', *Monthly Review*,
vol. 29, no. 3, August 1977, pp. 1-21; Harry Magdoff, 'The
Limits of International Reform', *Monthly Review*, vol. 30, no.
1, May 1978, pp. 1-11; Raimo Vayrynen, 'Interdependence vs.
Self-Reliance in Economic Relations', *Alternatives*, vol. 3,
no. 4, May 1978, pp. 481-514; Johan Galtung, *Poor Countries
vs. Rich; Poor People vs. Rich. Whom Will the NIEO Benefit?*
Occasional Paper 77/4, Vienna Institute for Development,
Vienna, 1977; D. Wadada Nabudere, *Essays on the Theory and
Practice of Imperialism*, Onyx Press, London, 1979, chapter 6;
and André Gunder Frank, op.cit.
(78) According to D.K. Fieldhouse colonial empires have, at different times, covered 85 per cent of world's land surface.
See his *The Colonial Empires*, Weidenfeld and Nicolson, London,
1966; and *Colonialism 1870-1945*, Weidenfeld and Nicolson,
1980.
(79) For a review of different theories of capitalist imperialism
see D.K. Fieldhouse, *The Theory of Capitalist Imperialism*,
Longman, London, 1967; T. Kemp, *Theories of Imperialism*,
Dobson, London, 1967; Benjamin Cohen, *The Question of Imperialism*, Macmillan, London, 1974; and Wolfgang J.Mommsen,
Theories of Imperialism, Weidenfeld and Nicolson, London,
1980.
(80) See J.M. Robertson, *Patriotism and Empire*, Grant Richards,
London, 1900; J.A.Hobson, *Imperialism: A Study*, Nisbett,
London, 1902; and N.N. Brailsford, *The War of Steel and Gold*,
G. Bell, London, 1914. For a more recent liberal analysis,
see A. Hodgart, *The Economics of European Imperialism*,
Edward Arnold, London, 1977.
(81) For a discussion of the relationship between imperialism
and the Marxist tradition, see George Lichtheim, *Imperialism*,
Allen Lane, London, 1971. Important Marxist interpretations
of imperialism include: Samir Amin, *Imperialism and Under-
development*, Monthly Review Press, New York/London, 1977;
Paul Baran, *Political Economy of Growth*, Monthly Review
Press, 1957; M. Barratt-Brown, *The Economics of Imperialism*,
Penguin, Harmondsworth, 1974; André Gunder Frank, *World Ac-
cumulation 1492-1789*, Macmillan, London, 1978, and *Develop-
ment Accumulation and Underdevelopment*, Macmillan, 1979;
P. Jalée, *The Pillage of the Third World*, Monthly Review
Press, 1967; Harry Magdoff, *The Age of Imperialism*, Monthly
Review Press, 1970; P.M. Sweezy, *The Theory of Capitalist
Development*, Monthly Review Press, 1968. For a specifically
Trotskyist analysis, see Michael Kidron, *Western Capitalism
Since the War*, Weidenfeld and Nicolson, London, 1968.
(82) Rosa Luxemburg, *The Accumulation of Capital*, Routlegde and
Kegan Paul, London, 1951 (first published 1913).
(83) See R. Hilferding, *Finanzkapital*, Verlag der Wiener Volks-
buchhandlung, Vienna, 1923 (first published 1910);

N.I. Bukharin, *Imperialism and World Economy*, International
Publishers, New York, 1929 (first published 1917); and V.I.
Lenin, *Imperialism, The Highest Stage of Capitalism*, Foreign
Languages Publishing House, Moscow, 1947 (first published
1916).

(84) Harry Magdoff, *The Age of Imperialism*, Monthly Review Press,
New York/London, 1970, p. 26.

(85) For general presentations of dependency theory, see the
papers in H. Bernstein (ed.), *Underdevelopment and Development: The Third World Today*, Penguin, Harmondsworth, 1973;
J.D. Cockcroft, A.G. Frank and D.L. Johnson, *Dependence and
Development: Latin America's Political Economy*, Anchor Books,
New York, 1972; K.T. Faun and D.C. Hodges, (eds.), *Readings
in U.S. Imperialism*, Porter Sargent, Boston, 1971; R.J. Owen
and R.B. Sutcliffe, (eds.), *Studies in the Theory of Imperialism*, Longman, London, 1972; R.I. Rhodes, (ed.), *Imperialism and Underdevelopment: A Reader*, Monthly Review Press,
New York/London, 1970; and. D. Slater, 'Underdevelopment and
Spatial Inequality', *Progress in Planning*, vol. 4, Pergamon,
Oxford, 1974. Dependency Theory is particularly associated
with Latin America and the *dependencia* school. The most prominent and influential of the theorists have been André Gunder
Frank, Theotonio Dos Santos and Celso Furtado. For a presen-
tation of their views see: André Gunder Frank: *Capitalism
and Underdevelopment in Latin America*, Monthly Review Press,
New York/London, 1969; *Latin Amercia: Underdevelopment or
Revolution*, Monthly Review Press, 1969; T. Dos Santos, 'The
Crisis of Development Theory and the Problem of Dependence
in Latin America', in H. Bernstein, op.cit., pp. 57-80;
Celso Furtardo, 'Elements of a Theory of Underdevelopment:
The Underdeveloped Structures', in H. Bernstein, op.cit.,
pp. 33-43; *Obstacles to Development in Latin America*, Anchor
Books, Garden City, New York, 1970; *The Economic Development
of Latin America: A Survey of Colonial Times to the Cuban
Revolution*, Cambridge University Press, Cambridge, 1970.
Their thesis is that the Spanish and Portugese colonies of
Latin America were so completely integrated into the world
capitalist system in the sixteenth century that they never
had the chance of achieving their own economic development.
They argue that the same processes of underdevelopment are
at work everywhere and in every age. In *Latin America: Underdevelopment or Revolution*, André Gunder Frank writes
(p. 225): "To extract the fruits of their labour through
pillage, slavery, forced labour, free labour, raw materials,
or through monopoly trade - no less today than in the times
of Cortez and Pizarro in Mexico and Peru, Clive in India,
Rhodes in Africa, the 'Open Door' in China - the metropolis
destroyed and/or totally transformed the earlier viable social and economic systems of these societies, incorporated
them into the metropolitan-dominated, world-wide capitalist

system and converted them into sources for its own capital
accumulation and development". Ernest Mandell has provided
quantitative support for this thesis. He has added up the
value of the gold and silver transported from Latin America
up to 1660, the booty extracted from Indonesia by the Dutch
East India Company from 1650 to 1780, the profits reaped by
the French in their eighteenth century slave trade, from
slave labor in the British Antilles and from half a century
of British looting in India. The total exceeds the capital
invested in all European industrial enterprises operated by
steam around 1800. See *Marxist Economic Theory*, Monthly Review Press, 1968, vol. 2, pp. 443-444. The processes of underdevelopment described by Latin American dependency theorists have since been described in other developing continents. For Africa, see Samir Amin, *Neo-Colonialism in West
Africa*, Penguin, Harmondsworth, 1973; Walter Rodney, *How
Europe Underdeveloped Africa*, Tanzania Publishing House,
Dar-es-Salaam, 1976; Justinian Rweyemamu, *Underdevelopment
and Industrialization in Tanzania*, Oxford University Press,
Nairobi, 1973; Immanuel Wallerstein, 'The Three Stages of
African Involvement in the World Economy', in P.C.W. Gutkind
and I. Wallerstein, *The Political Economy of Contemporary
Africa*, Sage, Beverly Hills, 1976; and Timothy M.Shaw, 'De-
pendence as an Approach to understanding Continuing Inequal-
ities in Africa', *Journal of Developing Areas*, vol. 13, no. 3
April 1979, pp. 229-246. For critiques of dependency theory,
see: P.J. O'Brien, 'A Critique of Latin American Theories of
Dependence', in I. Oxaal, T. Barnet and D. Booth, (eds.),
Beyond The Sociology of Development, Routlegde and Kegan Paul,
London, 1975; S. Lall, 'Is Dependence a Useful Concept in
Analyzing Underdevelopment?', *World Development*, vol. 3, no.
11, 1975; and C. Leys, 'Underdevelopment and Dependency:
Critical Notes', *Journal of Contemporary Asia*, vol. 7, no.1,
1977.
(86) P. Baran and P.M. Sweezy, *Monopoly Capital*, Monthly Review
Press, New York/London, 1969, p. 179.
(87) The role of the capitalist middle class has been most studied in Latin America. For a sample of reflections, see S.M.
Lipset and A. Solari, (eds.), *Elites in Latin America*, Oxford University Press, London, 1967. For a succinct analysis
of ways in which the consumption patterns of the elite dis-
torts the development process, see Celso Furtado, 'The Concept of External Dependence in the Study of Underdevelopment',
in C. Wilber, (ed.), *The Political Economy of Development
and Underdevelopment*, Random House, New York, 1973, pp. 118-
123.
(88) André Gunder Frank, 'The Development of Underdevelopment'
in R.I. Rhodes, op.cit., pp. 4-17, at p. 6.
(89) E. Laclau, 'Feudalism and Capitalism in Latin America',
New Left Review, no. 67, May-June 1971, p. 23.

(90) This process is well described by Samir Amin. See his *Unequal Development,* Monthly Review Press, New York/London, 1976.

(91) The center-periphery model used by dependency theorists has found a wide number of applications. It has been used by Johan Galtung to develop a structural theory of imperialism based upon dominance relations between collectivities, especially nations. See 'A Structural Theory of Imperialism', *Journal of Peace Research,* vol. 5, 1971, pp. 375-395. Immanuel Wallerstein has also developed the model in different ways, for example, through the elaboration of the concept of 'semi-periphery'. See his *The Capitalist World Economy,* Cambridge University Press, New York, 1979. For a collection of applications of the center-periphery model, see Jean Gottmann, (ed.), *Centre and Periphery: Spatial Variation in Politics,* Sage, Beverly Hills, 1980.

(92) For a comparison of the different streams, see: Helena Tuomi, 'Dependency Models in Western Development Research', in Eeva-Liisa Myllymäki and Brett Dellinger, (eds.), *Dependency and Latin American Development,* Finnish Peace Research Association, Turku/Tampere, 1977; Gabriel Palma, 'Dependency: A Formal Theory of Underdevelopment or a Methodology for the Analysis of Concrete Situations of Underdevelopment', *World Development,* vol. 6, 1978, pp. 881-924; and R. Janssen, 'Afhankelijkheidstheorieën. Het Dependenciamodel: Een Origineel Latijnsamerikaanse Bijdrage aan de Sociale Wetenschappen', *Intermediair,* October 20, 1978, pp. 17-21. Janssen argues that dependency theory can be conveniently subdivided into two main streams: a nationalist stream (represented by Furtardo, Jaguaribe, Pinto and Sunkel); and a Marxist stream (represented by Cardoso, Dos Santos, Weffort, Marini, Quijano, Stavenhagen, Faletto and Vasconi). The major difference is that the national stream places less emphasis on internal factors and more on external constraints on development whereas the Marxist stream stresses that the external factors become internalized and eventually become part of the internal social structure. The Marxist stream also stresses the systemic nature of dependence. The Marxist stream can be divided into sub-streams based upon whether dependence is viewed largely in terms of capitalist imperialism and exploitation on a world scale; as historically determined through the evolution of relationships with the metropolitan centers; or as a determining factor for the internal structure of the dependent country.

(93) The principal objections of some Marxists to dependency theory concern the stress placed on exhange relations rather than production relations and inadequate attention to the development of class relations. As some Marxists, like Kay, argue that dependency theorists "have turned their backs on the law of value" and this has meant that they are unable to

appreciate the real causes of underdevelopment. See G. Kay,
Development and Underdevelopment: A Marxist Analysis, Macmillan, London, 1975, viz. pp. 103-104. For Marxist critiques
of dependency theory, see: Robert Brenner, 'The Origins of
Capitalist Development: A Critique of Neo-Smithian Marxism',
New Left Review, no. 104, July-August 1977, pp. 25-92; E.
Laclau, 'Feudalism and Capitalism in Latin America', *New
Left Review,* no. 67, 1971; and J. Clammer, 'Economic Anthropology and the Sociology of Development: Liberal Anthropology
and its French Critics', in I. Oxaal, T. Barnet and D. Booth
(eds.), *Beyond the Sociology of Development,* Routledge and
Kegan Paul, London, 1975. As Aidan Foster-Carter has argued
only a few years ago it was possible to sketch out the dis-
tinctive features of a Marxist perspective to the problem of
underdevelopment. Today, Marxists are deeply and increasingly divided over fundamental issues. See his 'The Modes of
Production Controversy', *New Left Review,* no. 107, January-
February 1978, itself a good radical critique of dependency
theory. It is probably true to say that Marxists are being
compelled to proceed to a criticism of the ideology of development through a critique of Marxism itself. On this, see
P.R.D. Corrigan, H. Ramsay and D. Sayer (eds.), *Socialist
Construction and Marxist Theory,* Macmillan, London, 1978.
(94) A number of Marxists have challenged the thesis that capitalism cannot promote the development of peripheral areas.
See, for example, F.H. Cardoso, 'Dependency and Development
in Latin America', *New Left Review,* no. 74, 1972; and Bill
Warren, 'Imperialism and Capitalist Industrialization', *New
Left Review,* no. 81, 1974.
(95) See James A.Caporoso, 'Dependence, Dependency and Power in
Global Systems: A Structural and Behavioral Analysis', *International Organization,* vol. 32, no. 1, Winter 1978, pp.
13-43; and Raymond D.Duvall, 'Dependency and Dependencia
Theory: Notes Towards Precision of Concept and Argument,
International Organization, vol. 32, no. 1, Winter 1978,
pp. 51-78. That dependency theory is able to go beyond critique and to serve as a starting point for strategies of
national development is shown by Clive Y.Thomas in *Dependency
and Transformation; Economics of the Transition to Socialism,*
Monthly Review Press, New York/London, 1974.
(96) Harry Magdoff, 'The Limits of International Reform', *Monthly
Review,* vol. 30, no. 1, May 1978, pp. 1-11, at p. 4.
(97) This case has been argued by Immanuel Wallerstein, op.cit.
See also his 'Dependence in an Interdependent World: The
Limited Possibilities of Transformation Within the Capitalist
World Economy', *African Studies Review,* no. 1, 1974, pp. 1-26.
(98) Michael Harrington tells a revealing story of a dinner de-
bate he had with Third World ambassadors to the U.N. in New
York. Most of those present were "international technocrats
(who) believed in the market mechanism...(W)hen one in their

number voiced the classic left-wing, anti-imperialist position, the statement was rejected in a patronizing way as being fundamentally unserious". See *The Vast Majority: A Journey to the World's Poor,* Simon and Schuster, New York, 1977,
pp. 214-218, viz. p. 217.

(99) See Timothy M.Shaw, *Towards an International Political Eco-
nomy for the 1980s: From Dependence to (Inter)Dependence,*
Centre for Foreign Policy Studies, Dalhousie University,
Halifax, November 1980, pp. 27-33.

(100) Harry Magdoff, op.cit., 1978, p. 11

(101) For a historical review of stratification, see E. Luard,
Types of International Society, Free Press, New York, 1976.
An early presentation of the thesis that the international
system can be conveniently considered as a stratified social
system can be found in G. Lagos, *International Stratification
and Underdeveloped Countries,* University of North Carolina
Press, Chapel Hill, N.C., 1963.

(102) For a sympathetic but firm rejection of the theory of capitalist imperialism, see D.K. Fieldhouse, op.cit., 1967.
He notes that the theory "might have been true, but in fact
it was not". He considers it "surprising" that historical
evidence does not support the theory (p. 192).

(103) For a presentation of Mao's views on world order, see
Samuel S.Kim, *China, the United Nations and World Order,*
Princeton University Press, N.J. 1979; and 'China and World
Order', *Alternatives,* vol. 3, no. 4, May 1978, pp. 555-587;
and Edward Friedman, 'Maoist Conceptualizations of the Capitalist World System' in T.K. Hopkins and I. Wallerstein
(eds.), *Processes of the World System,* vol. 3, *Political
Economy of the World System Annals,* Sage, Beverly Hills,
1980, pp. 181-223.

(104) 'World in Great Disorder, Excellent Situation', *Survey of
the People's Republic of China Press,* no. 5537, January 18,
1974, p. 166.

(105) A headline in the New Years Day 1980 issue of *People's
Daily,* the official Chinese Communist Party newspaper, ex-
horts the Chinese to "make money for socialism".

(106) Samuel S.Kim, op.cit., 1978, p. 564.

(107) See 'Joint Ventures in China', *Newsweek,* May 5, 1980, p.46.

(108) Quoted in *Neue Zürcher Zeitung,* March 1, 1979, p. 35.

(109) See, for example, Charles Bettelheim, 'The Great Leap
Backward', *Monthly Review,* vol. 30, no. 3, July-August 1978,
pp. 37-130.

(110) OECD, *Facing the Future: Mastering the Probable and Managing the Unpredictable,* Paris, 1979, p. 198.

(111) International institution building in the twentieth century is more fully discussed in chapter 4. For a discussion
of the relationship between war and institution building,
see F.H. Hinsley, *Power and the Pursuit of Peace,* Cambridge
University Press, London, 1963; and J. David Singer and

Michael Wallace, 'Intergovernmental Organizations and the
Preservation of Peace, 1816-1964: Some Bivariate Relationships', *International Organization*, no. 3, 1970, pp. 520-
548.

(112) This conclusion is reached by Arnold J.Toynbee in his mam-
moth *A Study of History*, Oxford University Press, London,
1935-1961 (12 volumes). See the summary volume, 'Abridgement
in One Volume' published in 1960.

(113) Jan Tinbergen is among those who has forcefully argued
that institution-building cannot await catastrophe. See
'Building a World Order' in Jagdish N.Bhagwati, (ed.), *Economics and World Order. From the 1970s to the 1990s*, Free
Press, New York, 1972, pp. 141-157.

(114) Silviu Brucan, 'The World Authority: An Exercise in Political Forecasting', in A.J. Dolman, (ed.), *Global Planning
and Resource Management: Toward International Decision Making
in a Divided World*, Pergamon, New York, 1980, pp. 53-71, at
p. 53.

(115) On 'paths' to nuclear war, see Nigel Calder, *Nuclear Nightmares*, Viking Press, New York, 1980.

(116) Carl-Friedrich Weizsäcker, 'A Sceptical Contribution', in
Saul Mendlovitz, (ed.), *On the Creation of a Just World Order*,
Free Press, New York, 1975, pp. 111-150, at. p. 115.

(117) Bernard T.Feld writing in *The Bulletin of the Atomic
Scientists*, January 1981.

(118) According to Lt.-Col. Dmitry Rybakov, *Moscow News*, no. 52
(2936), December 28, 1980, p. 2.

(119) Convergence theory holds that the Western and Soviet systems will increasingly come to resemble each other. See Jan
Tinbergen, *Shaping the World Economy*, McGraw-Hill, New York,
1962, pp. 34-39. Marxists object to the thesis. For a Marxist
rejection, see Reinhard J.Skinner, 'Technological Determinism:
A Critique of Convergence Theory', *Comparative Studies in
Society and History*, vol. 18, no. 1, January 1979, pp. 2-27.
For an 'official' Soviet rejection, see S.A. Khavina, *A Critique of Socialist Economic Management*, M'isl, Moscow, 1968.

(120) The 'McCracken Report' was official OECD gospel for several
years. See OECD, *Towards Full Employment and Price Stability:
A Report to OECD by a Group of Experts*, Paris, June 1977.

(121) For arguments along these general lines, see: Michael
Harrington, *The Twilight of Capitalism*, Simon and Schuster,
New York, 1976; Andrew Gamble and Paul Walton, *Capitalism in
Crisis: Inflation and the State*, Macmillan, London, 1976;
Manuel Castells, *The Economic Crisis and American Society*,
Princeton University Press, Princeton, N.J. 1980; and Paul
Mattick, *Economics, Politics and the Age of Inflation*, M.E.
Sharpe, Inc., White Plains, N.Y., 1980.

(122) This is the conclusion reached by Rostow in *The World Economy: History and Prospect*, Macmillan, London, 1978. His
prescriptions for tackling the "greatest challenge to indus-

trial civilization" are presented in *Getting from Here to There: A Policy for the Post-Keynesian Age,* Macmillan, London, 1979.

(123) On this see Paul M.Sweezy, 'Whither U.S. Capitalism?', *Monthly Review,* vol. 31, no. 7, December 1979, pp. 1-12; and 'The Present Stage of the Global Crisis of Capitalism', *Monthly Review,* vol. 29, no. 11, April 1978, pp. 1-12.

(124) On the question of Islam and the Soviet Union, see R.S. Clem, 'Russians and Others: Ethnic Tensions in the Soviet Union', *Focus,* no. 1, September/October 1980, pp. 1-16; and A. Benningsen, 'Soviet Muslims and the World of Islam', *Problems of Communism,* March/April 1980, pp. 38-51.

(125) This theme is developed in Ted Robert Gurr, *Why Men Rebel,* Princeton University Press, Princeton, N.J. 1970.

(126) Jahangir Amuzegar, 'A Requiem for the North-South Conference', *Foreign Affairs,* October 1977, pp. 136-157, at p.157.

(127) This 'two wave' thesis is developed by Hannah Arendt in *On Revolution,* Winthrop, Englewood Cliffs, N.J. 1971.

(128) Julius Nyerere interviewed in *Utrechts Dagblad,* (Netherlands), December 24, 1980. His actual words were: "The real explosion will come when the poor refuse to stay poor".

(129) This view is developed by Elbaki Hermassi, *The Third World Reassessed,* University of California Press, Berkeley, Ca., 1980.

(130) For a discussion of the future of revolutionary movements in the Third World, see George Lichtheim, *Imperialism,* Allen Lane, London, 1971, viz. chapter 9; and Peter Worsley, *The Third World,* Weidenfeld and Nicolson, London, 1964, viz. chapters 3 and 4.

(131) On this see Rufus Miles, *Awakening from the American Dream: The Social and Political Limits to Growth,* Universe Books, New York, 1976, pp. 222 ff.

(132) It is by no means certain that a bipolar distribution of power promotes stability in the international system. For a presentation of the argument that stability is best served by a multipolar distribution of power, see K.W. Deutsch and J.D. Singer, 'Multipolarity, Power Systems and International Stability', *World Politics,* vol. 16, no. 3, April 1964, pp. 390-406.

(133) F.H. Hinsley, op.cit., shows how, for example, the search for solutions to the basic problems of war and peace have been simple minded. "Given the problem", he notes (p. 3), "every age will independently propound these solutions just as, given time, every civilisation will independently discover the wheel. What is surprising is the absence of development and refinement in the approach to the problem *within* the modern age. That a civilisation which has broken through barriers in almost every other direction, and which has surpassed all its predecessors on innumerable fronts, should still hold views and pursue programmes in international

politics that it held and pursued when it was young - this
is the outstanding failure of recent times. Only one thing
is more surprising: we do not yet recognise this failure".
(original italics).

(134) Immanuel Wallerstein, *The Modern World System*, Academic
Press, New York, 1974, p. 350.

(135) On this distinction, see Joseph S.Nye 'Independence and
Interdependence', *Foreign Affairs*, vol. 22, 1976, pp. 130-
161, viz. p. 145 ff.

(136) The Soviet Union, for example, has been able to purchase
almost all of the grain denied it by the U.S. following the
post Afghanistan embargo. It has cost the U.S. hundreds of
millions of dollars to store the grain it did not sell. For
a discussion of the limitations of economic sanctions as an
instrument of foreign policy, see Margaret P.Doxey, *Economic
Sanctions and International Enforcement*, Oxford University
Press, London, 1971; and Johan Galtung, 'On the Effects of
International Economic Sanctions', *Essays in Peace Research*,
Ejlers, Copenhagen, 1979, vol. V, chapter 4.

(137) This point is forcefully argued in P. Bachrach and M.S.
Baratz in their 'classic' essay 'Two Faces of Power', *American Political Science Review*, vol. 56, no. 4, 1962, pp. 947-
952. The thesis is further developed in their study of decision-making in a U.S. city. See *Power and Poverty: Theory
and Practice*, Oxford University Press, New York, 1970.

(138) On this, see Marina vN. Whitman, 'Leadership Without Hegemony: Our Role in the World Economy', *Foreign Policy*, vol.20,
Summer 1975, pp. 138-160.

(139) For a discussion of the problems involved in turning tigers
into vegetarians, see Silviu Brucan, 'World Politics in the
1980s', in David Krieger, *Disarmament and Development: The
Challenge of the International Control and Management of
Dual-Purpose Technologies*, Foundation Reshaping the International Order (RIO), Rotterdam, February 1981, pp. 111-121.

(140) On the question of 'group power' in international politics,
see W.P. Bundy, 'Elements of Power', *Foreign Affairs*, vol.23,
October 1977, pp. 1-26.

(141) William Safire, 'Sending in the Marines', *International
Herald Tribune*, February 15, 1980.

(142) For a discussion of the ways in which power impinges on
weakness, see Reinhold Niebuhr, 'Power and Ideology in National and International Affairs', in W.T.R. Fox, (ed.),
Theoretical Aspects of International Relations, Notre Dame
University Press, Notre Dame, West Bend, Ind., 1959, p.114 ff.

(143) On this relationship, see Denis Goulet, *World Independence:
Verbal Smokescreen or New Ethic*, Development Paper, 21, Over-
seas Development Council, Washington, D.C., March 1976; and
Idriss Jazairy, 'An Assessment of Prospects in the Light of
Recent Experience', in A.J. Dolman and J. van Ettinger, (eds.)
Partners in Tomorrow: Strategies for a New International Or-

der, E.P. Dutton, New York, 1978, pp. 46-60.

(144) J.O. Goldsborough, 'La Politique Etrangère des Etats-Unis', Politique Etrangère, vol. 45, no. 3, September 1980, pp.621-636 is among those who has pointed to the diverging interests of the U.S. and Western Europe. He argues that a more independent Western European line could actually serve to improve rather than undermine relations with the U.S. Immanuel Wallerstein has pointed to the complementary interests of Western Europe and the Soviet Union and argued that Western Europe will increasingly form an economic and thus a political threat to the U.S. See his 'Friends as Foes', Foreign Policy, Summer 1980, pp. 119-131.

(145) For a discussion of the potential importance of OPEC to the development of the bargaining power of the poor countries, see Mahbub ul Haq, The Poverty Curtain: Choices for the Third World, Columbia University Press, New York, 1976, chapter 9.

(146) The total oil bill of the non-oil producing developing countries increased from $ 8 billion in 1973 to approximately $ 70 billion in 1970.

(147) See 'OPEC's Helping Hand for the Third World', Far Eastern Economic Review, August 1, 1980, pp. 25-88.

(148) According to the World Bank's World Development Report 1980, p. 141, OPEC's official development assistance was 2.71 per cent in 1975 and 1.28 per cent in 1979. OAPEC performance fell from 4.99 per cent to 2.43 per cent in the same period. Against this it should be noted that OPEC has decided to pay $ 83.4 million to meet the contribution of the 35 poorest countries to the Common Fund, an institution to which the Third World has attached a good deal of importance.

(149) Interviewed in De Volkskrant (Netherlands), May 8, 1980, p. 2.

(150) See, for example, Hans Singer and J. Ansari, Rich and Poor Countries, George Allen and Unwin, London, viz. p. 26.

(151) Bruce R.Scott, 'OPEC, The American Scapegoat', Harvard Business Review, January-February 1981, pp. 6-30, at p. 28.

(152) Nicola Chiaromonte,The Paradox of History, London, 1966, p. 133.

(153) This is the starting point for Ali A.Mazrui's A World Federation of Cultures, The Free Press, New York, 1976. Denis Goulet is also among those who has argued passionately and persuasively about the need for a new ethic of development See his The Cruel Choice, Atheneum, New York, 1973.

(154) See Richard Barnet, The Roots of War, Atheneum, New York, 1972, viz. p. 237 ff.

(155) This duty has been clearly stated by Jean Ziegler in Une Suisse au-dessus de tout soupçon, Ed. du Seuil, Paris, 1976, viz. p.180.

(156) On this, see Michael Harrington, The Vast Majority: A

Journey to the World's Poor, Simon and Schuster, New York, 1977, pp. 127-128.

(157) For a discussion of the strategy of self-reliance, see Marc Nerfin, (ed.),'What Now. Another Development. The 1975 Dag Hammarskjöld Report on Development and International Co-operation', *Development Dialogue,* nos. 1 and 2, 1975; E. Oteiza and F. Sercovich, 'Collective Self-Reliance: Selected Issues', *International Social Science Journal,* no. 4, 1976, pp. 664-671; Samir Amin, 'Self-Reliance and the New International Economic Order', *Monthly Review,* vol. 29, no. 3, July-August 1977, pp. 1-21; W.K. Chagula, B.T. Feld and A. Parthasarathi, (eds.), *Pugwash on Self-Reliance,* Ankur Publishing House, New Delhi, 1977; Khadija Haq, (ed.), *Dialogue for a New Order,* Pergamon, New York, 1980, part IV; and the papers contained in Johan Galtung, Peter O'Brien and Roy Preiswerk, (eds,), *Self-Reliance: A Strategy for Development,* Bogle-L'Ouverture Publications, London, 1980.

(158) On self-reliance as a power strategy, see Johan Galtung, 'Power and Global Planning and Resource Management', in A.J. Dolman, (ed.), *Global Planning and Resource Management: Toward International Decision-Making in a Divided World,* Pergamon, New York, 1980, pp. 119-145. See also Carlos F. Díaz-Alejandro, 'Delinking North and South: Unshackled or Unhinged' in Albert Fishlow et al., *Rich and Poor Nations in the World Economy,* McGraw-Hill, New York, 1978, pp. 87-162.

(159) Denis Goulet, *World Interdependence: Verbal Smokescreen or New Ethic,* Development Paper 21, Overseas Development Council, Washington, D.C., March 1976, p. 22.

(160) For a powerful statement on the dangers of subordinating ideals of solidarity to the competition for power and resources, see Colin M.Turnbull, *The Mountain People,* Simon and Schuster, New York, 1972.

(161) On this see Philippe de Seynes, 'Prospects for a Future Whole World', *International Organization,* vol. 26, Winter 1972, pp. 1-17.

(162) For example, the outcome of North-South negotiations on commodity agreements has not been determined by the technical merits of the proposals which have been put forward. Proposals which can be shown to be technically superior do not necessarily have a greater chance of acceptance. Technical arguments are in fact often raised to obscure the main concerns of the negotiating parties. See Arjun Sengupta, 'Issues in North-South Negotiations on Commodities', *ODI Review,* no. 2 1979, pp. 72-86.

(163) On the idea of 'new coalitions', see Jan Tinbergen (coordinator), *Reshaping the International Order: A Report to The Club of Rome,* E.P. Dutton, New York, 1976, viz. pp. 106-107. For examples of possible Third World coalitions, see the section 'Third World Institutions' in chapter 4.

(164) Writing in *The Guardian,* May 13, 1980.

(165) See Paul M.Sweezy, 'The Crisis of American Capitalism',
      Monthly Review, vol. 32, no. 5, October 1980, pp. 1-13.
(166) The group of 'like-minded' countries has so far met on
      nine occasions, the first meeting being held in Stockholm
      in November 1975. Nine countries have attended the last six
      meetings: Austria, Belgium, Canada, Denmark, Finland, Ire-
      land, Netherlands, Norway and Sweden. Australia and New Zea-
      land have recently expressed a desire to participate in
      'like-minded' consultations on a more regular basis. For a
      description of the origins and evolution of the 'like-minded'
      forum, see Antony J.Dolman, 'The Like-Minded Countries and
      the New International Order: Past, Present and Future Pros-
      pects', *Cooperation and Conflict: Nordic Journal of Inter-
      national Politics,* vol. XIX, 1979, pp. 57-85. For a discus-
      ion of the possible roles they could play in North-South
      negotiations, see Antony J.Dolman, *The Like-Minded Countries
      and the North-South Conflict,* Foundation Reshaping the In-
      ternational Order (RIO), Rotterdam, February 1981.
(167) President Giscard d'Estaing presented his ideas on a lim-
      ited North-South dialogue at a press conference held at the
      Elysée Palace on 15 February 1979. Stressing the fundamental
      changes taking place in the world, he suggested that"it would
      be useful to reach an agreement whereby the solidarity be-
      tween Europe, Africa and the Arab States can be strengthened"
      An agreement could be reached, he suggested, which would re-
      flect bounds of solidarity and contribute to their mutual
      development. Giscard attempted to sell his ideas on a Euro-
      Africa-Arab summit at the EEC top held in Paris in 1979, but
      with little success.
(168) For a historical review of natural resource conflicts, see
      SIPRI, *Warfare in a Fragile World: Military Impact on the
      Human Environment,* Taylor and Francis, London, 1980, chapter
      8.
(169) This is argued in Richard J.Barnet, *The Lean Years: Po-
      litics in the Age of Scarcity,* Simon and Schuster, New York,
      1980.
(170) The thesis of S.R. Eyre's *The Real Wealth of Nations,* Ed-
      ward Arnold, London, 1978.
(171) See Denis Goulet, op.cit., pp. 19-20.
(172) In some respects the concept of the common heritage of man-
      kind approximates the notion of 'collective good' or 'public
      good' used by economists. Essential to the economists under-
      standing is that the benefits derived by a user of a collec-
      tive good do not result in a reduction of the benefits of
      another user and that their use and enjoyment cannot be di-
      vided up for individual benefits, i.e. 'collective goods'
      are indivisible. See John G.Ruggie, 'Collective Goods and
      Future International Collaboration', *American Political
      Science Review,* vol. 66, September 1972, pp. 874-893.
(173) For a discussion of some of the issues surrounding the

design of regimes for the 'global commons', see Seyom Brown
et.al., *Regimes for the Ocean, Outer Space and Weather,* The
Brookings Institution, Washington, D.C. 1977.

(174) See Richard N.Cooper 'A NIEO for Mutual Gain', *Foreign
Policy,* no. 26, Spring 1977, pp. 66-12.

(175) See C. Fred Bergsten, 'Interdependence and the Reform of
International Institutions', *International Organization,*
vol. 30, no. 2, Spring 1976, pp. 361-372, at pp. 366-367.

(176) Mahbub ul Haq, *The Poverty Curtain,* Columbia University
Press, New York, 1976, p. 173.

(177) This is argued in Ali A.Mazrui, *The Barrel of the Gun and
the Barrel of Oil in the North-South Equation,* Working Paper 5, World Order Models Project, Institute for World Order,
Inc., New York 1978.

(178) See U.N. document A/34/PV/11.

(179) From Lord Tennyson's poem 'Love Thou Thy Land'.

(180) On the relationship between national policy and global
reform, see Robert L.Paarlberg, 'Domesticating Global Management', *Foreign Affairs,* vol. 54, 1975-76, pp. 563-576. See
also Maurice F.Strong, 'Spaceship Earth: A Global Overview',
Paper presented at the 47th Annual Conference on 'Growth in
a Conserving Society', Geneva Park, Ontario, August 3, 1978
(mimeo).

(181) Karl W.Deutsch, 'Some Prospects for the Future', *Journal
of International Affairs,* vol. 31, no.2, Fall/Winter 1977,
pp. 315-326, at. p. 324.

(182) For a review of the global stimulation proposals made in
recent years, see R.E. Muller and D.H. Moore, 'A Description
and Preliminary Evaluation of Proposals for Global Stimulation', UNIDO, Vienna, March 1979 (mimeo); and Jan van Ettinger, 'A UN Industrial and Technological Development Fund',
Foundation Reshaping the International Order (RIO), Rotterdam (in preparation).

(183) Claude Cheysson, interviewed in *Le Nouvel Observateur,* no.
664, August 1-7, 1977. The EEC's thinking has recently been
presented in Michael Noelke, *Europe and the Third World: A
Study on Interdependence,* European Communities, Brussels,
1979.

(184) The Marshall Plan analogy is faulty for different reasons.
Firstly, the Marshall Plan was essentially a pump-priming
operation. All the human capital was already existing in
Western Europe; once the pump was primed, the machinery would
again operate. The situation is manifestly different in the
Third World. Moreover, the logic of the proposals assumes
that the developing countries see their own future in terms
of importers of Western goods, willing work horses for pulling
the rich countries out of recession, saviors of the system
which is the cause of a good deal of their grief. There are
obviously those who would refuse to accept such a role.
Secondly, the proposals probably would not help the developed

countries very much either. They provide no answer to 'supply side' problems - rigidities, inefficiences, weak competition, internal and external protection of various kinds -
all of which lead to reductions in productivity. As John
Lewis, Chairman of the OECD's Development Assistance Committee, has rightly observed: "The argument is not merely opa-
que to these supply side issues. It is positively hostile
to needed structural adjustments. It amounts to crypto-pro-
tectism". See John P.Lewis, 'A Possible Scenario for the
Development Strategy', *OECD Observer,* no. 101, November 1979,
pp. 3-11, at p.5-6.

(185) See Tony Smith, 'Changing Configurations of Power in North-
South Relations Since 1945', *International Organization,*
vol. 31, no. 1, Winter 1977, pp. 1-27. Joseph S.Nye, op.cit.,
pp. 158-161, similarly observes that U.S. exports to the
developing countries amount to only 1 per cent of the country's GNP and repatriated profits on foreign investment to
only 0.5 per cent of GNP.

(186) On the Third World's capacity for disruptive action, see
Bruce M.Russett, 'The Rich Fifth and the Poor Half: Some
Speculations About International Politics in 2000 A.D.', in
Bruce M.Russett (ed.), *Power and Community in World Politics,*
Freeman, San Francisco, 1974, pp. 145-170; P. Alpert, *Part-
nership or Confrontation? Poor Lands and Rich,* Free Press,
New York, 1973; and Richard A.Falk, 'Beyond Internationalism',
Foreign Affairs, no. 23, 1976, pp. 65-113.

(187) For evidence to this effect, see A.J.H. Latham, *The International Economy and the Underdeveloped World* 1865-1914,
Croom Helm, London, 1978.

(188) See, for example, E.H. Carr, *The Twenty Years' Crisis:
1919-1939. An Introduction to the Study of International
Relations,* Macmillan, London, 1939. Similarly, the importance
of aid as an instrument of foreign policy and as a means for
reducing the possibility of international conflict was realized in the very beginning of aid programs. For an early
statement of the case, see the papers in Lincoln Gordon,
(ed.), *International Stability and Progress,* American Assembly, New York, 1957.

(189) The estimate of P.N. Rosenstein-Rodan in 'The Have's and
Have-Not's Around the Year 2000', in Jagdish N.Bhagwati (ed.)
Economics and World Order: From the 1970's to the 1990's,
Free Press, New York, 1972, pp. 29-42 at p. 29.

(190) The 1:60 ratio results from a crude comparison of the gross
GNP per capita of the world's poorest and richest nations.
The RIO Report concludes that the decile ratio between the
world's richest and poorest 10 per cent is in the order of
13 : 1, the figure adjusted to take account of differences
in purchasing power. Leontief arrives at a similar figure
although through a different route. See Jan Tinbergen (coordinator), *Reshaping the International Order: A Report to*

The Club of Rome, E.P. Dutton, New York, 1976, chapter 6;
and W. Leontief, *The Future of the World Economy,* Oxford
University Press, New York, 1977. For a discussion of the
widening gap between rich and poor nations, see S. Kuznets,
'The Gap: Concept, Measurement, Trends', in G. Ranis (ed.),
The Gap Between Rich and Poor Nations, Macmillan, London,
1972.

(191) For presentation of the argument that relationships of
dominance and dependence are fundamental 'conflict formations'
see Peter Worsley, *The Third World,* Weidenfeld and Nicolson,
London, 1964, chapter 6; Peter Wallensteen, *Structure and
War: On International Relations 1920-1968,* Räben and Sjögren
Stockholm 1973; Helge Hveem, 'The Global Dominance System',
Journal of Peace Research, vol. 10, 1973, pp. 319-340; Die-
ter Senghaas, 'Conflict Formations in Contemporary Interna-
tional Society', *Journal of Peace Research,* vol. 10, 1973,
pp. 163-184; and Robin S.Jenkins, *Exploitation: The World
Power Structure and the Inequality of Nations,* McGibbon and
Kee, London, 1970.

(192) Henry Kissinger, 'America and the World: Principle and
Pragmatism', *Time,* December 27, 1976, pp. 43-45, at p. 45.

(193) See Robert McNamara, *The Essence of Security: Reflections
in Office,* Hodder and Stoughton, London, 1968. He notes that
in the period 1958-1968, 87 per cent of the very poor nations,
69 per cent of the poor nations, and 48 per cent of the
middle income nations suffered serious violence.

(194) This prospect has led a number of distinguished persons to
strongly advocate that the West promote the very rapid development of the poor countries. Andrei D.Sakharov has argued,
for example, that the industrialized countries should transfer
20 per cent of their national income to the Third World over
a 15 year period, a view which was shared by Lord C.P. Snow.
See Sakharov's *Progress, Coexistence and Intellectual Freedom,* W.W. Norton, New York, 1968. The same argument has been
advanced more recently. Paul and Anne Ehrlich have argued
that the rich world should transfer 20 per cent of its GNP
to the poor world, and René Dumont has argued that the developed countries should give - no strings attached - 5 per
cent of their GNP. See Paul R.Ehrlich, *The Population Bomb,*
Pan, London, 1971, and René Dumont, *Utopia or Else...,*
Deutsch, London, 1974. For a rejection of the argument that
growing inequalities in wealth and income constitute a threat
to world peace, see Robert W.Tucker, *The Inequality of Nations,* Martin Robertson, Oxford, 1977.

(195) Robert L.Heilbroner, *An Inquiry into the Human Prospect,*
W.W. Norton, New York, 1974, viz. p. 43.

(196) Ibid, p. 44.

(197) Joseph S.Nye, op.cit., p. 142.

(198) For a recent example of this new genre of apocalyptic fiction, see Colin Mandeville, *The Last Days of New York?,*

Springwood Books, London, 1980.

(199) Consider the following statement by Libya's Colonel Kaddafi, interviewed in *Newsweek,* June 18, 1979: "Socially speaking, America is not even living in the Middle Ages, but in the pre-Middle Ages. But because you're a superpower nobody dares to expel you from the United Nations and put you on trial where you deserve to be. That's the real truth. If the practices America resorts to were done by a small country, it would be voted out of the U.N. and blacklisted and boycotted by the rest of the world. But because its done by a superpower, you're immune". (p. 24) Kaddafi is, of course, committed to getting his hands on a thermonuclear bomb.

(200) Franz Fanon, *The Wretched of the Earth,* Grove Press, New York, 1966, p. 61.

(201) This section is derived from Anthony J.Dolman, 'Environment, Development, Disarmament: Three Worlds in One', paper prepared for the United Nations Non-Governmental Liaison Service, Geneva, November 1980 (mimeo).

(202) The most important information sources are Lester R.Brown, *Population and Affluence: Growing Pressure on World Food Resources,* Population Reference Bureau, Washington, D.C., 1973; and *The Twenty Ninth Day: Accomodating Human Needs and Numbers to the Earth's Resources*, W.W.Norton, New York, 1978; Barbara Ward and René Dubos, *Only One Earth*, Penguin Books, Harmondsworth, 1972; G. Barraclough, 'The Great World Crisis I', *The New York Review of Books,* January 23, 1975; Alden D.Hinckley, *Renewable Resources in Our Future,* Pergamon Press, Oxford, 1980; and the IUCN's *World Conservation Strategy,* 1980.

(203) These are modest estimates based upon a narrow definition of 'food'. Most people do not regard potato peelings as food, for example, yet the average family's yearly output of peelings contains the equivalent of the protein in 60 steaks, the iron in 500 eggs, and the vitamin C in 95 glasses of orange juice.

(204) According to the Smithsonian Institute, close to 10 per cent of the 20,000 plant species native to the continental United States are either "endangered" or "threatened". Half of Hawaii's native flora is thought to be imperiled. Reported in Erik Eckholm, *Disappearing Species: The Social Challenge,* Worldwatch Paper 22, Worldwatch Institute, Washington, D.C., July 1978. The problem of disappearing species is treated at length in Norman Myers', *The Sinking Ark,* Pergamon Press, Oxford and New York, 1979. See also K. Curry-Lindhal, *Let them Live: A Worldwide Survey of Animals Threatened with Extinction,* Wm. Morrow, New York, 1972.

(205) Reported in Harrison Brown, *The Human Future Revisited: The World Predicament and Possible Solutions,* W.W. Norton, New York, 1978.

(206) See 'The Shape of Fear', *The Economist,* November 29, 1980.

(207) This is one of the themes in Ernst Michanek's *The World Development Plan: A Swedish Perspective*, Almqvist and Wiksell, Stockholm, 1971.

(208) For a discussion of the differences between 'wellbeing' and 'welfare' and the moral and philosophical principles which underlie them see Erich Fromm, *To Have or to Be*, Abacus Books, London, 1979.

(209) For a discussion of the population-resource-environment equation, see Gerald O.Barney (Study Director), *The Global 2000 Report to the President of the U.S. Entering the 21st Century* (Volume 1: Summary Report), Pergamon, New York, 1980; Joseph Spengler, *Population Change, Modernization and Welfare*, Prentice Hall, Englewood Cliffs, New Jersey, 1974; Paul and Anne Ehrlich, *Population, Resources, Environment*, Freeman, San Francisco, 1970; Paul R.Ehrlich and R.L. Harriman, *How to be a Survivor: A Plan for Spaceship Earth*, Ballantine Books, New York, 1971; Paul R.Ehrlich, *The End of Affluence*, Ballantine Books, New York, 1971; Wayne H. Davis, 'Overpopulated America', in Daniel Callahan (ed.), *The American Population Debate*, Anchor, New York, 1971, pp. 161-167; and Nathan Keyfitz, 'World Resources and the World Middle Class', *Scientific American*, 235, July 1976.

(210) Books which have drawn attention to the increasing costs of economic growth include Ezra J.Mishan, *The Costs of Economic Growth*, Penguin Books, Harmondsworth, 1967; and *The Economic Growth Debate: An Assessment*, George Allen and Unwin, London, 1968; Herman Daly, *Toward a Steady-State Economy*, Freeman, San Francisco, 1973; and Tibor Scitovsky, *The Joyless Economy*, Oxford University Press, London, 1976. These volumes stress that economic growth should be viewed as a means of policy rather than an end in itself and that it can impede the attainment of important social objectives.

(211) As the RIO Report, op.cit., p.71 observes: "To conceive the objectives of development in terms of Western living standards may only compound confusion. The poor countries should reject the aim of imitating Western patterns of life. Development is not a linear process, and the *aim of development is not to 'catch up'*, economically, socially, politically or culturally. Many aspects of Western life have become wasteful and senseless and do not contribute to peoples' real happiness. For the poor nations to attempt to imitate the rich may only mean that they trade one set of problems for another and in doing so discard or destroy much that is valuable in terms of their human resources and values". (Original emphasis).

(212) On the idea of minima and maxima in consumption patterns, see Rajni Kothari, *Footsteps into the Future*, Free Press, New York, 1974, pp. 70-71.

(213) As Gunnar Myrdal observed in his Nobel acceptance speech: "The blunt truth is that without rather radical changes in

the consumption patterns in the rich countries, any pious
talk about a new world economic order is humbug", see 'New
Economic Order? Humbug!', *Sweden Now,* no. 4, 1975.
(214) This argument is developed in Lester R.Brown, *Resource
Trends and Population Policy: A Time for Reassessment,* Worldwatch Paper 29, Worldwatch Institute, Washington, D.C., May
1979; and *The Global Economic Prospect: New Sources of Economic Stress,* Worldwatch Paper 20, Worldwatch Institute,
May 1978.

4 International Institutions and Global Reform

If men's inclination to self-
interest makes their vigilance
against one another necessary,
their public sense of justice
makes their secure association
together possible.

John Rawls, *A Theory of Justice*,
1971, p. 5.

INTERNATIONAL INSTITUTIONS AND WORLD ORDER

"Once upon a time there was a town linked to the outside world
by only one paved road. Every morning, around sunrise, a crew of
men in a huge orange truck arrived and scattered nails on that
one road leading into town. No one knew why they did this. It was
their job and it had always been that way.

Unsuspecting motorists invariably could be seen along the side
of the road repairing flat tires. The townspeople didn't like
these drivers making tire tracks in the shoulders of the road and
slowing traffic. They finally asked the city council to do something about the problem of the huge influx of motorists with flat
tires.

The city council responded quickly to the demands of the people
by passing legislation that called for the construction of a service station along the road so motorists with flats could receive
help changing tires. This proposal was greeted with joy by the
people and the station was quickly constructed. Within a few
months the station was in operation advertising its speciality.

Drivers pulled into the station by the dozens each day, thankful
that the service was so conveniently located. The manager of the
station became an honored citizen of the town. Young people who
wanted to "help people" would often put their idealism into practice by working at the station.

The manager was a forward-looking individual who introduced various reforms at the station, improving the method used to fix
the flats and building a bigger station to handle the ever-in-
creasing amount of traffic.

But the number of needy motorists increased faster than the station could expand. And so the people of the town willingly taxed
themselves more to build another station a little further down
the road. Certainly the two stations could handle all the flats.

The two stations more or less managed to keep up with the demand.
Dissidents in the town would occasionally demonstrate against
the stations; they demanded that the service stations do a better
job. A few other townspeople saw that the problem would be solved
if only those people would stop having flats, but such radicals
were easily dismissed.

Meanwhile at 5:00 a.m. every morning the huge orange truck lum-
bered over nearby dirt roads and made its way to the one paved
road. There its crew scattered the nails on the road for another
day. It had always been that way". (1)

International institutions regulate the relationships between nations and, like service stations, help maintain an order. Unlike
service stations, however, they are not always visible. For although they may be formal, like organizations, they may also be
abstract which, like the 'hidden hand' and legal precedent, are
no less powerful even though they lack a physical presence.

Whether formal or abstract, institutions can either serve to ca-
talyse change or, perhaps unintentionally, to deny it. When they
become a vested interest and thus resistant to and suspicious of
change, they easily become - like the service station - a part
of the problem they were created to solve. At the national level,
for example, there are mental hospitals which drive people in-
sane (a situation exploited by totalitarian regimes), prisons
which spread crime, schools which encourage stupidity, and Departments of Defense which provoke violence and war. Similarly,
at the international level we have monetary institutions which
prevent monetary reform, a system of law which legitimizes injustices, and a system of 'free trade' which generates dependence.

There can be no order without institutions although institutions
do not in themselves provide order. In this century there have
been two main waves of institution-building for world order. Both
had their origins in terribly destructive wars and were guided
by the fear, far from unjustified, that even worse could follow. (2)

These attempts at global reform resulted in the creation of two
general purpose international institutions - the League of Nations and the United Nations - operating on the basis of very
general constitutional documents drafted by the nations which
emerged victorious from the wars which caused their creation.
These global master plans ambidextrously sought to freeze the
pattern of privilege and power then prevailing whilst providing
the chrysalis for a future world government.

The last wave has been followed by several ripples of institution-building. (3) The first came around 1960 when the European
Community, the OECD, the CMEA and - though barely noticed at the
time - OPEC were either established or transformed. The second
ripple has flowed through the 1970s, a decade which has seen the
creation of special institutions to deal with emergent problems
on the basis of technical specialization, such as UNEP, WFC, IEA
and Habitat. This second ripple has yet to show signs of subsid-
ing.

These attempts at global reform, general purpose institutions
supported by functional agencies, were not conceived as alternatives to the system of nation States, but as derivatives of and
dependent upon it. As a result, they have failed to produce any
transformation of the international order. Their role has essentially been one of legitimizing the system and of ensuring that
it works as smoothly as its structural imperfections allow it to
do so.

There is now growing recognition that something more is urgently
needed: that the existing institutional framework for grappling
with problems which defy national solution increasingly imperils
human survival. (4) There is a widespread feeling that present
forms of international organization, derived from historical experience, no longer work and will be subjected to ever growing
stresses and strains. (5) There is every reason for believing
that the answer to the institutional predicament cannot reside
in the careful application of 'relevant' past experience for the
simple but important reason that there is little experience which
can be considered 'relevant'. The experience became irrelevant
once mankind crossed unique thresholds which brought it face-to-
face with unprecedented problems of existence and survival. Unprecedented problems call for unprecedented responses. (6)

For the first time in history we can today talk of a world system,
a system shaped by the forces of science-based technology. (cf.
chapter 7) The world system has given us world problems. World
problems call for world institutions. What has yet to emerge -
if indeed it ever does - is a world society which may wish to
conduct its affairs through world institutions. We can legitimately define problems in such a way that the only solution is
global action through global institutions. The problem is that
we live in a world which is fragmented and disparate; it is not

a world society. (7)

How then can we strengthen the institutional presence at the international level? How can we promote institutional innovation
in a system which discourages innovation? How can we break out
of a service station mentality? Such questions are the subject
of this chapter. In discussing them we will first look at the
present and possible future role of the United Nations which,
barring war or other catastrophe, remains, despite its numerous
limitations, the only international instrument available for
shaping a better world. We will then go on to discuss strategies
for global institutional reform and, finally, the development
of an appropriate legal framework.

THE ORIGINS AND EVOLUTION OF THE UNITED NATIONS

The United Nations was originally conceived as a 'stop-Hitler'
organization and has its origins in a series of conferences which
took place during the Second World War. (8) The term 'United Nations' was first used by Franklin D. Roosevelt to denote the nations allied in opposition to the so-called Axis powers - Germany, Italy, Japan - and achieved world-wide prominence when the
Declaration by United Nations was signed by 26 States on January
1, 1942 setting forth the war aims of the allied powers.

The Second World War was a war which was fought by conference and
the evolution of the United Nations, because of its origins, can
be traced through the results of the war time negotiations between especially Churchill, Roosevelt and Stalin. The first important step in the direction of a United Nations organization
was the Inter-Allied Declaration signed by representatives of
14 governments in London in June 1941. The Declaration gave expression to its signatories intention "to work together, and with
other free peoples, both in war and peace".

Two months later Roosevelt and Churchill met at sea off the coast
of Newfoundland. At the conclusion of their discussions on August
14 they issued a joint declaration, to become known as the Atlantic Charter, in which they set forth "certain common principles
in the national policies of their respective countries" on which
they based their "hopes for a better future of the world". The
Charter refers to the need for all nations, "for realistic as
well as spiritual reasons", to abandon the use of force and calls
for "the establishment of a wider and permanent system of general
security". The Charter goes on to call for "fullest collaboration
between all nations in the economic field" to secure higher standards of living for the world. It served as a basis for the Declaration by United Nations of 1942.

The next important step was the meeting between the foreign ministers of the Soviet Union, United Kingdom and United States - Vyacheslav Molotov, Anthony Eden and Cordell Hull - and Foo Ping-sheung, Chinese Ambassador to the Soviet Union, in Moscow on October 18-30, 1943. The meeting endorsed a declaration, drafted earlier by Hull and already accepted by the Chinese, for "a general international organization, based on the principle of the sovereign equality of all peace-loving states, and open to membership by all such states, large and small, for the maintenance of international peace and security" and to provide for post-war collaboration between the allies. (9)

In the late summer of 1943 a number of important meetings of allied leaders took place. Churchill and Roosevelt met Chiang Kai-shek at Cairo November 23-27 and then travelled to Teheran for a separate conference with Stalin. They then returned to Cairo for five more days (December 2-7) of Anglo-U.S. consultations. During these various exchanges, devoted to the formulation of military strategy, time was found to discuss the question of establishing an international peace and security organization and of discharging, as the Teheran communiqué stated, "the supreme responsibility resting upon us and the United Nations to make a peace which will command the goodwill of the overwhelming masses of the peoples of the world and banish the scourge and terror of war for many generations". As a result of these conferences it was decided to convene a meeting during which a blueprint for such an organization could be drawn up. This meeting took place at Dumbarton Oaks, an estate in Washington D.C., between August 21 and October 7, 1944.

The Dumbarton Oaks talks, involving representatives of the 'Big Four', were officially designated 'conversations' to indicate that they were held below the foreign ministers' level and would constitute recommendations only, not binding decisions. The meeting laboriously (10) drafted a document entitled *Proposals for the Establishment of a General International Organization.* (11) The proposals were primarily concerned with the purpose and principles of the organization, its membership and principal organs, and arrangements for the maintenance of international peace and security and for international economic and social cooperation. According to the proposals, the key body in the United Nations for preserving world peace was to be the Security Council, on which the 'great powers' - China, France, U.K., U.S., and U.S.S.R - were to be permanently represented.

Although the Dumbarton Oak talks resulted in a remarkable degree of agreement between the 'Big Four', they failed to resolve differences on two essential points: the U.K. and U.S. could not agree with the Soviet Union on the voting procedures to be adopted in the Security Council nor could they agree to the Soviet demand that all its 16 constituent republics have seats in the General Assembly. Churchill, Roosevelt and Stalin were able, however, to resolve these differences at the Yalta conference, held

February 4-11, through a series of compromises. At the end of
the Yalta talks, the allied leaders were able to issue a report
which declared: "We are resolved upon the earliest possible establishment with our Allies of a general international organization to maintain peace and security ....We have agreed that a
Conference of United Nations should be called to meet at San
Francisco in the United States on 25th April 1945, to prepare
the charter of such an organization, along the lines proposed
in the informal conversations of Dumbarton Oaks". The invita-
tions to the Conference - extended by China, U.K., U.S. and
U.S.S.R. - were issued on March 5 to those nations which had
declared war on Germany or Japan by March 1, 1945 and had
signed the Declaration by United Nations of 1942.

Before the start of the San Francisco Conference, the Dumbarton
Oaks proposals were studied and discussed by the nations of the
world, both collectively and individually. From February 21 to
March 8, 1945, for instance, the representatives of twenty Latin
American nations met in Mexico City and adopted a resolution containing suggested modifications to the charter of the proposed
international organization. From April 4-13, 1945, talks were
held in London between representatives of the British Commonwealth, and a statement issued at the close of the meetings indicated agreement that the Dumbarton Oaks proposals provided,
with slight modification, the basis for a charter.

On April 25 delegates of 46 states assembled in San Francisco
for the conference known officially as the United Nations Conference on International Organization (UNCIO). Four other states,
including two Soviet republics as agreed by Churchill, Roosevelt,
and Stalin at Yalta, were admitted during the conference. The
Dumbarton Oaks proposals and the Yalta agreement on voting procedures - the unanimity rule, traditionally applied in diplomatic conferences, was abandoned in favor of a two-thirds majority
vote - together with 96 amendments, 24 proposed by the 'sponsoring powers' and 72 submitted by 40 other nations, were brought
together in a report of over 400 pages for consideration by the
assembled delegates. From this material and following two months
of negotiations in plenary sessions, committees, and behind
closed doors (12) the conference drew up the 111-article Charter
of the United Nations organization. Signed at the conclusion of
the conference on June 26, the Charter entered into force on
October 24, 1945 by which time the five 'great powers' and the
majority of other signatories had deposited their ratifications.
(13)

The San Francisco conference captured the imagination of the West
and a great deal of attention was devoted to it. It was, in the
words of one U.S. magazine, "the most important human gathering
since the Last Supper". (14)

The Charter closely follows the general lines of the Dumbarton

Oaks proposals. Its first article outlines the fourfold purpose
of the United Nations: "1. To maintain international peace and
security..... 2. To develop friendly relations among nations
based upon respect for the principle of equal rights and self-
determination of peoples..... 3. To achieve international cooperation in solving international problems of an economic, social,
cultural, or humanitarian character..... and 4. To be a center
for harmonizing the actions of nations in the attainment of these
common ends". (15)

The creation of the United Nations was thus the result of a long
process. It was also the product of the minds of a number of persons who championed the organization in the dark days of war and
whose names have become intimately linked to it. If the organization had a single master architect, then it was probably Cordell
Hull who, from 1933-1944, served under Franklin D. Roosevelt as
Secretary of State. During the Presidency of Woodrow Wilson,
Hull was noted for his views on peace and security issues. A
firm believer in the advantages of free trade, he argued that
the dismantling of trade barriers served the purpose of peace and
he believed that the U.S.'s rejection of the League of Nations
was one of the factors which helped plunge the world into the
Second World War. Under Roosevelt he was noted for his strong moral positions against nations whose actions seemed to threaten
peace in the 1930s. Throughout the Second World War, up to his
resignation after the 1944 presidential election, he used his office to advance the cause of an international peace and security
organization. He made no secret of the fact that he believed that
such an organization together with a new economic order would be
good for the U.S. "Leadership toward a new system of international relations in trade and other economic affairs will devolve
largely on the United States because of our great economic
strength", he argued. "We should assume this leadership and the
responsibility that goes with it, primarily for reasons of pure
national self-interest". (16)

Called by Roosevelt the "father of the United Nations", Cordell
Hull was awarded the 1945 Nobel Peace Prize for the role he played in its creation. (17)

The United Nations Charter and the Third World

The San Francisco Conference was thus a peace and security conference stage-managed by a handful of Western nations. In seeking
to establish an institution which would "save succeeding generations from the scourge of war", they no less sought to devise a
system which, in the words of Daniel P. Moynihan, "amounted to
arrangements by which a handful of nations very much in the ascendant in world affairs attempted to arrange those affairs so
that thier ascendancy should be enabled to persist". (18) Peace

was seen to be dependent upon continuation of the power realities
which prevailed in 1945 and the 'big five' of the victorious coalition thus awarded themselves a privileged position in the organization's governing structure. The primacy of politics is
clearly visible in practically all the articles of the Charter.

The San Francisco Conference was neither about development nor
world poverty. Nor could it have been. For one thing, the minds
of millions were seething with the horrors of a war which had
spread over four continents and claimed the lives of some 30
million men, women and children. It had been a savage and traumatic experience which inevitably determined perceptions of the
world and its problems. For another thing, at the time of the
founding of the United Nations, the Third World, as we understand it today, simply did not exist. Most of the world's people
lived under foreign suzerainty: the political liberation movement that was to sweep across the world in the following decades
was only gathering momentum.

As a consequence, the San Francisco Conference gave little articulation to the requirements of the poor world; its needs and
aspirations did not figure prominently - if indeed at all - in
the grand institutional design then drawn up.

The Charter does not condemn colonialism. It calls for sound colonial administration. Some of the colonial powers at San Francisco actually sought to equate colonialism with freedom. The
U.K. delegate, Lord Cranborne, told the Conference, for example,
that "The colonial empires have been welded into one vast machine
in defense of liberty. Could we really contemplate", he asked,
"the destruction of this machine and its separation into component parts". (19) History was to provide a very clear answer to
this question.

In the Charter little more than lip-service is paid to the rights
and welfare of colonial peoples. The administering authorities
simply accept a "sacred trust....to promote...the well-being of
the inhabitants". (Article 73) The Charter says nothing about
the supervision of dependent territories. It does not seek to
coerce colonial powers into relinquishing control over possessions and there is no mention of independence, even as a desired
future goal. There is a vague allusion to the promotion of self-
government but there are escape clauses to restrict progress in
this direction. No reference is made to the immorality of colonialism. In short, the language of the Charter was carefully calculated to assure as little interference as possible in the administration of colonial territories.

Despite all this, the Charter is an improvement on the Covenant
of the League of Nations. The Covenant not only sought to maintain the colonial system; it refused to recognize the principle
of racial equality. It was synonymous with the notion of white

supremacy.

There was a lively debate at San Francisco between the delegates from developing countries - 20 Latin American republics, 9 Asian and 3 African nations (20) - and those from the industrialized countries on the relationship between peace, the main principle and aim of the organization, and justice. (21) This debate in some respects foreshadows the 1970s debate on the New International Economic Order.

"Peace has different meanings for different nations", the Mexican delegate observed. "It does not mean the same thing to the oppressed as it does to the prosperous". He went on to speak of "the horrors of peace without hope, in which men would be subjected to humiliating privations and injustices. Blood, sweat and tears", he continued, "comprised the glorious but provisional rule of war. It must not become the rule of peace". (22) These sentiments were echoed by the Lebanese delegate. It was clear, he observed, "that certain outwardly peaceful and secure situations do not spring from genuine justice and therefore are not worth maintaining. Unless, then, the positive content of peace is determined in a foundation of real justice, there will be no real peace". (23) The developing countries were able to insist that 'justice' as well as peace serve as guiding principles in the settlement of disputes. They were also able to engineer modifications to the Dumbarton Oaks proposals in the provisions concerning human rights and social and economic progress.

In short, the Charter of the United Nations, whilst being less offensive to the developing countries than the Covenant of the League of Nations, had little to offer them. Their needs went unheard, their aspirations unrecognized. The Charter was not a mandate for world development. That it has become that is one of the most significant developments of the post-war period.

The Bretton Woods Negotiations

The late war years and early post-war period saw the creation of U.N. specialized agencies in the fields of economics (World Bank, and IMF), trade (GATT), agriculture (FAO), labor (ILO), health (WHO), education and science (UNESCO), civil aviation (ICAO), weather (WMO), telecommunications (ITU) and postal services (UPU). Some of these organizations, specially provided for in the U.N. Charter, were nourished by the ideas and agencies of the League of Nations and, like the ILO, ITU and WMO, have antecedents which predate the San Francisco Conference. (24)

These organizations institutionalized a world order. None were more important than those established to regulate international economic and trade relations. The centerpiece of the economic institutions were the IMF and the World Bank, established as a re-

sult of a series of conferences which began in September 1943 and
culminated in the United Nations Monetary and Financial Conference
held at Bretton Woods, New Hampshire in July 1944. The World
Bank, established to promote the economic development of its member countries by making loans available for commercially viable
projects, came into existence in December 1945 when 29 of the 44
nations which attended the conference signed its articles of
agreement. It commenced operations in June 1946. The articles of
IMF, established to promote international cooperation in monetary
matters, and to provide monetary stability through orderly exchange arrangements, similarly came into force in December 1945.
Ratification and appropriation of funds enabled the IMF to be
formally constituted in March 1946, the inaugural meeting of its
Board of Governors being held in that month together with that of
the World Bank, in Savannah, Georgia.

The Bretton Woods institutions were created to deal with the problem of post-war reconstruction and to establish a basis for sustained economic growth. The main functions of the order initiated
at Bretton Woods were to 'normalize' international economic relations, to rejuvenate Western European and Japanese capitalism, to
restructure the international monetary system, and to provide for
the expansion of international trade and investment. The U.S. dollar was enshrined as the chief means of international exchange.
The whole exercise was a commercial undertaking of major dimensions. In the words of Henry Morganthau, a former U.S. Treasury
Secretary, the Bretton Woods system provided for "a world in which
international trade and investment (could) be carried on by businessmen on business principles". (25)

The Bretton Woods system enabled the U.S. - as Roosevelt and Hull
had hoped - to secure its leadership in the post-war world. It
virtually legitimized U.S.-European world economic hegemony.

If the U.N. Charter had one main architect, the Bretton Woods
system had two: Harry Dexter White,the U.S. Assistant Secretary
of the Treasury, and Britain's John Maynard Keynes, then widely
regarded as the world's leading economic theorist. White and
Keynes argued their way to an agreement (26) and they more than
anyone else shaped the rules which governed the operation of the
international economy in the post-war years. Viewed from the
perspective of the U.S. and Western Europe, their work was a deli-
cate masterpiece that survived a quarter of a century.

The developing countries had little voice in determining the rules
of the international game and the Soviet Union soon felt obliged
to withdraw from the Bretton Woods negotiations. The U.S.S.R.
clearly planned to use the negotiations to obtain as much aid as
it could from the U.S. Stalin evidently believed that capitalist
economies would experience severe difficulties in a period of
peace and that it was, therefore, in the interests of the capitalist nations to shower the Soviet Union with all the assistance

it needed. The U.S. did not agree. It believed that the enormous
task of Soviet reconstruction would be impossible without its
help and support. U.S. negotiators, like Hull and White, thus
sought to link the question of aid to the opening of the Soviet
economy to U.S. business. Economic issues soon became inextricably mixed with political concerns and the Soviet Union withdrew
from the negotiations. (27)

The Trade Negotiations

Following the conclusion of the Bretton Woods agreement, the
United Nations turned its attention to the problem of trade. In
1946 it took decisions aimed at establishing an international
presence in this field. In that year ECOSOC decided to convene
an international conference on trade and employment, and it established a Preparatory Committee to prepare a draft convention for
an international trade organization. A draft charter, adopted by
the Committee in August 1947, formed the basis for the work of
the U.N. Conference on Trade and Employment, which was held in
Havana from November 1947 to March 1948. The Conference drew up
a charter, known as the Havana Charter, for an International
Trade Organization (ITO) which, as a specialized agency, was to
provide support to national policies for economic development
and full employment and to contribute to the gradual liberaliza-
tion of world trade.

While the Charter for the ITO was being worked out, the governments that formed the Preparatory Committee agreed to sponsor
negotiations aimed at lowering customs tariffs and reducing other
trade restrictions among themselves, without waiting for the ITO
to come into being. The first tariff negotiating conference was
held at Geneva in 1947, running simultaneously with the efforts
being made by the Committee to draw up the Havana Charter. The
tariff concessions resulting from these negotiations were embodied in a multilateral treaty called the General Agreement on
Tariffs and Trade (GATT). The Agreement, accepted by 23 countries,
was signed in Geneva on October 30, 1947 and became effective as
of January 1, 1948.

GATT was intended as an interim measure pending the formation of
the ITO which was meant to supersede it. The ITO, however, failed
to get off the ground. Of the 56 countries which participated in
the Trade and Employment Conference in Havana, 53 signed the
Charter, the U.S. being prominent in its refusal to do so. Only
one country subsequently ratified the Charter and plans for the
ITO - certainly one of the U.N.'s most ambitious proposals and
one of particular importance to the developing world - were abandoned in 1950. As a result of the failure to establish the ITO,
the decision was taken to amplify and enlarge GATT through a series of conferences - a process which continues today. Despite

the importance attached by the developing countries to trade
questions, it was not until 1964 that a special U.N. agency -
UNCTAD - was established to complement the work of GATT which,
from its beginnings, has focused on reconciling the trading problems of the industrialized nations.

ASSESSING THE RECORD

As a peace and security organization, the United Nations was to
function as a policeman. It was to be furnished with, in the
words of Roosevelt, the power "to act quickly and decisively to
keep the peace by force, if necessary". (28) As things turned
out, it proved to be a very ineffective policeman indeed.

The statistics of failure speak for themselves. Since the founding of the U.N. there has not been a single day in which the
world has been free of war. In the three decades up to 1976,
some 12 wars were taking place on an average day. In total, 133
wars were fought, involving the armies of more than 80 nations
and the territories of more than 70 states. (29) As many people
have been killed in wars in the post-war period as were killed
in the Second World War.

Established as a peace and security organization, its record in
this field must be judged its most spectacular failure. That our
world has been kept free from a Third World War can be attributed to the balance of terror and the fear of nuclear holocaust
rather than to the effectiveness of the United Nations.

Part of the answer for this failure can be found in the structural limitations of the organization. The 'big five' of the victorious coalition gave themselves, as we have seen, a privileged
position in the U.N.'s governing structure as permanent members
of the Security Council. The argument of the Charter's architects
was that the unanimity principle of the 'five' would limit their
freedom of action and thus help guarantee the peace. The practical consequence of this has been, however, that the U.N. has been
unable to take effective action when one or other of the great
powers has been involved in a conflict, which, given the growth
of superpower rivalries in the Third World, has been the rule
rather than the exception.

Even without this structural limitation, however, the U.N. could
never have succeeded as a peace and security organization for
the simple reason that its members have not sought to use it
as such. As noted earlier, the post-war period has been one in
which dominant powers saw their influence decline and the number
of nations multiplied. Old rivalries have been supplemented and
compounded by new conflicts between the strong and the weak, the
old and the new, and the rich and the poor. Problems which never

existed at the time of the founding of the U.N. now form part
of the consciousness of hundreds of millions of people and determine the motivation and action of States.

Today's world system is thus infinitely more complex than the
system which the drafters of the U.N. Charter set out to manip-
ulate. It is not characterized by carefully ordered power relations. It is rather an anarchic system and such a system is, by
definition, one in which imposed order is non-existent. The
world had undergone tumultuous changes in the post-war period
and the United Nations has mirrored them. In doing so, it has
become more a center of conflict than of common enterprise. It
has witnessed the demise of an order and been powerless to deal
effectively with the antagonisms, tensions and suspicions which
must come in its wake. In a very real sense, the U.N. has become,
not an instrument of peace, but a barometer of war and hostility.

Yeselson and Gaglione have shown how, in seeking to further their
own self-interest, nations have been able to use the U.N. as a
weapon in international relations, an arena of combat, a "part of
the armory of nations in conflict". (30) Disputes are brought to
the organization, not to have them subjected to dispassionate
analysis, but to weaken or embarrass an opponent, to strengthen
one's own side and to legitimize a cause, to prepare for war, to
denounce it, or to support it. (31) The adversary politics of
the U.N. may force nations, perhaps against their will, to
choose sides, thereby pushing them into blocks and progressively
eroding the possibilities for neutrality and impartiality. In
other words, the U.N. has become a battleground and this, like
other hostile acts, can contribute to the intensification rather
than defusing of disputes. And when it does, it diminishes the
prospects for peaceful solutions.

As the world has become more complex, so has the U.N. system. The
emergence of new problems has brought new organizations to deal
with them; new concerns require new fora in which they can be
voiced. Some U.N. organizations, notably those with their origins
in the Charter and Bretton Woods, still bear the indelible imprint of the power realities prevailing in 1945. Others, like
those created in the 1970s, are based on different power configurations and reflect different geo-political realities. Some organizations seek to defend and legitimize a world as it was; the
prime concern of others is the world as it is or should become.
Some organizations are impervious to demands for justice; others
function as 'justice constituencies' where claims of equity and
distributive justice can be asserted and internationalized. (32)

The United Nations has become an organizational supermarket. It
has something for everyone. It has its 'luxury' institutions, the
prerogative of the rich, and it has its bargain basement where
even the poorest can find an institution which fits them. This
plethora of organizations - organizations with overlapping man-

dates and jurisdictions - makes it possible for nations to shop
around in search of the organization where they pull the most
strings and which give greatest articulation to their needs and
preferred outcomes. (33) Motivated by self-interest, they know
that the same issue may come out quite differently in different
fora. Trade, for example, comes out differently in UNCTAD, which
is a 'justice constituency', than in GATT, which is not.

Nowhere has this shopping around phenomenon been more in evidence
than in the debate between the rich and poor countries on a new
round of negotiations on the New International Economic Order.
The world's nations were able to agree that there should be a
new round. They were even able to agree on some of the problems
which should be discussed. But they could not agree *where* they
should be discussed and *who* should have the final say on the proposals which would emerge. The rich countries sought to concen-
trate the negotiations and the responsibility for their outcome
in the specialized agencies, notably the IMF, World Bank and
GATT, which are Western dominated. The poor nations wanted a committee composed of all member-states to be the sovereign authority,
a procedure which would have given them decisive influence.

The use of the U.N. to further self-interest means that nations
are bound to try to drag a defendent before the judge who is
most sympathetic to their cause even though the favorable verdict
cannot be enforced. In such a situation, the U.N. will be unable
to exercise authority - and it may not necessarily be the intention that it should.

Crisis of Confidence

This situation is not one which engenders confidence in the United Nations. Confidence and the mutual trust which it implies are
the cement which holds an organization together. When trust is
high, an organization can withstand all manner of stresses and
strains; when it is low, it is extremely vulnerable for even a
seemingly innocuous incident can lead to irreparable damage to
its capacity to perform.

The cement which binds the U.N. together is slowly disintegrating
under the pressure of growing tensions and mistrust. Confidence
in the U.N. is probably at its lowest point in the history of the
organization. The dubiety and incertitude of both the rich and
poor countries are greater than ever before.

The mistrust of the Third World goes back, as we have seen, to
the very beginnings of the organization and to the knowledge that
the founding fathers were insensitive to its needs. The institutions required by the poor countries have, like the ITO, been denied them. Their attempts to democratize the organization have
failed to break the West's stranglehold; control which extends

through both political and economic institutions and organs. (34)

Western control of the U.N. takes many forms. Sometimes it is
direct and obvious, like veto rights in the Security Council. It
may take the form of threats to withdraw support from organizations and programs, threats which can become reality as they did
when the U.S. pulled out of ILO. More subtle are the hidden veto
rights which U.N. staffing gives the industrialized countries.
The U.S., U.K. and France command a disproportionate number of
posts in the U.N. Secretariat. In the mid 1970s more than one
half (54 per cent) of the professional staff came form Western
nations - 20 per cent from the U.S. alone - the Third World accounting for only one third of the posts. (35) The U.K. and
France each controlled as many positions as any of the major
Third World regions. The picture was even more skewed at the
level of directors, 57 per cent coming form the West and 31 per
cent from the Third World. In the important finance and personnel services, the U.S. had as many posts (25 per cent) as the
Third World (26 per cent). (36) Whereas it is nice to believe
that international secretariats are 'above politics', the servants of the interests of mankind as a whole, the truth is that
they are, in the words of someone who has a long experience of
the U.N., "constantly pushed and pulled by various pressures
coming from governments or others". (37) When an international
organization like the U.N. is a derivative of the nation-State
system, it is inevitable that the senior officials of the
organization will be agents of the states.

Western control of the U.N. is thus exercised through *de jure*
and *de facto* veto rights. The influence which this gives it
once led an Under-Secretary-General to remark that "the U.N. is
not an international body but rather a dependency of the U.S.".
(38)

The poor nations can take little comfort from past efforts to reform the U.N. These have sought to improve efficiency and have
left power positions untouched. The first major reform exercise
- the Jackson Report (39) - whilst extremely insightful in many
respects, focused on questions of control and coordination on an
administrative level. The most recent study - the Report of the
Group of 25 - similarly focuses on improvements in economic efficiency, not on ways in which the organization can be democra-
tized. (40)

For their part, the rich Western nations have steadfastly refused to relinquish control of the organization. They know that
without their financial support the U.N. would collapse. Since
they carry the financial burden of the organization, they refuse
to allow its policies to be dictated by nations so small that
five per cent of the world's population are represented by more
than two-thirds of the votes in the General Assembly.

The West has accused the Third World of irresponsibility in the way in which it has sought to use the U.N. to score Pyrrhic victories and of debasing the organization to the point where its credibility, already perilously low, threatens to become non-existent. The poor nations have been judged guilty of ideological confrontation, unnecessary 'politicization', the manipulation of the U.N. Charter and of exercising the now famous 'tyranny of the majority'.

Chastisements were much in evidence at the Sixth Special Session of the General Assembly held in 1974. The U.S. ambassador, John Scali, warned that the U.N. was fading into "the shadow world of rhetoric, abandoning its important role in the real world of negotiation....Support is eroding in our Congress and among our people. Some of the foremost American champions of this organization", he admonished, "are deeply distressed at the trend of recent events". (41) Ten Western ambassadors spoke in similar vein. "We cannot overlook", said Louis de Guiringaud, the French Minister for Foreign Affairs, "the drawbacks of adopting so many short-lived resolutions - each longer than the last, one a repetition of the other - virtually unreadable and sometimes not read, even by their sponsors. No newspaper in the world reproduces them. The United Nations", he continued, "runs the risk of living in a closed world". (42)

The view that the developing countries "can pass resolutions.... in the United Nations until hell freezes over, but none of them will have any important impact until they negotiate with the industrial states", (43) neatly summarizes the view of the majority of Western nations. Certainly, the West will not easily relinquish its control and has been quietly examining ways in which it can preserve its powerful position. (44)

Western concerns have been bathed in crocodile tears. Its condemnation of the irresponsibility and immaturity of the U.N.'s new majority must be considered somewhat bizarre in view of the West's long history of control over the General Assembly and its use of the organization as an anti-communist alliance, an alliance which, although it reached its zenith at the time of the Korean war, was still effective enought to bar China's admission to some of the specialized agencies for nearly 20 years. All that has happened is that the 'new majority' is able to use the U.N. to occasionally discomfort the West as the West traditionally did to rankle the Soviet bloc. The 'new minority' has yet to learn to accept this position. The U.N. was created for political reasons and the rich countries cannot object to the intrusion of politics - a new brand of politics - into the organization. What the 'new minority' still has to do is, in the words of one of its own spokesmen, learn "how to dialogue with people who were, only yesterday, directly under its control". (45)

This is not to suggest that the West's concerns are without legit-

imacy or that the crisis of confidence surrounding the U.N. is
contrived or imaginary. The crisis is very real and deepening.
It is, moreover, a crisis which has implications which are larger
than the U.N. itself. For the pessimism surrounding the U.N.
threatens to become a cynicism about international institutions
in general. Such cynicism breeds its own brand of disappointment
and frustration which become excuses for inaction.

THE RECORD RECONSIDERED

In assessing the record of the United Nations we have so far focused on disappointment and frustration. We have looked for reasons which help explain the organization's failure. We have suggested that, as a peace and security organization, it was doomed
from the beginning: the paint on its woodwork was barely dry when
the Cold War broke out, rendering it virtually powerless. The
U.N. mirrors world politics and if these are a mess we should not
be surprised if the organization is little better. Disorder and
confusion, we have suggested, are not the progenitors of trust
and confidence.

Despite its failures, frailties and imperfections, our world
would be in a much bigger mess without the United Nations. Even
a cursory examination of its record must lead to the conclusion
that it has served as an instrument for a better world order. Although its power is circumscribed, history has shown that the
U.N. can help defuse certain types of conflicts - those in which
the superpowers are either not involved or fear the threat of
eventual nuclear confrontation - and that it can promote positive-sum outcomes. Conflicts and zero-sum outcomes are not only
possible but probable in the absence of a global institution. (46)
The U.N. has also been able to influence the political processes
of States. It has encouraged governments to take more international approaches and it has strengthened the hand of outward-look-
ing leaders in dealing with domestic political opposition. It
has taken responsibility for compromises in situations where national leaders could not have taken responsibilities alone.

The most striking feature of the U.N. has been its evolution since
its creation. Today's organization bears little resemblence to
the one created 35 years ago. Its madate has been progressively
enlarged from peace and security to world development, reflecting
a trend in international society from a preoccupation with military security to economic security. The Declaration on the New International Economic Order was in many respects the confirmation
of this historical process, the culmination of some quarter century of change in the U.N. system. (47)

The U.N. Charter is not a mandate for the development of the poor

countries, but it has become the main concern of the organization. The Charter makes no reference to what we today call 'official development assistance'. The World Bank, the main development financing organization today, was conceived as a supplement to the private capital market to be used for mobilizing additional funds for investment in 'financially sound' projects:
it was not created for dispensing loans on concessional terms.
The first assistance programs - among the most effective ever
developed by the organization and in many respects a model for
what is required today - were not aimed at the developing countries but at providing emergency relief to those displaced by
war. (48)

The history of the United Nations is the story of the emergence
of a development organization; of a proliferation of efforts to
help new countries make sense of their political independence.
(49) The emergence of the U.N. has also legitimized 'development'
as a field of inquiry. At the time of the founding of the organization there was hardly a book with the word 'development' in its
title; there were neither special university courses, development institutes, nor development experts. (50) Which also meant
that there were no theories of development. This were not long
in coming, however. With their pedigree in, to use Dudley Seers'
term, "colonial economics out of political expediency" (51) and
their predilection for viewing the poor countries as rich countries at an earlier stage of development, they succeeded in sow-
ing seeds of confusion which are still being harvested. (52)

The U.N.'s emphasis on economic and social conditions has given
a new volition to its membership. For whereas the superpowers
may choose to exclude their discussions on disarmament from an
organization which has become too egalitarian for the conduct
of power politics - as indeed they have done - when it comes
to international economic affairs nations, even the most powerful, can no longer choose to be 'in' or 'out'. Objective interdependencies mean that nations have to be 'in' even though they
might prefer to be 'out'. As Moynihan has pointedly observed:
"This (world) order is already much too developed for the United
States or any other nation to think of opting out. It can't be
done. One may become a delinquent in this nascent world society.
An outcast in it. But one remains 'in' it. There is no escape
from a definition of nationhood which derives primarily from the
new international reality". (53)

The world knows few technological, economic or ecological sanctu-
ries. Global interdependence has given a legitimacy to the United
Nations that its architects could never have dreamt of.

The transformation of the U.N. can be illustrated in all manner
of ways. Particularly striking is the fact that, while established with the aim of prohibiting the use of force in the cause of
peace, the U.N. has actually legitimized its use in the cause of

justice, for example in the case of colonial domination and apart-
heid. The original concern of the organization, the promotion of
a negative peace - one based on the absence of war - has given way
to the desire to promote a positive peace - or one characterized
by the prevalence of justice and the absence of inequalities.

The U.N.'s record in the area of anticolonialism is not only one
of the organization's most notable achievements (54): its legitimization of anticolonialism has also served as an indication of
its capacity to promote the acceptance of international conduct
norms. The regular observance of such norms, no matter how mechanical it may be or become, affects the behavior of those who practice the observance and may eventually affect their motivation.
(55) U.N. resolutions can influence the behavior of nations and
the behavior of nations is the principle source of law.

The U.N. does not have the power to legislate, to formulate a
new legality. But it is able to bring about a new legitimacy
which can give rise to new concepts and further their acceptance.
So-called 'permissive resolutions', for example, do not seek to
establish duties but rather aim at granting rights by recommending action or non-action to U.N. members. Recommendations of this
kind, even though 'permissive', are able to create law. They
legitimate and stimulate the recommended action, opening the way
to the rapid growth of customary law, based upon international
collective opinion. (56)

The law-making function of the United Nations has received, outside of the legal community, surprisingly little attention. Yet
it could be its most significant contribution to international
order and the cause of justice. For whereas one might be excused
for believing that anarchy prevails in the law of nations, the
fact is that, to quote Louis Henkin, "almost all nations observe
almost all principles of international law and almost all of their
obligations almost all of the time". (57)

Coplin has suggested that an international organization can fulfill three main functions: they can function as a *forum* for negotiations and bargaining; they can play a *regulative* role through
which restrictions are placed upon the freedom of action of member States; and they can play a *distributive* role, making decisions
that are designed to distribute costs and benefits among States.
(58) We could argue that the forum function serves to articulate
and expand the collective knowledge base while the regulative and
distributive functions represent the institutional capacity for
collective policy formulation and implementation. (59)

The U.N. is all of this. It is a forum and it seeks to regulate
and distribute, to inform and formulate. It is in its forum function that it has achieved most success. Even something as powerless as a debating club - and the U.N. is certainly more than
that - can have a significant impact on international relations,

the impact being dependent upon the subject debated and the power of the debaters to influence affairs outside the forum of discussion. The U.S., for example, is said to take the U.N. more
seriously now even though it castigates the 'new majority' for
irresponsibility and admonishes its 'steamroller tactics' (60).
Through its forum function the U.N. has managed over time to contribute to the introduction of new concepts and data, to stimulate innovative theoretical work, to develop holistic perspectives of the complex of global problems and processes. In doing
so, it has expanded the collective knowledge base and contributed to the definition of issues that make up the negotiation agenda.

It is in the area of policy-making and the politicized processes
of regulating and distributing - of deciding who gets what, when
and how - that the organization has inevitably failed. Even here,
however, there have been modest successes in the cases where, like
air traffic control, the control of contagious diseases, postal,
telegraph and telephone services, the use of the radio spectrum,
things have to be regulated for everyone or they work for no one.

With such exceptions, general purpose international organizations
cannot go much beyond the forum function. When they try to do so
they run aground on the political and economic structures which
either control them or over which they have no control. In cases
where they are able to effectuate change, the change cannot, by
definition, be of a systems transforming dimension.

Certainly, the U.N. is chained to its own structure and to the
structures in which it must operate. To say that its scope for
activities is constrained is not, however, the same as saying
that there are no activities at all. (61) And, if there are activities, then the possibility exists that they may have consequences which are unintended and perhaps not even recognized by those
who initiate the action. Some international secretariats have been
able to influence the outcomes of political issues when they have
been prepared to stick out their necks and take risks. (62) Ruggie
has shown how something as innocuous as a statement drafted by a
group of 'independent experts' - the Cocoyoc Declaration - is able
to set all manner of processes in motion which, unenvisaged at the
time, effectively challenge the particularistic interests of both
the rich and poor countries. (63)

                    International Organization and
                              Leadership

The growing complexity of the international system and the need
to manage crises which threaten to consume the whole of mankind
can be expected to give a new legitimacy to global institutions.
Survival will depend upon finding ways of making them work. There

is no feasible alternative. As Alistair Buchan has observed: "If
one contemplates a world in which twenty or thirty powers, super,
great and middle-sized, try to maintain stability by means of bilateral diplomacy at four or five different levels of interaction,
some of which are vital to some but not to others, the prospects
of confusion and crisis increase exponentially, creating not only
international but domestic tensions also". (64) We will need international institutions to help cope with the confusion and to
help defuse the conflicts.

Complexity is the great enemy of play-it-by-ear approaches to diplomacy. In the past it was possible for politicians to 'persona-
lize' foreign policy: Nehru in India, Sukarno in Indonesia, Nas-
ser in Egypt, Benes in Czechoslovakia, Titulescu in Romania,
Lange in Norway, Spaak in Belgium and Luns in the Netherlands all
reigned for 20 years or slightly less. They dominated because they
either had the power to dominate - notably the case with Third
World leaders - or because there was a national consensus. In today's world it is becoming increasingly impossible for someone to
dictate policy - Kissinger tried it - and national consensus barely exists. (65) As complexity increases and the stakes become
higher, the scope for play-it-by-ear diplomacy will diminish and
the risks associated with it will become greater. It is safe to
assume that whereas the political issues which preoccupied the
minds of the founding fathers of the U.N. offered considerable
scope to talented individuals, today's economic problems are the
domain of international institutions.

It is true that our global institutions are not always fit to lead.
It may also be true, however, that they are no more unhealthy than
some of those whose names are associated with leadership. Caesar
was an epileptic, Lincoln had suicidal tendencies, Napoleon was
frequently incommoded by physical ailments. (66) More recently and
parochially, Eisenhower had a history of coronaries, strokes and
intestinal blockage, Kennedy relied on amphetamines and steroids,
Johnson had paranoid delusions during his second term, and Nixon
tended to bloodclotting in periods of strain. (67) There are no
reasons for believing that Soviet leaders are any more hale and
hearty. They also share the distinction of having presided over
the decline of 'their' order whilst fingering the nuclear button.
The destiny of mankind may be safer in the hands of institutions
which, despite their imperfections, are at least trying to think
and act globally.

Nations act in self-interest or what they believe to be self-interest. They will of course continue to do so. But as the world becomes more complex, issues more impacted and interpenetrated, the
risks of 'getting it wrong' greater, they will have no rigorous
way of knowing whether they are getting their sums 'right'. In
other words, of knowing what constitutes self-interest. In a world
in which traditional distinctions are blurred and historical ex-

perience is suspect or irrelevant, what is 'self' and what is
'interest'? Nations will no doubt find that resort to the United
Nations can affect which 'self' and which 'interest' ultimately
prevails. (68)

The exercise of self-interest cannot mean that nations dispose
of policy issues by simply turning them over to international
organizations. Nor could we expect that international organizations will become leaders in a leaderless world. Leadership will
not come from international organizations, but it seems both
likely and desirable that they be afforded a more important role
in international leadership. (69)

RESTRUCTURING ISSUES

We have noted that the U.N. of thirty years ago is very different
from today's organization and there is every reason to assume
that the U.N. thirty years hence will bear little resemblence to
the family we know today. What it will look like - assuming we
are still here to look - we can only guess at. What we can be
reasonably sure about, however, is that the organization will
continue to reflect the variety and complexity of the world with
all of its tensions, conflicts and antagonisms. Baring some historical mutation which gives birth to a new world organization,
international relations and the way in which nations choose to
conduct their affairs seem destined to exert greater influence
on the U.N. than any changes in the organization will have upon
the international system.

The future of the organization is intimately linked to the decisions of governments concerning which of their responsibilities,
their rights and their duties they wish to exercise through the
organization and, ultimately, how much of their own freedom of
action they are prepared to surrender to it. The answer to this
question will be largely determined by the way in which the international system evolves, how crises develop and are experienced.

This is not to suggest that the U.N. should simply sit back and
wait to see what role fate thrusts upon it. We have already suggested that the scope for 'leadership' is likely to be greater
as nations seek to make some sense out of their complex predicament and formulate collective responses to the management of
crises. There is very considerable scope for self-improvement and
the development of management capacities. Such self-improvement
could have a modest cause-effect relationship with changes in
international relations.

Even at the level of administration and coordination, the U.N.'s
deficiencies are so numerous that they conspire to present a bu-

reaucratic nightmare. Consider just some of the defects: too much unnecessary duplication between agencies and their programs; the incapacity to compare plans, programs and budgets; the lack of a central intelligence and guidance system which can define priorities and initiate planning; the desperate proliferation of committees, commissions, programs and funds within the organization itself and the uncontrolled growth of agency offices around the world; the inability and unwillingness of member governments to coordinate their approaches toward the U.N. as a whole; the incompetence and ineffectiveness of officials placed within the organization for reasons of who they are rather than what they know or can do; the inability of ECOSOC to perform its constitutional role - that of coordinating the coordinators - at the heart of the U.N. system. All this and much more. Any one of these deficiencies would be enough to seriously impede the functioning of the U.N. Together they conspire to make the organization an object of ridicule, a grotesque parody of what is needed. (70)

None of the defects noted above are 'new'. They have long been recognized and denounced and have been the object, as we noted earlier, of a number of well-conceived 'efficiency' studies. The proposals resulting from these studies, however, have perished on the battlefield of entrenched interests.

Even if some progress could be engineered in the areas of administration and coordination it should be recognized that the U.N. may not become much more efficient as a result. Efficiency has two main aspects: the willingness of governments to use an organization in the conduct of their affairs; and the ability of the organization to perform satisfactorily once it has been charged with a task. Here, the questions which are generally subsumed under the heading of 'political will' are a good deal more important than bureaucratic deficiencies. Only after an organization has been charged with the responsibility to perform does its capacity to perform become a primary consideration, although organizations with a proven capacity for performance are obviously more likely to be afforded new responsibilities than those in which there is little confidence.

Nor should efficiency be confused with 'democracy'. If the poor nations were to capture control of the main organs of the U.N. then it would not necessarily become more efficient as a result. It may become more representative, but that does not necessarily lead to increased efficiency. Since the U.N. is used as an instrument to advance national self-interest, any improvement may make it a more powerful weapon in international politics. (71) In other words, any change short of drastic change in the very structure of the organization may simply serve to advance the interests of one group of nations at the expense of those of another. In this sense, improvements in efficiency could serve to deny rather than advance the causes of peace and justice.

It would certainly be possible to improve efficiency without dis-
turbing vested power interests. If the aim, however, is to transform the organization into an effective instrument for global
planning and resource management - one which can advance the
construction of a more rational and equitable international order - then changes limited to the improvement of efficiency will
not be sufficient. (72) The U.N. is neither functionally stream-
lined nor structurally built to perform real planning and management tasks. And since function in a system cannot be dissociated
from its structure, it follows that changes must necessarily affect both. (72)

The U.N. derives its legitimacy from the system of nation-States.
It is the decisions of States which have resulted in the growth
and development of the organization and it will be national decisions which lead to its further evolution. Fundamental change in
the U.N. thus presupposes a transformation of the system of nation-States. For change in international organization is and
can only be a reflection of change in society as a whole.

STRATEGIES FOR INTERNATIONAL INSTITUTIONS:
GUIDELINES FOR A POSITIVE APPROACH

Institution building for global planning and resource management
will be a slow and painful process characterized by setbacks and
advances, progress and regression. That we need it is one thing,
that we can have it is quite another. As we noted in the previous
chapter, there is little or no space for deterministic blueprints
which presuppose the existence of a commanding or shared vision of
what the world needs or should look like. Despite their obvious
attraction, preoccupation with institutional master plans will
prove frustrating, even counter-productive. Rather, the emphasis
must be on the progressive democratization of existing institutions and the identification of those areas in which international cooperation appears possible, achieving some measure of consensus on the roles which institutions are to play and the power
they are to exercise. This implies a systematic exploration of
possible complementarities in the frequently diverging interests
of the world's nations, big and small, rich and poor, old and new.

There is no space for superagencies in institutional strategies.
Institution-building for global planning and resource management
does not mean megabureaucracies but mutually consistent sets of
internationally agreed principles and guidelines, supported by
action plans and programs hammered out within a global framework
by governments operating at the political level. Sometimes the
need will be to restructure established institutions, other times
to create new ones; sometimes it will be to transfer more power
and responsibility to international secretariats, other times to

bring government representatives together more often. Again, there can be no single master model. (74)

In designing institutional strategies we will have to make do with overall guidelines which, shaped by a perception of what needs to be done, and of the normative receptivities of decision-makers, may have a general relevance and application. It is to such guidelines that we will now turn.

Management Levels

It is essential that the right level of management be found for the problems to be addressed. In some instances effective action may require that problems be 'pushed down' to the national level, or even below, or 'pulled up' to regional or global levels. The guiding principle should be the need to ensure that all those who are affected by the decisions taken with respect to the problem are able to participate, through appropriate representation, in the making of those decisions.

The search for the right level implies parallel processes of centralization and decentralization of decision-making competences. There is nothing paradoxical or incompatible, however, with these opposing trends. Both are historically determined: the trend toward increased centralization is rooted in attempts to deal with the problem of 'external effects'; the trend toward increased decentralization being anchored in increased demands for participation and in line with such developments as anticolonialism.

The problem is one of finding optimum levels of decision-making. In searching for these we will need to bear in mind that in many areas of human affairs there may be no such thing as a real optimum and that even when it does exist, it is only in theory and seldom in practice.

Jan Tinbergen, who has done much to advance thinking on optimum levels of decision-making, has suggested a rule of thumb for the "political superstructure" of an organization required to handle a problem with 'external effects'. (75) He suggests that the aim should be to vest decision-making responsibilities for major problems in councils with about 10-15 members, the councils being linked in a matrix structure for the purposes of overall guidance and coordination. For global institutions, the membership would represent the world's regions in an equitable fashion.

Types of Problems

The terms of reference of the institution should be firmly related to the problems they are expected to deal with. While it is very difficult if not impossible to draw dividing lines between 'polit-

ical' and 'technical' problems, it may be possible to make basic
distinctions between those relationships and practices which,
because they benefit a large number of parties, can be institutionalized and those which must, at least for the forseeable future, remain strongly politicized. Experience tells us that technical and functional problems lend themselves more easily to coordinated decision-making than do more general political ones.

Attempts to build institutions which can play regulative roles
could be particularly rewarding. A large number of issues do revolve around technical concerns and require policies with a
strong element of regulation. The more that issues involve regulatory forms of management and the less they involve questions
of a distributive nature, the more likely it will be to engineer
an agreement. As noted earlier, there are problems which need to
be resolved for everyone or the answer works for no one, the reality behind such 'successes' as the regulation of the world's
airways and airwaves, and, in a different sense, the Law of the
Sea Conference.

Even modest progress in the area of building regulative institutions would serve two useful purposes: it would contribute to
the much needed processes of confidence-building; and it would
'catch' some problems which may become 'uncatchable' as new
sources of conflict emerge, and they become increasingly politicized.

The creation of regulative institutions should result from the
systematic search for the problems in which a regulatory approach
is sensible and a process of hard bargaining between the parties
involved. As such, it is not necessarily synonymous with lowest
common denominator decision-making. This, while usually but not
always preferable to no decision-making, easily leads to simple-
minded approaches to substantively and politically complex problems. Simple-minded approaches, shaped by lines of least resistance, may simply mean that difficulties have not only not been
faced but also pushed further into the future and made even more
complicated as a result. Nevertheless, there will be a need for
trade offs or, in the words of the *RIO Report*, "we must honestly
scrutinize the alternatives before us, be prepared to make compromises if failure to do so would result in no progress, and
to be wise enough to accept a second-best solution when the alternative is no solution at all". (76)

Regulative agencies do not and cannot exist in a political vacuum.
Even organizations which focus on comparatively straight-forward
technical and functional problems are immersed in their own political milieu. It is this which gives them form and substance. (77)
Ernst Haas has shown in different studies how the growth of international organizations with functional responsibilities depends,
not upon their technical competence and the possibilities for excluding 'politics' from entering their work, but upon the charac-

ter and dynamics of their political environment. (78) Regulative
agencies would thus react to rather than be immune to political
pressures and requirements. (79)

We have noted that the effectiveness of international institutions is determined first and foremost by questions of 'political
will' - notably the readiness of governments to charge an institution with decision-making responsibilities - questions relating
to such matters as technical competence being, at least in the
first instance, a secondary consideration. An institutional strategy aimed at going beyond forum institutions to regulative institutions is not a denial of this reality. It is rather a strategy which, while recognizing the primacy of politics, sets out
to challenge notions and definitions of political feasibility.

Membership of Institutions

The main problem here is to find a satisfactory relationship between efficiency and participation. The problem will be defined
by the nature of the task or the function to be performed. In
the case of institutions which are to fulfill a forum function
there may be no real tension between the need for efficiency and
the claims for participation. The problem will be much greater in
cases where institutions are to play regulative and distributive
roles. Here the challenge is to find ways in which expression can
be given to the legitimate rights of both rich and poor nations
without creating unmanageable institutions. (80)

In meeting this challenge there will be a great need for institutional innovation. Innovation may require that new ways be found
for involving specialists and non-governmental organizations
(NGOs) in the activities of international institutions. The dividing lines between specialists as advisers and politicians as decision-makers have become blurred by the complexity of many contemporary problems. (81) In order to take responsible decisions,
a decision-maker must be aware and take account of the consequences of his actions. In doing this he will in part be guided by
intuition and 'feeling'. But the substantive complexity of many
of the problems may well mean that he is more likely to crash
when he's flying by the seat of his pants than when he's navigat-
ing on expert opinion. (82)

In the past, specialists have often been reluctant to engage in
political debate or even to share their knowledge and fears with
ordinary people. Given social and political dilemmas, they have
often preferred to adopt neutral rather than value positions, to
tacitly advise rather than openly advocate. This generalization
no longer holds true. In many branches of science there are radical movements. Increasingly, both in the rich and poor worlds,
scientists are involved in active advocacy which they see as "the

intellectual and ethical duty of our age". (83)

All this suggests that specialists be provided with greater opportunities to participate in the making of decisions in areas
of vital importance to the future of mankind. This is not to
suggest the creation of a technocracy nor that political will
can ever be substituted by scientific opinion; only that it may
prove shortsighted not to more effectively use the insights and
understandings which both exist and are required to build roads
out of mankind's predicament. 'Wise council' is a valuable commodity and an essential ingredient of decision-making. It deserves more than the political wildernis of 'reports by independent experts'. (84)

Similarly, the involvement of NGOs in the work of international
organizations may, because they are less constrained by the need
to defend national interests and by the requirements of diplomacy, bring a fresh and new purpose to stale deliberations. It
will need to be recognized, however, that the NGO universe is
very diverse and that for every organization that is able to
bring an innovative and fresh approach there will be many more
who defend narrow, parochial interests and, in doing so, manage
to combine the worst features of amateurism with convention-
bound bureaucracy.

Guidance and Control Mechanisms

Large organizations, like the United Nations, tend to grow in a
haphazard, incremental and uncoordinated way as they respond to
new problems and government prodding. They develop into a loose
network which has various coordinating and integrating mechanisms
which operate independently. They do not grow into systems which
characteristically have a single guidance and control mechanism
which makes it possible to regulate the behavior of the system
through the evaluation of information flows and the linking of
feedback mechanisms to learning processes. (85) They function
like decapitated chickens which manage to run around and flap
their wings without the advantage of a brain.

The United Nations is very much a network rather than a system
(86) It has evolved without a central guidance and control mechanism. It has no 'brain'. Sir Robert Jackson looked for it "for
many years" but was forced to conclude that "the search has been
in vain. Here and there throughout the system there are offices
and units collecting the information available, but there is no
group (or 'Brains Trust') which is constantly monitoring the
present operation, learning from experience, grasping at all
that science and technology has to offer, launching new ideas
and methods, challenging established practices, and provoking
thought inside and outside the system. No general headquarters",

he went on, "could function without its intelligence (information) staff and its planning staff, for these form the military
brain. Yet the U.N. development system has tried to wage a war
on want with very little organized 'brain' to guide it. Its absence", he concluded, "may well be the greatest constraint of
all on capacity. Without it the future evolution of the U.N. development system could easily repeat the history of the dinosaur".
(87)

Without a central intelligence and guidance system it is impossible to provide for something as basic as coordination. Coordination is required for three main purposes: *rationalization,*
aimed at removing unnecessary duplication of policies, programs
and projects; *standardization,* aimed at coordinating procedural
matters on the basis of equity of treatment and comparability;
and *priority-setting* aimed at identifying which policies, programs and projects should be allocated what resources, when and
how, on the basis of an evaluation of their respective merits.
(88)

Priority setting is the most important type of coordination. Experience with national governments and large business corporations shows clearly that the activity requires the existence of
a mechanism which is hierarchically superior and vested with legal and financial powers to ensure compliance with its decisions.
The U.N. has no such mechanism. Effective priority-setting is
thus impossible.

Guidance and control mechanisms are not synonymous with bureaucracies and 'top heavy' organizations. They are perfectly compatible with decentralized structures - structures which have a
special need for institutionalized intelligence. In this respect
the general strategy for institution-building for global planning
and resource management should be guided by the need to move away
from conventional, hierarchical, centralized structures, to more
decentralized, horizontal, matrix organizations to encourage
flexibility and innovation and to provide for broader involvement
in decision-making. The decentralized structures should contain
provision for a central forecasting, guidance and control body
responsible for monitoring the implementation of policies, programs and projects, evaluating their effects, reviewing intercon-
nections, and defining priorities. To be able to function as a
'brain', the intelligence mechanism will require a measure of independence and its own authority.

Scientists and other specialists could be invited to play a significant role in the execution of this intelligence function.

The Question of Planning

Planning for and in anticipation of global crises is becoming a

matter of great urgency. As Mahbub ul Haq, one of the Third
World's most articulate spokesmen, has observed: "In a world becoming increasingly interdependent and often requiring adjustments which should be anticipated by decades, the needs and dimensions of international planning become probably just as important as those of national planning". (89)

Planning is, however, one of the most difficult of all management
functions and is traditionally a field in which practice bears
little relationship to theory. At the national level planning is
often conspicuous through its absence and the many constraints
on it intensify and multiply when attempted at the global level.
Even under reasonably closed systems with a high level of consensus on the goals and objectives to be pursued and the means
to be applied it is difficult enough. Most international organizations are not cohesive units built on shared value premises.
Their uncertainties with respect to direction (the goals and objectives to be pursued), are matched only by the confusion and
dissension surrounding what needs to be done (the problems to be
tackled), and how it is to be done (the means to be applied).

In this sense, the U.N. is hopelessly equipped to function as a
planning agency. The interests of its members are so diverse
that it excludes the possibility of consensus on all but the
most mundane of goals. It has neither the authority to balance
the ends/means equation nor does it have the compliance mechanisms to implement a plan even if it could be devised. Formal
planning models, whether marginal-inductive aimed at problem-
solving or rational-deductive aimed at goal-setting, will have
little place. The emphasis will need to be placed on the creation
of processes whereby conflicts can be identified and perceptions
of it compared. The conflicts will be resolved in the political
process of debate and contention organized in such a way that
answers to three questions - Who pays? Who benefits? Who decides?
- are made as explicit as possible. In other words, to coin the
old adage , justice should be seen to be done. The purpose of
planning becomes the process and the improvement of the process
becomes a worthy goal.

Against this background all that we can realistically hope for
is what Jan Tinbergen has called 'indicative planning' which
seeks to sketch out longer-term trends, indicating where processes are or could be heading, rather than seeking, as would 'imperative planning', to coerce nations into fulfilling specific
plan objectives. (90) Such planning would obviously need to be
linked in an organic fashion to the guidance and control mechanism discussed above.

Indicative planning would not aim at building a predetermined
'future' but rather at reducing uncertainties and at anticipating
crises. Its time-frame would thus need to be middle-range where
problems which need to be confronted now are piling up. It will

be messy planning, without a formalized theory and with little
scope for brilliant apercus either by individuals or computers.
It will, however, need to go beyond narrow specializations, becoming genuinely transdisciplinary and reflecting the new reality
that "you have to think about the situation as a whole if you
are going to act relevantly on any part of it". (91)

However the planning function is articulated, we shall need to
keep in mind that the planning horizon of most decision-makers
is a good deal less than ten years - two years for a U.S. Con-
gressman and four for a president - and in the case of about one
billion people it is temporally the next day and spatially the
next village. We shall also need to remember that planning does
not nor can it take place in a power vacuum. Planning is a process for determining future action through a sequence of choices.
In this process choice is ubiquitous, being involved at every
stage. (92) Choice implies preferences based upon value premises.
It also means that the contents of the policies, programs and
projects which finally emerge from planning institutions will be
biased in favor of those who have most power to influence the
process of choice. It follows that 'plans' because they give
stronger articulation to the interests of the strong, can serve
to deny the interests of the weak. In other words, 'plans', however defined, will reflect and be a function of the power structure.

It is also worth noting that although there is an urgent need
for longer-term planning, governments, especially industrialized
country governments, are practicing it less and less while advocating it more and more. The only institutional entities which
are involved in the formulation and implementation of longer-
term strategies are transnational corporations where, in the
words of the impeccably conservative U.S. Tariff Commission,
"planning and abstract monitoring of plan fulfillment have reached a scope and level of detail that, ironically, resembles more
than superficially the national planning procedures of communist
countries". (93) The planning of transnationals, because it is
closed system planning for limited objectives (profit maximization), is bound to be more successful than global planning for
development objectives (human welfare). Its very success, however, can be hostile to development and to the sharing of the
benefits of economic growth. As both developed and developing
countries seek to substitute planning mechanisms for market mechanisms, they will both, individually and collectively, need to
develop a countervailing planning capability.

                    The Need for Limited Approaches

We argued in chapter 3 that strategies for the future will need
to be guided by the principle of selectivity. This should be re-

flected in our institutional strategies and could find expression
in the following:

'Pioneering action' by limited numbers of countries. The creation
of a new institution need not be made dependent upon the agreement
of all nations. Small groups of countries could take the lead and
set the example. A small group of rich countries could, for example, choose to introduce a modest redistributive tax on consumer
durables (cf chapter 6) with the intention of gradually raising
and extending it to include more categories and of attracting
more countries. Similarly, groups of developed countries could
forge cooperative links with a group of developing countries for
a specific purpose, such as developing agriculture in the poor
countries or accelerating their technological transformation. (94)

Action at the regional level. Because the effective management
of resources requires institutions at different levels, decision-
making bodies at the regional or sub-regional level could be established prior to institutionalizing a capability at the world
level. A start at the regional level might be cheaper in terms
of transaction costs and simpler politically. (95) It could also
contribute to the process of confidence-building as a prerequisite for global institutions.

It is at the regional and sub-regional level where significant
progress is at present being made in the creation of regimes
for environmental protection and the management of renewable resources. Schachter has shown, for example, how attempts to develop regimes for the equitable apportionment of freshwater resources have produced "new legal concepts and arrangements that
combine ideas of distributive justice and of practical resource
management". (96)

Action could be linked to the notion of international resource
regions as developed by Young. (97) These are "geographical areas
demarcated in terms of the functional issues associated with the
management of natural resources and the maintenance of environmental quality". (98) the areas either have multiple sovereign
jurisdictions or fall outside the sovereign jurisdiction of any
given state, i.e. no single nation is responsible for their effective management. The management regimes created for international resource regions – which could include Beringa (the subject of Young's own detailed study), the North Sea, the Baltic
Sea, the Mediterranean Sea, the Caribbean Sea, the Sea of Japan,
the East China-Yellow Seas, the Artic and Antarctica – could be
responsible for functional areas (fish and marine mammals, transport and navigation, environmental quality, perhaps security and,
if available, hydrocarbons), physical domains (seabed and subsoil
resources, water column, surface water and surface-adjacent airspace) and horizontal domains (internal waters, territorial seas
and adjacent areas (contiguous zones, special fishing zones,
'economic zones', patrimonial seas, etc.)). (99) There is no

reason why such international resource regions could not be
linked to the U.N. network and thus at the global level. There
is also no reason why the notion of international resource regions could not be applied to terrestial areas, such a deserts,
drainage basins (hydrosystems) or even dominant ecosystems.

'Self-destruct'institutions. Experience has taught us that international institutions are prone to a cataleptic condition brought
about by their inability to advance and keep pace with changing
circumstances. Established to initiate and guide a process of
change, they can become a vested interest and consequently status
quo rather than change oriented, devoting less of their time to
dealing with the problem they were established to address and
more on justifying their own existence or enhancing their own
importance. (100)

The answer to the problem of 'institutional sclerosis' resides
in part in the creation of limited mandate institutions established to undertake a specific task or set of tasks rather than
as a permanent addition to the international institutional presence. Such institutions, at their inception, should be furnished
with a 'self-destruct' mechanism: periodic evaluation of the future need for the institution in the light of its performance
and changing political circumstances should be mandatory and result in decisions either to terminate operations or to adapt its
role or function. The guiding principle must be a greater determination to cast institutions onto the scrap-heap of history.

THIRD WORLD INSTITUTIONS

The development of Third World institutions is an essential element in the process of developing a planning and management capability at the world level and of shaping a more equitable international order. A stronger Third World institutional presence
is required for four main reasons. First and foremost, it is required for the purpose of autonomy building and to enhance the
positional and resource power of the developing countries vis-
à-vis the industrialized countries. (101) Second, Third World
institutions will be needed as a response to the inevitable failure of efforts aimed at democratizing the main organs of the
United Nations. Third, they will be required due to the fact that
it will be impossible to accommodate certain types of institutions
within the framework of the U.N. system, such as an organization
of non-aligned countries to challenge the bloc system, and an
organization of small countries to challenge the system of great
power dominance. (102) And fourth, they are required as part of
the process of intellectual liberation and self-reliance, a process which will lead to an increase in the ideological power of
the Third World. (103)

The lack of Third World institutions has no doubt damaged the
cause of the developing countries and weakened their bargaining
position. When the industrialized countries sit down to negotiate
with the developing countries they are usually better informed
and organized and able to bring more resources to bear on the
problems under discussion. (104) Its lack of institutional momentum has meant that the Third World has not been able to effectively follow up on the openings which have been created, or,
in its own words, "The Group of 77 has increasingly felt the absence of sustained technical support at a time when it is deeply
involved in complex negotiating processes".(105) The failure of
the developing countries to capitalize on the consensus which
emerged during the Seventh Special Session - the good old days
of the NIEO - can in part be explained by the fact that they had
no institutions which could help do it for them.

The role of Third World institution has been traditionally played by UNCTAD - a Third World 'justice constituency' - but its
scope in this direction is obviously limited. It is a U.N. organization funded largely by the rich countries and there are
limits upon what it can investigate and even greater limits upon
what it can recommend. As a member of the U.N. family it is mandated to furnish the information required to promote international cooperation and is required to avoid recommendations which
could lead to conflict or confrontation, or breaches of international conventions. As Helleiner has observed, "it is difficult
to imagine it preparing papers on means of defaulting on debt
and getting away with it, or on minimising compensation payments
in cases of nationalisation".(106) As a Third World institution,
UNCTAD is a prisoner of its own structural jail. It tends, moreover, to be 'economistic' and may not be entirely free of intellectual rigidity and innate conservatism. (107)

There are grounds for believing that the research required by
the Third World is not taking place in the Third World on anything like a significant scale. Studies have shown that the number of scholars working in the developing countries on international policy questions is and remains small. (108) It is even
less likely that the necessary research could be carried out on
any scale in the industrialized countries, and, assuming it were,
the results would inevitably be suspect.

There is thus an obvious need for a Third World Secretariat.
This need has long been recognized and steps are being taken to
fulfill it. (109) The Third World Forum, itself a comparatively
new institution, has initiated a study into the implications of
"an improved organizational framework for the Third World in the
context of international economic negotiations". (110) What the
Secretariat will eventually look like is not yet known. Indica-
tions are that it will not be a "fully fledged Secretariat but
a technical servicing facility" subservient to "the organizational and decision-making structure of the Group of 77". (111) A

proposal which suggests a string of political compromises.

The need is for an institution with a broad mandate: one vested with the authority to examine relations within and among the countries of the Third World with the aim of contributing to autonomy-building and the promotion of collective self-reliance, as well as relations with the First and Second Worlds. The Secretariat should be empowered to prepare background and briefing papers, not only for the formal process of negotiation, but also in connection with bilateral relations (as do First and Second World Secretariats). It would have a U.N. department with sections for U.N. organizations. It might even have a 'save the rich world' section devoted to the analysis of the social, political and economic predicament of the First and Second Worlds for the purposes of better understanding it and of bringing a new perspective and fresh approach to bear on problems where rich world theory and practice seem hopelessly inadequate.

A Third World Secretariat would be an obvious start but would be nowhere near enough. After establishing a general purpose organization the next step should be the creation, over time, of a large number of relatively small agencies serving limited groups of countries for specific purposes. (112) There is all kinds of scope for interesting alliances which can serve to promote collective self-reliance. Institutions could be established, for example, to serve neighbouring countries (at the regional or sub-regional level), countries with a similar level of development, countries with common problems (e.g. incidence of debt servicing, small island states, geographically disadvantaged), countries with common commodities (producer cartels), or countries with complementary products to exchange. (113) Much is already happening in this area and new organizations are beginning to emerge. (114) They are all parts of an overall strategy to institutionalize a new power structure.

All this is necessary but will be far from easy, as witnessed by the delay in creating a Third World Secretariat. History is not the most favorable augury for Third World institution-building. Attempts to forge cooperative links within the Third World, for example at the regional level, have given rise to more disappointments than success, and the process of institution-building is bound to alter the relative strengths of developing countries vis-à-vis one another which will itself give rise to tensions and conflicts. The experience within the rich world also sounds a cautionary note. The European Community, for example, is finding it increasingly difficult to reconcile the interests of ten industrialized countries within a single region. A Third World Secretariat may need to try to do the same for more than 100 countries at different levels of development spread around the world. (115)

NATION-STATES, NATIONAL SOVEREIGNTY
AND INTERNATIONAL INSTITUTIONS

Strategies of institution-building for global planning and resource management will need to recognize the primacy of the nation-State and the imperatives of national sovereignty. Whereas
it might be true that 'real' planning and management at the
world level would be easier without the inconvenience of nation-
States, there has never been a less promising moment in modern
history to advocate their disappearance. There can be no definition of world order and no strategy for its transformation that
does not have the system of nation-States as its starting point.

The nation-State is a Western invention with its roots firmly
planted in European history. Its emergence as the basis for world
order can perhaps be traced as far back as 732 AD and the repul-
sion of the Arab threat at the Battle of Tours. (116) The process
became autonomous following the defeat of the Ottomans in Europe
and institutionalized in the Peace of Westphalia concluded in
1648. This agreement brought to an end the Eighty Years War between Spain and the Netherlands, the German phase of the Thirty
Years War and resulted in the dissolution of the Holy Roman Empire
into sovereign entities. The product of French diplomacy, the
Peace of Westphalia declared governments equal and sovereign and
afforded them complete discretion to rule over national space
and to regulate external relations. It provided the basis for a
permissive and voluntaristic system of law which emphasized the
allocation of competences among States and which evolved into an
instrument which legitimized the privilege and served the interests of the rich nations. (117)

The nation-State came much later and has developed a different
significance in the 'South'. In some parts of the Third World,
nation-States are geometrical abstractions, their boundaries the
result of the application of rulers and compass wielded in the
'North', guided by questions of administrative convenience. The
Berlin Conference of 1884, called to formally carve up Africa
and to bring some semblance of order to the mad scramble for possessions on the continent, succeeded in drawing lines through
well over 100 African tribes.

Colonialism has meant that some developing countries, notably in
Africa, were created as artificial units, social and economic
'spaces' rather than entities. (118) This historical reality has
given a new dimension to the notion of sovereignty. Certainly,
it is something which must be exercised to redress power imbalances vis-à-vis the rich countries. But it is more than that. It
is the very essence of nationhood.

In many developing countries, especially those born on drawing
boards, the sense of national identity, when it exists, is some-

times rudimentary. (119) Populations have emerged from colonialism lacking what might be termed an affirmative attitude toward rules, persons and actions, a precondition for the consensus politics so much cherished in the West. Nations are more a constellation of kinship groups, castes and tribes than they are homogenous civil societies. They are, in the words of the sociologist, 'fissiparous', or inclined to split up into their constituent parts when subjected to stresses and strains. Neocolonialism and the growth of international capitalism has added to their internal incoherence. (120) Rapid social and economic change has tended to further fragment something already fragmented.

Inevitably, then, politics in many developing countries is preeminently a search for order. (121) Sovereignty, and a commitment to its principles, plays an important role in this process, serving as the glue which binds together disparate groups. Even when borders have been artificially drawn, sovereignty is a powerful force for unity and integration. It is something to be stressed and accentuated rather than downplayed or even given up. Indeed, there is an obvious and necessary relationship between sovereignty and nationalism. It was Karl Deutsch who stressed the relationship between 'nation' and the ability to communicate, and argued that nationalism can be defined in terms of the 'will' toward sovereignty on the part of a people. (122) It follows that the power to accomplish national goals is linked to the exercise of sovereignty. It some cases, this power can be rightly characterized as a scarce resource. (123)

The nation-State in the Third World thus assumes a significance unknown in the West. For the medium-term at least, it is the only framework in which independence can be exerted externally and social and economic development pursued internally. It is the institution which makes it possible to forge fragmented and divided societies into unified, reasonably coherent wholes, capable of self-identification and self-reliance. It is the institution which is able to mobilize the masses and, because it is rooted in a territory, can account to its people for its conduct and behavior. (124)

We can conclude from the above that the rich countries cannot be expected to relinquish their sovereignty and that the poor nations should not be expected to. The system of nation-States must thus constitute the foundation for world order even though it is essentially anarchical to order. (125) It is a system characterized by competing sovereignties giving rise to antagonisms and tensions and in which nations develop - to use Galtung's term - "porcupine-like defences" to protect themselves from the claims and assertions of others. (126) The very system may even be "the taproot of imperialism". (127)

Nation-States, however, are finding it ever more difficult to cope with the complexities of the international system. At this historical juncture, the birth of the modern nation-State has paralleled the emergence of a world system which, driven by the force of modern science-based technology and revolutions in transportation, communication and information processing, tends toward the integration of its component parts. This process is described in chapter 7 and will not be repeated here. Suffice it to note that within this system the behavior of subsystems - nation-States and groups of nations - is determined by the dynamics of the system as a whole. It is a system which, because it is genuinely global in scale, gives rise to problems which are similarly global in magnitude and implications. And because they are genuinely global problems, no nation, however powerful it may believe itself to be or how fiercely it may seek to exercise its sovereignty, can hope to deal with them in isolation.

A global system which brings global problems must also bring global responsibilities. Global responsibilities, if they are properly discharged, may well clash with national interests. Or, stated differently, national security calls for global security; and global security calls for global cooperation in the management of the world's resources.

Within the framework of global integration and global problems, the future existence of an anarchic system of nation-States will be determined by their capacity to engage in cooperation. Each nation must assume responsibilities for its own well-being and development based upon sovereignty over, and the creative utilization of, its own resources - the essence of self-reliance. To effectively discharge this responsibility a nation must have guarantees that its development efforts will not be jeopardized by the consequences of the actions of other states. These guarantees can only be provided by international agreements and thus the international fora in which they are negotiated. (128)

A precondition for the effective exercise of territorial sovereignty in a world of competing sovereignties and global problems is thus international institutions and international agreements. Without these, the belief that all aspects of sovereignty can be effectively exercised is at best an illusion, and at worst a precondition for more conflicts and tensions in a world which is already armed to the teeth.

Nations whose citizens are affected by the decisions of other nations and in whose decision-making process they have no part have, for all practical purposes, lost their sovereignty. The protest made by the Australian and New Zealand governments following the testing of French nuclear weapons in the South Pacific serves as a case in point. They contended that the deposit of radioactive fallout over their territory and its dispersion in airspace without their consent was a violation of their territorial sovereignty.

The failure to develop the cooperative machinery required to come to grips with a complex array of pressing global problems is not to exercise sovereignty but to default on the responsibilities which it brings. Refusal to attempt to develop the machinery, or to harmonize sovereignties, so as to deal with problems which defy national solution - even when these solutions call for limitations on sovereignty - can be interpreted as a decision which erodes rather than strengthens national prerogatives. In this sense, sovereignty takes on a dynamic character. It is, to quote Edward Heath, "not something to be hoarded, sterile and barren, carefully protected in a great coat with its collar turned up. Sovereignty is something for us as custodians to use in the interest of our country." (129) It is in exactly this sense that, in the words of Michael Manley, the question of "political leadership accepting a redefinition of the exercise of sovereignty (is) at the heart of the problem of a new world economic order". (130)

Failure to adjust the notion of sovereignty to changing geopolitical realities will damage the interests of all nations. The rich and powerful countries will be least vulnerable; the small and weak countries the most. Whether defined in terms of regional blocks, semiperipheral hegemonic centers, integrated parts of the world system, the future does not augur well for small developing nations. Viewed against the experience of the post-war period one is tempted to conclude, as Carlos Andrés Pérez has done, that "in today's world the survival of small nationalities is becoming impossible." (131) Their survival chances will be determined by their capacity to forge alliances through which they can defend and advocate their interests, by the benefits derived from collective Third World action and, last but by no means least, by the existence of strong international institutions which truly represent the community of nations and which can provide countervailing power to the hegemony of the rich and powerful nations. (132)

And this conveniently returns us to where we started: to the argument that the majority of international institutions, especially those founded at the end of and immediately following the Second World War, do not represent the 'community of nations', but rather give much greater articulation to the needs and desires of a handful of rich and privileged nations. No government can be expected to transfer some of its power - in the case of many developing countries newly acquired power at that - to organizations which they feel will be unable or unwilling to represent and defend its legitimate interests. (133)

Whereas the system of nation-States must be the foundation for world order strategies, the exercise of sovereignty is an insufficient basis for the shaping of a fairer world and the development of a capacity for global planning and resource management.

This requires international cooperation, strong international institutions and, in the longer-term, the readiness of nations to redefine notions of sovereignty. The scope for such a reinterpretation will itself in part be defined by the modalities of cooperation and the character of the institutions.

BUILDING THE LEGAL FRAMEWORK

Global planning and management institutions, if they are to be more than instruments of convenience, will need to be guided and supported by the force of international law. The evolution of international law, however, has faithfully followed the evolution of international relations and organization and thus mirrors their obliquities and biases.

Traditional international law originated in a Christian and essentially European world and has passed through a number of qualitative phases. (134) The first phase, the period of 'Christian Nations', came to an end in the middle of the nineteenth century when Turkey was invited by the Western nations "to participate in the public law and in the concert of Europe". The second phase the period of the 'Civilized Nations', was primarily directed at regulating the freedom of a small number of powerful nations which were assumed to make up the 'civilized world'. The third phase, the period of 'Peace-Loving Nations', followed the process of decolonization and the creation of the United Nations, the requirement that nations be 'peace-loving' becoming a condition for membership of the U.N. (article 4).

The development of international law has reflected changes in the world political scene and has sought to legitimize the concerns, privilege and power of the dominant or ascendant nations. The decision of the Western world to invite Turkey to join the 'inner circle', for example, was motivated less by the belief that the country could contribute to the process of law and more by the desire to maintain the European balance of power and to frustate Russian plans. Similarly, the law of Civilized Nations served to justify colonial domination. It legitimized the notion of ethnic superiority and sanctioned the bringing of the blessings of civilization to primitive savages and backward races. As such, international law raised legal entitlement to the position of hegemony.

International law thus has an inbuilt inclination to serve the interests of the powerful. It is sobering to note in this connection, for example, that until the mid 1970s very little attention was devoted in juridical literature to the place of the developing countries in the international economic order. (135)

International law is not the product of accident or chance. It is not something which 'just happens' and is found, for some

fortuitous reason, to have an intrinsic value. It is rather a
deliberate process which extends over centuries, a process which
obeys its own evolutionary laws. These laws are as strict as
their results are powerful.

International law provides a framework in which international relations are defined and nations conduct their affairs. It is, in
Henkin's words, "indispensable and inevitable" for both the
achievement and maintenance of order. (136) Much more than a few
prohibitory rules, it consists of a far-reaching set of provisions which indicate what nations can do and the procedures they
must follow in the pursuit of their goals. Because it is "indispensable and inevitable", nations generally observe international
law. Even developing countries, which have justifiably challenged
some of its tenets, have, by and large, chosen to accept the law
which they have inherited. That they have challenged it is part
of the political process which is both shaped by and has its own
outcome in law.

The legal problem is to transform a system of law based upon European traditions and which better articulates the interests of
the rich into a law of a world community and which articulates
the needs of the poor. In terms of the development of a capability for global planning and management, the legal challenge is
one of finding and applying concepts and arrangements which combine ideas of redistributive justice with practical resource
management. (137)

The period of Peace-Loving Nations has not only brought an increase in the number of nations covered by the system of law;
it has also brought a need for qualitative changes. The majority
of subjects are no longer strong and privileged; they are weak
and disprivileged. As such, they require much more from the law
than the regulation of freedom. They require provisions for the
sharing of freedom and protection from the powerful. This suggests that the new international legal order should provide for
rights of the weak, such as the right to determine their own socio-economic systems and, given prevailing inequities and power
imbalances, to form producer associations, to nationalize, and
to regulate foreign investment, as well as *duties of the powerful,* such as non-intervention and the non-imposition of sanctions
on the weak as they exercise their rights. (138)

Recent studies suggest that the evolution of international law
and the legal principles accumulated over five centuries provide
a sufficient basis for such a transformation. (139) The principles
of freedom, equity and solidarity are deeply rooted in international law and these are the cornerstones of an order under which
the world's resources are more equitably shared. The main question
concerning the process of transformation is whether the powerful
and privileged nations will allow international law to follow the
same path that law has followed at the national level; whether

the principles of equity, solidarity and welfare can be extrapolated beyond national boundaries. (140) This will not be brought
about easily. When and how it happens depends upon the way in
which the Third World formulates and organizes its legal challenge
It will need to fight. But, as Bert Röling observes, "a good law
should be fought for; that is a guarantee of its reality". (141)
And it is exactly international law which makes it possible to
engage in conflict without recourse to violence. (142)

The search for a new legal order will need to be conducted within the framework of the United Nations. Through its legitimization of new principle, its formulation of standards, its preparation of treaties and codification of law, it remains, in the
words of Innis Claude, "the most impressive and authorative instrument for the expression of the global version of the general
will". (143) If there is to be a new international legal order
it will be forged in the crucible of the United Nations.

There are a variety of ways in which development of international
law can be advanced in the forum of the U.N. There are principles
in a wide range of General Assembly decisions, resolutions and
other texts which can be used as legal building blocks in the
construction of a fairer world and of regimes for the management
of resources. The decisions and resolutions, and the principles
which they embrace, have been the subject of extensive discussion
and negotiation by the international community and are frequently
couched in reasonably precise and mandatory terms. Because they
have been accepted by the vast majority of states, the principles
must be recognized as reflecting rules of customary international
law, an obligation reinforced by the state's membership of the
U.N. And once accepted as a uniform practice, customary law is
legally binding. (144)

Even when resolutions are not accepted by all nations and grant
rights rather than impose duties, they contribute to the formation of law. 'Permissive resolutions' can, as we noted earlier,
bring about a new legitimacy which leads to a new legality. (145)

Conventions and custom are not the only sources of international
law. The decision of permanent international organizations, reflecting "the general principles of law recognized by civilized
nations", as well as the "judicial decisions and the teachings
of the most highly qualified publicists of the various nations"
are also recognized as "subsidiary means for the determination
of rules of law". (146) The law of existing regional organizations and of many specialized agencies similarly constitute a
source of law. (147)

Determined attempts will need to be made in the process of transformation to expand the application of accepted principle into
new domains. At one level, this is exactly what the U.N. Law of
the Sea Conference is doing (cf. chapter 5). At another level,

Schachter has shown that the concept of 'needs' can be taken out
of the area of charity and linked to the notion of justice. 'Legitimate expectations' and historic entitlement are concepts
which are grounded in international law. Demands based on needs
can thus be linked to entitlements derived from accepted principles. (148)

The Need for a Framework Treaty

There are thus many instruments which can be used to progressively transform the international legal order. It will need to be
recognized, however, that international law has never distinguished itself as a forerunner of progress; and it never will,
for that is not its function. Positive law, while it can prod
and push, characteristically sanctions social and economic change
a posteriori. It will also need to be recognized that developments in international law in the past two decades - a period
which has witnessed as much legal activity as in the previous two
centuries - have resulted in an increase in the number of reservations made by states to the treaties adhered to by them. Parties to multilateral treaties have become more numerous while the
legal content of treaties has become 'shallower'. New uncertainties concerning the legal content of treaties may in fact have
added obstacles to the transformation of the international legal
order.

Something more than the 'due process of law' will thus be required to accelerate the transformation of the international legal
order and establish the basis for a more peaceful and equitable
world. If it is true, as Manuel Pérez Guerrero has suggested,
that "this is the great hour of international law", (149) it may
be legitimate to search for a legal solution which matches the
problems confronting us.

Arvid Pardo and the RIO Report have suggested an appropriate
response. (150) They argue that current legal problems could
most effectively be overcome through the negotiation and subsequent adoption by the rich and poor nations of a framework treaty
which clearly lays down the ground rules for international cooperation and the guiding principles to be adopted by nation-States
in the shaping of a more equitable international order. It would
constitute an umbrella treaty which would specify the principles
and mechanisms to be used in the negotiation of agreements for
specific problems or sets of problems. The treaty would thus be
concerned with procedures and define the mechanisms on the basis
of which substantive issues could be subsequently and progressively negotiated.

The framework treaty would not, therefore, constitute an attempt
to legislate a new world order in a single stroke. That would

obviously be absurd. Rather, its basic purpose would be, in
Pardo's words, "to make an unmistakable initial step toward international economic - and social - solidarity, and hence toward
a world order based upon cooperation rather than competition between States". (151) In serving as a legal foundation for a more
equitable international order "it would represent a binding commitment to peaceful structural change and to the elaboration of
a law of nations that serves the interests of all peoples, poor
as well as rich." (152)

The core of the treaty would contain provisions on three major
subjects. Firstly, the procedures to be used in the progressive
negotiation of substantive issues. Secondly, the establishment
of a flexible but also comprehensive, compulsory and binding
system for the settlement of the disputes arising from the interpretation or application of the treaty. And thirdly, the
treaty should contain provisions acceptable to states on matters
directly affecting international economic relations. Once ratified by a nation, the treaty would, in accordance with the legal
principle *pacta sunt servanda,* be legally binding.

Since the negotiation of a treaty could be used as a delaying or
diversionary tactic by enemies of a more equitable international
order, it would need to be organized in such a way that it does
not interfere with ongoing or planned North-South negotiations,
a point stressed by both Pardo and the RIO Report.

In addition to laying the legal foundation for the fairer sharing
of the world's resources, the framework treaty would carry several advantages. It might make it easier for - perhaps even encourage - Western governments to go to their people on a whole range
of policy choices which could be discussed in a broad perspective.
It would serve to demonstrate the readiness of the industrialized
countries to take seriously the claims of the developing countries for more equity in international economic relations and the
willingness of Third World nations to link the reform of the international order to changes in national orders. Moreover, since
the treaty would lay the foundations upon which a new order could
be progressively constructed, it would be very difficult for the
centrally planned economies to exclude themselves from its negotiation.

Transformation of the Charter
of Economic Rights and Duties of States

In drawing up the provisions of the framework treaty it would
neither be necessary nor desirable to begin with a fresh sheet
of paper. Pardo and the RIO Report suggest that it could be conveniently modelled on the Charter of Economic Rights and Duties
of States, adopted by the vast majority of nations in the U.N.
General Assembly on 12 December 1974. (153)

The Charter seeks to establish "generally accepted norms to govern international economic relations systematically" and "to
promote the establishment of a new international economic order,
based on equity, sovereign equality, common interest and cooperation among all States." Initiated by President Echeverría of
Mexico and prepared over a seventeen month period by a working
group of representatives from forty nations under the auspices
of UNCTAD, the Charter elaborates standards that would "protect
the rights of all countries and in particular the developing
states" and presents fifteen fundamentals which should govern international economic relations.

Although a very useful guide to the international community, the
Charter is a far from perfect document. A recent important Dutch
study has pointed to its many gaps, its lack of system and its
internal contradictions. (154) Notable deficiencies include its
failure to provide for the fundamental rights of all citizens
(as developed in earlier resolutions) and for the rights and duties of transnational corporations, main actors in the shaping
of international economic relations. The Charter fails to recognize that the use of sovereign rights can be limited by international law and thus does not acknowledge that functional sovereignty on specific subjects can be transferred to international
organizations. The Charter is also surprisingly weak in introducing new forms of the equity principle. On all these points,
the Charter can be judged to lag behind the actual state of development of international economic law. The Charter is also
strangely silent on such matters as the monetary order, food,
energy, the oceans and outer space. (155) All these and other
deficiencies lead the Dutch study to conclude that the Charter
might actually damage the interests of the developing countries
more than they do those of the industrialized countries.

Perhaps the biggest limitation when viewed in terms of its usefulness as a framework treaty is that the Charter is neither explicit with respect to the instruments and mechanisms to be used
in building a more equitable international order nor does it contain clear provisions for dispute settlement. The first of these
is particularly surprising in view of the Charter's implicit position that the market mechanism is an insufficient basis for a
NIEO.

Certain of the Charter's articles caused a good deal of gnashing
of teeth in the industrialized countries when they were discussed during the Twenty-Ninth Session of the U.N. General Assembly.
Article 2, the permanent sovereignty and nationalization provisions, and Article 28, the 'indexation' article, were particularly unpalatable to the developed countries and caused them, with a
single exception, to either abstain or to vote against the Charter.
(156) Their recalcitrance, however, was not alltogether justified.
With respect to nationalization, the legal system of property

rights in all Western nations is primarily a matter of national law, as provided for in the Charter. Similarly, in the case of raw materials the Charter simply applies the current practices of the Western nations on agricultural commodities to all raw materials. And the indexation principle has its legal roots firmly planted in the Western world. That these articles need not constitute a permanent obstacle to a reformulation of the Charter is evidenced by the preparedness of the developing countries to make them 'negotiable'. On the occasion of the Seventh Special Session, held just nine months after the adoption of the Charter, the developing countries chose to omit contentious issues, including that of permanent sovereignty over natural resources, from its working paper. This tactical concession was instrumental in engineering success and the then much heralded shift from confrontation to cooperation.

The Charter is subject to periodic review. Article 34 calls for five-yearly evaluations when "any improvements and additions which might become necessary" can be made. The transformation of the Charter into a framework treaty is thus provided for in the Charter. Such a transformation would be an ambitious undertaking - perhaps too ambitious given the prevailing political climate. In line with the idea of 'second best' solutions and a step-by-step approach to the development of a global planning and management capability, it might be more appropriate and realistic to seek to negotiate, not a single framework treaty, but a series of mini framework agreements, each covering one or a set of issue area(s). An agreement on ground rules, procedures and mechanisms could be negotiated, for example, with respect to the international monetary order, international trade, transnational corporations science and technology, raw materials and commodities, food production and distribution, and operational development assistance. In all these cases, the mini framework agreement would lay down and clarify the rules of the international game - rules which would subsequently be applied to the negotiation of substantive agreements. Alternatively, mini framework agreements could be negotiated on the basis of what Johan Kaufmann has called "institutional clusters" or of the "world economic communities" proposed by Elisabeth Mann Borgese. (157)

NOTES AND REFERENCES

(1) Jeffrey Schrank, *Snap, Crackle and Popular Taste: The Illusion of Free Choice in America*, Delta, New York, 1977, pp. 130-132.

(2) See Richard Falk, 'The Institutional Dimension of a New International Order', in A.J.Dolman (ed.), *Global Planning and Resource Management: International Decision-Making in a Divided World*, Pergamon, New York, 1980, pp. 87-102. For a short history of institution-building in the post-war

period and of the role of the developing countries in the
process, see Lars Anell and Birgitta Nygren, *The Developing
Countries and the World Economic System*, Frances Pinter,
London, 1980, chapter 1.

(3) See C.Fred Bergsten, 'Interdependence and the Reform of International Institutions', *International Organization*,
vol. 30, no. 2, Spring 1976, pp. 361-372.

(4) This view is cogently argued by Richard Falk, *This Endangered
Planet*, Random House, New York, 1971.

(5) This conclusion is reached by F.H.Hinsley after reviewing
attempts made in history to find institutional solutions to
the problems of war in his excellent *Power and the Pursuit
of Peace*, Cambridge University Press, London, 1963.

(6) For an argument of this case see the essays of Silviu Brucan
and Harlan Cleveland in A.J.Dolman, op.cit., pp. 53-71 and
pp. 72-86.

(7) See Ralph Dahrendorf, *Not the Westminster Model*, Third World
Monograph 2, Third World Foundation, London, 1979.

(8) For a review of the history of the United Nations, see Inis
L.Claude, *The Changing United Nations*, Random House, New
York, 1967.

(9) If the declaration had a historical precedent it was the
Quadruple Alliance of 1815 when Austria, Britain, Prussia
and Russia expressed their determination to maintain re-
settlement of Europe negotiated under Metternich's Congress
of Vienna, with its international peace-keeping machinery.

(10) Because the Soviet Union was neutral in the war with Japan,
it refused to meet directly with China. The talks were therefore arranged in two phases: between August 21 - September
28, the Soviet Union, U.K. and U.S. drafted proposals; between September 29 - October 7, British and U.S. experts
met with the Chinese to discuss and, eventually, to endorse
them.

(11) For the text of the Dumbarton Oaks proposals, see U.S.
Department of State, *Bulletin*, vol. XI, no. 276, October 8,
1944.

(12) Considerable influence was exerted on the conduct and outcome of the Conference by the private consultations of China,
the Soviet Union, U.K. and U.S., later joined by France, in
the penthouse apartment of Edward R.Stettinius, Jr., who
had replaced Cordell Hull as U.S. Secretary of State.

(13) The San Francisco conference had its own secretariat which
daily distributed documents in Chinese, English, French,
Spanish and Russian. The chairmanship of the plenary sessions rotated among the 'Big Four' sponsoring powers. The
Conference formed a Steering Committee, composed of the
heads of all the delegations, which decided all matters of
major principle and policy. An Executive Committee of 14
heads of delegations was chosen to prepare recommendations
to the Steering Committee.

(14) Quoted in Bert V.A.Röling, 'The United Nations - A General
     Evaluation', A.Cassese (ed.), in *UN Law/Fundamental Rights:
     Two Topics in International Law*, Sijthoff & Noordhoff,
     Alphen aan den Rijn, the Netherlands, 1979, pp. 23-38, at
     p. 23.
(15) The Charter contains 19 chapters, covering Purposes and
     Principles (Articles 1-2), Membership (Articles 3-6), Organs
     (Articles 7-8), The General Assembly (Articles 9-22), The
     Security Council (Articles 23-32), Pacific Settlements of
     Disputes (Articles 33-38), Action with Respect to Threats
     to the Peace, Breaches of the Peace, and Acts of Aggression
     (Articles 39-51), Regional Arrangements (Articles 52-54),
     International Economic and Social Cooperation (Articles
     55-60), The Economic and Social Council (Articles 61-72),
     Declaration Regarding Non Self-Governing Territories
     (Articles 73-74), International Trusteeship System (Ar-
     ticles 75-85), The Trusteeship Council (Articles 86-91),
     The International Court of Justice (Articles 92-96), The
     Secretariat (Articles 97-101), Miscellaneous Provisions
     (Articles 102-105), Transitional Security Arrangements
     (Articles 106-107), Amendments (Articles 108-109) and
     Ratification and Signature (Articles 110-111).
(16) Quoted in Gabriel Kolko, *The Politics of War: The World and
     United States Foreign Policy, 1943-1945*, Random House, New
     York, 1968, p. 251.
(17) For an analysis of Hull's contribution to the creation of
     the United Nations, see J.W.Pratt, *Cordell Hull: 1933-1944*,
     Cooper Square, Totowa, New Jersey, 1964.
(18) Daniel P.Moynihan, 'Party and International Politics',
     Commentary, vol. 63, no. 2, February, 1977, pp. 56-59, at
     p. 57.
(19) See UNCIO, vol. VIII, 1945, p. 146.
(20) The developing nations which attended the Conference were:
     (i) *Africa*: Egypt, Ethiopia and Liberia; (ii) *Asia*: China,
     India, Iran, Iraq, Lebanon, Philippines, Saudi Arabia,
     Syria and Turkey; (iii) *Latin America*: Argentina, Bolivia,
     Brazil, Chile, Colombia, Costa Rica, Cuba, Dominican Repu-
     blic, Ecuador, El Salvador, Guatemala, Haiti, Honduras,
     Mexico, Nicaragua, Panama, Paraguay, Peru, Uruguay and
     Venezuela.
(21) See Röling, op.cit.
(22) UNCIO, vol. I, 1945, pp. 552 and 706.
(23) Ibid, pp. 15 and 252.
(24) 'Oldest' of the specialized agencies are the ITU, which
     was originally established in 1865, the UPU whose origins
     go back to 1875, and the WMO, which has its origins in the
     International Meteorological Organization, a non-govern-
     mental body founded in 1878. The ILO was established in 1919
     under the Treaty of Versailles and functioned autonomously
     in the League of Nations system, eventually to become the

first of the U.N.'s specialized agencies. Similarly, the
WHO, which became operational in 1948, inherited various
duties from the League's Health Organization and from the
International Office of Public Health, a Paris based organization established before the First World War. 'New'
specialized agencies included the FAO (established 1945),
UNESCO (1946) and ICAO (1947).

(25) Quoted in Kolko, op.cit., p. 257.
(26) For a discussion of the differences between Harry Dexter
White and John Maynard Keynes before, during and after the
Bretton Woods conference, see Armand van Dormael, *Bretton
Woods: Birth of a Monetary System*, Macmillan, London, 1978.
(27) See Herbert Feis, *Churchill, Roosevelt, Stalin*, Princeton
University Press, Princeton, N.J., 1967, viz. pp. 648-657;
and Lloyd C.Gardner, *Architects of Illusion: Men and Ideas
in American Foreign Policy*, New Viewpoints, New York, 1972.
(28) 'American Foreign Policy', Address by the President, *The
Department of State Bulletin*, no. 278, 22 October 1944,
pp. 447-449.
(29) The figures are quoted in Frank Barnaby, 'Arms and the
Third World', *New Scientist*, 7 April 1977, p. 30.
(30) Abraham Yeselson and Anthony Gaglione, *A Dangerous Place:
The United Nations as a Weapon in World Politics*, Grossman,
New York, 1974, p. X. In their opinion "the United Nations
contributes about as much to peace as a battleship or an
atomic bomb." (p. X).
(31) Yeselson and Gaglione, op.cit., refer to the use of the
U.N. for what they term, politics of embarrassment, politics
of status, politics of legitimization, and politics of socialization. Under politics of embarrassment nations bring
disputes to the U.N. with the purpose "to inflict some
gratuitous hurt, to gain a symbolic victory where no other
is possible, to express frustration and anger" (p. 31)
rather than with the intention of seeking a settlement.
Politics of status refers to the use of U.N. "forums, processes and decisions in order to advance legal positions
that have some bearing on the conflictual political purposes of member states." (p. 59) Politics of legitimization
can take various forms all of which are designed to show
that a state has the right on its side, a right which should
be reflected in the use of U.N. machinery. By politics of
socialization reference is made to the bringing of issues
to the U.N. "by those who hope to add some legal, moral,
or even material support to their cause because they do
not otherwise possess sufficient means to win." (p. 123)
(32) The term 'justice constituency' is taken from Oscar Schachter, *Sharing the World's Resources*, Columbia University
Press, New York, 1977, p. 3.
(33) See Joseph S.Nye, 'Independence and Interdependence',
Foreign Affairs, vol. 24, 1976, pp. 130-161, viz. pp. 146-

147; and Seymour M.Finger, 'United States Policy Toward International Institutions', *International Organization*, vol. 30, no. 2, Spring 1976, pp. 347-360. The argument that nations should selectively participate in the U.N. system, making use of only those agencies and programs which advance their interests is advanced by David A.Kay, 'On the Reform of International Institutions: A Comment', *International Organization*, vol. 30, no. 3, Summer 1976, pp. 533-538.

(34) For a Third World appraisal of Western control of the U.N., see Mohammed Bedjaoui, *Towards a New International Economic Order*, Holmes & Meier, New York/London, 1979, viz. Part II, chapter 1 and 2.

(35) See Marc Nerfin, 'Is a Democratic United Nations System Possible?, *Development Dialogue*, vol. 2, 1976, pp. 79-94. Nerfin believes that similar skewed patterns could be found in the specialized agencies.

(36) The collapse of the Bretton Woods institutions may be helping to redress this situation. According to a report in the *Frankfurter Allgemeine* (14 March 1979, p. 10), developed country representatives are leaving the U.N. because, following the fall in the value of the dollar, the U.N. no longer pays them enough to keep them there.

(37) Johan Kaufmann, whose experience with the U.N. extends over nearly 20 years. See 'The United Nations as a World Development Authority', in A.J.Dolman, op.cit., pp. 103-115, at p. 108.

(38) Hernane Tavares de Sà, quoted by Nerfin, op.cit., p. 90.

(39) The Jackson report was published by the U.N. under the title *A Study of the Capacity of the United Nations Development System*, document DP/5, 2 vols., Geneva, 1969.

(40) See United Nations, *A New United Nations Structure for Global Economic Cooperation. Report of the Group of Experts on the Structure of the United Nations System*, document E/AC.62/9, New York, May 1975. This report was the result of a decision taken at the Sixth Special Session. It is well aware that its focus on economic efficiency leaves power positions intact. It notes (para 10) that "Every serious reform proposal (as opposed to marginal proposals that amount to mere 'tinkering') is bound to cut across someone's vested interest in the *status quo*. A meaningful reform of the system, to take account of new requirements and developments, may involve the foregoing of some short-term interests and entrenched habits in favour of long-term interests in a workable international economic order".

(41) See U.N. document A/PV 2231.

(42) See U.N. document A/PV 2229.

(43) A "top American economic official" following the Colombo Non-Aligned Summit, quoted in *U.S.News and World Report*, 16 August 1976.

(44) Bedjaoui, op.cit., pp. 161-167, for example, refers to a mimeographed U.S. document entitled 'Report of the Secretary of State to the President on Reform and Restructuring of the United Nations System', of 28 February 1978, which reviews alternative ways whereby the developed countries can shield themselves from 'automatic majority' and preserve their present privileged position.

(45) Gaston Thorn, quoted in Bedjaoui, op.cit., p. 145.

(46) See C.Fred Bergsten, 'Interdependence and the Reform of International Institutions', *International Organization*, vol. 30, no. 2, Spring 1976, pp. 361-372.

(47) See Bo Huldt, 'Institutional Dependence: Sweden and the United Nations - History and Future Perspectives', Paper prepared as part of the project 'Sweden in the World Society', Secretariat for Futures Studies, Stockholm, Sweden, September 1976 (mimeo).

(48) The first major assistance program of the U.N. was the United Nations Relief and Rehabilitation Administration (UNRRA). It was established as a result of an international agreement signed by 44 nations at the White House on November 9, 1943 after a series of negotiations that began in London in 1940. UNRRA was created to assist the war damaged nations in greatest need and unable to finance the imports required to meet the needs of those displaced by war. In today's terminology it could be called a basic needs organization. It operated in 25 countries and its programs, which were aimed at "helping people to help themselves", are said to have reached more than one billion persons. At its peak, the staff employed by UNRRA numbered 25,000. Special funding targets were formulated for the organization. All United Nations countries not invaded during the Second World War, were asked to contribute 1 per cent of their national income for the fiscal year ending 30 June, 1943. In the 4 years of its existence, UNRRA's budget exceeded $ 4 billion, the U.S., U.K. and Canada being the largest contributors. UNRRA discontinued activities in 1947, handing over its uncompleted projects and unexpended assets to the International Refugee Organization, UNICEF and WHO.

(49) The first step in the direction of creating programs specifically designed to meet the needs of the developing world was a General Assembly resolution passed in 1946 which called for the establishment of machinery within the Secretariat for the provision of technical assistance. As a consequence of this decision, the Expanded Programme of Technical Assistance (EPTA) was established which became operational when approved by the General Assembly in 1949. It was financed by voluntary contributions from member States, pledges being made at an annual conference convened for that purpose. In the period 1950-1956, annual expenditures were typically in the order of $ 25 million.

In the mid 1950s the United Nations took several steps to
increase the flow of funds for the financing of development
projects. In July 1956 it established the IFC as an affili-
ate of the World Bank for the purpose of encouraging the
growth of productive private enterprise, particularly in
the developing countries. Established to supplement the activities of the World Bank, the IFC was able to make direct
loans available for private enterprise projects which failed
to meet the Bank's 'commercial' requirements for loans.
Loans can be extended by the IFC, for example, for projects
without government guarantees.
In 1957, the General Assembly established a Special United
Nations Fund for Economic Development (SUNFED) for the
special purpose of financing projects which were considered
'commercially unattractive'. The Special Fund became the
U.N.'s most important instrument for funding development
oriented projects. By 1965 it was supporting 59 projects
in the non-agricultural field, involving $ 55 million in
Fund allocations.
During the late 1950s it became increasingly clear that the
World Bank, because of its commercial practices, was in many
respects an unsatisfactory mechanism for funding development
projects. Many such projects, with their necessary emphasis
on social as well as economic development, failed to achieve
the status of 'bankable proposals' and thus failed to quali-
fy for World Bank support. It was a recognition of this
problem which had led to the creation of the IFC. As far
as many developing countries were concerned, however, the
IFC was still too rigid in its banking and loan procedures.
The particular problems of a growing number of developing
countries led the General Assembly to establish, in September 1960, the International Development Association (IDA).
The IDA was specifically created to finance any project
"which will make an important contribution to the development of an area or areas concerned, whether the project is
revenue producing or directly productive". It was authorized
to pursue this goal by extending 'soft' loans to developing
countries, i.e. by providing finance on terms which are
more flexible and bear less heavily on the balance of payments of recipient countries than do conventional loans.
It was during the 1960s, with the first U.N. Development
Decade, that U.N. efforts in the development field intensified and diversified. At the beginning of the '60s, both
EPTA and SUNFED continued to assume a central importance,
ECOSOC urging in 1962 the "prompt attainment" of the tar-
get, contained in the proposals drawn up by the Secretary-
General for DD I, of $ 150 million for both EPTA and SUNFED.
It was in 1965, when the failures and disappointments with
DD I were becoming increasingly evident, that the General
Assembly decided to combine EPTA and SUNFED into a single

program to be known as the United Nations Development Pro-
gramme (UNDP).
(50) See Osvaldo Sunkel, 'The Development of Development
Thinking', *Liaison Bulletin*, no. 1, OECD Development
Centre, Paris, 1977, pp. 9-17.
(51) Dudley Seers, 'The Birth, Life and Death of Development
Economics', *Development and Change*, vol. 10, no. 4,
October 1979, pp. 707-719, at 708.
(52) The best known representatives of linear approach to
development are probably Daniel Lerner in sociology and
Walt Rostow in economics. See Lerner's, *The Passing of
Traditional Society*, Free Press, New York, 1964; and Ros-
tow's, *The Stages of Economic Growth. A Non-Communist
Manifesto*, Cambridge University Press, Cambridge, 1960.
For a radical review of early development theories, see
T.Szentes, *The Political Economy of Underdevelopment*,
Akadémiai Kiadó, Budapest, 1976.
(53) Daniel P.Moynihan, 'The United States in Opposition',
Commentary, March 1975, pp. 31-44, at p. 40.
(54) See Irving L.Horowitz, 'The United Nations and the Third
World: East-West Conflict in Focus', in R.Gregg and M.Bor-
kun (eds.), *The United Nations System and its Functions*,
Van Nostrand, Princeton, N.J., 1968, pp. 350-357; and Inis
L.Claude, Jr., *The Changing United Nations*, Random House,
New York, 1967.
(55) See Herbert J.Spiro, *World Politics: The Global System*,
Dorsey Press, Homewood, Ill., 1966, p. 129.
(56) For a discussion of the power of U.N. resolutions, see
A.J.P.Tammes, 'Decisions of International Organs as a
Source of International Law', *Recueil des Cours*, vol. 94,
no. 11, 1958, pp. 265-284; Rosalyn Higgins, *The Development
of International Law Through the Political Organs of the
United Nations*, Oxford University Press, London/New York,
1963; Jorge Castañeda, *Legal Effects of United Nations
Resolutions*, Columbia University Press, New York, 1969;
Oscar Schachter, 'Toward a Theory of International Obligation', in Stephen Schwebel (ed.), *The Effectiveness of International Decisions*, Sijthoff, Leiden, 1971; Bert V.A.
Röling, 'International Law and the Maintenance of Peace',
Netherlands Yearbook of International Law, vol. IV, 1973,
pp. 1-103; and Maurice Mendelson, 'The Legal Character of
General Assembly Resolutions: Some Considerations of Principle', in J.K.Hossain (ed.), *Legal Aspects of the New International Economic Order*, Frances Pinter, London, 1980,
pp. 95-107. See also the collection of papers (including
that of Tammes, and the ones by Higgins and Schachter) in
Richard A.Falk and Saul H.Mendlovitz, *The United Nations*,
World Law Fund, New York, 1966, part 2.
(57) Louis Henkin, *How Nations Behave: Law and Foreign Policy*
Columbia University Press, New York, 1979, p. 47.

(58) William Coplin, 'International Organizations in the Future
Bargaining Process: A Theoretical Projection', *Journal of
International Affairs*, vol. 25, 1971, pp. 287-301.
(59) For a discussion of the differences between 'knowledge
base' and 'institutional capacity', see John G.Ruggie,
'On the Problem of 'The Global Problematique': What Roles
for International Organizations?', *Alternatives*, vol. V,
no. 4, January 1980, pp. 517-550, viz. pp. 526-549.
(60) See Charles W.Maynes, 'A U.N. Policy for the Next Administration', *Foreign Policy*, vol. 54, 1975-76, pp. 804-819.
The 'next administration' was of course the Carter administration in which Charles Maynes served as Under-Secretary
of State for International Organizations. Did the Carter
administration have a U.N. policy?
(61) See Ruggie, op.cit., pp. 526-527.
(62) Cases where secretariats have been able to influence outcomes include the Stockholm Human Environment Conference
(1972) where the secretariat, under the direction of
Maurice Strong, achieved a great deal through the way in
which it organized the preparatory process and participated
in negotiations. The secretariat's record is assessed in
Ruggie, op.cit., pp. 538-540. The most notable institutional
'success story' may well be UNCTAD. The way in which it was
able to influence the outcome of the 1970 agreement on the
Generalized Scheme of Preferences is described in Anindya K.
Bhattacharya, 'The Influence of the International Secretariat: UNCTAD and Generalized Tariff Preferences', *International Organization*, vol. 30, no. 1, winter 1976, pp. 75-
90. Other evaluations of UNCTAD's performance are Branislav
Gosovic, *UNCTAD: Conflict and Compromise*, Sijthoff, Leiden,
1972; and Robert L.Rothstein, *Global Bargaining: UNCTAD and
the Quest for a New International Economic Order*, Princeton
University Press, Princeton, N.J., 1979.
(63) Ruggie, op.cit., pp. 544-548. The Cocoyoc Declaration was
drafted by a distinguished group of 32 scientists and U.N.
officials who attended the UNEP/UNCTAD Symposium on 'Patterns of Resource Use, Environment and Development Strategies', held at Cocoyoc, near Mexico City, on 8-12 October
1974. The text of the Declaration is contained in U.N.
document A/C.2/292, 1974. It has been widely reprinted,
among others in *International Organization*, vol. 29, summer
1975, pp. 893-901; *Alternatives*, vol. I, nos. 2-3, July-
September, 1975, pp. 396-406; and *Development Dialogue*,
no. 2, 1974, pp. 88-96.
(64) Alistair Buchan, *Change Without War: The BBC Reith Lec-
tures 1973*, Chatto and Windus, London, 1974, p. 106.
(65) On the personalization of foreign policy, see Robert L.
Rothstein, *The Weak in the World of the Strong: The Developing Countries in the International System*, Columbia
University Press, New York, 1977, chapter 4.

(66) The physical handicaps and physic abnormalities of some of history's 'greats' are described by Antonia Fraser in *Heroes and Heroines*, Weidenfield, London, 1980.

(67) See Hugh l'Etang, *Fit to Lead?*, Heinemann Medical, London, 1980. He argues that men get to the top often only at the cost of physical and psychic injury, much of it self-inflicted through compulsive overwork, adrenalin dependence, alcoholism and self-medication. When they reach the top they may become unfit to lead. The state of the international system would seem to suggest that a good many of them are unfit while still at the bottom.

(68) See Joseph S.Nye, 'Transnational and Transgovernmental Relations', in G.L.Goodwin and A.Linklater (eds.), *New Dimensions of World Politics*, Croom Helm, London, 1975, pp. 36-53.

(69) See Joseph S.Nye, 'Independence and Interdependence', *Foreign Affairs*, vol. 24, 1976, pp. 130-161, viz. p. 157 ff. See also the essays of Silviu Brucan, Harland Cleveland, Richard Falk, and Johan Kaufmann in A.J.Dolman, op.cit., pp. 53-71, 72-86, 87-102 and 103-115.

(70) For a discussion of the coordination issue, see Robert I. McLaren, 'The UN System and its Quixotic Quest for Coordination', *International Organization*, vol. 34, no. 1, winter 1980, pp. 139-148.

(71) This thesis is developed in Yeselson and Gaglione, op.cit.

(72) There are those who argue that the structure of the U.N. is basically sound. Martin Hill, an Assistant Secretary-General for Inter-Agency Affairs, for example, argues this case in *The United Nations System: Coordinating its Economic and Social Work*, Cambridge University Press, Cambridge, 1978. In his view, the U.N. requires "the care of the physician rather than the knife of a surgeon". (p. 148)

(73) See Silviu Brucan, op.cit., viz. pp. 58-59.

(74) On this see Miriam Camps, *The Management of Interdependence: A Preliminary View*, Council on Foreign Relations, Inc., New York, 1974.

(75) See Jan Tinbergen, 'The Need for an Ambitious Innovation of the World Order', *Journal of International Affairs*, vol. 31, no. 2, Fall/Winter 1977, pp. 305-314, viz. pp. 308-309.

(76) Jan Tinbergen (Coordinator), *Reshaping the International Order: A Report to The Club of Rome*, E.P.Dutton, New York, 1976, p. 104.

(77) See Albert Tévoédjrè, *Poverty: Wealth of Mankind*, Pergamon, New York/Oxford, 1979, pp. 145-150 for a discussion of this point.

(78) Ernst Haas, *Beyond the Nation State*, Stanford University Press, Stanford, Ca., 1964; and *The Uniting of Europe*, Stevens, London, 1958.

(79) David A.Morse, former Director-General of ILO, was fond of pointing to the organization's political character. "I think

politics will always be with us in the ILO", he told the
International Labour Conference in 1956. "It is time", he
went on, "that we cast aside any remaining illusions that
this could ever be a purely technical body". He returned to
this theme at the 1957 Conference. "We cannot assume", he
said, "that the objectives for which this organization was
established are universally accepted or that where they are
accepted people mean the same things by them". Quoted in
Tévoédjrè, op.cit., p. 146 and p. 147.

(80) For an interesting example of the institution-building
required, see Brian Johnson, *Whose Power to Choose? International Institutions and the Control of Nuclear Energy*,
International Institute for Environment and Development,
London, 1977. Johnson presents a strategy for restructuring
and improving the effectiveness of international energy institutions with the aim of overcoming some of the risks of
a plutonium economy as well as of offering developing countries a greater choice in planning for their energy needs
than presently available in international institutions.

(81) The distinction between decision-makers (those who prepare
through analyses and recommendation, for decisions) and
decision-takers (those with formally constituted responsibilities for taking decisions) is more useful. In this sense,
the decision-makers (specialists) determine the choices of
decision-takers (politicians), the difference frequently
being one of *de facto* and *de jure* decision-making.

(82) As the RIO Report, op.cit., p. 118, points out, the usefulness of scientific opinion is illustrated by the experience
of the Pugwash Conferences. On some issues of arms control
the scientists involved reached agreement before politicians,
simply because they had a sounder understanding of the subject matter, including, for instance, the discovery possi--
bilities and limitations of nuclear testing. Specialist
opinion has also played a particularly important role in
shaping political opinion in the case of the Law of the Sea
conference.

(83) Hasan Ozbekhan, quoted in E.Jantsch, *Technological Forecasting in Perspective*, OECD, Paris, 1967, p. 291.

(84) There are of course cases where expert opinion plays an
important role in framing policy, such as the U.N. Committee
for Development Planning.

(85) This is well covered in Ervin Laszlo, *A Strategy for the
Future: The Systems Approach to World Order*, Braziller, New
York, 1974.

(85) For a discussion of the differences between systems and
networks, see Anthony Judge, 'International Organization
Networks: A Complementary Perspective', in P.Taylor and
A.J.R.Groom (eds.), *International Organization: A Conceptual Approach*, Francis Pinter, London, 1978, 381-413, viz.
pp. 387-391.

(87) Jackson Report, op.cit., vol. 1, p. 13.

(88) See R.I.McLaren, op.cit.

(89) Mahbub ul Haq, *The Poverty Curtain: Choices for the Third World*, Columbia University Press, New York, 1976.

(90) See Jan Tinbergen, *Central Planning*, Yale University Press, New Haven, 1964. For a shorter description of indicative planning and the way it has been used by French national planners, see Lester R.Brown, *The Twenty-Ninth Day*, W.W. Norton, New York, 1978, pp. 305-310.

(91) Harlan Cleveland, op.cit., p. 80.

(92) See Paul Davidoff and Thomas A.Reiner, 'A Choice Theory of Planning', *Journal of the American Institute of Planners*, vol. 28, May 1962, pp. 103-115.

(93) The Commission's report goes on to compare the planning employed by capitalist corporations with centrally planned States: "There are general goals set by top management, against which far-flung affiliates generate plans for a year's, 5 years' or 10 years' activity. These local plans then are fought out at the regional headquarters level, where goals, inputs, outputs and financial needs are recommended. The regional executive then carries "his" plan to a confrontation with his colleagues and top management at "the Kremlin" (U.S. headquarters), where still more recommendations and compromises are made." U.S. Tariff Commission, *Implications for World Trade and Investment and for U.S. Trade and Labor of Multinational Corporations*, Senate Finance Committee, Washington, D.C., 1973, p. 159.

(94) Ways in which the so-called 'like-minded countries', a group of small industrialized countries with a 'progressive' reputation, could seek to assist a group of poor developing countries in their technological transformation is the subject of Antony J.Dolman, *The Like-Minded Countries and the Industrial and Technological Transformation of the Third World*, RIO Foundation, Rotterdam, 1979.

(95) For a general discussion of the problem of transaction costs, see E.J.Mishan, 'The Post-War Literature on Externalities: An Interpretative Essay', *Journal of Economic Literature*, vol. IX, 1971, pp. 21-24. He argues that transaction costs "increase with the numbers involved, probably at an exponential rate", (p. 22) a thesis which has generally been borne out by the experience of the 1970s.

(96) Oscar Schachter, *Sharing the World's Resources*, Columbia University Press, New York, 1977, p. 65.

(97) See Oran Young, *Resource Management at the International Level: The Case of the North Pacific*, Frances Pinter, London/Nichols Publishing, New York, 1977. He argues that international resource regions could be the most appropriate managerial unit for resource management. He believes that there are compelling reasons for stopping at the level of the region rather than treating the entire global system

as the managerial unit for resource problems.

(98) Ibid, p. 22. The argument for regional arrangements in the
realm of resource management and environmental quality is
judged by Young to be "analytically parallel to the argument for customs unions in the realm of standard economic
interactions. The essential idea is to supplement other
administrative or managerial units rather than to replace
them". (p.25)

(99) In the case of Beringa, Young believes that the most appropriate institutional regime would be a regional authority
based on loose confederal arrangements encompassing a set
of specific institutional arrangements for individual functional areas tied together and integrated through the operation of an overreaching umbrella agency.(pp. 203-213)

(100) This process is described in Anthony Downs, *Inside Bureaucracy*, Little, Brown, Boston, 1967.

(101) For a definition and discussion of positional and resource
power, see Johan Galtung, 'Power and Global Planning and
Resource Management', in A.J.Dolman (ed.), *Global Planning
and Resource Management: Toward International Decision-
Making in a Divided World*, Pergamon, New York, 1980, pp.
119-145.

(102) On this see Johan Galtung, 'Nonterritorial Actors and the
Problem of Peace', in Saul H.Mendlovitz (ed.), *On the Crea-
tion of a Just World Order: Preferred Worlds for the 1990s*,
Free Press, New York, 1975, pp. 151-188.

(103) For a definition and discussion of ideological power,
see Galtung, op.cit., 1980.

(104) This is sometimes a matter of sheer numbers. For example,
the U.S. had about 160 staff working solely on the GATT
Tokyo Round of negotiations in Geneva.

(105) See 'A Third World Secretariat', *Third World Forum Newsletter*, June 1979, p. 1.

(106) G.K.Helleiner, in his introduction to *A World Divided:
The Less Developed Countries in the International Economy*,
Cambridge University Press, London, 1976, p. 17.

(107) The view of Johan Galtung, op.cit., 1980, p. 138.

(108) See, for example, James W.Howe et al., *The Developing
Countries in a Changing International Economic Order: A
Survey of Research Needs*, Occasional Paper No. 7, Overseas
Development Council, Washington, D.C. 1973. The recently
published OECD *Register of Development Research Projects
in Latin America*, Paris, 1979, lists more than 400 research
projects. Of this only 5 have as their subject the New International Economic Order.

(109) Sri Lanka's Mrs. Bandaranaike called for the creation of
a Third World Secretariat at a meeting of the Group of 77
held in Geneva in 1975. In 1976 a working group was established to examine alternative organizational models, its
results being published by UNCTAD, *Report on the Proposal*

for the Establishment of a Secretariat of the Group of 77,
document CA/843, GE 76-64251, Geneva, 1976. Since then a
stream of Third World leaders and spokesmen, including
Julius Nyerere, Shridath S.Ramphal, Mahbub ul Haq and
Ismail Sabri Abdalla, have called for its creation, as have
such First World scholars as Johan Galtung and Gerald K.
Helleiner. For a sample of views see Mahbub ul Haq, *The
Poverty Curtain: Choices for the Third World*, Columbia
University Press, New York, 1976, p. 182 ff; Julius Nyerere,
'Unity for a New Order', Inaugural Address to the Ministerial Conference of the Group of 77, Arusha, 12 February,
1979, reprinted in *IFDA Dossier*, (Nyon), no. 5, March 1979;
Shridath S.Ramphal, 'Not by Unity Alone: The Case for a
Third World Organization', *Third World Quarterly*, vol. 1,
no. 3, July 1979, pp. 43-52; G.K.Helleiner, 'An OECD for
the Third World', *IDS Bulletin*, vol. 7, no. 4, April 1976,
and Johan Galtung, op.cit., 1980.
(110) *Third World Forum Newsletter*, June 1979, p. 35.
(111) See 'Third World Secretariat', *Third World Forum Newsletter*, March 1980, pp. 4-6, at p. 5.
(112) On this see John White, 'International Agencies: The Case
for Proliferation', in G.K.Helleiner, op.cit., 1976.
(113) The RIO Report suggests (p. 107), for example, that OPEC
countries in the Middle East, a water deficit area, and
countries in South Asia with a water surplus could possibly
benefit from mutual cooperation. Interestingly, Japan is
currently examining the feasibility of shipping water to
the Middle East in part exchange for oil.
(114) An example of such a new organization - a Third World
regional secretariat - is SELA (Latin American Economic
System) based in Caracas. SELA draws up policies which
Latin American nations could adopt in negotiations with,
for example, the EEC and in various U.N. fora.
(115) In this context it can be legitimately asked whether the
interests of the smallest developing countries might not
best be served in democratic global institutions rather
than in Third World regional institutions dominated by
hegemonic powers.
(116) See Hugh Seton-Watson, *Nations and States*, Methuen, London, 1979 for a 'history' of the evolution of the nation-
State.
(117) The relationship between the Peace of Westphalia and the
evolution of international law is discussed in Richard A.
Falk, 'The Interplay of Westphalia and Charter Conceptions
of International Legal Order', in Richard A.Falk and Cyril
E.Black, *The Future of the International Legal Order.
Volume I: Trends and Patterns*, Princeton University Press,
Princeton, N.J., 1969, pp. 32-70.
(118) Kwame Nkrumah of course argued that the carving up of
colonial empires into artificial units - "into small non-

viable states which are incapable of independent development" - was a deliberate policy followed by the colonial
powers aimed at ensuring that the resulting external and
internal weaknesses would serve to maintain situations of
dependence. See *Neo-Colonialism: The Last Stage of Imperialism*, International Publishers, New York, 1965 (quotation
p. xii).

(119) On this see Edward Shils, 'On the Comparative Study of
the New States', in Clifford Geertz, (ed.), *Old Societies
and New States*, Free Press, New York, 1963, viz. p. 22.

(120) This process has been stressed by such radical scholars
as Samir Amin. See, for example, his *Unequal Development*,
Monthly Review Press, 1976, chapter 4. Less radical scholars
have argued that the fissiparous character of poor and weak
States has been the reason why they have been unable to
establish satisfactory relationships with the international
system. It aggravates the problem of being 'small' in a
'big' world. This view is expounded by Robert L.Rothstein,
*The Weak in the World of the Strong: The Developing Coun-
tries in the International System*, Columbia University
Press, New York, 1977.

(121) For a discussion of this, see Gerald A.Heeger, *The Politics
of Underdevelopment*, Macmillan, London, 1974.

(122) See Karl W.Deutsch, *Nationalism and Social Communication*,
John Wiley, New York, 1953, viz. chapter 8.

(123) It is worth noting that it is only comparatively recently
that industrialized countries have emerged as reasonably
homogeneous units. Britain, for example, likes to refer to
the signing of Magna Carta in 1215 as the date at which the
freedom of its citizens was recognized and guaranteed. Yet
in the fifteenth century, the North and South of England
(to say nothing of Wales and Scotland), were barely able
to communicate with each other. Even in the middle of the
nineteenth century, as Britain was beginning to consolidate
its Empire, there were two distinct cultures and ways of life
in the North and South - worlds that existed virtually in
isolation to each other. This is well described in Elisabeth
Gaskell's novel *North and South*, first published in 1855
(Penguin Books, Harmondsworth, 1970). Nor are the industrialized countries all that homogeneous today. Many
threaten to be torn apart by minority groups determined to
assert their cultural identity or economic power. France
has its Bretons, Corsicans, Alsatians and the Occitanians
of Gascony; Spain its Basques and Catalans; Belgium its
Flemings and Walloons; the United Kingdom its Scots and
Welsh; Canada its Quebecois and 'Westerners'. In the U.S.S.R.
Georgians protest Russion domination, and Abkhazians the
heavy hand of the Georgians.

(124) See Jean Piel, 'The Current Role of the Nation-State', in
Immanuel Wallerstein (ed.), *World Inequalities*, Bertrand

Russell Peace Foundation, London, 1975, pp. 98-111.

(125) See the argument in Hedley Bull, *The Anarchical Society: A Study of Order in World Politics*, Columbia University Press, New York, 1977.

(126) Johan Galtung, op.cit., 1975, p. 187.

(127) The view, not shared by radical circles, of Benjamin Cohen, *The Question of Imperialism*, Macmillan, 1974, p. 245.

(128) See the RIO Report, section 5.8 for a discussion of the need for cooperation in defense of sovereignty.

(129) Edward Heath, quoted in *Time Magazine*, April 21, 1975.

(130) Michael Manley, ex premier of Jamaica, quoted in *Development Forum*, June-July 1975, p. 5.

(131) Carlos Andrés Pérez, ex President of Venezuela, interviewed in *Time Magazine*, 3 November 1975.

(132) For a discussion of the role and problems of small states in international politics, see, for example, David Vital, *The Inequality of States: A Study of the Small Power in International Relations*, Clarendon Press, Oxford, 1967; and *The Survival of Small States: Studies in Small Power/Great Power Conflict*, Oxford University Press, Oxford, 1971. The question is also discussed in Robert L.Rothstein, op.cit., and *Alliances and Small Powers*, Columbia University Press, New York, 1968.

(133) In this context, the developing countries can take little comfort from recent reports of the ability of transnational corporations to penetrate, and to influence decisions within, the United Nations. Through close links between themselves and with government officials and ministers, corporations have been able, for example, to either weaken or postpone some U.N. initiatives designed to curb their power. See the report of the Swiss-based Declaration of Berne, *The Infiltration of the UN System by Multinational Corporations*, Berne, 1978.

(134) For a description of these phases see Bert V.A.Röling, *International Law in an Expanded World*, Djambatan, Amsterdam, 1960, chapters 3-5.

(135) See P.Verloren van Themaat, *Rechtsgrondslagen van een Nieuwe International Economische Orde*, Asser Instituut, The Hague, 1979, pp. 1-2. Typical of the limited attention is the fact that Wolfgang Friedmann's avant-garde and widely quoted work *The Changing Structure of International Law*, (Columbia University Press, New York, 1964) has only a few pages devoted to the issue.

(136) Louis Henkin, op.cit., p. 314.

(137) See Oscar Schachter, *Sharing the World's Resources*, Columbia University Press, New York, Part II. For a discussion of ways in which the challenge could be met, see the collection of papers in Kamal Hossain (ed.), *Legal Aspects of the New International Economic Order*, Frances Pinter, London, 1980.

(138) See the RIO Report, p. 115.

(139) See especially the very comprehensive study coordinated
      by P.Verloren van Themaat, op.cit. The study involved some
      20 experts and advisers over a period of several years.
(140) The need and inevitability of such an extrapolation is
      discussed in Röling, op.cit., 1960.
(141) Röling, op.cit., 1960, p. 122.
(142) On this, see William D.Coplin, *The Function of Inter-
      national Law*, Rand McNally, Chicago, 1966, p. 100 ff.
(143) Inis L.Claude, *The Changing United Nations*, Random House,
      New York, 1967, p. 58.
(144) This is discussed in Christopher Pinto, 'Toward a Regime
      for International Public Property', in A.J.Dolman, op.cit.,
      1980, pp. 202-224.
(145) See the references listed under footnote 56.
(146) Article 38 of the Statute of the International Court of
      Justice.
(147) Interesting examples of possible instruments include the
      quasi-legislative procedure of the International Labour
      Office, the use of conditional financial incentives
      by the World Bank, the International Monetary Fund and the
      European Communities, the refined system of sanctions of the
      International Monetary Fund, the persuasive force of the
      Annual Review procedures and escape-clause supervision in
      the Organization for Economic Cooperation and Development,
      and the concept of 'enforceable community rights' enabling
      individuals to request the national courts in the European
      Communities to apply community law so as to force the
      national administration to abide by their international
      obligations under that law.
(148) Schachter, op.cit. He argues that the linking of needs and
      entitlement is "not merely a matter of "dialectics" or
      rhetoric. It reflects a political judgement that as an
      international criterion the maxim "to each according to
      his need" is too impractical and far-reaching in its impli-
      cations to win acceptance as a general principle; but that
      when this maxim is conjoined with and limited by a principle
      of legitimacy, it becomes more acceptable because less
      threatening to the international order. In short, the Aris-
      totelian principle of distributive justice may be seen as
      implicit in the normative assumptions of governments and
      as providing a counterpoint to competing egalitarian con-
      ceptions." (p. 20)
(149) Manuel Pérez Guerrero, 'The New International Economic
      Order and the International Law', Paper presented to The
      Third World and the International Law, 20th International
      Seminar for Diplomats, Salzburg, 1 August 1977, p. 23
      (mimeo).
(150) See the RIO Report, pp. 116-117; and Arvid Pardo, 'Buil-
      ding the New International Order: The Need for a Framework
      Treaty', in A.J.Dolman, op.cit., 1980, pp. 195-201.

(151) Arvid Pardo, op.cit., p. 198.

(152) Ibid, p. 200.

(153) The Charter of Economic Rights and Duties of States, Resolution 3281 (XXIX), adopted at the 2315th plenary session, 12 December 1974. A comprehensive history of the Charter has been published in Spanish. See Robert Ríos Ferrer et al., *Exégesis de la Carta de Derechos y Deberes Económicos de los Estados*, Editorial Porrúa, Mexico, D.F., 1976.

(154) See the evaluation in Verloren van Themaat, op.cit., chapter IV. The review contains useful references to other assessments. See also Subranta Roy Chowdhury, 'Legal Status of the Charter of Economic Rights and Duties of States', in K.Hossain, op.cit., pp. 79-94; and A.Rozenthal, 'The Charter of Economic Rights and Duties of States in the New International Economic Order', *Virginia Journal of International Law*, vol. 16, Winter 1976, pp. 309-322.

(155) The RIO Report suggests (p. 117) that the Charter could be expanded to include the following provisions: (a) All States shall facilitate access to technology and scientific information; (b) All States have the obligation to expand and liberalize international trade; (c) Ocean space and the atmosphere beyond precise limits of national jurisdiction are the common heritage of all mankind: as such they shall be administered exclusively for peaceful purposes through international mechanisms with the participation of all States and their resources shall be exploited with particular regard to the interests of poor countries; (d) Developed countries have the duty to ensure that net flows of real resources to poor countries shall not be less than the targets established by the United Nations General Assembly; (e) No State shall allow itself to be permanently and greatly dependent on others for its basic food-stuffs; (f) All States shall encourage the rational utilization of energy, with particular attention being given to non-renewable resources, and develop new sources of non-conventional energy which would particularly contribute to reinforcing the self-sustained growth of the poorest countries; (g) All States shall accept an international currency to be created by an international authority; (h) All States shall accept the evolution of a world organization with the necessary power to plan, to make decisions and to enforce them.

(156) Of the Western industrialized nations only Sweden adopted the Charter. The U.S., Western Germany, U.K., Denmark and Luxemburg voted against it, the others abstaining. For a review of the negotiations, see Karen Hudes, 'Towards a New International Economic Order', *Yale Studies in World Public Order*, vol. 2, no. 1, 1975, p. 88 et seq.

(157) See the essays of Johan Kaufmann and Elisabeth Mann Borgese in A.J.Dolman, op.cit., 1980, pp. 103-115 and 181-194.

Kaufmann proposes the formation, through the restructuring
of the U.N. and its specialized agencies, of four institutional clusters: one dealing with basic production sectors
(industry, agriculture, resources); one dealing with trade
and current monetary problems; one dealing with basic infra-
structural sectors (for example health, education, intellectual property, telecommunications); and one dealing with
operational development assistance. Mann Borgese advocates
the creation of 'world economic communities' or 'modules'
for such areas as the oceans, outer space, energy, food,
mineral resources, science and technology, international
trade - the whole system being drawn together in a restructured ECOSOC.

5 The Common Heritage of Mankind and Global Reform*

> The sea indeed is assuredly common to all.
>
> Titus Maccius Plautus (254-184 BC), *Rudens*, Act 4, Scene 3.

INTRODUCTION

In this chapter our central concern is with a concept which has the power to transform the relationship between rich and poor countries and which must form the basis for international regimes aimed at the rational and equitable management of renewable and non-renewable resources: the concept of the common heritage of mankind. Although the concept has its ancestral home in outer space it has been nurtured by and has evolved within the Third U.N. Conference on the Law of the Sea. This conference, arguably the most important law-making process ever devised, has given birth - painful and protracted birth to be sure - to solutions unique in the field of international resource management. These solutions have been shaped by the concept of the common heritage. In looking at both the history and possible future of the concept it is thus necessary to take a close look at the ongoing attempt to fashion a regime for the world's oceans.

The sequence of this chapter is as follows. We first look at the origins of the concept of the common heritage of mankind and then go on to define it. We next examine the experience of the Law of the Sea Conference and attempt to distill the most important lessons for the international management of resources. Fi-

---

*This chapter has been prepared in close cooperation with Elisabeth Mann Borgese.

nally, we look at ways in which the common heritage concept can
be expanded and at their implications for the progressive development of a global resource management capability. (1)

THE ORIGINS OF THE CONCEPT OF THE
COMMON HERITAGE OF MANKIND

It was in the early 1960s that the international community came
to recognize the immense potential of the oceans - an enormous
envelope, largely unexplored, covering two-thirds of the earth's
surface and with all the features of emerged land. This recognition was clearly reflected in a U.N. General Assembly resolution adopted in 1966 which expresses "the need for a greater
knowledge of the oceans and of the opportunities available for
utilisation of their resources, living and mineral". It went on
to suggest that the "effective exploitation and development of
these resources can raise the economic level of peoples throughout the world, and in particular of the developing countries".
(2)

It was also recognized, however, that differences in technological capabilities between the rich and poor countries could easily mean that a handful of industrialized nations would be the
main beneficiaries of attempts to unlock a storehouse of immense
wealth. Rather than raising "the economic levels of peoples
throughout the world", the exploration and exploitation of the
oceans could result in new types of colonial relationships and
in a further aggravation of the inequalities between the rich
and poor nations. Such a possibility was expressly referred to
by President Johnson in a speech made in July 1966. "Under no
circumstances", he observed, "must we ever allow the prospects
of rich harvest and mineral wealth to create a new form of colonial competition among the maritime nations. We must be careful
to avoid a race to grab and to hold the lands under the high
seas. We must ensure", he went on, "that the deep seas and the
ocean bottoms are, and remain, the legacy of all human beings".
(3)

It was with this and related issues in mind that on 17 August
1967 the Maltese delegate to the United Nations, Ambassador Arvid
Pardo, filed a *note verbale,* requesting the inclusion of a sup-
plementary item on the agenda of the Twenty-Second Session of the
General Assembly. The item was entitled "Examination of the question of the reservation exclusively for peaceful purposes of the
seabed and the ocean floor, and the subsoil thereof, underlying
the high sea beyond the limits of present national jurisdiction,
and the use of their resources in the interest of mankind". (4)

On 1 November 1967 Ambassador Pardo rose in the First Committee
of the U.N. General Assembly to introduce the item. In a four

hour presentation he drew the attention of the Assembly to the
vast riches hidden on the deep floor of the world's oceans which
the technological revolution was rapidly making accessible to exploration and exploitation, and which did not belong to any nation. He pointed to the dangers of a military competition to
dominate the deep seas. He saw a race developing to carve up the
no-man's land of the ocean floor in the way the black continent
had been carved up by the colonial powers in past centuries, a
race which would give rise to acute conflict and pollution. He
explained how the old law of the sea, based on the premises of
the sovereignty of coastal States over a narrow belt of ocean
along the coasts and of the freedom of the seas beyond this, was
being eroded. He suggested that a new concept, the common heritage of mankind, must take the place of the old freedom of the
sea. He stressed the ecological unity of ocean space and the interactions between all areas and all uses of ocean space. He
concluded that the United Nations General Assembly declare the
seabed and its resources beyond the present limits of national
jurisdiction a common heritage of mankind, elaborate a set of
principles to govern activities relating to the seabed, and then
proceed to negotiate a treaty which would both clearly define
the limits of the international seabed and create a new type of
international organization to administer and manage its wealth
for the benefit of all mankind. The common heritage of mankind
would be used for peaceful purposes only, thus excluding the
arms race from an area that comprises over two-thirds of the
surface of the globe. (5)

Few speeches heard at the United Nations General Assembly have
triggered off as much activity as Arvid Pardo's address. An ad-
hoc committee of thirty-five nations was formed to study the
question and make recommendations to the General Assembly. A
year later, in December 1968, the committee was reconstituted
as a permanent Committee on the Peaceful Uses of the Seabed and
Ocean Floor Beyond the Limits of National Jurisdiction, with a
membership of forty-two states, which had become ninety-one by
1973. A moratorium resolution, proposed originally by Pardo in
1967, and a resolution declaring the 1970s the first decade of
ocean exploration, proposed by the U.S.A., were adopted in 1969.

In the meantime, the Soviet Union and the United States submitted to the committee proposals for the demilitarization of the
seabed. These were then transferred to the Disarmament Committee
in Geneva, and eventually resulted in the Seabed Treaty of 1972.
(6)

During the summer of 1970, the United Kingdom and France submitted working papers on the regime for the international seabed
area, while the United States introduced an elaborate draft convention. In the autumn of the same year, the Twenty-Fifth General
Assembly of the United Nations adopted a Declaration of Principles governing the seabed beyond the limits of national juris-

diction, which spelled out and enlarged the Pardo proposals and elevated the principle of the seabed as a common heritage of mankind to a norm of international law.

The General Assembly also took another important decision in 1970: it decided to convene in 1973 a Conference on the Law of the Sea which, in addition to dealing with the question of the seabed beyond the limits of national jurisdiction, would also examine "a broad range of related issues including those concerning the regimes of the high seas, the continental shelf, the territorial sea (including the question of its breadth and the question of international straits) and contiguous zone, fishing and the conservation of the living resources of the high seas (including the question of preferential rights of coastal states), the preservation of the marine environment (including, *inter alia*, the prevention of pollution) and scientific research". (7)

DEFINING THE COMMON HERITAGE
OF MANKIND

In his statement of November 1, 1967, Arvid Pardo argued that a new treaty on the Law of the Sea should incorporate the following principles:

(1) The seabed and the ocean floor, underlying the seas beyond the limits of national jurisdiction as defined in the Treaty, are not subject to national appropriation in any manner whatsoever.

(2) The seabed and the ocean floor beyond the limits of national jurisdiction shall be reserved exclusively for peaceful purposes.

(3) Scientific research with regard to the deep seas and ocean floor, not directly connected with defense, shall be freely permissible and its results available to all.

(4) The resources of the seabed and ocean floor, beyond the limits of national jurisdiction, shall be exploited primarily in the interests of mankind, with particular regard to the needs of poor countries.

(5) The exploration and exploitation of the seabed and ocean floor beyond the limits of national jurisdiction shall be conducted in a manner consistent with the principles and purposes of the United Nations Charter and in a manner not causing unnecessary obstruction of the high seas or serious impairment of the marine environment.

In a later statement, he went on to elaborate the concept of the common heritage of mankind which he presented as "a new legal principle which we wish to introduce into international law". (8) The concept of the common heritage of mankind, he explained,

"implies the notion of peaceful uses, since it is clear that
military use of the ocean floor might impair or endanger the
common property. The common heritage concept implies freedom of
access and use on the part of those having part in the heritage,
but also regulation of use for the purpose of conserving the
heritage and avoiding the infringement of the rights of others;
inherent in the regulation of use is, of course, responsibility
for misuse. The concept finally implies the equitable distribution of benefits from exploitation of the heritage. It is possible to go further", Pardo went on: "the notion of property
that cannot be divided without the consent of all and which
should be administered in the interest and for the benefit of
all is a logical extension of the common heritage concept".

Since then the international legal community has sought to define the common heritage of mankind. This task it has yet to
complete: there is no universally accepted definition. The term
was a new one to the legal community and lawyers have struggled
to define 'common', 'heritage' and 'mankind'. Some lawyers des-
paired of a definition. "The common heritage of mankind", one
argued, "no matter how well motivated, in a legally binding document... carries no clear judicial connotation, but belongs to
the realm of politics, philosophy, morality, and not law". (9)
At the first substantive session of the Third U.N. Law of the
Sea Conference some 40 States presented their interpretation of
the concept.

The main issue in finding an accepted definition for the common
heritage has been whether it should be defined in terms of a
property relationship. The term 'common heritage' has been vari-
ously interpreted to mean 'common property' and 'common sovereignty', confusion resulting in part from the U.N. Secretariat's
translation of 'common heritage' into French and Spanish as *pa-
trimoine commun* and *patrimonio comun* respectively. These trans-
lations established a non-existent relationship with Roman law
and the modern property law of States. (10)

The non-property interpretation is essential to the concept. As
Arvid Pardo observed in 1970, the expression 'common heritage'
is much preferable to the term 'common property'. (11) "We do
not think it advisable to use the word 'property'", he observed.
"Property is a form of power. Property as we have it from the
ancient Romans implies the *jus utendi et abutendi* (right to use
and misuse). Property implies and gives excessive emphasis to
just one aspect: resource exploitation and benefits derived there-
from". The content of the common heritage, he suggested, ought
to be "determined pragmatically in relation to felt international
needs". It is not limited by a complex of real or potential resources. "World resources", he went on, "should not be conceived
in a static sense. New resources are being constantly created by
technology". The common heritage of mankind, however, also includes *values*. "It includes also scientific research". Thus if

there were a set of ethical and legal rules to be derived from
the principle of the common heritage, these would have to be applicable to science policy as well.

In the same statement Pardo suggested three characteristics of
the common heritage of mankind. First of all, "the absence of
property". The common heritage engenders the right to *use* certain property, but not to *own* it. "It implies the management of
property and the obligation of the international community to
transmit this common heritage, including resources and values,
in historical terms. Common heritage implies management. Management not only in the sense of management of resources, but management of all uses". Thirdly, common heritage implies sharing
of benefits. "Resources are very important; benefits are very
important. But this is only a part of the total concept".

There are important precedents for such a concept. In religious
doctrine, economic theory as well as law there are practices
upon which the common heritage can draw. Such practices could be
universalized and endowed with legal and economic content at a
time in which absolute ownership and absolute sovereignty have
to be reconsidered in the light of ecological, economic, and
technological interdependence and of a new perception of the individual as part of the community and of the human species as a
part of nature.

The Roman Catholic Church spiritually never quite moved into the
era of the nation-State and of the capitalist system based on
private property. Today she is among the most evolved advocates
of the common heritage concept. In *Populorum Progressio*, the
encyclical that does to "property" what *Pacem in Terris* did to
"sovereignty", Pope Paul VI stated: "...private property does
not constitute for anyone an absolute and unconditioned right.
No one is justified in keeping for his exclusive use what he
does not need when others lack necessities...the right to property must never be exercised to the detriment of the common good.
If there should arise a conflict between acquired private rights
and primary community exigencies, it is the responsibility of
public authorities to look for a solution, with active participation of individuals and social groups..... It is unfortunate
that in these new conditions (of the industrialization) of society a system has been constructed which considers profit as
the key motive for economic progress, competition as the supreme
law of economics, and private ownership of the means of production as an absolute right that has no limits and carries no corresponding social obligation".

A couple of decades earlier, a Prelate of the Anglican Church,
Hewlet Johnson, the Dean of Canterbury, declared all the waters,
not only the high seas, together with all the other "elements of
life" to be "common property". "There are four requisites for
life which are provided by nature, even apart from man's labor:
air, light, land and water... I am not persuaded that the right

way to deal with this question is by nationalization of the land
...but I am sure we need to assert the prior interest of the
community respecting land and water with a vigor of which recent
political history shows no trace. Here, supremely, the principle
of the old Christian tradition holds good that the right of property is the right of administration or stewardship, never the
right of exclusive use".

Boodhan, the Hindu doctrine whose followers achieved the voluntary distribution of 2,100,000 acres of land in India, adheres
to a similar pre-capitalist concept of common property. Following Gandhi's teaching, *Boodhan* advocates the transformation of
"legal ownership" from "private" to "community". Ownership is
considered here as a "bundle of rights". Of these, usufruct, the
right to inheritance, and the right to alienation or transfer
remain intact. But property must be used in the common interest,
and at least one-twentieth of it must be given away for community use or redistribution.

The common land system traditional of large parts of Africa is
another example. As one often-quoted Nigerian chief once remark-
ed: "The land belongs to a big family of which many members are
dead, some are living, and innumerable others are still to be
born". In this system of landholding, a man cannot own the land,
because he did not make it. It was always there, a gift from the
gods, in trust for the lineage. A man can own the fruits of the
earth - crops and trees which he himself planted and tended. But
he cannot dispose of his plot or sell it since there is no individual title to land.

There are also important precedents in Saxon and Germanic law,
Roman law and Slavic law.

Perhaps the closest approximation to the concept of the common
heritage of mankind can be found in Yugoslav political theory,
as embodied in the Yugoslav Constitution, from 1958 on. That is
the concept of social ownership. This is how Jovan Djordjević,
one of the main architects of the constitution, defined the concept: "The term 'social property' has a negative meaning: it in-
dicates the *negation of the right to ownership* to each and all.
It prohibits the power monopoly over the means of production and
the produce of labor. No one - neither State nor community nor
enterprise, neither the working collective nor the individual -
has ownership rights with regard to the social means of production and the product of labor, nor can he dispose of them as his
property, on the basis of power". (12)

In the same essay, Djordjević observes: "...the concept of social ownership is organically tied to the concept of management.
Social property and its complementary regime of management represent a theoretical, political, and legal whole. In a functional sense, management implies specific action with respect to the
maintenance, conservation and use of the objects of social pro-

perty, i.e., an economic-technical and social usage which presupposes a corresponding regime of investment and distribution of
products obtained by the economic-technical use of the means in
social property. Politically managing means not only administering, transacting, and conserving but also planning, developing,
and distributing. All of this calls for a special socio-legal
regime which needs specific definitions. Furthermore - and this
is the political aspect - that regime must include machinery for
management which guarantees integrity, social function, and social use of those objects which enter the regime as social and
thereby international social property."

The parallels with the common heritage of mankind are indeed
striking.

The concept of ownership developed by the authors of the *Bari-
loche Report,* regarded as an example of Third World thinking,
similarly approximates that of the common heritage of mankind.
"What is the role of property in the world described in (our)
model?", the report asks. "It is clear that, in our context, the
concept of property loses much of its meaning. The private ownership of land and the means of production do not exist, but, on
the other hand, neither does the State own them as is currently
the case in many centrally planned economies. The present-day
concept of private ownership of the means of production should
be replaced by the more universal concepts of the *use and management* of the means of production..." (13)

A whole new theory of economics can indeed be built on this distinction between the right to *ownership,* which is rejected, and
the right to *utilize* and to *manage,* which is here upheld. The
building of such a new system has been attempted by Orio Giarini
in a recent report to The Club of Rome. (14) The source of wealth,
in that report, is called the "patrimony" and it comprises all
the natural, biological, man-made and monetarized assets from
which we derive our means of livelihood. It is a "stock" or an accumulation of assests which have "utilization" value. This notion
of a value is thus related to a "stock" and not, as in the conventional economic process, to a "flow" (where the notion of value is linked with the transformation process of products and services). A "flow" can in fact have also *negative* effects (deducted
values) rather than added values in terms of real wealth and welfare. The real value of products and services cannot be measured
by their cost/exchange value at a given moment, but by their utilization value over a period of time.

Such a theory of value would be most applicable to a common heritage regime. A common heritage system would similarly emerge as
the logical outcome of applying such a theory of value. For that
which cannot be owned can have no cost/exchange value; and that
which can be utilized and managed must have a utilization value.

Given the revolutionary character of the concept of the common

heritage of mankind it must be considered surprising that the
Law of the Sea Conference has failed to give it clear definition
in legal and economic terms. For the outsider or newcomer to the
Law of the Sea, it remains difficult to state precisely what is
meant by the concept. Yet the main elements of a definition are
all to be found in the Draft Convention currently before the Conference. (15) One can use five different articles (136, 137, 140,
141 and 145) to formulate a definition in two basic articles:

First Article

The Area and its resources are a Common Heritage of Mankind.

Second Article

Common Heritage of Mankind means that:

1. No State shall claim or exercise sovereignty or sovereign
rights over any part of the Area or its resources, nor shall any
State or natural or juridical person appropriate any part thereof...

2. Activities in the Area shall...be carried out for the benefit
of mankind as a whole, irrespective of the geographical location
of States, whether coastal or land-locked, and taking into particular consideration the interests and needs of the developing
States...

3. The Area shall be open to use exclusively for peaceful purposes by all States, whether coastal or land-locked...

4. Necessary measures shall be taken in order to ensure effective
protection for the marine environment from harmful effects which
may arise (from activities).

These paragraphs express the five legal and economic attributes
of the common heritage concept as they have developed in discussions and writings since the concept was first proposed by Arvid
Pardo in 1967. These attributes, more succinctly, are:

- non appropriability

- shared management

- benefit sharing by mankind as a whole

- use for peaceful purposes only

- conservation for future generations.

THE THIRD UNITED NATIONS CONFERENCE
ON THE LAW OF THE SEA (UNCLOS III)

The first session of UNCLOS III was held in New York in December
1973. (16) It was limited to matters of procedure. Three Committees were established: Committee 1, entrusted with the task of

building an international regime for the deep seabed; Committee 2, entrusted to deal with issues related to coastal State sovereignty; and Committee 3, responsible for such matters as pollution, scientific research and the transfer of technology. The Sri Lankan diplomat Shirley Amerasinghe was elected President of the Conference and Chairman of the Plenary Sessions.

Since then UNCLOS III has moved through ten laborious, quarrelsome, frustrating sessions. Sessions burdened with all the political problems which beset our world as well as those arising from the Conference's own many concerns. The sessions have been heated by personality conflicts and not infrequently shaken by political changes in distant countries. Although the results of UNCLOS III will have a considerable bearing on the future of the relationship between the rich and poor countries and the prospects for a New International Economic Order, the traditional distinction between 'North' and 'South' is blurred by geographical and functional considerations. The more than 160 nations participating in the Conference are spread over ten 'blocs' some of which have unique combinations of countries. The interests of the Soviet Union, for example, make it a maritime and fishing State. By comparison, its allies in Eastern Europe are all landlocked and geographically disadvantaged States. In UNCLOS III, East and West Germany are members of the same group.

In spite of itself, UNCLOS III has slowly and painfully progressed, often by untried and unprecedented methods, and succeeded in producing a number of landmark documents. The first of these was the draft Informal Single Negotiating Text (ISNT) produced by the three committees at the end of the Third Session of UNCLOS. (17) Most of the Fourth Session was held in plenary meetings and devoted to the revision of the ISNT. The result was the Revised Single Negotiating Text (RSNT). (18) The Fifth and Sixth Sessions were devoted to the revision of the RSNT and resulted in the Informal Composite Negotiating Text (ICNT). The ICNT, negotiated in the summmer of 1977, was essentially a draft Ocean Space Convention. Although full of incongruities, holes, and technical weaknesses, it was a document the likes of which the international community had never before been confronted with. It was, in Arvid Pardo's words, "a remarkable document (and) a momentous achievement". (20)

At the Seventh and Eighth Sessions of the Conference efforts were made to narrow the remaining areas of - in some cases very considerable - disagreement. These Sessions resulted in two revisions of the ICNT. (21) The Ninth Session, held in New York in March 1980 and resumed in Geneva in August of that year succeeded in turning the revised ICNT into a Draft Convention on the Law of the Sea. (22) The existence of the Draft Convention, although still an informal and negotiating text, suggests that the end of UNCLOS III is now finally in sight.

The world is thus still considering the ideas launched by Arvid
Pardo well over a decade ago. Pardo himself has not been as active in the UNCLOS III process as he should have been. The nationalist government of Malta was defeated by the Labour Party
of Dom Mintoff in 1971. The inevitable changes in the conduct
of the country's foreign affairs meant that when UNCLOS III opened at the end of 1973 Pardo was not a member of the Malta delegation. The man who almost single-handedly had set into motion perhaps the greatest law-making conference ever, a conference which
has brought forth a document unique in history, was out on the
sidelines, an observer rather than an actor in the drama of the
oceans. (23)

The Conference has also lost its President. Shirley Amerasinghe
who more than anyone else steered UNCLOS III away from the rocks
of failure unexpectedly died in December 1980. It is indeed a
tragedy that he was unable to witness the end of a process to
which he had contributed so much.

The Draft Convention on the
Law of the Sea

The Draft Convention is a very comprehensive document. Its 320
Articles spread over 17 parts, supported by 8 annexes, extend
over 180 closely typed pages. Of special interest to us here are
the two children which the Conference has spawned: the Exclusive
Economic Zone (EEZ) and the regime for the deep seabed.

Under the Convention coastal States will enjoy exclusive economic rights to a zone extending 200 miles from their baselines (in
the drawing of which they will have considerable latitude). Inhabited islands, however small, will bring them similar 200 mile
zones as well as their own shelves and margins. In their EEZs,
coastal States will have "sovereign rights for the purpose of exploring and exploiting, conserving and managing the natural resources, whether living or non-living, of the sea-bed and subsoil
and the superjacent waters, and with regard to other activities
for the economic exploitation and exploration of the zone, such
as the production of energy from the water, currents and winds".
(Article 56)

Under the traditional law of the sea, coastal State national sovereignty extended three miles - a limit which, based upon the
range of the cannon ball, was derived pragmatically. Under the
provisions of the Draft Convention, national sovereignty will be
effectively extended to 200 miles and possibly beyond. Many
coastal States have already declared their EEZs in anticipation
of the results of UNCLOS III. The conflicting claims that this
was given rise to has made the grab for the world's oceans, in
the words of *The Economist,* "the biggest can of worms ever opened", and has assured the legal community of gainful employment

for many years ahead. (24)

Coastal State EEZs will account for at least 25 per cent of the
world's oceans. More significantly, they will contain most of
the ocean's riches. As far as we know today, nearly 90 per cent
of all potentially recoverable oil and gas is to be found within
EEZs. The value of these reserves is not known but estimates made
in the mid 1970s placed oil reserves at $ 25 trillion. It is a
similar story with fishing. About 90 per cent of fish stocks are
to be found within 200 miles of the coast.

The Draft Convention thus gives coastal States, through their
EEZs, exclusive rights to much of the ocean's immense wealth.
This has changed the conceptions which Arvid Pardo so eloquently
enunciated.

Let us now turn to the regime for the deep seabed. The area and
its resources beyond the limits of national jurisdiction are designated "the common heritage of mankind" (Article 136) and not
subject to appropriation by States. Under the provisions of the
Draft Convention all rights to the resources of the Area are
vested in mankind as a whole (Article 137). These rights are represented by the proposed International Seabed Authority, the
centerpiece of the Draft Convention, and an international institution unique in the area of resource management.

The powers of the ISA are regulated by the Draft Convention. Its
principal organs are an Assembly, a Council, and a Secretariat.
The ISA is to have an operational arm, called the Enterprise,
which will be responsible for carrying out activities in the international area. The most important of these activities is mining and, more particularly, mining for the much publicized manganese nodules. Nodules were first dredged up by the British
Challenger expedition in 1872, between Honolulu and Tahiti. The
richest deposits are known to exist in a narrow band, about 200
km across and 1600 km long, running roughly east-west along the
southern edge of the equatorial belt at a depth of about 1500 to
4000 metres, in the Pacific, Atlantic and Indian oceans. They
contain iron, nickel, copper, cobalt and traces of two dozen
other metals, in addition to manganese, often in concentrations
comparable to those in land ores. Rich beds contain about 74 ki-
los of nodules per sq.km of ocean floor. As they vary in composition, so they vary in shape and size. Many look like potatoes,
and there are trillions of tons of them scattered on the sea-bed
- 1.5 trillion tons in the Pacific alone.

Manganese nodules can legitimately be classified as 'renewable
resources' since they keep re-forming. Growth rates may be a lei-
surely 1-100 millimetres per million years, but the very vastness
of the oceans means that perhaps 16 million tons of nodules are
formed every year.

The regime for the deep sea-bed detailed in the Draft Convention

is a so-called 'parallel system' in which both the Enterprise
and other entities - governmental and private (notably a handful
of transnational consortia) (25) - would be entitled to mine the
deep sea-bed. The entire system would be under the control of
the ISA. Those wishing to explore or exploit the deep sea-bed in
the international area can only do so if the ISA extends permission through a contract. Mining entities which meet financial
and technical criteria specified in the Draft Convention would
be guaranteed access, except when the ISA decides for economic
reasons - notably the earnings of mineral exporting nations - to
limit the production of sea-bed minerals.

To obtain a contract, an applicant would have to prospect the
area (or have it prospected) and then present the ISA with two
mineral-bearing areas of equal commercial value. The ISA would
select one, leaving the other for the successful applicant, who
would mine it in accordance with a plan of operations which the
ISA would be empowered to approve. The ISA's sites would constitute a reserved area for exploitation by the Enterprise or by
developing countries.

This parallel system, a system which effectively places the Enterprise in hopeless competition with 'big business', would be
established for an initial period of 20 years. At the end of
that period a review conference would be called to decide whether
the system should be modified.

Under the proposed regime, two main problems remain unresolved:
the financing of the Enterprise and its acquisition of the technology required to exploit the reserved area. As far as financing is concerned, there is general agreement that the Enterprise
should be provided with funds for at least its first mining project - a figure that could amount to one billion dollars. The
Conference's answer to the question of who is to pay and on what
basis is, however, dubious. It remains obscure whether the very
elaborate provisions will ever be implemented.

LESSONS FROM UNCLOS III FOR THE INTERNATIONAL
MANAGEMENT OF RESOURCES

What resource management lessons can be drawn from the Third U.N.
Conference on the Law of the Sea and from the ongoing attempt to
fashion an ocean regime shaped by the concept of the common heritage of mankind? In attempting to answer this question we will
look firstly at issues related to EEZs and the extension of national jurisdiction over ocean space and, secondly, at issues
relating to the regime for the deep sea-bed.

Exclusive Economic Zones:
National Jurisdiction and Functional Sovereignty

It is clear that under the Draft Convention by far the greatest
advantage from the acquisition of the 200 mile EEZ will accrue
to a few, already rich, coastal States, while the majority of
poor developing states, including the poorest among them, get
nothing. Apart from Micronesia, whose huge area can be calculated in various ways, the United States, acquiring an economic
zone of 2,222,000 square nautical miles, is the principal bene-
ficiarcy. Five of the next six - Australia, New Zealand, Canada,
USSR and Japan - are industrialized countries, each of which
will acquire EEZs in excess of one million square nautical miles
(26) Under the Draft Convention some 25 States will acquire 76
per cent of the total area of all economic zones. Of these, 13
are industrialized States which together will gain one half of
the total area of all EEZs. The 12 developing countries will together gain 28 per cent of the total area. About 80 countries
will gain nothing.

The question, however, is what do we mean by 'gain'? The rich
and powerful coastal States 'gain' what they already have: for
the former freedom of the high sea bestowed on their might the
right to exploit marine areas as far as their technologies, and
their national interests, would reach - 200 miles out or further.
Developing coastal States, on the other hand, formerly at the
mercy of the fishing fleets and factory ships of wealthy distant
water fishing States free to deplete and pollute their coastal
waters, will be, at least theoretically, protected against these
inroads. They will still, of course, be dependent on a handful
of industrialized nations for the technologies required to exploit the minerals and hydrocarbons they might find in their EEZs.

One is forced to conclude that the new Law of the Sea will in
many respects look like the old. The rich countries will continue
to rule the waves and to exploit the resources of the sea: within
their own economic zones, the no-man's land of the High Seas and
in the economic zones of poorer coastal States. In these zones
the rich States and their companies, whether national or multinational, will have made suitable bilateral arrangements, paying
rent or royalties. This, however, will not be substantial enough
to make any dent in the economic and social status quo. Production, as heretofore, will be geared to the needs and interests
of the industrialized countries, not to the needs of the poor,
not toward a redistribution of resources, technologies and skills.
If the economic zones of poor coastal States are not exploited by
the companies of the rich, they will be underexploited: for it
will take a considerable time for poor coastal States to develop
the technologies and social infrastructures needed to manage large
expansions of ocean space. Who, under these circumstances, will
be able to resist the pressures and blandishments of the rich?

Nature abhors a vacuum.

The more important aspect of the establishment of the EEZ, however, is not where boundaries are drawn but it is that it imple-
ments at the national level the transition of a laissez-faire
system to a system of management which is at least initiated in
the international area with the establishment of the ISA. Additional institutions are, however, needed for the management of
ocean space, especially living resources. It is an illusion, for
example, to believe that fisheries can be managed successfully
within national ocean space, no matter how large that space, if
the traditional freedom of the high seas reigns in international
open space, leaving nations and their industries free to over-
fish and pollute beyond the limits of national jurisdiction.
Arvid Pardo, in his 1967 speech, went to lengths to stress that
the oceans are a single space, an ecological unity, in which
'boundaries' cannot be artificially drawn. It follows that rational fisheries management in national ocean space requires
equally rational management for international ocean space, with
the two management systems cooperating and interacting.

The inadequacies of the EEZ as an instrument of management and
of distributive justice can be overcome not by going back - a
return to the laissez-faire system of the high seas - but by
moving forward. There are several sets of measures which could
be taken, both inside and outside UNCLOS III, to make the EEZ a
useful part of a NIEO and of a system of international resource
management. The first is the tidying up of the boundaries of the
EEZ. The second is the establishment of strong public international institutions to cooperate with developing coastal States
in the management of the resources of their economic zone. The
third set of measures relates to regional cooperation and integration.

The Limits of the Exclusive Economic Zone. The sets of measures
should be aimed at forestalling further extensions of national
claims. The least that must be done here is to achieve a more
precise definition of the baselines from which the EEZ is measured. These are at present very losely defined, making it possible to enclose large marine spaces as 'internal waters' and
pushing the boundary of the EEZ out much further than 200 miles
from shore. The geopolitical theories on which the Draft Convention's definition is based is pseudo-scientific. It is to be re-
gretted that the proposal first put forward by Malta in 1971 and
then endorsed by a large number of States, including the group
of Arabic States and many African, that the boundaries of the
legal continental shelf should coincide with those of the economic zone, i.e. 200 miles from clearly defined baselines, has not
been accepted by the Conference. Its day may yet dawn some years
from now, years very likely characterized by cumbersome legal
squabbles arising from the ambiguities of the present legal provisions.

International Institutions. If the EEZ is to be of use to developing countries and to serve as an instrument for rational resource management then developing countries should have access to public international institutions which can render relevant assistance. This requires that, in many cases, existing international institutions be restructured, on a global and regional basis, and new ones established wherever necessary.

This applies, in the first place, to the international institutions dealing with fisheries. The body established within the United Nations to deal with fisheries on a global scale is the Committee on Fisheries (COFI) of the Food and Agriculture Organization (FAO). This institution should be upgraded, restructured and strengthened so that it can operate at the same level of, and in cooperation with, the future International Seabed Authority. This process of restructuring is already in course. To be complete and effective it should cover at least (a) universalization of membership (which presently is limited to members of FAO and thus excludes the Soviet Union); (b) establishment of a system of licensing for fishing in the international area (regulation of catches in the exclusive economic zone is impossible unless catches are equally regulated in the international zone); (c) establishment of an independent Secretariat, separate from that of FAO; (d) establishment of an operational arm or "Enterprise system", somewhat analogous to that of the International Seabed Authority, to manage living resources in the international area and assist developing coastal States in the exploration and exploitation of the resources of their economic zones; (e) establishment of an independent international fisheries research capacity; (f) establishment of dispute settlement machinery as required by the Draft Convention; and (g) independent financing, preferably through international taxes.

Besides the restructuring and strengthening of COFI, it is essential that the regional fisheries commissions be reorganized and adapted to the requirements of the new Law of the Sea and that the system of regional commissions be properly coordinated with COFI.

Developing coastal States will need increasing assistance from the Inter-Governmental Maritime Consultative Organization (IMCO) for the regulation of navigational traffic and the provision of navigational aids in the waters under their jurisdiction where they now bear the responsibility for the safety of ships in transit. This means that IMCO must be strengthened and the participation of developing countries in all its organs must be increased. This process is already in course and will continue. Furthermore, the problems of the economics of shipping and of a more equitable participation of developing countries in freight carriage can only be solved by structural changes in the international machinery.

Similar considerations apply to scientific research and to the protection of the environment. Most coastal States do not have the marine scientific capacity for the research needed as a basis for rational ocean management. Either they have to rely on the great powers to carry out such research in their waters and on their shelves, which often may be politically undesirable, or there will be no research. The only way out of this dilemma is to internationalize scientific research as far as possible; that is, to give to international scientific institutions an independent research capacity.

While the Law of the Sea Conference can give, and is giving, an initial impulse to the process of restructuring and strengthening of the international institutions dealing with the major uses of ocean space and resources and to the creation of some integrative machinery for the harmonization and integration of their policies, this development, obviously, points beyond the scope of the Conference. (27) It must be carried out by the institutions themselves.

Regional Cooperation and Integration. An important additional measure for improving the usefulness of economic zones is to merge them, where appropriate, into *regional economic zones* or 'matrimonial seas'. This is the only solution for enclosed or semi-enclosed seas, like the Mediterranean or the Caribbean, where national economic zones would be exceedingly complicated to delineate and would make rational resource management totally impossible. Cooperation, through an appropriate regional institutional framework, should extend to all marine activities, from the management of living resources and the protection of the environment to scientific research, from navigation to the mining of minerals. The Draft Convention provides for regional cooperation in enclosed and semi-enclosed seas but omits reference to oil drilling and seabed mining, taking account of the particular sensitivities of States with regard to their sovereignty over their continental shelves. Yet, the regionalization of the continental shelf would, in some cases, be the only hope for the maintenance of peace and the effective exploitation of the resources.

The establishment of regional regimes need not be limited to enclosed or semi-enclosed seas; (28) they can be conceived as part of land-based regional economic development, such as the EEC or African or Latin American common markets. The extension of such common markets to 'matrimonial seas' holds by far the greatest promise for the solution of the problems of landlocked and geographically disadvantaged States which would participate in the marine common markets on an equal footing. The development of regional regimes, likewise, transcends the scope of the Law of the Sea Conference. Such regimes must be established by the countries belonging to the region.

National Jurisdiction and Functional Sovereignty. The coastal
State does not exercise territorial sovereignty over the EEZ
where important rights relating to navigation and communication
are reserved to other States. The coastal State exercises *functional* sovereignty, i.e. jurisdiction over determined uses rather
than geographical space. This transformation of the concept of
sovereignty is in line with the transformation of the concept of
ownership explicit in the common heritage of mankind. Functional
sovereignty permits the secure accommodation of inclusive and
exclusive uses of the sea or, in other words, the interweaving
of national and international jurisdiction within the same territorial space.

It also opens the possibility of applying the concept of common
heritage of mankind within marine areas under national jurisdiction and management, i.e. of compensating for the territorial
shrinkage of the concept with a functional expansion.

An important first step in the functional expansion of the common heritage concept would be for the international community
to agree that manganese nodules are a common heritage no matter
whether they are found in ocean space under international or under national jurisdiction. (29) If this were agreed upon, nodule
deposits in areas under national jurisdiction could be explored
and exploited in joint venture arrangements involving the International Seabed Authority and the coastal State in which the
latter might have a controlling interest. In this case, the ISA
would receive a part of the profits which could be used for
agreed international purposes. Such an arrangement would be more
profitable for the world community and for developing countries
than if the coastal State were to engage a private consortium
for the exploitation of these resources. In the latter case,
profits would go largely to a private company.

Since a number of manganese nodule sites are in areas under national jurisdiction their exploitation is only a matter of time.
To declare them the common heritage of mankind would be to greatly enhance the importance of the International Seabed Authority,
which could become a most useful instrument to assist developing
countries in the exploration of their mineral resources in general. That there is a great need for international assistance in
this area has been pointed out by many writers on the NIEO, most
explicitly by the Brandt Commission.

Developing countries will not and shall not retreat from their
solemnly affirmed inalienable right over their natural resources,
but it is the concept of sovereignty that is undergoing a transformation, and through international cooperation all countries,
developed and developing, may gradually extend common heritage
status to resources and technologies in those cases where it is
necessary for the building of a NIEO.

Ambassador Shailendra K.Upadhyay, the Nepalese delegate to UN-
CLOS III, has suggested that the erosion of the concept of the
common heritage could in part be compensated for by the establishment of a *Common Heritage Fund*. His proposal called for
coastal States to make payments or contributions in kind to the
Fund from the proceeds derived from the exploitation of the non-
living resources - notably hydrocarbons - of the exclusive economic zone. The rate of payment to the Fund would be determined
by the ISA, taking into account the relative capacity of States
to make such payments and contributions. The ISA would make disbursements to States parties to the Law of the Sea Convention
on the basis of equitable sharing criteria. It would also be allowed to make disbursements to protect the marine environment,
to foster the transfer of marine technology, to help finance the
Enterprise, and to promote the work of the United Nations in the
management of ocean space and marine resources. (31)

The idea of a fund based upon the exploitation of non-living
resources in EEZs was first raised at the first substantive session of UNCLOS III held in Caracas in 1974. The idea is again
before the Conference in the form of the Nepalese proposal. Afghanistan, Austria, Bolivia, Lesotho, Singapore, Uganda, Upper
Volta and Zambia joined Nepal in submitting the proposal to the
Eighth Session.

It should be noted in this context that a more ambitious proposal
was made in 1970 by the International Ocean Institute for an
Ocean Development Tax. (32) Under this proposal, a small levy
(one per cent) would be collected by States on the value of all
major uses of ocean space, whether within or outside national
jurisdiction. This would apply to commercial fisheries (value of
landed catch); hydrocarbon production (wellhead value); shipping
(value of cargoes; use of cables per word); etc. The sums collected by States would be paid to the International Seabed Authority and to other intergovernmental organizations whose major
activities are focused on the marine environment, in agreed proportions and for clearly specified purposes.

The Regime for the Deep Sea-bed

Let us now turn to questions relating to the development of an
international regime for the deep seabed. In order to derive
resource management lessons from the experience gained it is
necessary to briefly consider the conceptual origins of the ISA
and particularly its operational arm, the Enterprise.

The idea of an Enterprise, as embodiment of the principle of
common heritage, has by now a rather long history. The California
based Center for the Study of Democratic Institutions was the
midwife who attended its birth. "Ocean Enterprises" were discussed in the Center's Ocean Regime project as early as 1968.

The first Center model draft treaty (33) provided for the representation and participation of companies in management decision-making in a multi-chamber Assembly: thus attempting to integrate political and economic decision-making and to bring private management under public control. A revised Center Draft
(34) proposed, in addition, a system of "Maritime Corporations"
for ocean mining, fisheries, navigation, and the mangement of
scientific research, to be half financed and governed by the
Ocean Authority, and half by companies. Although potentially already extending the concept to all areas of marine resource exploitation and services, this proposal anticipated proposals introduced in the Law of the Sea Conference several years later.

The Committee on the Peaceful Uses of the Seabed entertained a
number of proposals for a seabed mining Enterprise which was to
be the operational arm of the Authority and would have a monopoly
on seabed mining. The first proposal came from the Latin-American
Group and was inspired by the experience of the nationalization
of the copper mines in Peru. It was incorporated in a Working
Paper submitted by Chile, Colombia, Ecuador, El Salvador, Guate-
mala, Guyana, Jamaica, Mexico, Panama, Peru, Trinidad and Tobago,
Uruguay, and Venezuela. (35) Article 33 of this paper provides
that "The Enterprise is the organ of the Authority empowered to
undertake all technical industrial or commercial activities relating to the exploration of the area and exploitation of its
resources (by itself, or in joint ventures with juridical persons
only sponsored by States)". Article 34 specifies that "The Enterprise shall have an independent legal personality and such legal
capacity as may be necessary for the exercise of its functions
and the fulfillment of its purposes". Article 35, which was to
deal with questions relating to the structure and functions of
the Enterprise, was not elaborated in the Draft.

The Latin-American proposal gained the support of all developing
countries. They all agreed that resources which are the common
heritage of mankind have to be *managed* and that *management* has
to be embodied in an Authority which has to be provided, for this
purpose, with an operational arm.

The industrialized countries demurred. Common heritage to them
meant, if anything, a sharing of financial benefits, not joint
management. (36) It also meant an Authority which left the economic structures, including the consortia, intact and unchanged.

The gap appeared unbridgeable. The introduction of the 'parallel
system', now the 'logic' behind the regime for the deep seabed
did not close it. It merely displaced it to another level of discussion. In doing so it has left the key questions of how the
Enterprise is to be financed and how it is to obtain the technologies required to enable it to compete successfully with the
consortia unanswered. (37)

Negotiations were stifled by two basic, inherent contradictions: one is tempted to say tragic contradictions.

The first arose from underlying disagreement on the very purpose of the Authority, which the industrialized countries wanted limited in scope and powers while the developing countries wanted it wide in scope and powerful. After all, one of the main reasons that pushed the industrialized countries to develop their costly and sophisticated deep-sea mining technologies was that they wanted to decrease their dependence on some developing countries, considered politically unstable - especially for strategic metals such as cobalt and mangenese or molybdenum, besides copper and nickel. While trying to gain independence from those countries, they found themselves slipping under the control of an International Seabed Authority, dominated by those very same countries they had tried to elude. Some developing countries, on the other hand, soon discovered that seabed mining was to be a source of competition for land-based mining and that, far from benefiting them, it was going to decrease their export earnings. Total losses over a 20-year period, as calculated by UNCTAD, might run as high as 4 billion dollars. The powers with which they wanted to see the Authority endowed, therefore, were to include, above all, the power to control and limit seabed production. Canada, as a large-scale nickel producer, although not a developing country, played a leading role in giving expression to this concern.

The second stemmed from self-contradictory attitudes among the developed countries themselves: fear of Third-World domination suggested distrust in the Authority that was being established. No discretion was to be left to it in decision-making, lest such decisions were dictated by the majority of developing countries and incompatible with the interests of the minority of rich nations which were to invest huge sums of money in seabed mining. Every detail, about modes of operation, rules and regulations, amounts of payments, had to be pre-arranged and inscribed immutably in the text of the Convention. Thus, the text grew longer and more complicated with every year that passed. At the same time, however, these same nations, loyal keepers of the proprietary secrets of their companies, avowed to know nothing, nothing at all, about the ways this totally new and untried industry might work out, in technological, managerial, and financial terms. How the Conference was to elaborate minute details and technicalities for a period of 25 years, about the running of an industry about which it could know nothing, was never explained.

These basic contradictions both determined and frustrated the technical work of UNCLOS III in three main areas: production policy; the financing of the Enterprise; and the transfer of technology to the Enterprise.

Production Policy. Negotiations on limitations on production eventually led to a formula acceptable to the largest consumer

country (USA) and to the largest producer country (Canada).
This formula has a certain mathematical magic. Although unscrut-
able to the majority of delegates, it could not hide its real
weakness in the long run.

The formula is to be found in Article 151 ('Production Policies')
of the Draft Convention:

"(b) The production ceiling for any year of the interim period
beginning with the year of the earliest commercial production
shall be the sum of (i) and (ii) below:

(i) The difference between the trend line values for annual
nickel consumption as calculated pursuant to this subparagraph,
for the year immediately prior to the year of the earliest
commerical production and the year immediately prior to the
commencement of the interim period; plus

(ii) Sixty per cent of the difference between the trend line
values for nickel consumption, as calculated pursuant to this
subparagraph, for the year for which the production authorization is being applied for and the year immediately prior to
the year of the earliest commercial production;

(iii) Trend line values used for computing the nickel production ceiling pursuant to this subparagraph shall be those
annual nickel consumption values on a trend line computed
during the year in which a production authorization is issued.
The trend line shall be derived from a linear regression of
the logarithms of actual nickel consumption for the most recent
15-year period for which such data are available, time being
the independent variable."

The difficulties that arose were partly exposed in a report by
Ambassador Nandon, Chairman of a Committee of Experts appointed
to deal with them, during the Seventh Session of the Conference.
Attempts to solve these difficulties were very tentative, coun-
seling greater flexibility and more discretion for the Authority
in planning and decision-making.

The overriding difficulty arose from the fact that the power of
the Authority in limiting production is confined to "activities
in the area". It is meaningless, however, to limit "activities
in the area" if they cannot be so limited in areas under national jurisdiction. The opening of any new mine, in areas under national jurisdiction, potentially may have the same unsettling
effect on the volatile mineral market as the opening of seabed
mining. It should be noted, furthermore, that "land-based production" now explicitly includes production off-shore in areas
under national jurisdiction. This is a point that was stressed
repeatedly during the Eight Session. Considering, however, the
looseness of the definition of the boundaries of the international area in the Draft Convention (boundaries are determined

unilaterally by coastal States who merely have to declare and
register their claims), it is quite certain that if production
is limited in the international area while it is free in areas
under national jurisdiction, boundaries will simply be extended
as necessary, and production will take place under national jurisdiction. The effects on the metal market will be the same -
the International Seabed Authority will simply have limited itself out of production.

The second major difficulty arises from the fact that production
policy and limitation is pegged to the demand of one single metal, nickel. This is undoubtedly due to the fact that Canada, a
nickel producer, is the driving force behind the limitation policy. It is of small solace, however, to the producers of cobalt
and manganese, nor does it take into account current shifts of
attention by the industry, from nodules with a high nickel content to nodules of different metal and mineral composition. Ambassador Nandon's committee attempted to cope with the question
by proposing that even if no nickel is produced by a mining operation, the non-extracted nickel content determines the limit on
the other metals: but this leaves wide open the possibility of
a wild over-production of cobalt and manganese.

And, all the while, industrialized States were demanding that
there be not only a ceiling but also a floor for production, in
an attempt to rescue at least a limited access to the resources.
At the same time it became clear that the present depression of
land-based production will not encourage a rush into seabed mining in the near future.

The Financing of the Enterprise. Discussions on the financing of
the Enterprise, under the chairmanship of Ambassador Tommy Koh
of Singapore, have led to another complex set of provisions. An
application fee of $ 500,000 was provided for, to cover the costs
of processing the application of a contractor. An annual fixed
fee of $ 1,000,000 was set, to be paid from the date of entry
into force of the contract and that of commencement of commercial
production. This is to prevent speculative occupation of seabed
real estate. Upon commencement of production, the contractor is
either to continue to pay the annual fee or a production charge,
whichever is greater. The production charge can be paid in either
of two forms: a production charge (single system) or a combination between a production charge and a share of net proceeds
(mixed system). A detailed schedule of payments and percentages
was established: "net proceeds" and "gross proceeds" as well as
"attributable net proceeds (AMP)" were painstakingly defined.
The latter was necessary because "activities in the area" are
supposed to cover only exploration and exploitation, whereas subsequent stages of an integrated project - transportation, processing and marketing - are not to be accounted for by the Authority. This, in turn, gave rise to another set of complications,

since the Enterprise, through the Authority, is explicitly empowered to engage in transportation, processing, and marketing,
that is, in an area beyond its own limits of jurisdiction.

A range of figures has been negotiated up and down but, thus far,
no acceptable compromise has emerged. Either the charges were
low enough to be acceptable to the industrial States, but then
the Authority's income was too low to be of any benefit to developing States or to the Enterprise; or charges were high enough
to be of some use, but then they were totally unacceptable to
the industrial States, In no case, however, would the Authority's
revenue exceed $ 1.2 billion per contract over a 20-year period.
This is about $ 60 million per year; obviously totally inadequate
to start the Enterprise on its own operation.

An agreement had, therefore, to be reached on the financing of
the Enterprise, which had to cover, at least, the investment capital needed for one integrated mining operation, including exploration, exploitation, transporting, processing and marketing
- an investment which might run to roughly a billion dollars. The
question of how this amount was to be raised reamined unanswered.
Prospective sea-mining countries wanted the burden distributed
among all States parties to the Convention, according to the U.N.
scale of payments. Developing and socialist countries, presumably
not among the first sea-miners, advocated a system under which
the sea-mining countries that will be the primary beneficiaries
of sea-mining, would have the responsibility for providing this
capital. They also insisted on a 1:1 rate between cash payments
and guaranteed loans, whereas the industrialized countries took
the position that the cash/loan ratio might well be 1:2.

A host of additional difficulties cropped up which will almost
certainly turn out to be insoluble. They all derive from the
fundamental error of trying to establish a system in which the
Authority and its Enterprise are in direct competition with established industry. It is easy to show, in a simple mathematical
model, (38) that this kind of 'parallel system' is the most expensive and cost-ineffective of all conceivable systems: burden-
some to industrialized countries, developing countries, and the
Authority alike.

Technology Transfer to the Enterprise. The principal agents of
technology transfer to the Third World are transnational corporations. The history of transfer is a history of abuses, from
eightfold overcharging to such restrictions as so-called 'black-
box' technologies, and the sale of 'inappropriate' or obsolete
technologies. Waste, aggravation of differences between rich and
poor within a country, and growing dependence on the industrialized countries for spare parts and technicians, interference in
domestic politics on the part of the foreign company providing
the technology have been among the best known consequences of
technology transfer malpractices.

There is nothing to suggest that poor countries would fare better at sea than they have on land or that the transfer of the
highly sophisticated seabed mining technology would be more successful and more beneficial to developing countries than the
transfer of other industrial technology. Hence the seriousness
of the issue of technology transfer from the "contractor" - industrialized State or consortium - to the Authority, its Enterprise, and developing countries: an issue considered by Third
World countries to be absolutely crucial for success or failure
of the whole Conference.

The Draft Convention defines technology as "the specialized
equipment and technical know-how, including manuals, designs,
operating instructions, training and technical advice and assistance necessary to assemble, maintain and operate a variable
system and the legal right to use these items for that purpose on
a non-exclusive basis".(Annex III, Article 5 (8)). The definition
is thus a broad one and the Draft Convention makes elaborate
provisions for what appears to be mandatory transfer.

These provisions are too strict to be acceptable to industrialized countries which have been quick to take refuge behind the
shield of patent laws and the private-property based free-enter-
prise system. They are, however, not stringent enough for the
developing countries. They fear, rightly or wrongly, that the
conclusion of each "contract" with a "contractor" may give rise
to long drawn-out negotiations and arbitration procedures regarding the transfer of technologies. The result would be that they
remain *without* the technologies for the whole of the interim
period of two decades, up to the planned Review Conference.
Whether they would do better at the Review Conference than they
are doing now is an open question.

The difficulties surrounding the issue of technology transfer
stem, like those surrounding the financing of the Enterprise,
from the faulty conception of the 'parallel system' - a system
that places the ISA in a conflict situation with established industry.

Lessons for International
Resource Management

Many of the lessons learned during the course of the long and
difficult negotiations to build the prototype of an international
resource management authority are applicable, or adaptable, to
future international resource management institutions in other
areas. They may be summarized as follows:

(i) International resource management cannot be based on the
classical Roman-law concept of private ownership and on the
classical, static concept of national sovereignty. Both the con-

cepts of ownership and of sovereignty are being transformed by
the new, revolutionary concept of the common heritage of mankind.
This must form the basis of international resource management for
a NIEO just as it must constitute the basis of the International
Seabed Authority.

(ii) International resource management cannot be restricted to
the commodities (metals and minerals) of the international area
alone. In the discussions on the International Seabed Authority
it became amply clear that either the Authority has a voice in
planning the production and distribution of the minerals it is
managing - on a global basis, through commodity agreements or
other mechanisms - or it will not be able to do very much at all.
International resource management must follow functional rather
than territorial lines, which means essentially that it can just
as well be applied to resources other than those of the international or extranational areas. From the viewpoint of strategies, however, resources "beyond the limits of national jurisdiction" are the most obvious starting point.

(iii) It is futile to try to regulate the production of *one* commodity - nickel, in the case of the International Seabed Authority - and to peg the production of the other metals contained in
the nodules - copper, cobalt, mangenese and others - to the demand for nickel. Production and distribution must be planned for
all metals: nodules must be stockpiled and metals extracted according to the conditions of the market. The stockpiling of millions of tons of tailings may of course cause some serious environmental problems.

(iv) A public international resource management system cannot be
built *in competition* with established industry, whether State
enterprises or private consortia. It is the latter that have the
capital, the technology and the managerial skills required. They
must be *built into the new system* in such a way that they can
continue to operate effectively while maximizing the benefits to
the international community. Negotiations at the Law of the Sea
Conference indicate that a joint-venture system would come closest to providing a solution of this kind. Under such a system,
the consortia would provide half of the investment and operating
capital, the International Seabed Authority, the other half. The
Authority would appoint half of the Directors of the Board governing the Joint Venture, the consortia would appoint the other
half, in proportion to their investments. Profits would be shared
in the same proportion. The joint venture might comprise one or
all phases of an integraged operation, from exploration to exploitation, processing and marketing. The Board members appointed by the Authority could all come from developing countries or
from small industrialized countries without a seabed mining capacity of their own. It would constitute a new form of economic
cooperation, facilitating enormously the transfer of technologies and the financing of the international authority.

It would, for the first time, bring transnational corporations
under public international control. It would, in fact, create a
new type of public international company: it would be a significant contribution to the building of a New International Economic Order.

(v) International management of *resources* must be complemented
and integrated with international management of *technologies*.
Without such integration international resource management would
be both unpractical and unacceptable. There are a number of con-
verging reasons for this. Resources and technologies are interdependent. Resources become exploitable as the technologies,
from simple to highly complex, from 'labor-intensive' to 'capital-intensive', become available and their cost can be borne by
the market. Without 'appropriate' technology, therefore, there
cannot be any resource management at all. The generation of
wealth through resource management has four component factors:
resource, capital, labor and technology; each factor assuming a
variable proportion of importance throughout history. Industries
based on highly developed technologies are *less* resource-inten-
sive than industries based on less developed technologies, in as
much as substitution, synthesizing and recycling reduce the
original amount of raw materials required. It is, therefore, essential for developing countries that the international management (in which they participate) of resources and of technologies are balanced and integrated. Finally, there is a political
reason for this integration. Resources, in today's post-colonial
extraction economy, are located largely in developing countries.
Technologies are the monopoly of industrialzed countries. If developing countries are asked to accept a common heritage status
for resources over which they hold sovereign rights, industrial
States, as counterpart, must accept the same status for their
technologies.

(vi) Effective ways have to be found of raising international
capital for development purposes. In the case of the ISA its investment share in the joint ventures would have to be raised -
at least in the early period before it becomes revenue generating. Perhaps the most practical solution would be the adoption,
on the basis of international agreement, of an international tax
based upon the use of the oceans. (39) Reference has already been
made to the proposal for a Common Heritage Fund and to the International Ocean Institute's proposal for an Ocean Development Tax.
Other proposals for taxes based upon the use of the oceans have
been made over the years. (40) 'Benchmark' documents, like the
so-called Cocoyoc Declaration, have also supported the idea. (41)

Whan can be extrapolated from these lessons learnt? What would
be the best approach to the development of a global planning and
resource management capability? The most appropriate approach
would appear to be to take the best available International Sea-

bed Authority model - that is, the 'unitary joint venture system' - and apply it, with the necessary modifications, across the board to all transnational corporations involved in a significant way with basic resource management as well as to State enterprises and private consortia similarly involved. This would effectively amount to an *international chartering,* under U.N. auspices, of such companies and consortia, providing a degree of international public control and participation, including the participation of developing countries and, more broadly, the representation of consumers and of labor on the boards of the companies thus chartered. The *Statute for European Companies,* though still on the drawing board, could be studied as another 'prototype' for this kind of arrangement. The chartering could be made obligatory, or it could be voluntary. In the latter case, there should be such legal and financial incentives as to make it effectively the new *modus operandi.*

The building of an 'Enterprise system' under U.N. auspices, and with the participation of the competent Specialized Agencies (FAO, IAEA, INTELSAT, INMARSAT, UNIDO, IOC, etc.) would have another advantage. Besides providing a necessary and long eluded control of the transnationals, this 'Enterprise system' would also enhance the restructuring of the U.N. system of organizations as it would require, in each case, the *adding of an operational arm* to the agencies, patterned on the 'Enterprise' of the Seabed Authority. If they are to be effective in the last quarter of this century and the beginning of the next, the U.N. agencies must indeed become 'operational'. This is surely one of the requirements of the New International Economic Order.

Transnational food companies would be chartered by FAO. One part of FAO, the Committee on Fisheries (COFI) will, in the wake of UNCLOS III, undergo a structural transformation making it more operational. Changes in COFI are, in turn, bound to affect FAO as a whole. FAO could eventually be made responsible for chartering food transnationals. With these enterprises FAO could establish 'Enterprises' in the way in which the ISA establishes 'Enterprises' with the mining consortia. This might provide a new instrument for effectively limiting the impact of the major food crises which have been predicted for the 1980s.

The nuclear reactor industry must go public under charters provided by IAEA. The provisions of the charter would incorporate all the safety measures recently discussed in the context of the Non-Proliferation Treaty and the International Nuclear Fuel Cycle Evaluation (INFCE). (42)

Multinational oil companies could be chartered by UNIDO: that is, UNIDO could establish 'Enterprises' with the participation of producer and consumer States, developed and developing countries. A precedent for this kind of arrangement is the newly established Arab Drilling and Workover Company (ADWC), with a

private company (Santa Fe) holding 40 per cent and the Arab
Petroleum Services Company (APSC) holding 60 per cent. APSC was
established as an operational arm by OAPEC. ADWC is APSC's first
subsidiary or 'Enterprise'.

As a final example, the space industries might be chartered by
INTELSAT or INMARSAT. The establishment of 'Enterprises' to manage satellite-based factories would be a most appropriate case
for the application of the common heritage principles and Enterprise system since the moon and other celestial bodies have already been declared by the United Nations to be the common
heritage of mankind (see below).

An Enterprise system of this kind would be very much decentralized operationally. Each Enterprise would be responsible for its
own production policy. There would be special institutions within the system, on a regional and global basis, to integrate and
harmonize policies and plans.

The Draft Convention (Articles 275 and 276) proposes the establishment of national and regional marine scientific and technological centers. The concept could be enlarged and applied to
the building of regional scientific and technological centers in
general. Such centers could play three major roles: undertaking
environmental monitoring and environmental impact studies; training as a basis for technology transfer; and exercising a planning
function through the preparation of economic/technological models
for resource production and distribution, providing a basis for
the integration and harmonization of the policies and plans prepared by the 'Enterprises'. Financing for such centers could be
provided by international taxes on the pattern of the ocean development tax as well as from the revenues of the Enterprise system.

The unitary joint venture formula has the advantage of being
very flexible. The proportion between public/international share-
holding and representation and private/State share-holding and
representation could vary on a sliding scale. The more commercial
the Enterprise, the greater could be private or State participation (e.g. the food industry). The greater the security aspects
of an Enterprise, the greater should be public/international participation (e.g. the nuclear reactor industry).

The descriptions and prescriptions presented above have an un-
deniable utopian ring. Certainly, the difficulties in the path
toward the realization of such systems are enormous. Some of the
industries mentioned - the nuclear reactor and space industries
for instance - are among the most sensitive. The free enterprise
system is still resiliant and the industrialized nations can be
expected to resist international controls as long as they can.
Yet the ideas expressed here do not come out of 'thin air'. The
idea of a U.N. Charter for transnational corporations has been

vented on many occasions. It may be an idea whose time has come.
The Charter for European Companies has been drawn up and adopted
by the Commission of the European Communities. Private (national)
and public (international) sectors work harmoniously together in
the space industry; and the long negotiations on the International Seabed Authority, the prototype for international resource
management institutions, are drawing to a close. None of the proposals made here are really new. They are merely projections of
ongoing trends.

Towards a Functional Federation of
International Organizations

Experience with the Law of the Sea clearly suggests that the
most effective way of restructuring the U.N. system through
the creation of a functional federation of international organizations, some established, others to be created, linked
through appropriate integrative machinery. This essentially involves creating an institutional 'module' for ocean space and
marine resources.

This would suggest that a 'module' system could constitute the
most effective way of progressively developing a global planning
and resource management capability. Modules could be created,
for example, for each of the issue areas for which the international community must eventually formulate a response.

One module could be developed, for example, for the outer space
sector. A large number of U.N. agencies, organizations, and commissions as well as other intergovernmental, regional and non-
governmental organizations are presently engaged in outer space
activities. The U.N. Committee on the Peaceful Uses of Outer
Space (COPUOS) has the mandate to coordinate these activities,
which are regulated by a number of legal instruments, the most
important of which is the so-called Outer Space Treaty of 1967.
The Treaty, which provides a code of conduct, does not provide
for any kind of decision-making machinery nor does it take much
account of the economic and development potential of space and
satellite technology. As this potential becomes more obvious and
given the fact that the common heritage principle has been applied to the resources of the moon and other celestial bodies,
it becomes necessary to create machinery through which all nations can share in policy-making as well as in the management
of programs and technologies.

One could imagine a periodic Outer Space Conference or Assembly
(every three, two, or one year/s), which might either consist
of all member States or, if the model of a functional federation
of international organizations were to be followed, of representatives of all the international organizations active in outer

space. (Which, in turn, are composed of States). COPUOS might
serve as an Executive Council, or the Conference itself might
elect an Executive Council which would supersede COPUOS and
would be chosen on a strictly regional basis ensuring equitable
representation of all parts of the world. (43) Obviously there
would have to be some kind of common Secretariat which might
well be the U.N. Secretariat. Such an *International Outer Space
Authority* would have to have an operational arm, although it may
be difficult, at this stage, to say whether it would be more
functional to create it *ex novo,* following the pattern of the
Seabed Authority, or whether the operational arm should be even
more decentralized, utilizing existing operational organizations
such as INTELSAT, INTERSPUTNIK, INMARSAT, ESO, which, in this
case would have to be brought under the policy of the Authority.

Supposing there were six or seven such 'modules' or 'world economic communities' (in the meaning given to the word 'communities' by the 'European Economic Communities') dealing with oceans
outer space, energy, food, mineral resources, science and technology, international trade - the whole system could be drawn
together in a restructured ECOSOC, which might be composed of
Delegations from these various module Conferences or Assemblies.

EXPANDING THE COMMON HERITAGE

The ideas formulated above might be looking a bit too far - and
too logically - into the future. History will no doubt fumble
along its own way: far less logical, far less straightforward.
In terms of strategies, the essential task is to look for new
domains and new opportunities to apply the concept of the common heritage of mankind.

In doing so we should recognize that we are dealing with a concept whose time has come and one which is powerful. The concept
has crept into international law. Although it still lacks a rigorous definition, it has become, through the Law of the Sea Conference, an accepted norm of international law. Its acceptance
by the international community has slowly transformed it from a
moral concept into a legal concept. (44) Its evolution within
the framework of UNCLOS III has given a new legitimacy to demands for justice and equity.

In this final section we still look at some of the opportunities
for expanding the common heritage. We will look first at its
further functional expansion to include living resources and
then at the opportunities for applying the concept to two domains
which fall outside national jurisdiction: outer space and the
Antarctic continent.

Common Heritage and Living Resources

We have already referred to the need for a functional expansion
of the concept to include non-living resources, notably manganese nodules, within EEZs. A parallel step must be its expansion
to include living resources in international as well as national
ocean space.

A signpost in this direction is a statement made by the delegation of the Holy See at the Seventh Session of UNCLOS III in the
Spring of 1978. "The Contribution which the Holy See can make to
the Conference does not consist of technical proposals", the
statement reads, "but rather principles which may guarantee just
and equitable solutions for the whole international community
and, in the first line, the principle which is universally accepted, at least on the theoretical level, namely that the sea
is 'the common heritage of mankind'." It should be noted that
the statement says "the sea", not "the seabed beyond the limits
of national jurisdiction".

"Moreover", the statement continues, "this view constitutes a
part of a larger principle of 'The universal purpose of created
things'. It is already applied by States on their territory, not
as a restriction of their sovereignty, but as an exploitation or
use of their natural resources which shall take into consideration the needs of the whole humanity and, above all, of States
which are most deprived of them".

In particular the statement points out that while "the principle
of delineation of maritime areas adjacent to the coast into economic zones entrusted to the coastal State is acceptable", on
the contrary, "the strictly speaking appropriation of the living
resources of these areas is not admissible because they do not
constitute res nullius but they represent goods which belong to
the community of nations and, in addition, because the argument
of contiguity which is invoked as a justification for such appropriation does not represent a sufficient basis for it".

The statement was well received by many - especially African -
developing countries as well as the Socialist States. It represents a moral force and contributes toward a conceptual breakthrough. The application of the ideas expressed to exclusive
economic zones would ensure that land-locked and geographically
disadvantaged countries have access to and are able to participate in regional joint management regimes.

Common Heritage and Outer Space

Outer space has long been recognized as a candidate for the common heritage. The Outer Space Treaty of 1967 defines outer space
as "the Common Province of Mankind", and astronauts as the "en-

voys of mankind". No treaty has ever used such language. The
concepts, however, remained in the realm of the poetic. With
the limits of outer space undefined, and the economic potential
of space technology as nebulous as the more remote stars, there
appeared to be no urgent need to endow the poetic expression
with a precise legal content.

That situation has now fundamentally changed. Technological developments in recent years have brought outer space 'nearer'
and the economic potential of space and satellite technologies,
and their impact on development, have become more and more evident. It was thus of considerable importance that on 3 July 1979,
after seven years of deliberations, the U.N. Committee on the
Peaceful Uses of Outer Space approved a draft international
agreement which declares the natural resources of the moon and
other celestial bodies the common heritage of mankind. The so-
called Moon Treaty bars any claim to national ownership of any
part of the moon and contamination of the moon's environment.
It declares that the moon is to be used for peaceful purposes
only and that State parties to the Treaty will pool all information resulting from exploratory activities.

The Moon Treaty was approved at the 34th Session of the U.N.
General Assembly at the end of 1979 and is now open for ratification. (45)

The next essential step is to apply the common heritage concept
to the products of space activity. This would ensure that the
information gathered by satellites, for example, on earth resources, on pollution, on weather, or on military activities
would become available to, and used in the interests of, all
nations rather than the space superpowers. (46) Recents developments in this area are discussed in chapter 7.

Common Heritage and Antarctica

The Antarctic continent has a total area of some 14 million
square kilometres. Occupying one tenth of the world's land surface, it is far larger than Australia, larger than Europe, than
the U.S. and Mexico combined, even larger than India and China
taken together. It is also the coldest, driest, windiest, least
accessible, worst known and generally the most unpleasant of all
the seven continents. (47)

Since 1959 the 'cold continent' has been governed by the Antarctic Treaty. The Treaty was negotiated by 12 nations, all of
whom had participated in the International Geophysical Year,
at a special conference convened by the U.S. and held outside
the United Nations. It became operative on 23 June 1961 when
the 12 signatory powers, called "consultative parties" in the
Treaty, ratified it. Seven of the signatories (Argentina, Aus-

tralia, Chile, France, New Zealand, Norway and the U.K.) have
- in some cases conflicting - territorial claims to the continent; the other five parties (Belgium, Japan, South Africa, USA,
and USSR) do not. Since its coming into force, nine other nations (Brazil, Bulgaria, Czechoslovakia, Denmark, German Democratic Republic, Netherlands, Poland, Romania and West Germany)
have acceded to the treaty, although they do not have full consultative powers. (48)

The Antarctic Treaty is a rather modest document of 14 Articles.
It recognizes that "it is in the interest of all mankind that
Antarctica shall continue forever to be used exclusively for
peaceful purposes". "Measures of a military nature" are banned
as are nuclear explosions and the dumping of nuclear wastes.
Freedom of scientific investigation is ensured and there are
provisions for the exchange of information. Appointed observers
from consultative treaty powers have the right of free access
to any area and may inspect all stations, installations and
equipment. (49)

The Treaty applies to "the area south of 60° south latitude,
including iceshelves". It thus includes vast areas of ocean
space, the Southern Ocean. Of great importance is Article IV of
the Treaty which freezes the legal status quo in Antarctica.
New claims are banned during the period the Treaty is in force.
The Treaty may be reviewed after 30 years have elapsed since
its entering into force, which would mean a review in mid 1991.

The Treaty has no machinery or dispute settlement procedures.
Consultative meetings are held approximately once every two
years for the purpose of modifying or amending the Treaty. (50)
Recommendations are only effective when they receive the unani-
mous agreement of all consultative parties. (51)

Drafted at the height of the Cold War the Antarctic Treaty is
in many respects a significant achievement. Despite its obvious
shortcomings - its institutionalization of an elite 'Antarctic
club', its lack of provisions for resource management, and its
lack of real machinery, for example - the Treaty, until comparatively recently, worked reasonably well. It has helped keep
Antarctica demilitarized, internationalized and pollution-free.
Territorial claims have been suspended; scientific bases have
been open to surprise inspection; nations have cooperated in
scientific research and results have been freely published and
exchanged. It may be no exaggeration to suggest, as Jon Tinker
has done, that "a continent half as big again as the United
States has been under the nearest thing to a world government
yet known". (52)

When Antarctica's main export was scientific information, the
Antarctic Treaty made sense. It was, as Elisabeth Young observed,
"agreeable, sensible and harmless, and risked no one". (53)

The world's chancelleries have never been too enamered with science and were prepared to leave the cold continent to those who were eccentric enough to want to study the growth of lichens in temperatures of -50°C.

This situation has now fundamentally changed and the Antarctic Treaty is under unprecedented attack. The reason for this is that the Antarctic continent and its surrounding seas may well constitute a great treasure trove of resources, renewable and non-renewable.

Although none has yet been discovered, there seems little doubt that Antarctica posseses important deposits of oil and gas. Privately, many oil companies are convinced that oil will be found and some have speculated that there may be as much as or more than there is in Alaska. (54) The technology required for exploratory drilling already exists, having been developed in the Arctic, and a number of countries - the U.S., Australia, Canada, France and Japan among them - have demonstrated a great deal of interest in the commencement of drilling operations. (55)

The hard mineral resources of Antarctica are unknown. The continent is virtually uncharted geologically and there has been little exploration either on land or at sea. By 1964, 14 minerals with a commercial value had been found, including significant deposits of iron ore and what may be the world's largest coalfield. Analogy with other continents suggests that Antarctica could have 900 major mineral deposits. (56)

Of no less interest are the living resources of Antarctica. Although its land mass is almost lifeless, its seas are among the most biologically productive in the world. Fin fish, which is being intensively fished by the Soviet Union, East Germany and Poland, is plentiful, as are squid, crabs and lobsters. Of particular importance is krill (euphausia superba), a shrimp-like crustacean which grows up to a length of some 7 cm. There may be up to one quadrillion - one thousand million million - of them in the Southern Ocean. Being around 15 per cent protein, roughly the same as beefsteak, shrimp or lobster, they could have a tremendous significance in meeting world food needs in the years ahead.

Estimates of the annual sustainable yield of krill have been as high as one billion tons. More recent estimates suggest a yield of 110-115 million tons. (57) Although considerably less than first estimates, a yield in this range would triple the total world fish catch (around 70 million tons in 1977). Scientists are still discussing the question of sustainable yield. Given the fact that krill provides the major food supply of five species of whale, three species of seal, 20 species of fish, three species of squid and numerous bird species, the risks of possible overfishing, a fate that befell the Peruvian anchoveta, cannot be taken lightly. (58)

Antarctica's hydrocarbons and living resources are concentrated within 200 miles of subantarctic islands or the Antarctic mainlands. The seven claimant States, once prepared to suspend their claims in the interests of scientific research, have proven less principled when the issue is oil and fisheries. They all consider, to varying extents, that their dubious territorial claims entitle them to establish exclusive economic zones in the Southern Ocean. They evidently feel that if they do not declare sovereignty over Antarctic waters they are in effect abandoning full sovereignty over the land. The non-claimant States cannot accept the validity of Antarctic EEZs without admitting mainland sovereignty, which they have always resolutely denied. This development has driven a wedge through the Antarctic club. It also threatens to drive limited internationalism out of Antarctica and to wreck the Antarctic Treaty.

The rush to carve up Antarctica and to appropriate its resources is on. It is one which must be resisted at all costs. The Antarctic continent must be used and managed for the benefit of and in the interests of everyone. Its minerals, hydrocarbons and living resources are the common heritage of mankind.

Calls for a regime which better reflects the interests of the international community are not new. These calls have, however, intensified as the developing countries have come to recognize the importance of Antarctica. In 1975, the issue of Antarctica was raised in the U.N. by Shirley Amerasinghe. "There are still areas on this planet", he observed, "where opportunities remain for constructive and peaceful cooperation on the part of the international community for the common good of all rather than the benefit of a few. Such an area is the Antarctic continent... There can be no doubt", he went on, "that there are vast possibilities for a new initiative that would redound to the benefit of all mankind. Antarctica is an area where the now widely accepted ideas and concepts relating to international economic cooperation with their special stress on the principle of equitable sharing of the world's resources, can find ample scope for application..." (59)

In 1976 India requested the U.N. to take up the issue of Antarctica. Guinea, Sri Lanka, Cuba and Peru are among the developing countries that have called for a new Antarctic Treaty. Third World concern was expressed by Sri Lankan ambassador Christopher Pinto in 1977 when he observed that every effort must be made to prevent marine resources becoming the "subject of selfish and irresponsible exploitation by those who, for the time being, possess the technology for the purpose". The international community, Pinto noted, had an "undoubted and continuing interest" in the Southern Ocean and called for "a regime of rational management and utilization to secure optimum benefits for mankind as a whole, and in particular, for the developing

countries, in accordance with appropriate global international
arrangements, and within the framework of the new international
economic order". (60) Similar sentiments were expressed two
years later by Alvaro de Soto, a Peruvian diplomat active in
UNCLOS III. Critical of the "exclusive attitude" and "secre-
tative style of consultation" of the Antarctic Treaty powers,
he warned them not to "set aside private hunting grounds" in the
Antarctic. The Antarctic Treaty, he argued, "should be understood as an eminently provisional arrangement..." It cannot purport... to prejudge the definitive status of Antarctica... The
silence of the (international) community regarding the treaty",
he observed, "can hardly be understood as a form of acquiescence".
(61)

The Treaty powers have so far turned a deaf ear to the voice of
the Third World and have been successful in opposing moves to
raise the issue of Antarctica. In 1975, for example, they prevented UNEP from even discussing Antarctica, and they have also
managed to dilute a large-scale FAO project aimed at developing
Antarctic fisheries. They have also negotiated, among themselves,
a so-called 'Krill Convention' which seeks to regulate fishing
of this valuable, protein rich resource. The Convention, negotiated in great secrecy, is a compromise document which attempts
to balance the interests of claimant and non-claimant States.
In line with the tradition of 'exclusiveness', non-members of
the Antarctic Treaty will only be allowed to join the proposed
'Krill Commission' by invitation of the consultative parties.(62)

As the tremendous potential of the cold continent becomes ever
clearer, the consultative powers will not be able to prevent
discussion of Antarctica and its resources. As conflicting interests become more marked, the Treaty powers will themselves
be compelled to search for new international arrangements.
Scientific research, demilitarization, peaceful coexistence and
environmental protection are valuable and complementary goals.
The exploitation of living and non-living resources does not fit
within this framework, nor does the idea of competition for
those resources. In the past decade, Antarctica has come to en-
capsulate many of the key political issues of our time - rich
versus poor, strong versus weak, transnational corporate interests versus the interests of the international community, exploitation versus conservation. (63)

These conflicts revolve around two interrelated issues: how
should the area be used; and who should decide how to use it.
The answer is becoming increasingly obvious. Antarctica should
be used and managed for the benefit of all mankind and all nations should participate in the making of decisions. In other
words, the need is for a common heritage regime.

There are positive signs that such a regime could be built.
Norway, for example, has suggested that the krill of the South-

ern Ocean be declared the common heritage of mankind. The two
superpowers have no territorial claims. New Zealand has stated
that it is prepared to forego its claim. Belgium and the U.K.
have also been sympathetic. In a paper presented in April 1977,
Brian Roberts, for many years in charge of U.K. Antarctic foreign
policy and one of the architects of the Treaty, observed that:
"Anyone who seriously considers the future of the Antarctic
Treaty Area must take into account the emergent hopes and wishes
now finding expression in many nations which are not themselves
active in the Antarctic. There is a widespread belief that this
very large region possesses immensely rich resources which are,
or should be, part of the common heritage of mankind". (64)

As far as minerals are concerned there is some evidence to suggest that nearly all consultative parties are being influenced
by these "hopes and wishes". At the Ninth Antarctic Treaty consultative meeting in 1977, representatives recommended to their
governments that they endorse the principle that "Consultative
Parties, in dealing with the question of mineral resources in
Antarctica, should not prejudice the interests of all mankind
in Antarctica" (Recommendation IX.1.1977).

If the Law of the Sea negotiations are any guide, the job of
building a rational and equitable international regime for the
Antarctic continent and the Southern Ocean will be long and difficult. The conference itself, however, offers a tentative solution. As a first step toward a regime, the International Seabed Authority could be given the power, through UNCLOS III, to
establish provisional limits for the international area in the
Antarctic region following consultations with Antarctic Treaty
powers. It should be noted in this respect that a group of Arab
countries has already proposed that the ISA take Antarctica
under its wing, and manage the offshore oil reserves. (65)

Other Domains for the Application
of the Common Heritage of Mankind

The need for rational resource management and a more equitable
international order suggests that, in the longer-term, the concept of the common heritage of mankind should be applied to
those resources where uneven distribution threatens world peace
and security. Food falls into this category. Harlan Cleveland
has, in this context, already raised the question of whether the
U.S.'s "amber waves of grain" may not need one day to be designated common heritage. (66) Energy would similarly fall into
this category.

Another candidate for the common heritage are technologies which
have a dual-purpose character, i.e. those with an intrinsic potential for good and for evil. The question of building a 'dual-
purpose' technology system is the subject of chapter 7.

NOTES AND REFERENCES

(1) The chapter draws upon a number of published sources. The most important are: by Elisabeth Mann Borgese: *The Drama of the Oceans*, Harry N.Abrams, Inc., New York, 1975; 'The Age of Aquarius', in A.J.Dolman and J.van Ettinger (eds.), *Partners in Tomorrow: Strategies for a New International Order*, E.P.Dutton, New York, 1977, pp. 193-204; 'Expanding the Common Heritage' in A.J.Dolman (ed.), *Global Planning and Resource Management: Toward International Decision-Making in a Divided World*, Pergamon, New York, 1980, pp. 181-194; 'Introduction' in Arvid Pardo, *The Common Heritage: Selected Papers on Oceans and World Order 1967-1974*, International Ocean Institute Paper No. 3, Malta University Press, 1975; by Arvid Pardo and Elisabeth Mann Borgese: *The New International Economic Order and the Law of the Sea*, International Ocean Institute Occasional Paper No. 4, Msida, Malta, 1976; and 'The Common Heritage of Mankind and the Transfer of Technologies', paper prepared for the IOI training course on the management of exclusive economic zones, held in Malta in spring 1980 (mimeo).

(2) U.N. General Assembly Resolution 2172 (XXI), 6 December 1966.

(3) Statement made by President Lyndon B.Johnson on 13 July 1966 on the occasion of the commissioning of the marine research vessel 'Oceanography'.

(4) See U.N. document A/6695.

(5) See U.N. document A/C.P.V. 1515-1516, 1 November 1967. The most important statements made by Arvid Pardo on matters related to ocean management and the common heritage of mankind are reprinted in Arvid Pardo, *The Common Heritage: Selected Papers on Oceans and World Order 1967-1974*, International Ocean Institute Occasional Paper No. 3, Malta University Press, 1975. For the statement made to the First Committee on 1 November 1967, see pp. 1-41.

(6) Or to give it its full title, the Treaty on the Prohibition of the Emplacement of Nuclear Weapons and Other Weapons of Mass Destruction on the Seabed and the Ocean Floor and the Subsoil thereof, 1972.

(7) Resolution 2750C (XXV).

(8) Statement before the First Committee of the General Assembly, October 29, 1968, reprinted in Arvid Pardo, op.cit., pp. 51-65.

(9) S.Gorove, 'The Concept of the Common Heritage of Mankind: A Political, Moral or Legal Innovation', 9 *San Diego Law Review*, 390, 1970, p. 402.

(10) See Arvid Pardo, 'Ocean Management and Development', paper presented to the IX Pacem in Maribus Convocation, Yaounde, January 1979, (mimeo).

(11) See his statement made at a Pacem in Maribus seminar held
     in Rhode Island, January/February 1970, reprinted in Elisa-
     beth Mann Borgese, (ed.), *Pacem in Maribus*, Dodd, Mead &
     Co., New York, 1972, viz. pp. 161-2.
(12) Jovan Djordjević, 'The Social Enterprise of Mankind', in
     Pacem in Maribus, op.cit.
(13) See Amilcar O.Herrera et al., *Catastrophe or New Society:
     A Latin American World Model*, International Development
     Research Centre, Ottawa, 1976, p. 26.
(14) Orio Giarini, *Producing Value for Wealth - The Role of
     Capital and Capital Needs*, The Club of Rome, October 1979.
(15) United Nations, *Draft Convention on the Law of the Sea*,
     document A/CONF.62/WP.10/Rev. 3, 22 September 1980.
(16) The *First* U.N. Conference on the Law of the Sea was held
     in Geneva in 1958. It agreed on four conventions: on
     fishery conservation; on the high seas, declaring the free-
     dom to fish, navigate, flyover, and lay submarine cables
     and pipelines; on the territorial sea and the contiguous
     zone, defining a new contiguous zone, up to 12 miles from
     shore, within which coastal States had some jurisdiction;
     and on the continental shelf, extending seabed jurisdic-
     tion to 200 metres or to a depth "which admits of the ex-
     ploitation of the natural resources". The *Second* U.N. Con-
     ference on the Law of the Sea was convened in Geneva in
     1960. It met to discuss fishery limits and the settlement
     of disputes, but its proposals failed (by one vote) to get
     a required two-thirds majority.
(17) U.N. document A/Conf.62/WP.8/Part 1.
(18) U.N. document A/Conf.62/WP.8/Rev. 1/Part 1.
(19) U.N. document A/Conf.62/WP.10/Add. 1.
(20) See Arvid Pardo, 'Justice and the Oceans', in John L.Logue
     (ed.), *Peace, Justice and the Law of the Sea*, World Order
     Research Institute, Villanova University, Villanova, Pa.,
     1978, pp. 51-57, at p. 51.
(21) U.N. documents A/Conf.62/WP.10/Rev. 1 and A/Conf.62/WP.10/
     Rev. 2.
(22) U.N. document A/Conf.62/WP.10/Rev. 3, 22 September 1980.
(23) Deprived from being a member of an official delegation,
     Arvid Pardo has been able to attend most of the UNCLOS III
     sessions in various consultative capacities.
(24) See *The Economist*, 30 December 1978, pp. 35-36.
(25) The main commercial actors are eight consortia of enter-
     prises, six of which are engaged in operations. The main
     consortia are: *Kennecott Exploration Corporation* (known as
     the Kennecott Group), established 1974 with 6 enterprises
     from U.S., U.K., Canada and Japan; *Ocean Mining Associates*
     (known as U.S. Steel Group or Deepsea Ventures Group),
     established 1974 with 3 enterprises, 2 from U.S. and 1
     from Belgium; *Ocean Management Incorporated* (known as INCO
     Group), established in 1975, with 6 enterprises from Canada,

U.S. and West Germany; *Ocean Minerals Company* (known as Lockheed Group), established 1977 with 4 enterprises from U.S., Netherlands and U.K.; *Association Française pour l'Etude et la Recherche des Nodules* (AFERNOD) (known as French Group), made up of French enterprises and government agencies; *Continuous Line Bucket (CLB) Syndicate* (known as CLB Group) with 20 enterprises from 6 countries; *Deep Ocean Minerals Association* (DOMA) (known as Japanese Group), with 35 Japanese enterprises and various government agencies; and *Eurocean*, established 1970, with 24 European enterprises (from France, Belgium, Netherlands, U.K., Italy, Sweden, Norway, Spain and Switzerland), directed to scientific research and survey rather than commercial activities. For brief descriptions of each of these consortia, see 'The U.N. Puts to Sea', *Development Forum*, June-July 1979, p. 9.

(26) For figures on the area of EEZs, see *Neptune: Independent News at the Law of the Sea*, Number 3, April 14, 1975, (Geneva), pp. 4-6.

(27) On the question of the international institutional machinery required for the management of ocean space see two essays by Arvid Pardo and Elisabeth Mann Borgese: 'Ocean Management' in Jan Tinbergen (coordinator), *Reshaping the International Order: A Report to The Club of Rome*, E.P. Dutton, New York, 1976, pp. 305-317; and *The New International Economic Order and the Law of the Sea*, IOI Occasional Paper No. 4, International Ocean Institute, Msida, Malta, 1976.

(28) Of importance here is the idea of international resource regions discussed in chapter 4.

(29) It might be noted here that under the Euratom Treaty nuclear resources are 'common heritage' even though they are in areas under national jurisdiction.

(30) On this see W.Riphagen, 'Some Reflections on "Functional Sovereignty"', *Netherlands Yearbook of International Law*, vol. VI, 1975, pp. 121-165, viz. pp. 143-148.

(31) See document A/Conf.62/65.

(32) See International Ocean Institute, *Proceedings of the First Pacem in Maribus Convocation*, Malta, June 28-July 3, 1970, Volume 3: 'Planning and Development in the Oceans', International Ocean Institute, Msida, Malta, 1970.

(33) See Elisabeth Mann Borgese, *The Ocean Regime*, Center for the Study of Democratic Institutions, Santa Barbara, Ca., October 1968.

(34) See Elisabeth Mann Borgese, op.cit., 1972.

(35) Document A/AC.138/49, entitled 'The Regime for the Seabed and Ocean Floor and the Subsoil Thereof Beyond the Limits of National Jurisdiction'.

(36) This was very evident in, for example, the U.S. trusteeship proposal. In an attempt to reconcile the EEZ with the

common heritage concept the U.S. in 1970 proposed exclusive
coastal State jurisdiction down to the 200 metre depth line,
with a trusteeship zone over the remainder of the continental shelf, within which the coastal State would act as a
trustee for the international community, paying half to
two-thirds of the revenues derived from international funds.
Although an important proposal it made no provision for
joint management responsibilities.

(37) On these questions, see Elisabeth Mann Borgese, *The Enterprises*, IOI Occasional Paper No. 6, International Ocean
Institute, Msida, Malta, 1977.

(38) See Elisabeth Mann Borgese, 'The Impact of Seabed Mining
on Developing Countries: Four Models', Paper presented to
a seminar held at the Institut Universitaire des Hautes
Etudes Internationales, Geneva, August 1979.

(39) The subject of international taxation is discussed in
chapter 6.

(40) Reference should be made to the revenue sharing provisions
of the U.S. trusteeship zone proposal (see footnote 36) and
the proposal made by Canada in the U.N. Seabed Committee
for an international tax on, or payment with regard to, seabed minerals (including oil), beyond the limits of the
territorial sea.

(41) The Cocoyoc Declaration, the result of a UNEP/UNCTAD Symposium on 'Patterns of Resource Use, Environment, and
Development Strategies', held in Mexico in 1974, advocates
the need for strong international regimes for exploiting
the common heritage, and emphasizes the importance of the
oceans. Among the proposals made is one for the levying of
tolls on vessels using the high seas. The Declaration is
reproduced in *Development Dialogue*, no. 2, 1974, pp. 88-96.

(42) See the discussion of nuclear technologies in chapter 7.

(43) The principle of regional representation, which is becoming
increasingly important in the United Nations system, ought
to be elaborated and refined. The four 'regions' - Asia,
Africa, Latin America and 'Western Europe and others' - are
clearly inadequate as a basis for equitable regional representation. The concept of 'region' has many meanings and is
nowhere clearly defined. As a basis for equitable representation, the 15 regions established in the *Leontief Report*
might offer a fair, balanced, and workable solution: e.g.
in a Council of 36 members, at least two members would have
to be chosen from each of these 15 regions, while six might
be chosen at large, to have more flexibility. See Wassily
Leontief, *The Future of the World Economy*, Oxford University
Press, New York, 1977.

(44) On this see Christopher Pinto, 'Toward a Regime Governing
International Public Property', in A.J.Dolman (ed.), *Global
Planning and Resource Management: Toward International
Decision-Making in a Divided World*, Pergamon, New York,

1980, pp. 202-224.

(45) Five States need to ratify the Treaty before it comes into force. Unless ratified by the two space powers it will, of course, have little impact.

(46) See on this the important statement made by W.Riphagen, Netherlands delegate, before COPUOS on 23 March 1978 (document A/AC.105 C.2/Sr290, 23 March 1978).

(47) For informative reviews of the main issues surrounding the Antarctic continent, see Barbara Mitchell and Jon Tinker, Antarctica and its Resources, International Institute for Environment and Development, London, January 1980; and K.D. Suter, Antarctica: World Law and the Last Wilderness, Friends of the Earth, Sydney, 1980.

(48) With the exception of Poland. Poland became a consultative party in 1977, two years after beginning a regular Antarctic research expedition and five months after establishing a permanent scientific base.

(49) This provision (Article VII of the Treaty) was the first time that the two superpowers agreed on an on-site inspection system to ensure against unauthorized military activity.

(50) Consultative meetings are held in the capitals of the various treaty nations. The tenth meeting - on the 20th anniversary of the Treaty's signature - was held in Washington, D.C. in September 1979. The eleventh meeting will be held in Buenos Aires in 1981.

(51) 141 recommendations were adopted at the first ten consultative meetings held. Many have, however, been adopted on a voluntary basis as 'interim guidelines' before coming into force.

(52) Jon Tinker, 'Antarctica: Towards a New Internationalism', New Scientist, 13 September 1979, pp. 799-801, at p. 799.

(53) Elisabeth Young, A Farewell to Arms Control?, Penguin Books, Harmondsworth, 1972, p. 131.

(54) The US research ships Eltanin and Glomar Challenger found thick layers of unmetamorphosed tertiary sediments - more then 2,000 metres thick - in the Bellingshausen, Weddell and Ross Seas. Such sediments are frequently associated with oil. Glomar Challenger drilled four holes in the Ross Sea in 1972-73, in shallow water around 470 metres. In three of the holes ethane, ethylene and methane were found - in spite of the fact that the sites were chosen to avoid the most likely oil-bearing structures (because Glomar Challenger could not prevent an oil blowout). These hydrocarbons are evidence for the possible formation of petroleum hydrocarbons: methane is common in deep sea cores, but ethylene often occurs with petroleum.

(55) See M.W.Holdgate and J.Tinker, Oil and Other Minerals in the Antarctic, The Scientific Committee on Antarctic Research (SCAR), Cambridge, 1979.

(56) Some of the speculation surrounding Antarctic minerals
     revolves around the Grondwanaland hypothesis. This assumes
     that in the early Mesozoic era, some 200 million years ago,
     Antarctica was joined to Latin America, Africa, Australia
     and India in a single land mass, called Grondwanaland. If
     this hypothesis is correct - and it is widely accepted -
     then the mountains of the Antarctic Peninsula, once con-
     tinuous with the Andes, may have deposits of lead and cop-
     per (similar to those of Peru and Chile). Structural simi-
     larities between the East Antarctic shields and parts of
     Australia and South Africa suggest the presence of uranium.
     Similarly, oilfields found off New Zealand, Argentina and
     in the Bass Strait may point to the existence of oil
     deposits.
(57) It is worth noting here that in 1976 only 10 fisheries in
     the world recorded catches in excess of one million tons,
     the highest being the Alaska pollock at 5.1 million tons.
     Even if the estimates of maximum sustainable yield were to
     be greatly reduced, krill would still be one of the world's
     largest fisheries. For a discussion of the management of
     stocks of krill, see Barbara Mitchell and Richard Sandbrook,
     The Management of the Southern Ocean, International Insti-
     tute for Environment and Development, London, 1980, chapters
     7-10.
(58) On the question of krill, see Earthscan Press Briefing
     Document no. 15, 1979, available from the International
     Institute for Environment and Development, London. Important
     reports on krill have been produced under the FAO/UNDP
     Southern Oceans program. See I.Everson, *The Living Resources
     of the Southern Ocean*, FAO publication GLO/55/77/1, 1977;
     G.C.Eddie, *Harvesting of Krill*, pub. GLO/50/77/2, 1977; and
     G.J.Grantham, *The Utilization of Krill*, pub. GLO/50/77/3,
     1977.
(59) See U.N. document E/AC.24/SR 555-581, and A/PV.2380.
(60) Pinto, addressing an Earthscan press briefing, is quoted
     in Mitchell and Tinker, op.cit., p. 80.
(61) De Soto, addressing another Earthscan press briefing, held
     in Washington D.C. in September 1979, is quoted in Mitchell
     and Tinker, op.cit., p. 81.
(62) For a description and evaluation of the 'Krill Convention',
     see Barbara Mitchell and Richard Sandbrook, op.cit., viz.
     chapter 11.
(63) For a discussion of these conflicts, see Barbara Mitchell
     and Lee Kimball, 'Conflict Over the Cold Continent',
     Foreign Policy, Summer 1979, pp. 124-141.
(64) See B.Roberts, 'International Cooperation for Antarctic
     Development', *Polar Record*, vol. 19, no. 119, pp. 107-120.
(65) See 'Why Does the Polar Bear Intrude into Antarctica?',
     Hsinhua News Agency, 30, April 1976.

Common Heritage of Mankind 267

(66) See Harlan Cleveland, 'Does Everything Belong to Every-
    body?', *The Christian Science Monitor*, 19 December 1978,
    p. 22.

6 International Taxation and Global Reform

Government officials, it is your
concern to mobilize your peoples
to form a more effective world
solidarity, and above all to make
them accept the necessary taxes
on their luxuries and their wasteful expenditure, in order to bring
about development and to preserve
peace.

Pope Paul VI, *Encyclical Populorum
Progressio*, para 84.

INTRODUCTION

We have suggested that the automatic mobilization of resources
- or, more simply, international taxation - is an important
means for bringing about a more rational and equitable international order. We have further suggested that it may be an area
in which, because of its distinct advantages and attraction,
some progress could be engineered in the difficult years ahead.
The progress would be important progress for it would give expression to the principle that access to resources is as important as their distribution and that the world's riches belong
to all the world's inhabitants on the basis of priority needs
rather than geographical accident or the capacity to extract,
exploit and to consume them. Progress in the building of international systems of taxation would give a new legitimacy to the
United Nations and real expression to the notion of solidarity
with present and future generations. It would be synonymous with,

and a stepping stone in the direction of, conscious planning
and management practices for the benefit of all rather than a
privileged few.

In this chapter we will look at alternatives and possibilities
in the field of international taxation. We will do so as follows.
We begin by taking a brief look at the history of the idea of
international taxation and document its emerging support. We
next look at the main requirements for a system of international
taxation and go on to list some of the main taxation alternatives.
Criteria for the evaluation of the alternatives are then formulated and used to identify the alternatives which appear to hold
out most promise.

EMERGING SUPPORT FOR
INTERNATIONAL TAXATION

The history of the idea of redistributive international taxation
extends, like so many other ideas central to the creation of a
more rational and equitable international order, over a long
period. Inevitably, the United Nations has served as a focus for
much of the interest and activity. That this interest is a well
established one is evidenced by the fact that it was Trygve Lie,
the organization's first Secretary-General, who initiated activities by setting up a coordinating committee to consider the
principle of international taxation.

There was a great deal of interest in the subject in the early
1960s when international taxation mechanisms were presented and
discussed as ways of effectively dealing with commodity price
fluctuations and as alternatives to commodity agreements. Proposals made under this general heading include the introduction
of a tax on petroleum products (1) and for the conversion of
tolls on important waterways into international taxes for the
principal benefit of the developing countries. (2) The proposal
made by the French government prior to UNCTAD I for the introduction of refundable import levies on commodities exported from
developing countries also belongs to this group. (3)

It was not until 1970 that the idea started to be taken seriously. In that year, the U.N. Committee for Development Planning,
at its sixth session, considered a proposal for a tax on a range
of durable consumer goods - motorcars, pleasure boats, television sets, refrigerators, washing machines and dishwashers -
the possession of which was considered indicative of high levels
of material wellbeing. (4) Seen as a "world solidarity contribution", the tax was to have a uniform rate of about 0.5 per
cent of the purchase price. The tax was to be collected by national authorities and the proceeds to be used to finance international development, primarily through multilateral channels.

Elaborated as part of the Committee's preparatory work for the
strategy for the Second Development Decade, the "world solidarity contribution" was conceived as a means, not only of raising
revenue for the purposes of development, but also of "identifying the public with the spirit and objectives of the decade".
Inevitably, some members of the Committee expressed doubts about
the feasibility of the tax and although a follow-up study of the
proposal was recommended, it was not taken up.

During the 1970s, however, as Third World demands for the 'decolonization of aid' and a NIEO became more strident, interest in
automatic resource mobilization intensified. Third World insistence on the principle of automaticity was soon to find its way
into U.N. declarations and resolutions. The resolution adopted
by consensus at the conclusion of the Seventh Special Session
calls for flows of concessional resources which are "predictable,
continuous and increasingly assured". (5) A year later, in December 1976, the General Assembly, in reviewing ways in which
resource flows to the Third World could be accelerated, repeated
the requirement that transfers should be "predictable" and "increasingly assured". (6)

In recent years various proposals have been made within the U.N.
system for the introduction of systems of international taxation.
At the 31st and 32nd sessions of the General Assembly, for example, the representative of Saudi Arabia proposed the introduction of such a mechanism as a means of providing additional funds
required to meet global environmental and other needs. He specifically suggested a levy of one cent on a barrel of oil and a voluntary tax of 0.1-0.2 per cent on arms sales. (7) Other OPEC members have also shown a readiness to support the principle of international taxation. Venezuela, for example, proposed to OPEC
that the price of oil be increased by 5 per cent, the proceeds
being used to help reduce the external debt of the poorest developing countries. While these and other proposals were being
made, the Third U.N. Conference on the Law of the Sea, a conference which started in 1973, was struggling to devise the institutional mechanisms for taxing the exploitation of the seabed
beyond the limits of national jurisdiction which has been declared the common heritage of mankind. (8)

An important development in the acceptance of the principle of
automatic resource mobilization was provided by the U.N. Conference on Desertification, held in Nairobi from 29 August - 9 September 1977. The Plan of Action adopted by the Conference refers
specifically to "fiscal measures entailing automaticity". (9)
The Plan was subsequently approved by the U.N. General Assembly.
(10) The resolution adopting the Plan invited the Governing Council of UNEP to commission a study by a group of "high level specialists" of "additional measures and means of financing for the
implementation of the Plan of Action". The group of 17 distin-

guished experts subsequently formed by UNEP to undertake the
study submitted its report in March 1978. (11) The group considered a variety of automatic financing mechanisms, including
revenues derived from the use and exploitation of the 'international commons', taxation of arms expenditures and sales, taxation of international trade flows, and the SDR-development 'link'.
The group concluded that:

"(T)he establishment of these new sources could generate considerable funds, of a magnitude far surpassing those generated
through any present means of raising development capital, and
would thus go a long way towards meeting the needs of development and environmental protection. While the establishment and
utilization of these resources are undoubtedly complex matters,
the practical difficulties can be resolved, in the same way that
they have been in the case of the revenue-raising mechanisms
employed by national governments. The question is one of political will - whether the United Nations General Assembly is prepared to pursue what is clearly the avenue with the greatest
potential for the mobilization of funds for development." (12)

Although recognizing the long-term nature of the proposal they
had made, the members of the group called for urgent and immediate action.

Activities within the United Nations have been supported by and
have drawn upon the work of a number of non-governmental organizations. The most important and comprehensive study so far undertaken on the subject of international taxation was published by
The Brookings Institution in 1978. (13) This study served as an
essential input into the work of UNEP's expert group. Other,
more modest, studies have also recently been completed. (14)

The principle of automaticity in resource transfers through the
mechanisms of international taxation has been endorsed by an
array of studies involving distinguished groups of experts from
both sides of the North-South divide. To give just four examples:

What Now?, published in 1975 as the 1975 Dag Hammarskjöld Report
on Development and International Cooperation, (15) argues that
U.N. resources for development "should be progressively generated
in an automatic manner". (p.120) It specifically calls for the
introduction of a tax on the exploitation of the deep seabed, a
tax or levies on the movement of goods and persons over the global commons (the high seas and the atmosphere), and the establishment of a link between SDR creation and development financing.
(p.120)

RIO Report, published in 1976, contains a range of taxation proposals. (16) It advocates an international tax on "undesirable
forms of consumption" in the rich countries and on armaments
spending (p.132) and contains more detailed proposals for (i)
a stronger link between SDR creation and development financing;

(ii) a tax on the kilowatt hours of nuclear fission energy produced, the proceeds to be used to help fund research into 'soft'
sources (p.149); (iii) a system of world taxation on profits
derived from the trade of fossil fuels and on the value of production of mineral ores, the system to in part replace national
taxation (pp.148-149); (iv) the development of a regime for exploiting the resources of the international commons (p.165) and,
more specifically, a regime for the oceans which includes provisions for a tax on all uses of the oceans, within and outside
the limits of national jurisdiction on the basis of the concept
of the common heritage of mankind (pp.173-175). The Report further calls for the gradual application of the common heritage
concept to all the world's mineral resources, means of production,
science and technology, and "other sources of wealth" (pp.82-83,
123). The report proposes that in the long-term the revenues
derived from international taxation could be used to support a
World Treasury which would have the task of promoting "equitable
world development and the eradication of world poverty" (pp.133-
134).

Brandt Commission Report (17), published in 1980, argues
the need for "a worldwide effort to raise automatic funds, which
would make a beginning in mobilizing international resources
with a built-in growth potential" (p.244). It makes special reference to the special advantages of a tax on international trade
and of the revenues which could be derived from "new global enterprises", such as one created for seabed mining. Like *What Now*
and the *RIO Report,* the *Brandt Commission Report* supports the
proposal for a stronger link between SDR allocation and development financing.

IFDA's Third System Project Report (18), published in 1980 as
the main result of a $ 3 million exercise aimed at formulating
an extragovernmental contribution to the preparatory process
for the International Development Strategy for the 1980s, sees
the introduction of international taxation as an essential
ingredient in the process of "decolonizing aid". It refers to
the possibilities of taxing "internationally undesirable activities" (armaments, pollution, destabilizing exchange rates) and
of introducing revenue generating taxes (sales or turnover tax
on international trade, tax on energy and minerals, and revenues
derived for the use and exploitation of ocean space) (pp.57-58).

Support for automatic resource mobilization through international taxation mechanisms has been no less in evidence in international conferences convened to discuss the future of North-South
relations. A few examples of such support:

The Cocoyoc Declaration (19), resulting from the UNEP/UNCTAD
symposium on 'Patterns of Resource Use, Environment and Development Strategies' held in Mexico in October 1974, was in many
respects a landmark statement. (20) It calls for the creation of

a regime for the 'international commons'. The revenue derived through the regime is presented as "a first step towards the establishment of an international taxation system aimed at providing automatic transfers of resources for development assistance". It argues that international taxation together with the funds released through disarmament should eventually replace traditional assistance channels.

The Algiers Symposium (21), held in Algiers in October 1976 during which the RIO Report was 'presented' to the international community - close to 200 persons from government and extragovernmental organizations in the First, Second and Third Worlds. The participants "fully accepted" the principle of international taxation, although certain doubts were expressed concerning its "immediate political feasibility. The introduction of international progressive taxation was seen as a long term process which should be started now". (22)

The Scheveningen Symposium (23), was convened in the Netherlands in July 1979 at the request of the U.N.'s Director-General for Development and International Economic Cooperation to discuss the aims and the scope of the International Development Strategy for the 1980s. Participants called for international taxation as part of a system of automatic resource transfers operating according to "universally acceptable and socially responsible criteria". (24) The system of international taxation proposed would be universal, progressive and start at low rates and initially applied to the global commons and to "internationally undesirable activities" (arms expenditures and arms trade, pollution and the accumulation of destabilizing exchange reserves).

The general support to be found in studies and conferences for the principle of automatic resource mobilization has in recent years been supplemented by a range of proposals for ambitious systems of international taxation - 'grand designs' aimed at accelerating the flow of concessional resources to the developing countries. Noteworthy among such proposals are:

Ocean Development Tax, proposed by the International Ocean Institute as early as 1970, calls for a small levy on all major uses of the oceans in ocean space both under and outside coastal state jurisdiction. (25)

World Solidarity Tax, proposed by the Club of Dakar in 1977, calls for the introduction of a value-added tax on trade in energy, minerals and agricultural products. The rate of taxation would be graduated, ranging from 1-3 per cent (the lowest rates applied to basic foodstuffs, the highest to minerals extracted from the oceans). The rates would be further differentiated to account for rates of depletion and would be applied world-wide. Proceeds would be collected by national governments and transferred to a World Agency which would disburse the funds on the basis of agreed principles and programs. (26)

World Fund for Employment and Development, proposed during a
meeting held in Mexico City in November-December 1977 devoted
to discussion of the RIO Report. The revenues for the fund were
to be obtained from a tax of approximately one per cent on consumption in developed countries and would be directed to financing projects in the fields of agriculture, energy, basic industries, mass transporation and in other high priority areas
in the developing countries. (27)

It has been suggested that the principle of automaticity through
the mechanisms of international taxation is one of only four
areas in which there is a great deal of North-South consensus on
what could and should be done to stimulate the flow of concessional resources to the Third World. (28) Indeed, no report on
the future of the new international order can today be considered complete without some reference to the 'need for automaticity'
and the 'promise of international taxation'. And it is clear why
this should be so. Its logic is compelling. It provides an opportunity to move away from the present aid order which, shroud-
ed as it is in controversy and uncertainty, no one really wants.
It makes it possible to substitute the principles of justice,
equity and obligation for the vagaries of philanthropy, pater-
nalism and voluntarism. It provides for deliberate and visible
mechanisms for channeling flows of resources to the Third World,
thereby helping to counter-balance the working of systematic but
invisible mechanisms which channel the benefits and rewards of
the international economic system to a core of rich countries.

One of the advantages of international taxation is that it is
guided by the same principles which are accepted by all nations
virtually without question. As the Brandt Commission Report
rightly observes: "In the welfare states taxes are progressive
in incidence, social expenditures are redistributive and links
between tax payers and beneficiaries are indirect. It may seem
ambitious to internationalize this model, but the concept itself
is intelligent and already accepted on a national scale". (29)

International taxation is ultimately a matter of international
law and international law requires precedents. (30) The first
precedent was the acceptance by the world's nations of the principle of automaticity in the General Assembly of the United Nations. The resolution adopted gives a legitimacy to attempts to
fashion regimes for international taxation and helps to pave the
way for the development of customary international law. This
development should be facilitated by the fact that the concepts
in question are "intelligible and already accepted".

There are many who believe that the time for international taxation, if it has not yet come, cannot be far away. This was particularly evident in the discussions and negotiations which took
place as part of the process for formulating an international
development strategy for the 1980s. A number of U.N. agencies

strongly argued the case for the automatic mobilization of resources and fought to have the principle included in the strategy. The U.N. Secretariat, for example, stressed the need for
automaticity so as to free the flow of real resources "from the
vagaries of government decision-making". (31) UNCTAD similarly
argued that the Strategy "should contain provision for the establishment of new arrangements... such as international taxation, for the automatic mobilization of additional financial
resources for accelerating the development process". (32) The
viewpoint of the non-governmental system was summarized by IFDA
as follows: "If the international community were to take a decisive step in the 1980s for the establishment of an international tax this would be a real breakthrough toward genuine international cooperation". (33)

MAIN REQUIREMENTS FOR A SYSTEM
OF INTERNATIONAL TAXATION

What should a system of international taxation provide for?
There is a wide measure of agreement that its principal elements
should include:

Requirement 1: A Sound Legal Basis. The system of taxation should
have a basis in an international treaty which is accepted, at
least in principle, by a large number of nations so as to guarantee adequate participation. The participation could, however,
be graduated and differentiated so as to provide for different
degrees of involvement over time. This implies the existence of
progressive rates of taxation. The legal instrument upon which
the system is based should thus lay the foundations for a system
of taxation which could be progressively applied at the global
level rather than provide for the introduction of a single tax.

Requirement 2: National Control. As a general rule the collection of taxes would be entrusted to national authorities where
an established tax collecting capability exists. A major exception to this rule would be international bodies which, like the
proposed International Seabed Authority, are specifically created for the purposes of managing and taxing the use and exploitation of areas designated the common heritage of mankind. The
exceptions would, however, be accommodated in legally constituted and tailor-made international regimes.

Requirement 3: Development Orientation. In the case of national
authorities the proceeds collected would be transferred to an
international authority empowered to use and distribute the funds
for internationally agreed development purposes. There are a number of alternatives for such an authority. It may be an existing
institution modified to implement the funds, such as a democra-
tized World Bank; or a new institution, such as a World Develop-

ment Fund (as proposed by the Brandt Commission) (34), or even
a World Treasury (one of the more ambitious proposals of the
RIO Report). (35) The modalities would be laid down by Treaty.

Requirement 4: International Supervision. A specially constituted standing body would need to be empowered, through the provisions of the treaty, to supervise, monitor and enforce the
system, to judicate in cases of violation, to arbitrate in cases
of dispute, by the decisions it would be vested to take, to further develop the system within the framework of prescribed limits.

THE MAIN TAXATION ALTERNATIVES

The general agreement on the need for and the main elements of
a system of international taxation does not extend to cover what
should actually be taxed. The main options here reside essentially in the areas of direct or indirect taxation. (36) Candidates under each of these headings could include:

Direct Taxation

Income Tax. A tax on income earned could take the form of a surcharge on income tax (it might be called a 'development tax') or
tax deductions of voluntary contributions for development purposes, extending a principle already recognized under most systems of national taxation. The surcharge on income, which could
be made progressive, would be mandatory; tax deductions would be
voluntary. The first alternative could constitute an important
initial step towards a genuine international income tax or a
'guaranteed income plan for the nations of the world' which has
been advocated in different circles. (37) Precedents for development taxes already exist. Between 1964 and 1974, for example,
Norway levied a separate development tax on incomes which financed most of its aid program in the period.

'Brain Drain' Tax. An additional tax could be levied by the industrialized countries on the incomes earned by the 'brains
drained' from developing countries. There are a number of ways
in which such a tax could be organized. (38) The revenues derived could be remitted to the migrant's country of origin, in
which case the tax would have a bilateral character, or used for
more general purposes and involve multilateral channels. From
the viewpoint of international taxation, the latter is clearly
preferable.

'Bread and Games' Tax. A tax could be levied on those activities
which are genuinely symbolic of 'fiddling while Rome burns'.

Candidates for such a tax, which is clearly guided by moral considerations, would seem to include gambling (lotteries, total-
izers, casinos, etc.) and certain types of professional sports
where there appear to be few restrictions on the finances which
can be raised for the purposes of 'keeping the fans amused'.
Such a tax might be extended to cover other sections of the 'en-
tertainment industry', especially those in which profits made
are or can be out of all proportion to the effort involved. It
should be noted in this context that precedents for such a tax
already exist. There is a tradition in a number of industrialized
countries of using the proceeds derived from gambling and 'games
of chance' for charitable and humanitarian purposes. In some
cases there is even a direct link between such taxes and international development. Belgium, for example, diverts 10 per cent
of the revenues derived from the National Lottery to its development program.

Tax on International Investment. Such a tax could take several
forms. At its most ambitious it could aim at taxing interest
derived and profits remitted from international capital flows
(private and public credits, private overseas direct investment).
A more modest but practical proposal would be to tax the activities of transnational corporations operating in the Third World.
A tax on the profits of transnational activity would, however,
need to address the problem of possible evasion and be organized
in such a way that it did not result in a reduction in the supply
of capital for international investment.

Common Heritage Taxes. Revenues can be derived from the institutional regimes developed to manage the common heritage of mankind. The concept of common heritage, already applied to the
seabed beyond the limits of national jurisdiction, could be functionally expanded to include living and non-living resources
within and beyond the waters of coastal States, thereby bringing
offshore oil and gas production and commercial fisheries within
the range and scope of taxation systems. It can also be applied
to new domains which fall outside national jurisdiction, such as
outer space and Antarctica. (39) In the case of the upper atmosphere, taxes could be levied on international air travel and
freight transport. Taxes related to outer space could include
the use of radio and telecommunications frequencies and channels,
the use of space orbits and, most importantly, the information
derived by satellites from the use of space. It might also, one
day, be possible to derive revenues from the exploitation of the
moon, which has already been declared common heritage. Antarctica's
resources include minerals, hydrocarbons and the living resources
- notably krill - of the Southern Ocean. It has been suggested
that a surcharge could be levied on passports since possession
implies a commitment to travel the 'global commons'.

Pollution Taxes. Taxes could be levied on activities which run

counter to the rational management of resources, threaten global
life-support systems, and which carry the world closer to the
'outer limits' imposed upon it by the natural environment. There
are many alternatives for such taxes. They could, for example,
focus on activities with long-term negative impacts, such as the
production of highly toxic radioactive wastes. Alternatively,
taxes could be levied on activities which further undermine the
workings of natural cycles which, indispensable to life on earth,
are already known to be under unprecedented attack. Such cycles
include the oxygen cycle, where problems associated with the
process of photosynthesis are becoming ever more serious. These
problems would justify a tax on, for example, marine pollution.
Similarly, the carbon dioxide cycle is threatened by the burning
of fossil fuels, a situation which may justify a tax related to
their consumption.

Indirect Taxation

Tax on Luxury Goods. A tax could be levied on forms of conspicuous consumption, i.e. on luxury consumer durables the possession
of which is conditioned more by questions of prestige and status
than the meeting of basic material needs. Goods falling into
this category could include jewelry, furs, 'haute couture', per-
fumes, exotic foods, certain types of household equipment, and
'gas-guzzling' automobiles.

Tax on 'Undesirable Forms of Consumption'. 'Undesirable' in this
context can be given a threefold meaning: undesirable for the
individual consumer in that the consumption carries certain risks
for his health and well-being; undesirable for the nation given
the social costs associated with the consumption; and undesirable
for the world as a whole in that the consumption is antithetical
to the goals of development and diverts much needed resources
required to raise the living standards of the poor. The first
type of consumption could give rise to additional taxes on such
items as alcohol and tobacco; the second type to taxes on, for
example, the negative effects of mass motorization; the third
type could give rise to taxes on indirect grain consumption and
on 'throw away' articles which cannot be easily recycled.

Tax on International Trade. A tax could be levied on all transactions involving international trade and on international services
associated with trade, for example, shipping, insurance, telephone and postal services. Such a tax would have a twofold justification: international trade makes use of the world's oceans
and airspace, domains which 'belong' to mankind as a whole; and
it is only possible under 'peaceful' conditions, the use of the
proceeds of the tax contributing directly to the creation of
such conditions.

Tax on Minerals. The taxation of minerals could take different forms. A tax could be levied, for example, on the value of minerals traded internationally, perhaps on the basis of metal content. A fairer but more complicated tax would be one levied on the total production of minerals, whether for export or for local use. A still more ambitious tax would be one based upon an index of the total consumption of mineral resources. Not only would a tax on mineral resources be guaranteed a large tax base, it could also be modulated to account for scarcities and rates of depletion. It could thus serve to directly promote the more rational utilization of the world's resources.

Tax on Energy. As in the case of mineral resources, taxes on energy could take different forms. The simplest case would be a tax on oil exports. More attractive, because of its more equitable coverage, would be a tax on all oil production. Also conceivable is a tax on the generation of nuclear (fission) power, although the proceeds derived from this tax would probably need to be used to fund research into 'soft' sources. As in the case of minerals, the most equitable tax would be one based upon total energy consumption. Taxing energy would also ensure that a very extensive tax base was combined with a sound management practice: an inducement to save a valuable and non-renewable resource; a resource which could conceivably give rise to international conflicts in the far from distant future.

Tax on Armaments. Such a tax could be based upon total armaments spending, the possession of nuclear weapons and/or a delivery capability, or on weapons with an undisputed offensive character. As an alternative to armaments spending, a tax could be levied on the trade in armaments. The argument for such taxes rests upon the widely accepted fact that the present level of armaments spending constitutes a permanent impediment to the pursuit of alternative opportunities for economic growth and development. (40) Military expenditures - and as a direct consequence the military use of scarce material and non-material resources - have grown sharply and the rate at which resources are being diverted from constructive civilian use is increasing. The arms race is incompatible with equitable access to and distribution of the world's resources and hence with the New International Economic Order.

EVALUATING THE ALTERNATIVES

Although the above list has no pretence as to completeness, it seems safe to conclude that there is no shortage of candidates for international taxation. The list is something of a menagerie, a highly variegated collection resplendent with its exotic as well as more mundane species. Some of the entries are 'obvious',

other much less so. Some are motivated by practical considerations, the foundation of others is moral indignation. Some are
overreachingly ambitious, others are modest in scope and aspiration. Some are principled and contoured, others more arbitrary
and capricious.

Which of the candidates is most fit for the job? 'Best' in this
context must be a matter of choice rather than fact and choice
implies value judgements based upon normative criteria. 'Best'
is thus a measure of the extent to which the alternatives meet
the criteria. There can be no hard and fast rules, however, for
drawing up the criteria for they themselves will be a matter of
debate. It is suggested here that highest priority should be afforded the following eight criteria: the tax should be admini-
stratively convenient, it should be politically feasible, it
should be equitable, it should draw upon an extensive revenue
base, it should be flexible, it should have 'packagability', it
should have growth potential, and it should be principled rather
than arbitrary in its intention. It is to each of these that we
will briefly turn. (41)

Administrative Convenience. A first requirement is that the tax
should be simple to administer and that its economic effects be
predictable. As a general rule it will be easier to administer
a modest direct tax through authorities with a proven tax collecting capability, such as nation-States. There is also an obvious relationship between administrative convenience and the
complexity of the tax. An additional tax on income will be easier
to implement than a general, indirect tax, such as one on international trade, due to such problems of assessment, exemptions
and double taxation. By the same token, value-added taxes, such
as those on total energy and mineral consumption, will be still
more complicated to administer than turnover taxes.

Administrative convenience also decreases as possibilities for
tax evasion increase. There is thus a strong relationship between
convenience and control. In this sense, taxes on income and purchase taxes are relatively straightforward whereas taxes on
transnational activities, such as the operations of large enterprises with possibilities for manipulating transfer prices and
for making use of the differences in national taxation systems,
will be considerably more difficult to implement. It should be
recognized, however, that convenience is not synonymous with costs
for the costs of administering comparatively simple direct taxes
can become prohibitive. High costs of collection was one of the
reasons why Norway discontinued the levying of its development
tax in 1974.

High levels of convenience and acceptable costs can legitimately
be expected from regimes specifically designed to administer and
to tax the common heritage of mankind - the oceans, outer space,
and Antarctica. In such cases the modalities of the taxation

system can be specifically geared to the substantive taxation
problems and opportunities and the systems would be unified
rather than made up of sometimes highly divergent national regimes.

Political Feasibility. Political feasibility is traditionally
defined to mean that proposals should fall within the normative
receptivities of government and opinion leaders. At this point
in time there is clearly little receptivity for additional direct
(domestic) taxation, a situation typified by the 'California tax
revolt' syndrome. It is worth noting that all the OECD's DAC members reacted negatively when questioned by the U.N. Secretary-
General on the desirability and feasibility of introducing an
income-related special development tax. (42) The reactions varied.
Canada and Germany argued that such a tax lacks political support.
Denmark, the Netherlands, Norway, Sweden and the United Kingdom
went further, arguing that the tax would have an adverse effect
on public opinion. France and the United Kingdom questioned the
efficacy of the proposal and Sweden suggested that international
taxation should be deemed preferable to domestically levied taxes.
It might also be noted that there appears little popular support
among the Belgian population for the use of the country's National Lottery for financing development. (43) Given these considerations, it appears safe to assume that at this point in time
the criterion of political feasibility points clearly in the
direction of indirect rather than direct taxation.

Political feasibility will also be enhanced when the object to
be taxed is non-proprietary, i.e. is owned by neither individuals, enterprises, nor nations. At present only the common heritage of mankind enjoys the status of non-ownership, and this has
so far been conferred on the oceans, the moon and other celestial bodies, and it could conceivably be conferred upon outer
space and the Antarctic continent. The so-called 'global commons' would thus appear to have a special attraction when viewed
against the criterion of political feasibility.

There is also a relationship between feasibility and convenience,
for proposals are more likely to meet with support when it can
be shown that the costs of administering the tax are low, efficiency is high, and the legal basis firm. These conditions will
be met in situations where the taxation system is strongly rooted in especially constituted regimes - which brings us conveniently back to the common heritage of mankind - and where it
can be painlessly meshed with existing national systems.

Equity. A fair tax will be one in which the burdens do not fall
on the poorest and most disprivileged groups within nations and
on the poorest nations within the world community. The most attractive taxes in this respect are those based upon progressive
and sliding scales and, especially, those which bypass the poorest altogether, as would, for example, a tax on luxury goods and

conspicuous consumption.

Estimates of burden imply a knowledge of the economic effects
of the tax and of the way in which it is likely to be absorbed.
Additional taxation would result in a reduction of national tax
revenues which would need to be made up from other sources.
There will be some cases, however, where the tax can be absorbed
without the need to pass it on, directly or indirectly, to the
consumer. This could be the case with a levy on oil exports, the
oil producer being in a position to incur small losses. As noted
earlier, Saudi Arabia has already suggested that oil producers
should be prepared to introduce a self-imposed levy of one cent
on every barrel of oil produced for the purpose of helping to
fund activities aimed at coming to terms with environmental problems of global dimensions.

Certain kinds of taxation can no doubt be shown to be inflationary and inflation is an enemy of the poor. Taxation could also
result in a reduction of GNP and the poor are the main victims
of shrinking economic pies. Yet taxation rates can be organized
to ensure that negative economic effects would be negligible or
marginal. Even in the case of energy, regarded in many circles
as an inflationary force and an economic drain down which to
pour the fruits of national endeavour, it has been shown that a
narrowly defined tax of one per cent on all hydrocarbon consumption - surely an ambitious proposal - would constitute a burden
of 0.05-0.09 per cent of the GNP of the industrialized countries,
being considerably smaller for developing countries with their
less energy-intensive economies. (44)

Particularly attractive will be the alternatives which set out
to tax that which is not yet the subject of taxation. Such taxes
will neither need to be absorbed or passed on. Especially interesting in this respect will be taxes levied on the exploitation
of the 'new' resources of the oceans, such as ocean minerals,
and of Antarctica's resources, both of which are yet to start
in earnest.

Revenue Base. There should be an extensive tax base so that even
low rates of taxation still generate large revenues. There can,
of course, be no general rule for defining what constitutes 'low'
Acceptable tax rates could easily range from 0.1 per cent in the
case of broad turnover taxes, through say 5 per cent for specific
types of taxation, to up to 50 per cent or more in the case of
profits derived from the exploitation of the common heritage of
mankind. The rate of taxation is obviously of no little importance: different assumptions with respect to rates could mean
the difference between a bagatelle or bonanza. The $ 25 million
that could be generated by a 0.1 per cent surcharge on air travel
is considerably less interesting than the $ 250 million that
would result from a 1.0 per cent tax. Similarly, it would not be
worth the effort to attempt to collect the $ 50 million which

could theoretically be generated by a 0.1 per cent tax on international investment income. A 1 per cent tax yielding $ 500 mil-
lion could, however, make the enterprise worthwile, adding, as
it would, the equivalent of Belgium's ODA disbursements to the
flow of development finance.

In terms of the size of the revenue base there are four 'big
ones': a tax on international trade, on energy, on minerals, and
on military spending. The value of international trade is currently in the order of $ 1,300 billion. Even a very modest flat
rate of 0.1 per cent would thus generate an interesting $ 1.3
billion, the equivalent of the United Kingdom's ODA program.
The more ambitious rate of 1 per cent - if it could be justified
on the grounds of equity and feasibility - would yield a bumper
$ 13 billion, a figure comparable to the total ODA disbursements
of all DAC countries in 1977.

A 1 per cent tax on oil exports, which would be relatively
straightforward to implement, would, following the recent round
of oil price increase, yield in the order of $ 3.5 billion. By
way of comparison, this would be equivalent to having two new
Scandinavias on the development financing scene. A 1 per cent
tax on all internationally traded minerals could be expected to
yield well in excess of $ 1 billion, with steel, iron ore and
zinc accounting for nearly 60 per cent of the revenues.

With world military expenditures now in the order of $ 1 million
per minute, a 1 per cent tax would generate an interesting $ 4
billion a year. A 5 per cent tax on the export of armaments, at
present running in the order of $ 20 billion a year, could be
expected to yield about $ 1 billion.

Flexibility. In introducing international taxation there will be
considerably more scope for step-by-step approaches than for
'grand designs', however appealing and seductive the latter may
be. The introduction of the taxation system need not be made an
all or nothing affair which sets out to involve all the world's
nations. There will undoubtedly be clear advantages in taxes
which can be implemented in phases, each new phase resulting in
an expansion of the system through such measures as increased
rates of taxation, greater country participation, and an extension of the system to include a greater number of goods and services to be taxed.

A gradualist approach will make it possible for groups of pioneering and like-minded countries - for example those in the
North which have declared their commitment to the principle of
automaticity - to initiate action and to establish precedents.
Others may follow. Clearly, the system should have a potential
for world-wide application. A gradualist approach would make it
possible to monitor performance, search for improvements and
thus to sharpen cutting edges prior to more universal application.

One of the keys to flexibility is thus the careful introduction
of progressive rates of taxation which make it possible to dif-
ferentiate involvement over time; to 'fit' the tax to the changing positions and possibilities of participating nations.

'Packagability'. Related to the criterion of flexibility is the
requirement that taxes should preferably cover well defined objects on the basis of well defined procedures. In this sense
taxes which are 'exclusive' rather than 'inclusive' can be considered more attractive, even though they may involve a reduction in the size of the tax base. 'Inclusive taxes' covering
large areas characterized by their diversity and differentiation,
as would be the case with a levy on all international trade and
on all energy and mineral consumption, would not only give rise
to inevitable problems of assessment and implementation; they
could also frustrate rather than facilitate attempts to construct,
over time, an extensive and well-articulated system of taxation
involving a growing tax and higher levels of country participation.

General and broad taxes would appear to have little to offer
when viewed in terms of their packagability: it will prove difficult to treat them as individual elements which can be effectively combined in taxation 'packages' articulated to meet the
changing needs of the international community and changing perceptions of political feasibility. General and broadly based
taxes run the risk of becoming so riddled with exceptions, conditions and escape clauses that they become virtually unworkable.
Unworkable taxes in the early stages of introducing a world system of taxation will simply add to existing resistance rather
than create useful precedents. Preferable would be taxation
packages made up of sets of mutually reinforcing and supporting
taxes involving different groups of countries and different types
of tax base. The taxes which together make up the package could
be conceptually interlinked but operationally autonomous, each
possessing their own modalities and time scales. A taxation
package could, for example, be made up of an OPEC surcharge on
oil exports, a tax levied by the rich countries on the worst
forms of conspicuous and energy-intensive consumption and on the
production of nuclear power, and the proceeds of a marine pollution tax levied on the basis of oil 'lost' during transport.

Growth Potential. There should be a potential for raising revenues on a sustained and reliable basis, preferably on an increasing scale. In this context, taxes designed for the dual purpose
of raising development revenues and redressing undesirable activities have a limited attraction. A marine pollution tax of
say $ 10 on every ton of oil lost during transport, for example,
would today yield around $ 20 million a year. More effective pol-
lution control and enforcement measures could conceivably mean
that revenues decrease as the capacity to collect them grows.

Certain high yield taxes may also have limited growth potential.
The spectacular proceeds which could be derived from a modest
flat rate levy on international trade, for example, could not
be sustained if Third World countries are successful in their
declared intention of implementing strategies designed to
strengthen their self-reliance, reduce their dependency on the
rich countries, and generally extricate themselves from the international system which is the cause of much of their misery.
A tax on oil imports might similarly have a limited growth potential as would most certainly taxes related to incomes in the
industrialized world.

Taxes with a high growth potential would definitely include those
levied on the exploitation of the resources of the oceans and
Antarctica since, as noted earlier, such exploitation has still
to get under way. The potential value of these resources is at
present a matter of much speculation. Some estimates suggest that
the revenues which could be derived from the mining of manganese
nodules alone could be close to $ 250 million by the mid 1980s.
(45) That would be a start. The oceans will become more important
as the technology required to exploit their resources - hydrocarbons, hard minerals, energy, food, etc. - becomes available
and as mankind turns to the oceans to meet a larger share of its
needs. Similarly, the 'cold continent' undoubtedly conceals vast
quantities of oil and minerals (to say nothing of its enormous
quantities of fresh water) and its surrounding seas are among the
most biologically productive in the world. Both are real growth
areas.

Competition for the resources of outer space - access to the
radio spectrum, satellite orbits (especially geostationary orbits), the products of remote sensing technologies - is also
bound to intensify in the years ahead, although it is difficult
to see how the potential revenue base will ever come to rival,
at least in the forseeable future, that of the oceans and Antarctica.

Only the brightest optimist would fail to see armaments spending
as anything other than a 'growth area'. Measured in constant
prices, world military expenditures have more than doubled in
the past two decades while the trade in arms has increased nearly tenfold in the same period. (46) Current orders for arms are
estimated to stand at over $ 29 billion. (47) Given the dynamics
of world militarization, the end is far from being in sight.

Management Principle. Last, but certainly not least, is the requirement that the tax contribute toward the rational management
of resources. The tax should thus serve to promote the rational
and equitable use of the world's resources and help to safeguard
the interests of the unborn through the legacy of a habitable
planet. Taxes which are guided by or reflect this requirement
include those related to the consumption of energy and minerals,

the reduction of armaments spending, pollution, those aimed at reducing waste and conspicuous consumption and, especially, those related to the use and exploitation of the common heritage of mankind. When viewed against the requirement that taxes should contribute to the sensible husbandry of planetary resources some candidates, such as taxes on brain drain, on international investment, on incomes earned and on international trade, appear somewhat arbitrary. This is not to suggest, however, that such taxes might not give expression to important other principles.

Having briefly looked at the eight criteria it is evident that there is no single tax which effectively meets all of the requirements formulated. Are there candidates which do better than others? An attempt to provide a first and tentative answer to this question is made with the simple matrix shown in the figure. The matrix compares types of taxes with the evaluation criteria, indicating positive and very positive relationships. It should be stressed that the assessment of the relationships is not based upon rigorous analysis; it is indicative only and designed to present an overall picture rather than detail.

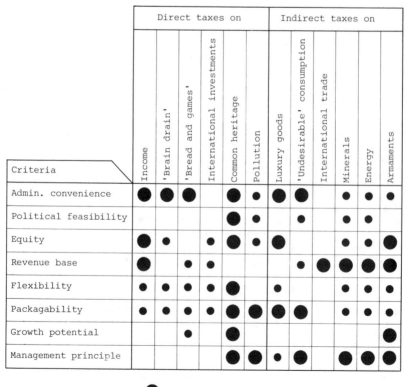

● Very positive   ● Positive

The matrix confirms some of the observations made earlier. It suggests that the administrative convenience of direct taxation is generally higher than that of indirect taxation, but that the revenue base of possible indirect taxes is generally larger than that of direct taxes. It further suggests that the criterion of equity is met by a range of direct and indirect taxes, as are the requirements of flexibility and packagability. The matrix further suggests that few of the taxes listed have a large growth potential and it seems to leave little doubt that indirect taxes are better able to incorporate resource management principles than direct taxes.

Certain taxes score better than others. Taxes related to income, such as development tax surcharges, meet the requirements of administrative convenience, equity and large revenue base and, to a lesser extent, the demands of flexibility and packagability. They have, however, little or no political support. Of the indirect taxes, those on luxury goods and 'undesirable' forms of consumption score generally high, and those on energy and mineral consumption and armaments expenditures even higher. The tax on international trade offers the advantage of an enormous revenue base but seems to have few other attractions.

The matrix does, however, have a clear 'winner': taxes related to the use and exploitation of the common heritage of mankind, which we have defined to include the oceans, space beyond the limits of national jurisdiction, and the Antarctic continent and its surrounding seas. Taxes related to the common heritage meet, with a single exception, all the criteria listed, including, it is suggested, the central one related to political feasibility. The exception is caused by the limited size of the present revenue base. Limitations in this respect, however, may be more than compensated for by the growth potential of the tax base.

Besides, in the early years of building a system of international taxation the revenues derived, while certainly not unimportant, are a secondary consideration. Even if it proves possible to move rapidly from 'theory to practice', the revenues derived will initially need to be seen as a valuable supplement to rather than as an alternative for present assistance channels and mechanisms. More important in the early years will be the legitimation of the process, of building support for the ideas and principles involved, of creating precedents upon which can be built. This is where the main challenge lies. For, as the Brandt Commission has rightly observed: "Even if the first results at the international level are modest, they will have a profound value in demonstrating global solidarity and partnership in the process of development". (48)

These words echo the same sentiments expressed by the Committee for Development Planning ten years earlier. The world has changed in the intervening period. Demands for a more equitable inter-

national order have been made and will be with us in the years
ahead. The new order must include the principle of automaticity
in development financing and automaticity must eventually lead
to international taxation. When the Committee formulated its
proposals for such taxation, the concept of the common heritage
of mankind was in its infancy. It was being nurtured by a few
for the future of the many. The concept has now come of age and
in its maturity it is becoming the centerpiece of discussions
in a range of United Nations fora. If international taxation
does belong to the alchemy of the new international order, the
common heritage of mankind could well prove to be the catalyst
for turning principle into practice.

NOTES AND REFERENCES

(1) See Boris Swerling, *Current Issues in Commodity Policies*,
    Princeton University Press, Princeton, New Jersey, 1962.
(2) Boris Swerling, 'Financial Alternatives to International
    Commodity Stabilization', *Canadian Journal of Economics and
    Political Science*, vol. 30, November 1964, pp. 526-537.
(3) The proposal is discussed in Gerda Blau, *International
    Commodity Arrangements and Policies*, FAO Community Policy
    Studies 16, FAO, Rome, 1964.
(4) See U.N. Committee for Development Planning, *Toward Accel-
    erated Development: Proposals for the Second U.N. Develop-
    ment Decade*, New York, 1970, pp. 27-28. The proposals were
    originally published as Official Records of ECOSOC, 49th
    Session, Supplement no. 7 (document E/4776).
(5) Resolution 3363 (S-VII), 16 September 1975, para II/1.
(6) Resolution A/31/436, 21 December 1976.
(7) See documents A/C.2/31/SR.45 and A/C.2/32/SR.23.
(8) See chapter 5 for a presentation of the concept of the
    common heritage of mankind and for a discussion of the
    various taxation proposals made within the framework of
    the Third U.N. Conference on the Law of the Sea.
(9) Report of the United Nations Conference on Desertification,
    document A/Conf. 74/36, para 104 (e).
(10) Resolution 32/172, 19 December 1977.
(11) See UNEP, *Additional Measures and Means of Financing for
    the Implementation of the Plan of Action to Combat Desert-
    ification*, document GC.6/9/Add. 1, April 1978.
(12) Ibid., pp. 21-22.
(13) See Eleanor B.Steinberg and Joseph A.Yager, *New Means of
    Financing International Needs*, Brookings Institution,
    Washington, D.C., 1978. For an interesting earlier study
    on possible sources of finance for development purposes
    see Nurul Islam, *New Mechanisms for the Transfer of Re-
    sources to Developing Countries*, United Nations, document
    E.AC.54/1.83, 13 November 1975. Undertaken as part of the
    work of the Committee for Development Planning, the study,

although it contains no specific references for international taxation mechanisms, contains a range of suggestions concerning the mobilization of funds for
development.

(14) See, for example, Horst P.Wiesenbach, *Mobilization of
Development Finance: Promises and Problems of Automaticity*,
paper prepared as part of the IFDA Third System project,
IFDA, Nyon, May 1979 (mimeo). This and the Steinberg and
Yager studies have served as important sources for this
introductory section on international taxation.

(15) Marc Nerfin (ed.), *What Now. The Dag Hammarskjöld Report
on Development and International Cooperation*, Dag Hammarskjöld Foundation, Uppsala, Sweden, 1975.

(16) Jan Tinbergen (coordinator), *Reshaping the International
Order: A Report to The Club of Rome*, E.P.Dutton, New York,
1976.

(17) *North-South: A Programme for Survival*, Pan Books, London
and Sydney, 1980.

(18) IFDA, *Building Blocks for Alternative Development Strategies*, IFDA Dossier 17, Nyon, May-June 1980.

(19) The Cocoyoc Declaration (U.N. document A/C.2/292, 1974)
is reprinted in *International Organization*, vol. 29, Summer
1975, pp. 893-901; *Alternatives*, vol. 1., nos. 2-3, July-
September, 1975, pp. 396-406; and *Development Dialogue*,
no. 2, 1974, pp. 88-96.

(20) For an evaluation of the importance of this statement, see
John G.Ruggie, 'On the Problem of 'The Global Problematique':
What Roles for International Organizations?', *Alternatives*,
vol. V, no. 4, January 1980, pp. 517-550, viz. pp. 544-548.

(21) See *Towards a New International Order: An Appraisal of
Prospects*, joint report published under the auspices of the
Governments of Algeria and the Netherlands and in coopera-
tion with the RIO Foundation, Netherlands Government
Printing Office, The Hague, 1977.

(22) Ibid., p. 44.

(23) Symposium report reprinted in *IFDA Dossier*, no. 13, November 1979, pp. 4-26.

(24) Ibid., p. 18.

(25) The Ocean Development Tax is described in chapter 5. For
details of the tax, see International Ocean Institute, *Proceedings of the First PIM Convocation, Malta, June 28 -
July 3, 1970*, vol.3 : 'Planning and Development in the
Oceans', Msida, Malta, 1970.

(26) See E.Pisani, 'Here's to Utopia. A Global Tax on Natural
Resources', *CERES*, January-February, 1977. The proposal is
most fully described in Mohamed T.Diaware, *Une Taxation
Mondiale de Solidarité: Project TERRE*, Club de Dakar,
Senegal, 28 July 1977 (mimeo).

(27) For a description of the tax, see Jorge Lozoya, Jaime
Estevez and Rosario Green, *Alternative Views of the New*

International Economic Order: A Survey and Analysis of Major Academic Research Projects, Pergamon Press, Oxford and New York, 1979, p. 53.

(28) See Jorge Lozoya et al., op.cit., pp. 48-53.

(29) *North-South: A Programme for Survival*, p. 244.

(30) See 'Redistributing the World's Wealth', interview with Jan Tinbergen, *Development Forum*, April 1978, p. 3.

(31) United Nations, *Development and International Economic Cooperation: Preparations for the Special Session of the General Assembly in 1980*, document A/34/596, 23 October 1979, p. 13.

(32) UNCTAD, *Preparation of a Draft for the Contribution of UNCTAD to the Formulation of the International Development Strategy for the Third United Nations Development Decade*, document TD/B/AC.31/2, 15 January 1980, p. 8.

(33) IFDA, op.cit., p. 58.

(34) *North-South: A Programme for Survival*, pp. 252-254.

(35) *RIO Report*, pp. 131-132.

(36) Linkage type proposals for guaranteeing automaticity in the flows of concessional assistance are not discussed here. Under 'linkage' proposals is understood such ideas as using a larger share of SDR creation for the purposes of development and relating the growth of GNP to the expansion of development cooperation budgets either through the mechanisms of taxation or through the application of budgetary planning in relation to aid targets. For a discussion of this so-called 'incremental approach', see Wiesenbach, op. cit., and his 'Mobilization of International Development Finance: Automaticity and the Incremental Approach', *IFDA Dossier*, 9, July 1979.

(37) On the idea of a world income plan, see, for example, Arnold Simoni, *Beyond Repair: The Urgent Need for a New World Organization*, Collier-Macmillan, Canada, 1972; and Hanna Newcombe, 'Annual Guaranteed Income Plan for the Nations of the World', *Bulletin of Peace Proposals*, vol. 6, 1975, pp. 77-84.

(38) UNCTAD has been looking carefully at the possibilities of taxing the brain drain. See the study undertaken by Jagdish N.Bhagwati, *The Reverse Transfer of Technology (Brain Drain): International Resource-flow Accounting, Compensation, Taxation and Related Policy Measures*, document TD/B/C.6/AC.4/2, January 1978; UNCTAD's 'view' is given in *Development Aspects of the Reverse Transfer of Technology*, document TD/B/C.6/41, November 1978.

(39) Ways in which the common heritage of mankind can be expanded to new domains was discussed in chapter 5.

(40) See United Nations, *Economic and Social Consequences of the Arms Race and of Military Expenditure*, U.N. sales no. E.72. IX.16, New York, 1972; and United Nations, *Economic and Social Consequences of the Armaments Race and its Extremely*

Harmful Effects on World Peace and Security, document A/32/88, August 1977.

(41) Steinberg and Yager, op.cit., pp. 91 ff, give highest priority to the criteria of economic effects, fairness, administrative convenience and revenue raising potential. Wiesenbach, op.cit., pp. 28-29, stresses the importance of simplicity, fairness, low rates, high yields, reliability and wide participation.

(42) See Wiesenbach, op.cit., p. 13.

(43) According to Wiesenbach, p. 12, a 1975 opinion survey indicated that only 8 per cent of those questioned were in favor of the use of 10 per cent of the lottery's profits for development purposes.

(44) Steinberg and Yager, op.cit.

(45) Ibid., pp. 136 ff.

(46) SIPRI, *World Armaments and Disarmament: SIPRI Yearbook 1979*, Taylor and Francis, London, 1979, pp. 34-35 and pp. 172-173.

(47) Ibid., p. 169.

(48) *North-South: A Programme for Survival*, p. 244.

7 Technology and Global Reform

> Why does this magnificent applied
> science which saves work and
> makes life easier bring us so
> little happiness? The simple ans-
> wer runs: Because we have not yet
> learnt to make sensible use of it.
>
> Albert Einstein,
> Address, California
> Institute of Technology,
> 1931

THE IMPORTANCE AND ROLE OF TECHNOLOGY

Any statement about resources is an implict statement about technology; any statement about the future availability and use of
resources is a statement about the future availability and use of
technology. It follows that the development of a global planning
and resource management capability implies the strengthening of
the capacity to control and manage technology at the world level.

Technology has more than anything else shaped the world in which
we live. From mankind's earliest beginnings, technology has been
the main agent in the struggle upwards from subsistence toward
a decent, healthy and longer life. From the shaping of the first
bone and flint tools, the discovery of the wheel, the lever, the
plough, the use of fire, the smelting of the first metal ores,
mankind has assiduously, and by empirical means, shaped a technology to serve its material needs. Technology, then, is no new
phenomenon. What is different today is that the discovery of natural laws through scientific research has given a new dimension

to technology - a dimension of such massive impact that it not
only offers infinite promise for the relief of poverty and hunger, but also, as a consequence of its distorted development
and lack of systematic control for human welfare, threatens
patterns of life, the ecology of the globe, and even the survival of the human race. (1)

Modern science-based technology has been the main engine of
growth and has constituted the major instrument in the process
of industrial growth and development. It has been the major
force in the dramatic growth of global interdependence and the
interpenetration of societies. It has, in the words of Miriam
Camps, "eroded the traditional insulators of time and space"
(2) and given rise to such notions as 'spaceship earth' and
the 'global village' (3). It has changed man's notion of resource frontiers, taking him into the darkness of outer space and
into the depths of the oceans.

Modern technology has also given us, for the first time in history, a 'world system', a 'world economy', perhaps even a 'world
civilization'. (4) Immanuel Wallerstein has elegantly shown how
the size of the world economy is a function of the state of
technology, and in particular of the possibilities for transport
within its bounds. (5) The 'world system' has also given us
'world problems'. It is true that mankind has always known war,
hunger, poverty, ecological disruption and resource scarcities.
Until comparatively recently, however, these were not world problems. They could not become so because there was no world system to account for their global scope. Today problems are made
global by a world system which, shaped by the forces of science
and technology, has effectively integrated its component parts.
(6)

The revolution in communications, information processing, transportation, and weaponry has undermined traditional concepts of
sovereignty and security and reshaped the environment in which
international politics is perceived, formulated and conducted.
Henry Kissinger, writing in 1968, observed that changes in the
relative power of nations has become more a function of technological proficiency than territorial conquest and hence that
the capacity to use technology for military ends was of fundamental political significance. (7) Technology has given us weaponry which is planetary in its implications and which has blurred conventional distinctions between war and politics. Politics
have become geopolitics and geopolitics have become 'high politics'. These have given rise to a global power game which has
created its own logic, a logic so powerful that it transcends
all other considerations, even ideological ones. (8) For in a
world in which two nations maintain the means for mutual geno-
cide in the name of freedom, peace and security, ideological considerations become subservient to questions of human survival.

The spread and complexity of modern technology has also eroded
the power of those charged with decision-making - the politicians. Since most modern technology is developed in the laboratories of Western transnational corporations, it has elevated
their influence to a point which often exceeds the capacity of
governments to control it. The concentration of the sources of
new technology may already be such that no more than a few hundred people in the corporate boardrooms of large Western transnationals are able to decide who is going to get what part of
much advanced technology and under what conditions. (9) This is
power which can assume life and death proportions. The very
complexity of much modern technology has also increased the influence of those who purport to understand it - scientists. The
rapid growth of modern technology has given us, to use Ralph
Lapp's phrase, a 'new priesthood' of scientists who have taken
decision-making prerogatives out of the hands of politicians.
(10) In today's world, corporate executives rub shoulders with
scientists in the corridors of power.

Not surprisingly, the importance of technology is recognized by
those in the North and South, the East and West. Few disagree
that technological developments and the pace and direction of
technical change are crucial to understanding the kind of future
mankind is to have; whether indeed, it is to have any future at
all. Whether the need is more food, better education, improved
health care, increased industrial output, more efficient and
safer transportation, even the monitoring of peace, technology
will play a vital role. The question which confronts us is surely whether we have the wisdom to direct the development of science and technology in directions which are genuinely worthwhile
or whether we allow, as we have done to date, the feasible to
become the permissable, ranking 'can' higher than 'ought':
whether we foreclose the future or succeed in opening new perspectives on human welfare and wellbeing.

                        TECHNOLOGY AND THE ARMS RACE

The origins of modern technology can be traced back through the
natural sciences to empiricism and the inductive method, established as a reaction to the Greek and scholastic traditions of
learning. (11) The first empiricists, like Francis Bacon, hoped
to discover, through their experiments, the artlessness and innocence which Adam is supposed to have had before the Fall. The
scholastic tradition, they believed, constituted a continuation
of Adam's sin of pride. "We clearly empress the stamp of our own
image on the creation and works of God", Bacon wrote, "instead
of carefully examining and recognizing in them the stamp of the
Creator himself". (12)

Despite its noble origins, empiricism - the 'New Learning' - did not retrieve man's lost innocence. Instead, it has given, not artless power, but the dreadful power to destroy himself and all other creatures. Instead of innocence it has given us a world in which one of the most prominent practitioners of science has admitted that "we have known sin". (13)

History has known scientists, like Archimedes, Leonardo da Vinci and Napier who kept secret the knowledge of the terrible weapons which they had invented. Leonardo wrote in his secret diary of his "underwater boat" and speculated on its usefulness for practising "assinations at the bottom of the sea". He decided to suppress his invention "on account of the evil nature of men". Napier invented a mysterious machine which, according to testimony, "could clear a field of four miles circumference of all the living creatures exceeding a foot in height". Given "the malice and rancour rooted in the heart of mankind", he decided, like Leonardo, to take his secret with him to the grave. (14)

When the invention of weapons was the work of a single man, such a decision was the prerogative of the inventor. Today, the production of weapons is the work of a complex, hierarchical, centralized, and specialization-oriented network which links together governments, military establishments, industries, universities and research institutions into a highly interpenetrated and mutually reinforcing whole. The maintenance of this network requires vast amounts of resources - resources which might otherwise be used for peaceful and development-oriented purposes. World military expenditures are today in the order of $400 billion a year - more than $1 billion every day - and increasing at the rate of about 5 per cent per annum. (15) Since the Second World War, the direct costs of the arms race have exceeded $6000 billion, equivalent to the combined GNP of the entire world in the mid 1970s.

The arms race not only deprives mankind of vast financial resources, it also consumes vast human resources. About 25 per cent of the world's scientific manpower is engaged in military research and development at a cost of between $20-25 billion, or nearly 50 per cent of all, public and private, research and development expenditures. World militarization also stakes a large claim on available supplies of depletable natural resources. In the U.S. in 1970, for example, military purposes accounted for 14 per cent of all bauxite and copper consumption, 11 per cent of all lead and zinc, and 10 per cent of all nickel and molybdenum. (16) World military consumption of liquid hydrocarbons (excluding petroleum products used in the production of weapons and equipment) has been estimated to be about 700-750 million barrels annually - twice the annual consumption of the whole of Africa and about 4 per cent of total world consumption. (17)

The highly interpenetrated global network of industry and R & D
institutions which sustains the competitive armaments race is
thus voracious in its appetite for human and material resources.
Not only does it divert a treasure trove of resources from civilian applications and peaceful purposes. It also perverts schol-
arship and the development of science and technology. The arms
race has made science and technology the masters of war rather
the servants of peace. Like some demonic prism, it has deformed
and distorted the knowledge and techniques we can bring to bear
on questions of human welfare, even survival.

TECHNOLOGY AND DEVELOPMENT

Technology is one of the keys to understanding the future of
the rich and poor countries and of the relationship between them.
It is the root cause of international inequality and the prime
force behind the ever growing disparities between the rich and
poor nations. The 'widening gap' was once thought to have its
origins in unequal trading relationships. That has been found
to be only partly true. The fundamental advantage of the rich
countries is not only that they produce and trade certain
types of commodities but also that they have the capacity for
technological change and innovation, a capacity to a large extent vested in transnational corporations. It is because of this
that they are the main beneficiaries of any type of commercial
trannsaction with the Third World, be it in the area of trade or
investment. (18) If we are to talk in terms of 'gaps', then the
gap between the rich and poor countries is a technological one.
Technology is the force which is pushing the rich and poor worlds
ever further apart.

In a world of imposed North-South asymmetry, nowhere are the disparities between North and South more in evidence than in the
crucially important field of scientific research and technological development. Some 90 per cent of all the scientists and tech-
nologists who have ever lived are alive today and 9 out of 10 are
employed in the industrialized countries. The vast majority of
these - more than 90 per cent - are involved in either the development of military systems or in finding solutions to rich world
problems and converting these solutions into protected industrial
processes. The rich minority thus commands an overwhelming proportion of the infrastructure - material and human - required to
'get ahead'. (19) In this race to 'get ahead', the poor nations
are, in the words of Ali Mazrui, condemned to 'scientific margin-
ality" and to lagging ever further behind. (20)

In its national context technology comprises a system of knowledge, skills, experience and organization required to produce,
utilize and control services and the tools which we can call
techniques. This technique-centered part of the social system

is critical to development for four main reasons: it is a resource and the creator of new resources; it is a powerful instrument of social control; it bears on the quality of decision-
making to achieve social change; and it constitutes a central
arena in which new meanings must be created to counter alienation, the antithesis of meaningful existence. (21) Technology
is not merely a mode of production and therefore neutral. It
incorporates and reflects value systems. It embodies deeply
rooted assumptions about the organization of knowledge, space
and time, of human relations and relations with nature. Johan
Galtung has suggested that every technology carries its own
code - economic, social, cultural, and cognitive. (22) The economic code of Western technology, he argues, requires that
techniques be capital-intensive, research-intensive, organiza-
tion-intensive, and labor-extensive. The social code creates
a center and periphery and thus perpetuates a structure of inequality. In the cultural arena, the code presents the West as
entrusted by destiny with the historic mission of molding the
world in its own image. And in the cognitive field, it sees
man as the master of nature, the vertical and individualistic
relations between human beings as normal and natural, and history as a linear process.

Clearly, technology both embodies and perpetuates structures,
both intranationally and internationally. It is both an agent
of change and a destroyer of values. It can promote equality
of opportunity or systematically deny it. Technology thus
plays a political role in society, nationally and globally, a
role intimately related to the distribution of power and the
exercise of control. Because technology and social processes
are organically linked, reinforcing each other in both material
and ideological ways, it follows that choices concerning technology imply choices concerning a type of society. It follows
also that society imposes limits on the choice and development
of technology. Technology is thus a preeminently political matter. Once the political nature of modern technology is recognized it becomes apparent that a brave new world, however defined, cannot result form the judicious manipulation of techniques alone. It is no less apparent that an alternative technology can only be developed - at least on any significant
scale - within the framework of an alternative society. (23)
Technological development and social change are part of the
same dialectical process. You can't have one without the other.

In the West, modern science-based technology has brought undreamt of levels of material prosperity to hundreds of millions
of people. It has helped rescue them form ignorance and free
them from crippling diseases. But at a cost. It has also helped
shape a productive system which, through mindless and repetitive
work, deforms the minds and destroys the initiatives of countless
numbers of people. The alienation brought about by much modern

technology and the soul-destroying nature of the productive system have been described by such distinguished scholars as Jacques
Ellul, Erich Fromm, Jurgen Habermas, Ivan Illich, Herbert Marcuse,
Lewis Mumford, Theodore Rozak and E.F. Schumacher. (24) They have
argued that much modern technology has succeeded economically only because it has been allowed to fail socially; that technological means have come to shape human ends and that man-the-tool-
maker has become man-the-tool. They view with deep skepticism
both the legitimacy and efficacy of technocratic authority and the
commitment of capitalism and socialism to progress defined in
terms of bigger and better technology. (25) Ecologists have also
pointed to the destructive and wasteful character of modern technology, a technology with a rapacious appetitive for renewable
resources and which treats pollution as an 'externality'. In
their view, "the new technology is an economic success only because it is an ecological failure". (26)

Such criticisms are barely heard in Eastern Europe where scientists and scholars have a commitment to the notion of technological progress now virtually unknown in the West. (27) According to
Soviet scientists the world 20 years hence will be one with unlimited energy (nuclear) which will unlock the door to infinite
supplies of natural resources. There will be no hunger in the
world. Technology will have turned deserts into gardens, made
it possible to harvest food from the sea, to modify climate and
to produce synthetic foods on an industrial scale. Technology,
rather than degrading the environment, will have restored ecological equilibrium. By 1990, Russians will be liberated from house-
work since this will be fully automated. This will give them the
chance to take tourist trips to the moon (there will be an extensive network of railways on the moon by 2030). According to Soviet scientists, Russians will be living to the ripe old age of
100 by the year 2000 thanks to control of aging processes. (28)

Although presented as Soviet repudiations of Western 'burgeois
futurology', the picture painted by Soviet academicians bears a
striking resemblance to the promised lands of such burgeois futur-
ologists as Herman Kahn, Anthony Wiener and Daniel Bell. (29) Indeed, one is tempted to believe that the only difference between
a capitalist and socialist post-industrial society is the road
chosen to get there. Moreover, it has been argued that much
technical change in the Soviet Union has been based, not upon
indigenously developed technologies, but upon imported Western
technologies, i.e. on technologies which embody the structure -
economic, social, cultural and cognitive - of a capitalist rather
than a socialist society. (30) If this is so, the socialist post-
industrial society will in part be built upon a foundation of
capitalist forms of social organization and control. (31)

The developing countries have little time for such speculation.
Their urgent task is to bring some of the benefits of modern tech-

nology to the hundreds of millions of people who live in a world
of hunger, disease, soul-destroying poverty and premature death
- a world left untouched by the miracles of modern science. In
addition to using technology to raise the living standards of
the poor, they must seek to use it to combat the ever-present
risk of natural disaster; to rid the heavens of the four Horsemen of the Apocalypse who forever ride over the skies of the
Third World.

The developing countries have become acutely aware of the importance of technology in the process of development. They know
that without a capacity for technological change and innovation
they are condemned to penury and stagnation. Their attempts to
shape meaningful strategies of change, however, are forever running aground on the rocks of technological dependence.

The technological dependence of the Third World has many dimensions and aspects. At one level it results form the fact that
the source of modern technology is highly concentrated. The U.S.
at present supplies about 55-60 per cent of all traded technology and 80-90 per cent of the technology acquired by developing
countries is supplied by Western transnationals which are motivated by business (profit maximization) rather than development
(social welfare) considerations. At another level, technological
dependence is but one aspect - albeit a particularly crucial
one - of the general pattern of dependence into which the poor
countries are locked. As such, it can only be comprehended within the overall framework of the legitimization and reproduction
of political systems and social and economic structures. (32)

At its worst, technological dependence is a structural-cultural
invasion which results in the reproduction of rich country structures and value premises. It is a subtle invasion for the combat-
ants are systems which promise progress. But once established
they create societies in their own image and require imported
supplies to sustain them. In this situation, weakness reinforces
dependence and dependence creates weakness.

Clearly, there can be no such thing as technological independence. But there must be technological self-reliance. For a developing country this must include the capacity to unlock the
code of Western technology, ridding it of its rich world ethno-
centricity, and stamping it with the societal imprint of the
developing country. It must go well beyond the capacity to regulate the flow of imported technology. The mainspring of self-
reliance is the autonomous capacity for innovation. This requires much more than formal arrangements, new institutions and
programs. It requires the mobilization of the creative energies
and problem-solving capacities of ordinary people, conscious
efforts to trace the knowledge 'hidden' in local communities,
among the peasantry, and in the experience of women. (33)

All this implies national self-confidence and the exercise of

political will. It also raises the question of whether it is
possible for all developing countries to embark upon their
technological transformation without a corresponding and parallel social and political transformation.

TOWARD A MANAGEMENT RESPONSE:

THE CONCEPT OF DUAL-PURPOSE TECHNOLOGIES

What can we conclude from the above? Simply, that the development of modern science-based technology has changed out of all
recognition not only the face of the world but also the way in
which we perceive it. It is the key to understanding the future
of the rich and poor countries and of the relationship between
them. And given its incredible destructive power, it has the
greatest possible bearing on the future of the human race.

Science-based technology preempts the future. It shapes our conception of problems and our understanding of what is possible.
It creates resources and denies their existence. It is, in short,
both servant and master. Clearly, there can be no capability for
global planning and resource management without an enhanced capacity for effectively wrestling with technological issues and
questions; without the capacity to influence the growth and development of modern technology. But how? Science and technology
and their social consequences are, short of catastrophe, irreversible: we cannot go back; we cannot even stand still. Their
impact is indivisible and their future unpredictable: we can
neither put limits on scientific inquiry nor can we anticipate
the results of it.

Modern technology is pervasive. It refuses to recognize sectoral
distinctions, scientific specializations, ministerial competences, national frontiers. It overflows all the vessels created
by man to contain it. Indeed, of all the areas in which we may
recognize the need for a planning and management capability, it
is difficult to conceive of one in which problems would be greater than in science-based technology. Technology is just about
the most difficult thing one could set out to plan for. But we
must try.

We will argue that the concept of *dual-purpose technologies*
could be used to engineer a breakthrough: that part of the technological dilemma could be resolved by determined attempts to
plan and manage technologies with a dual-purpose character.

By dual-purpose technologies we understand those which:

● are applicable to the fabrication of weapons of massive destruction;
● have an economic development potential or can be used for
peaceful purposes;

- carry serious environmental risks, even in their peaceful uses;
- are transnational in their effects.

In a sense, virtually all technologies can be considered dual-purpose: a knife, for example, can be used to feed a hungry man or to arm a soldier. The technology spectrum is wide. At the one end, however, there is a set of industries and technologies which has become or is becoming responsible for the worst of the weapons of massive destruction. These technologies have carried the arms race into the reaches of outer space and into the depths of the ocean. They are genuinely transnational in their effects. These same technologies also have a potential for economic development through peaceful uses and all countries thus stress their inalienable right of access to them. And even in their peaceful application, these technologies, if unregulated and unmanaged, can cause environmental damage almost as catastrophic as their planned diversion for military purposes.

It is upon such technologies that we will focus in the following pages. We will look specifically at:

- nuclear technologies
- chemical and biological technologies
- space and satellite technologies
- marine technologies
- laser technologies
- environmental modification technologies.

We present this list not in the belief that it is in any way comprehensive but in the hope that a discussion of it will reveal the problems inherent in, and the rewards which could result from, the effective management of dual-purpose agents.

In each case we will look at the military applications and the peaceful applications of the technologies and at the institutional arrangements which exist to control and manage them. In doing so, we hope to demonstrate that dual-purpose technologies have invalidated traditional approaches to both disarmament and development and to processes of institution-building and the development of a planning and management capability at the world level. (34)

NUCLEAR TECHNOLOGIES

In terms of the Nuclear Age, our world is just 35 years old. In that time, mankind has been haunted by the ever-present threat of nuclear war (35) and has speculated on the advent of an era in which energy "would be too cheap to meter". All but 140,000 people have survived a nuclear holocaust. The era of cheap energy never arrived.

And it looks as though it never will. Recognition of the nightmare risks associated with the development of nuclear fission
reactors - thermal pollution, radiation leaks, the problem of
storing radioactive wastes, the risk of a catastrophic accident,
and the proliferation of nuclear weapons - together with its
poor economics have placed the future of nuclear energy in
doubt. (36) Few societies, with the notable exception of the
Soviet Union, the country which has so far had the most spectacular nuclear accident, (37) appear ready to uncritically accept it.

Nuclear technologies have found a number of other peaceful applications. In medicine, radioisotopes are used in the diagnosis
and treatment of cancer. In industry nuclear technologies are
used to measure and control the density, thickness and height
of industrial materials, and in agriculture they have found a
limited application in studies on plant growth and energy ab-
sorption. Nuclear explosions for large-scale excavations, once
thought "as an answer to the increasing demand for energy, water,
minerals, transportation links and food supply" (38), no longer
generate much enthusiasm due to the inevitable problem of radiation release, and this particular application has more or less
come to a standstill.

It is safe to assume that the ending of nuclear energy research
and development would not put an end to research into technologies for peaceful purposes. Nuclear technology, a Promethean
bequest, is a dual-purpose technology *par excellance* and must
be dealt with accordingly.

The dual aspect of the mass destruction and peaceful uses potential of nuclear technology was fully understood at the very beginning of the Nuclear Age. To cope with this unprecedented situation, Lilienthal and Baruch presented a plan at the first
meeting of the Atomic Energy Commission on 14 June 1946 for an
international regime for the management of nuclear technology.
(39) The plan recognized the importance of vesting a single
institution with responsibilities for both disarmament and development. "Since the exploitation of atomic energy for peaceful purposes necessitates operations which are, in the initial
stages, identical with those needed to make atomic energy available for destructive purposes". Bernard Baruch observed, "both
of these functions.... should be assigned to the same agency.
Furthermore, an international agency with responsibilities for
fostering the beneficial uses of atomic energy as well as responsibilities for preventing its misuse, will be more effective,
constructive, and workable than if it has merely duties of inspection and policing. The activities of such an agency might
even result in establishing beneficial patterns of international
cooperation of a new and hopeful kind". (40)

The International Atomic Development Authority, as conceived
by Lilienthal-Baruch, would have been the first international
resource management institution and, in this respect, a forerunner of the International Seabed Authority discussed in
chapter 5. Its powers and functions, with regard to the management of nuclear resources and technologies, would have been
even more sweeping than those proposed, more timidly, for the
Seabed Authority today. For the Atomic Development Authority
would have had control over all phases of the development and
use of atomic energy. It would have managerial control or ownership of all atomic energy activities potentially dangerous to
world security and the power to control, inspect, and license
all activities. It was to have the duty of promoting the peaceful uses of atomic energy. The Authority was to conduct continuous surveys of supplies of uranium and thorium and bring the
raw materials under its control. It was to possess the exclusive right both to conduct research in the field of atomic explo-
sives and to produce and own fissionable material. All other
nuclear activities were to be permitted only under license of
the Authority, which would lease, under safeguards, denatured
fissionable materials. Dangerous activities of the Authority
and its stockpiles were to be decentralized and strategically
distributed. All nations were to grant the freedom of inspection
deemed necessary by the Authority. Baruch stressed the importance of immediate punishment for infringements of the rights
of the Authority and maintained that: "There must be no veto
to protect those who violate their solemn agreements not to develop or use atomic energy for destructive purposes". Once a
system of control and sanctions was effectively operating,
further production of atomic weapons would cease, existing
stocks would be destroyed and all technological information
would be communicated to the Authority.

At the time the proposal was made the United States not only
had a monopoly of nuclear technology, it also controlled the
votes in the United Nations. The Authority, hence, was to be established under U.S. hegemony and control, which is precisely
why it could not happen. This, however, does not detract from
the validity of the principles for the management of a technology for both disarmament and development.

History has shattered the great design, but bits and pieces of
it keep surfacing. The dual-purpose character of nuclear technology is enshrined today in a number of Treaty provisions and resolutions, urging, on the one hand, the limitation, control and
final elimination of nuclear weapons and, on the other, international cooperation in the promotion of the peaceful uses of
nuclear technology, under international safeguards, control, and,
at least partially, management.

Attempts to control the spread and use of nuclear weapons have

resulted in more than a dozen agreements involving either all
the world's nations or the superpowers. (42) Given the number
of agreements, to say nothing of the effort which has gone into
their negotiation, one could be excused for believing that there
has been some nuclear arms control. Nothing could be further
from the truth.

Consider the record. (43) The Antarctic Treaty (1961) was sensible but harmless and risked no one. The Partial Test Ban Treaty (1963), concluded in the afterglow of the Cuban missile crisis, did nothing to impede the nuclear arms race nor the proliferation of nuclear weapons. More nuclear weapon tests have in
fact been carried out in the period following the partial test
ban than the one before it. The Treaty banning nuclear weapons
in Latin America (Treaty of Tlatelolco, 1967) does not ban non-
military nuclear explosive devices, a consequence of the dual-
purpose character of nuclear technologies. Neither the U.N. resolution of 1963 which banned weapons of mass destruction in
outer space (44) nor the subsequent Outer Space Treaty (1967) succeeded in preventing the extension of the nuclear arms race into
space. The success of the Seabed Treaty, which prohibits the
'emplacing' or 'emplanting' of nuclear and other weapons of mass
destruction on the seabed, resides in the fact that the technique was abandoned by the superpowers in the early sixties in
favor of submarine systems about which there is no agreement.
The Non-Proliferation Treaty(1970) has also singularly failed
to halt the spread of the technology required to manufacture
nuclear weapons. Non-nuclear powers have refused to accept an
agreement which, by its very nature, gives a cartel of great
powers a monopoly of the means of mass destruction, thus stabi-
lizing the existing balance of power in the international system. The potential usefulness of the NPT has been consistently
undermined by the failure of the great powers to come to terms
with the nuclear arms race among themselves and, perversely,
by their readiness to sell nuclear technologies to the Third
World.

The history of attempts to control the nuclear arms race is one
of noble men and women wrestling with forces which are too big
for them. The consequence has been an ever more virulent race,
a race with an inevitable outcome. It would seem fair to conclude, as Elizabeth Young has done, that efforts at arms control "have had about as much bearing on the life of nations as
a Mafioso's crossing himself as he loads his gun, has on his
hopes of going to heaven". (45)

There can be little doubt that the dual-purpose character of nuclear technologies has greatly hampered the negotiation of effective arms control agreements. The NPT, for example, stresses
in Article IV, that nothing in this Treaty shall be interpreted
as affecting the inalienable right of all the Parties to the

Treaty to develop research, production and use of nuclear energy for peaceful purposes; and that all the Parties to the Treaty undertake to facilitate, and have a right to participate in,
the fullest possible exchange of equipment, materials, and
scientific and technological information for the peaceful uses
of nuclear energy. Parties to the Treaty in a position to do
so shall also cooperate in contributing, alone or together with
other States or international organizations, to the further development of the applications of nuclear energy for peaceful
purposes, especially in the territories of non-nuclear-weapon
States Parties to the Treaty, with due consideration for the
needs of the developing areas of the world.

The Non-Proliferation Treaty Review Conference went one step
further in recommending some measure of common management. The
Final Declaration issued by the Conference recognizes "that regional multinational nuclear fuel cycle centres may be an advantageous way to satisfy, safely and economically, the needs
of many States in the course of initiating or expanding nuclear
power programmes, while at the same time facilitating physical
protection and the application of the IAEA safeguards and contributing to the goals of the Treaty".

Forty States from the First, Second, and Third World met in
Washington D.C. in October 1977 and initiated an International
Nuclear Fuel Cycle Evaluation (INFCE), a huge project that picks
up a number of bits and pieces of the Lilienthal-Baruch design.
(46) The participants in the project are still convinced that
nuclear energy for peaceful purposes should be made widely
available because of the urgent need to meet the world's energy
requirements. They are also convinced that effective measures
can and should be taken, at the national level and through international agreements, to minimize the danger of the proliferation of nuclear weapons without jeopardizing energy supplies or
the development of nuclear energy for peaceful purposes. They
stressed that special consideration should be given to the specific needs of and conditions in developing countries. While
INFCE was to be a technical and analytical study and not a negotiation, the participants expressed the hope that the International Atomic Energy Agency will play an active role in the
conduct of the project at all levels. "The participants acknowledge in this connection the dual responsibility of the IAEA
in promoting and safeguarding nuclear activities". (47)

In outlining the technical and economic scope of the project
and the methods of work, the Final Communiqué of the Organizing
Conference time and again refers to "multinational or regional
fuel cycle centers or similar arrangements", "multinational or
international mechanisms guaranteeing timely deliveries in case
of delays or cut-off of supplies", and "international control
of separated plutonium (including storage under the auspices

of the IAEA and related availability criteria)".

If the spectre of the military uses of nuclear technology is to
be exorcised, the peaceful uses of nuclear technology must be
managed internationally for the benefit of all mankind, with
particular consideration to the needs of developing countries.

What form this international management system may take in the
future may depend, partially, on the future of atomic energy
itself. Should atomic energy production become a major economic
factor (particularly in the form of nuclear *fusion* reactors),
the IAEA might be restructured and strengthened as an Atomic
Development Authority, endowed with regulatory and managerial
capacity and the responsibility of coordinating and integrating
regional networks such as Euratom. Such an Atomic Development
Authority could become a major instrument for, and part of, a
global energy production and distribution system which is needed for world development as part of a New International Economic
Order. Alternatively, the regulatory and control functions could
be split off and entrusted to an International Disarmament Agency. Experience at the national level (for example in the U.S.),
however, points in the opposite direction. The question obviously needs further study.

CHEMICAL AND BIOLOGICAL TECHNOLOGIES

Chemical and biological technologies are so integrated into the
fabric of society that it is difficult to imagine a civilized
community existing without them. They have constituted the foundation upon which advances in such fields as sanitation, health
care and nutrition have been built. They have reached a level
of complexity that tends to make us forget that our well-being
is very dependent upon their wise use and they have provided
mankind with an array of products for industrial, domestic and
agricultural uses.

Biotechnologies especially have received a good deal of attention in recent years. With their potential in the field of energy generation, medecine, food production, industrial processes
and their general ability to produce new products from new processes, they are considered by some to hold more promise for
human development than almost any other scientific advance in
mankind's history. (48) Biotechnology is enabling mankind to
unravel genetic strands of deoxyribonucleic acid and to recom-
bine them with others, altering the instructions that govern
living cells. In laboratories all over the world, scientists
are taking genes from one organism - the human organism has
100,000 genes in every cell - and planting them into another.
Single-celled organisms are being used to produce protein which

could help nourish the hungry of the world. Genetically engineered bacteria are being designed to eat their way through oil spills and to extract scarce minerals from the soil. Biotechnology is being used to produce cellulose enzymes for processes of biomass conversion, a development which will make it possible to combine both food and energy production within the same agricultural system, instead of making competing demands on it as has been widely feared. Biotechnology will also make it possible for mankind to harvest some of the riches of the ocean and to fulfill the promise of aquaculture.

The same technologies, however, can be used to construct weapons - even 'poor man's weapons' - with a capacity for massive destruction. Unlike nuclear weapons, chemical and biological weapons are relatively cheap and simple to develop. They are, however, dangerous to handle and difficult to control. Their killing power is horrendous and they pose threats comparable to those of nuclear technologies. (49)

The destructive capacity of chemical and biological weapons has been recognized for decades and some progress has been made in the negotiation of international agreements aimed at controlling their use. The horrors of the First World War led to the Versailles Treaty of 1919 prohibiting the use of poisonous gases. This prohibition was expanded to include bacteriological weapons in the Geneva Protocol of 17 June 1925. 103 States have so far signed the Protocol.

While the Protocol prohibits the use of chemical and biological weapons, it does not prohibit their research and development. Inevitably, then, the arms race in chemical and biological weapons has continued unabated. The science and technology applicable to the manufacture of these weapons are diffuse, penetrating a large sector of industrial production. They are not costly and are generally available to, or easily developed by, the world's nations, rich and poor. This conspires to make both the control of military uses and international cooperation in the advancement of peaceful uses every bit as difficult as in the case of nuclear technology.

Some progress has, however, been made. A Biological Weapons Convention (50) has been negotiated and was opened for signature in London, Moscow, and Washington on 10 April 1972. It entered into force on 26 March 1975 and has so far been signed by 118 States. The Convention can be considered the only real disarmament agreement negotiated since the Second World War: it provides for real disarmament as opposed to arms control. It is also distinguished by the fact that it imposes equal obligations on all parties (unlike, for example, the Nuclear Non-Proliferation Treaty). Parties to the Convention undertake never under any circumstances to develop, produce, stockpile or otherwise acquire and retain microbial or other biological agents, or toxins, whatever their origin or method of production, other than for prophylactic protection or other peaceful purposes. Signatories similarly undertake to foresake weapons, equipment or means of delivery designed to use such agents or toxins for hostile purposes or in armed conflict. Parties further undertake to destroy or to convert to peaceful purposes all biological warfare agents, toxins, equipment and means of delivery within, at the latest, nine months of the Convention coming into force. The Convention thus fully recognizes the dual-purpose character of biological technologies.

The Convention contains no provisions for inspection or enforcement, although states, should they suspect another state of violation, may lodge a complaint with the U.N. Security Council. Each state party agrees to cooperate in carrying out any investigation initiated by the Security Council as a result of a complaint. It further undertakes to provide or to support assistance to a state in cases where the Security Council decides that it has been exposed to danger as a result of the violation of the Convention.

At the same time, the Convention provides (Article X) that parties to it undertake "to facilitate and have the right to participate in the fullest possible exchange of equipment, materials and scientific and technological information for the use of (biological) agents and toxins for peaceful purposes". Implementation of the Convention is to be carried out in such a way as not to interfere with the economic and technological development of its signatories nor with international cooperation aimed at promoting peaceful applications.

There is no Treaty machinery of any kind. The lack of effective mechanisms for dealing with complaints and violations is increasingly regarded as a major deficiency which may be examined by the Review Conference.

Although an enormous amount of effort has gone into the negotiation of a chemical weapons convention very little tangible progress has been made since the Geneva Protocol in 1925. The lack of progress must in large part be explained by the fact that nations have not greatly wanted it. For chemical agents make 'better' weapons than biological agents. They are more predictable (these is less likelihood of killing your own troops or civilian population), they have a longer shelf life, and may be easier and safer to handle. Their effects are also more immediate which is a military advantage.

Despite this, some steps in the direction of a chemical weapons convention have been taken. A draft convention was submitted to the Committee of the Conference on Disarmament (CCD) by nine socialist States in 1972. This was followed by a Japanese draft convention in 1974, and a British one in 1976. The Non-Aligned

members of the CCD have also prepared a working paper on the
subject. (51) A number of informal meetings with experts have
also yielded much valuable background material. (52) The United
States and the Soviet Union have been conducting bilateral
talks since 1976 which, so far, have failed to produce concrete
results. A group of 21 States has been established by the CCD
to facilitate parallel negotiations in the Committee and between the two superpowers. The group has proposed the establishment of an ad hoc committee to elaborate a new draft Convention.
This proposal, however, has met with opposition from both the
U.S. and the USSR. Bones of contention remain the definition of
a chemical weapon (should it include, for example, high explo-
sives, smoke bombs, tear gases and herbicides all of which have
been used in warfare) and appropriate methods of verification.
(53)

Recent steps taken by the Federal Republic of Germany and the
United Kingdom in the area of verification may contribute to
the much needed process of confidence-building. Both countries
have unilaterally opened their borders to groups of experts and
diplomats from other nations who are free to inspect major converted chemical weapons plants and other chemical installations.
This is a significant development since it touches on the most
sensitive questions of national sovereignty and industrial property rights.

What lessons can be drawn from the decades of experience of
trying to negotiate a treaty to ban chemical weapons? Three
main recognitions have surfaced.

● Firstly, it has been generally recognized that, as a Delegate
of Japan formulated it, it may not be possible at all "for any
chemical agents available for weapons purposes to be prohibited
outright without hindering the peaceful uses of that agent".
(54) The dual-purpose character of chemical technologies has
thus been clearly established. This recognition is further evidenced in, for example, the statement made by Kamanda Wa Kamada,
Zaire's Delegate, "Zaire was deeply preoccupied by the problem
of chemical weapons. As a developing country", he observed,
"Zaire believed that the resources to be released as a result
of disarmament could be used in solving the socio-economic problems of the Third World". (55)

● Secondly, and related to the above, the need has been stressed, especially by developing countries, to couple prohibitory
measures with provisions dealing with the peaceful uses by sti-
pulating that States which are parties to a future Convention
should cooperate in contributing to the further development and
application of scientific discoveries for peaceful purposes.

● Thirdly, the convergence of development and environmental
protection measures and disarmament measures in the field of

chemical and biological weapons has been recognized. Multi-pur-
pose monitoring systems, embodying an entirely new type of
science policy, an entirely new approach to resource inventori-
zation and management, and a new combination of national and
international measures and structures, would simultaneously
serve the causes of disarmament, development and environmental
protection. (56)

SPACE AND SATELLITE TECHNOLOGIES

The Space Age began on 4 October 1957 when the Soviet Union
launched its first satellite, Sputnik 1, as its contribution to
the International Geophysical Year. A few months later, the U.S.
launched Explorer 1, its first satellite. Since then, both
countries have established themselves as the world's only space
powers, although some nations, individually and collectively,
have recently sought to challenge this absolute supremacy. (57)

The peaceful uses of space and satellite technologies are numerous. (58) Communication satellites have revolutionized telecommunications and broadcasting. Telecommunications via satellites are much cheaper, more reliable, extensive, of better
quality and can be installed more quickly than traditional means
of communications. They are especially attractive to developing
countries since, as a U.N. report notes, "a modern, highly capable communications system can be installed without the need
for intermediate development of extensive land based facilities
and real estate for cable or microwave links". (59) The use of
telecommunications satellites is spreading rapidly and two
commercial telecommunications systems, INTELSAT and INTERSPUT-
NIK, already link most of the world's capitals. Regional and
national systems are now being developed or expanded. (60)

Meteorological satellites have revolutionized the state of the
art of weather forecasting, with enormous economic benefits
and saving of human lives. (61) Because they can "see" larger
areas of the earth, meteorologists are able to monitor weather
patterns and to measure, with infra-red sensors, changing temperature patterns. More accurate weather predictions are the
result.

Remote sensing, satellites, or more accurately Earth Resources
Technology Satellites (ERTS), have been another major breakthrough. Thier photographic and electronic devices make it possible to locate mineral deposits, pollution, crop and forest
diseases, and to estimate food production (crop forecasting).
Their potential has been described by Peter Jankowitsch, Chairman of the U.N. Committee on the Peaceful Uses of Outer Space
as follows: "Among the other uses of ERTS images are geological

surveys, off-shore and on land. Oil companies are among the big
users of this technique. While no oil strikes have thus far been
reported that could be specifically attributed to information
supplied by satellite, geologists expect such finds within a
short time. In searching for other minerals, prospecting from
space has already produced actual discoveries". Turning to other
applications he notes that "other experiments with ERTS indicate
that the satellite could make an important contribution to a
worldwide survey of food production. Greater accuracy would lead
to more efficient planning in all aspects of commodity processing
and distribution, and tend to force down prices". (62)

Other areas in which technologies are either operational or ex-
perimental include geodetic satellites for mapping, and navigational satellites for more efficient and safer transport by aircraft and ships.

New areas of application are currently under investigation. Studies are being made of the feasibility of solar power satellites
which would collect electricity and transmit it to earth via
microwaves. (63) The possibility of manufacturing and processing
in outer space, (reduced atmospheric pressure and gravity facili-
tates the fabrication of precision products like cathodic lamps
and certain electronic equipment) is being explored by those who
believe that the industrialization of space will be both feasible
and beneficial by the end of the century. (64) Indeed, the end-
less physical, psychological, technical and scientific frontiers
of space seem likely to stimulate the development of new systems
in such areas as transportation, communication, education and
health care. Whether we realize it or not, space and satellite
technology has already become an integral part of our lives and
it has a vast potential for further contributing, directly and
indirectly, to man's knowledge and welfare. (65)

Space and satellite technologies, however, are intrinsically dual-
purpose. The very same technologies which promise so much also
have enormous potential for massive destruction. It was of course
military considerations which provided the first stimulus to the
development of space technology. It was an ICBM, with its origins in the V-2 rockets of the Second World War, which placed
the first artificial satellites into earth orbit. Of the 4,500
objects which have been fired into space since the beginning of
the Space Age, about 1500 have been military satellites. The
military use of space is, however, increasing, as witnessed by
the fact that about 60 percent of all satellites launched in recent years have been for military purposes.

Civilian communication satellites can be used for military communications. (66) Civilian navigation satellites can be used to
guide warships and warplanes, or a single system cna be used for
both civilian and military purposes, as is the case with the
U.S.'s MARISAT System. Geodetic satellites can provide pinpoint

guidance to ICBMs, military aircraft and other bombardment systems, and remote sensing technologies can be used for purposes
of photographic or electronic guidance. The dual-purpose nature
of space and satellite technology is evidenced by the fact that
the Soviet Union conducts all of its space activities within
the framework of a single organization. (67)

Testifying before the Committee on Science and Technology of the
U.S. House of Representatives on the U.S. LANDSAT program in
January 1978, Howard Kurtz pointed out: "Do 'eye in the sky' satellites involve 'military' or 'civilian' policy? One of the
emerging satellites will contain instruments which will measure
the temperature of the surface water of the oceans, hundreds of
metres below, to within a fraction of a degree. This will be of
added value for *civilian* seastate and weather forecasting. But
this same instrument at the same moment will be able to detect
the faint trail of slightly warmer water rising to the surface,
heated by the friction of the propellor of a silent nuclear submarine, against the surrounding water, leaving a telltale trail
of warmer surface water to mark the path of this *military* submarine. *From here on out 'military technology' and 'civilian
technology'increasingly will overlap*..... Satellites monitoring
crops along national borders, simultaneously will be monitoring
troop movements across that border. Satellites monitoring pollution of rivers from sewage or oil spills, also will detect
pollution of the same river from production of nuclear or other
weapons". The U.S. LANDSAT", Kurtz stressed, "covers the entire
Earth in eighteen days, garnering information and forwarding it
to U.S. computers. Only 1.8 percent of its time is spent over
U.S. territory, however, 98,2 percent of the time this American
LANDSAT is gathering and storing information from areas that are
foreign to the United States". (68)

There are, of course, technologies which are used exclusively
for military purposes. The satellite telecommunications systems
operated by national defense departments and military alliances,
reconnaissance satellites, the Fractional Orbital Bombardment
System (FOBS) are just a few examples. (69) There are also the
weapons and weapon systems which were formerly the domain of the
science fiction writer. Killer satellites, equipped with powerful laser beams which can be used to 'blind' spy satellites, are
already under development. Both the Soviet Union and the U.S.
are also aggressively developing laser and charged particle
beams which can be carried by ASAT (anti-satellite system) satellites, fired from space platforms or from the ground. These
'death rays' could be directed at enemy satellites, ballistic
missiles, thermonuclear warheads and, ultimately, human beings.
(70)

The military potential of space has long been recognized and ever
since the beginning of the Space Age suggestions have been made

concerning ways in which the use of outer space for peaceful
purposes *only* and for the benefit of all mankind could be
guaranteed. The aspiration to demilitarize space was expressed
by the U.N. General Assembly just a few days after the launching of the first satellite. Resolution no. 1148 (XII) of 14
November 1957 calls for steps aimed at ensuring that space be
used "exclusively for peaceful and scientific purposes". Resolution no. 1348 (XII) of 13 December 1958 reaffirms that "it
is the common aim that outer space should be used for peaceful
purposes only".

Other important resolutions have since been passed. A number of
them were incorporated in the Outer Space Treaty of 1967. (71)
This Treaty, so far signed by 113 nations, is the principal legal instrument for regulating the peaceful uses of outer space.
It provides that the exploration and use of outer space, including the moon and other celestial bodies, "shall be carried
out for the benefit and in the interest of all countries, irrespective of their degree of economic or scientific development".
It guarantees to all States freedom of exploration and scientific research. It declares outer space "the province of all mankind" (Article I) and astronauts the "envoys of mankind" (Article V), and establishes that outer space, including the moon
and other celestial bodies, cannot be subject to appropriation
by nations (Article V). At the same time the Treaty prohibits
"the establishment of military bases, installations and fortifi-
cations, the testing of any type of weapons and the conduct of
military manoeuvres on celestial bodies". No "objects carrying
nuclear weapons or any kind of weapons of mass destruction" are
to be placed in orbit around the earth, but the use of military
personnel for scientific research or other peaceful purposes is
explicitly permitted. (Article III) The obligation of use for
exclusively peaceful purposes is restricted to the moon and
other celestial bodies and does not apply to the use of outer
space as such.

The Outer Space Treaty fails to define outer space (72) and contains no specific reference to its economic development potential. It is, however, cleverly worded and full of loopholes. It
has unfortunately resulted in the establishment of two regimes:
one for the moon and other celestial bodies, which are to be
used *exclusively* for peaceful purposes (Article IV); and one
for outer space since nowhere in the Treaty is it stated that
this is to be used *exclusively* for peaceful purposes. (73) This
inconsistency has given rise to different interpretations of the
Treaty and to a fierce debate on what exactly constitutes military uses of outer space. The debate has not only divided the
two superpowers; it has also split the international legal community. (74) A continuous stream of suggestions concerning ways
in which the controversy could be reconciled has failed to bring
an end to this unfortunate situation. The failure to reach agree-

ment has resulted in the militarization of outer space.

It has also meant that it has proven impossible to develop an
institutional framework for the management of outer space and
for the sharing of the benefits resulting from its use. (75)
Although there are two international organizations (INTELSAT
and INTERSPUTNIK) and a large number of intergovernmental organizations (ITU, WMO, FAO, WHO, UNESCO, IMCO, IAEA, WIPO, ICAO,
ASTRA, INMARSAT), regional organizations (ESA, ARABSAT) and international non-governmental organizations (ICSU and COSPAR,
IAF, IISL, ILA) which are involved in one way or another in
space activities, there is as yet no global agreement on rules
to govern telecommunication by satellites; and no rules to
govern the use of earth resource satellites. The international
treaties which have been negotiated are essentially nothing
more than the product of mutual agreement between the two superpowers. (76) The rest of the world has been asked or is required to either adhere or to adopt them.

There are, however, some signs that nations realize the necessity to demilitarize outer space and to establish a regime for
its management. The Delegation of Italy, for example, recently
introduced a working paper in the CCD in which it proposes a review of the regime established under the Outer Space Treaty to
include explicitly measures to prohibit the launching and sta-
tioning in orbit, or anywhere in outer space, of *all* weapons,
not merely nuclear weapons and other weapons of mass destruction. (77) Such a ban, the document suggests, could be embodied
in an Additional Protocol to the 1967 Treaty.

The most advanced and detailed proposal to use outer space and
satellite technology for peaceful purposes was introduced by
the Delegation of France in the Ad Hoc Committee of the Tenth
Special Session of the United Nations General Assembly held in
1978. (78) The French paper notes that the progress space technology has made in the field of earth observation satellites
constitutes a new development in international life. Satellites,
particularly those of a military type, have already attained a
very high level of precision in their observation capability,
and further progress will undoubtedly be made. At present the
information secured by means of such satellites is collected by
two countries which have the greatest experience in space technology and are in a position to make observations of the surface
of the earth at such places and for such observation periods
as they choose. The satellites available to those two countries,
moreover, play an important role in the verification of their
bilateral disarmament agreements.

France considers, the paper continues, that, within the framework of current disarmament efforts, this new monitoring method
should be placed at the service of the international community.
An *international satellite monitoring agency (ISMA)*, as a Spe-

cialized Agency of the United Nations, should be come an essential adjunct to disarmament agreements and to measures to increase international confidence and security by providing interested parties with information that they were entitled to demand. The Agency would be responsible for collecting, processing and disseminating information secured by means of earth observation satellites. Membership would be open to any State Member of the United Nations or of a Specialized Agency. The decision-making and deliberative bodies of the Agency would include at least a plenary organ and a restrictive organ having balanced representation of all regions of the world. It also would have the personnel required for the accomplishment of its tasks, including in particular, qualified technical personnel to process and analyse the data collected by observation satellites, as well as machinery for the settlement of disputes. To that end, the French paper suggests, an arbitration committee would be established, and arrangements for its composition and operation would be incorporated in the statute of the Agency.

The U.N. General Assembly, in its Resolution no. 33/71 of 14 December 1978, requested the Secretary-General to undertake a study of the technical, legal and financial implications of the establishment of the ISMA. (79) A group of governmental experts was appointed and it has published its report. (80) Whether the ISMA can get off the ground will of course largely depend upon the positions of the two superpowers. The omens do not augur well. The U.S. has declared itself against the proposal. (81) The Soviet Union remains silent. In the meantime, all other members of the United Nations have declared themselves in favor of the French proposal. (82)

Another recognition of the economic development potential of outer space is the approval on 3 July 1979, after seven years of deliberations, by the U.N. Committee on the Peaceful Uses of Outer Space of a draft international agreement which declares the natural resources of the moon and other celestial bodies the Common Heritage of Mankind. The draft agreement bars contamination of the moon's environment or any claim to national ownership of any part of the moon. It was approved by the U.N. General Assembly at its thirty-fourth session in 1979 and is now open for ratification. (83)

But there is still a long, long way to go. Where to? The experience of the United Nations Law of the Sea Conference suggests an answer. It may reside in a periodic Outer Space Conference or Assembly (every one, two or three year(s)),which might either consist of all member States of the United Nations or, if the model of a functional federation of international organizations were to be followed (cf. chapter 5), of representatives of all the international organizations active in outer space (which in turn are composed of States). The Committee on the Peaceful Uses of Outer Space (COPUOS) might serve as an Executive Council, or

the Conference itself might elect an Executive Council which
would supersede COPUOS and would be chosen on a strictly regional basis, ensuring equitable representation of all parts of
the world. (84) There would be an obvious need for some kind of
common Secretariat which might well be provided by the U.N.
Secretariat.

Such an *International Outer Space Authority* would require an
operational arm, although it would be difficult at this stage
to say whether this should be created *ex novo*, following the
pattern of the International Seabed Authority, or whether the
operational arm should be even more decentralized, using existing operational organizations such as INTELSAT, INTERSPUTNIK,
INMARSAT, ESO, which, in this case, would have to be brought
within the policy framework of the Authority.

A new order for outer space will eventually be born out of necessity. As satellite systems - international, regional and national; military and civilian - proliferate, pressures on space
once considered infinite will mount. Already, there are problems
of overcrowding in the geostationary orbit. Satellites placed
in this orbit, at an altitude of 36,000 km, are able to remain
in a more or less fixed position, rotating along with the planet. (85) Some 100 satellites already use the geostationary orbit - 'the most valuable parking place in space' - and are
joined by 15-20 new satellites every year. The popularity of
the geostationary satellite is increasing the pressure on the
radio frequency spectrum. Since certain frequencies and certain
orbital positions - notably those above the equator - are much
preferred to others, the problem of overcrowding is already
deadly serious. (86) Most of the satellites using the geostationary orbit are operated by the U.S. and the Soviet Union.
This has led to inevitable and justifiable charges of superpower monopoly of a 'limited natural resource'. It has also resulted in a number of equatorial states - Colombia and Venezuela for example - declaring their sections of the geostationary
orbit to be national space and thus subject to national territorial sovereignty. (87)

Whereas most of the satellites currently in geostationary orbit
are for general communication, there are also national reconnaissance satellites fulfilling military pruposes. Considered
vital to national security, these satellites would be the obvious targets of hunter-killer devices and would thus be the
main priority in the development of ASAT systems. In other
words, military demands on the geostationary orbit can be expected to increase considerably, adding to the pressures placed
on it by general communication satellites.

Without interference-free radio frequencies, space activity,
even for the superpowers, becomes impossible. As more and
more nations 'take to the air' the choice will increasingly be

between chaos or a system that works. It striving to build a
system that does work, one which reconciles competing claims
and assigns frequencies in an equitable manner, the great need
will be to go beyond efficiency into the realm of human survival.
Of designing a system which, recognizing the dual-purpose character of much space and satellite technology, provides for the
progressive demilitarization of space and its use for exclusively peaceful purposes.

MARINE TECHNOLOGIES

Of the many types of technology developed for use in areas related to the sea, Anti-Submarine Warfare (ASW) technologies are
particularly important and have a strong dual-purpose character.
In terms of their military applications, they have both a strategic and a tactical significance. (88) Strategic uses include
the detection and tracking of enemy balistic missile carrying
submarines (SSBNs), the monitoring and defense of trans-ocean
supply lines vital to national security (such as oil tanker
routes to and from the Persian Gulf), and the denial of large
areas of ocean space to enemy forces. Tactical applications include direct protection of individual surface ships, offshore
stations, convoys, coastal and harbor defenses, and the protection of SSBNs from enemy attack. Strategic ASW systems are
operated by the superpowers and a few of their close allies;
tactical ASW systems are used by many nations, both developed
and developing.

Like those in outer space, military developments underwater
challenge the imagination. Consider the following picture
sketched some years ago by Leitenberg: "Bottom-mounted acoustic
surveillance systems may soon be mounted on seamounts or table-
guyots in mid-ocean. The United States NR-1 and the Dolphin are
precursors of the next generation of United States ballistic
missiles and 'hunter-killer' nuclear submarines, and are reported to have depth capabilities of 6,000 to 10,000 feet. The United
States DSSP (Deep Submergence System Project) and DSRV (Deep
Submergence Rescue Vehicles) programmes are essentially for the
development of vehicles and equipment to inspect, install, repair or serve bottom-mounted surveillance or weapon systems.
ASWEPS (Anti-Submarine Warfare Environmental Prediction System)
has peppered the ocean surface and depth with various sensor
and buoy systems. The United States plans one atmosphere-manned
bottom station in the coming years at depths of 1,000 feet and
more. Project Rocksite hopes to adapt techniques for dry tunnel-
ling under the sea to great depths from under the continental
land mass itself". (89)

Some of these developments will change the rules of war. They

will transfer the second - and perhaps even the first! - strike
capability of the superpowers from land to sea, thereby threatening to make the oceans the hub in the balance of terror. Although
the direct destructive potential of ASW technologies is very
small - usually the destruction of one or several submarines -
their indirect potential through their intimate involvement with
strategic missile systems is very high. This makes them a supporting actor in the deadly serious war game.

The costs of ASW technologies are extremely high. Total spending
in the ASW market in the U.S. from 1978-1983 is expected to be
in the order of $46 billion, roughly eleven times the combined
annual budget of the United Nations *and* all its specialized agencies. (90) Of this expenditure, approximately 60 per cent is
being spent on 'platforms' (aircraft, ships, submarines) while
approximately 13 per cent, or $5 billion, is being spent direct-
ly on sensors, for an average of $1 billion a year.

The peaceful applications of ASW technologies are very numerous.
They include geophysical mapping of ocean areas (so important
in oil exploration), the location of foundering ships and rescue operations, operations of and communications with undersea
research vehicles, cable-laying, ocean drilling, undersea archae-
ology, fish resource monitoring, pollution detection and prevention, the management of exclusive economic zones, and an extensive array of marine scientific research.

The benefits which could be derived from the operation of ASW
surveillance and tracking devices on a global scale are even
more impressive. The development of a global system would make
it possible to keep a permanent eye on all merchant ships (by
monitoring their 'accoustical fingerprints'), to monitor fish
stocks and fishing operations, to undertake rescue operations
more quickly and effectively, and to warn specific vessels of
impending hurricanes, tsunamis or other such phenomena. The
peaceful application of ASW technologies could be instrumental
in the establishment of peace zones or seas of peace, such as
proposed for the Indian Ocean, as called for by the Resolution
adopted by the Tenth Special Session of the U.N. General Assembly. (91) All this would save lives and money as well as help
develop a real global resource management capability and promote
the cause of peace.

There are at present no international institutional arrangements
aimed at controlling or managing the use of ASW technologies.
(92) Because the primary functions of these technologies consist
of monitoring and surveillance, and because they are in themselves not very destructive, ASW technologies do not fall within
the provisions of the Seabed Treaty of 1972. (93)

LASER TECHNOLOGIES

Laser (an acronym for light amplification by stimulated emis-
sion of radiation) technologies are barely 20 years old but
they have already found their way into the military arsenal.
(94) The most publicized military application is the development of the so-called 'death ray' whereby intense laser radiation (95) is focused upon a target (aircraft, satellite or missile) with the aim of burning through its metal skin, of disrupt-
ing a vital function (such as guidance, solar energy conversion, transmitting and receiving) or, in the case of an ICBM,
triggering the warhead. Like ASW technologies, the destructive
power of lasers is limited. Their application in 'smart bombs',
precision guidance systems, and as a triggering device for
thermonuclear bombs, however, intimately links them with weapons of massive destructive. The application of laser technology
in inertial confinement fusion processes and in isotope separation may also open the way to the development of even more destructive fusion bombs.

The science fiction image generated by 'death rays' suggests
that the use of lasers for military purposes is still a long
way off. This is not so. The Pentagon recognized their military potential in 1959, shortly after the laser principle was
discovered by A.L. Schawlow and C.H. Townes and a year before
T.H. Maiman produced an operating laser. The U.S. Defense Department began a laser weapons project in 1961 and by 1972 the
U.S. Air Force was testing laser guns on unmanned aircraft.
Laser guidance systems were used by the U.S. to aim conventional bombs in Vietnam as early as 1972. Today, the U.S. Air
Force is testing a carbon dioxide gas dynamic laser carried
aboard a modified Boeing 707. It plans to use the laser, reportedly capable of developing one million watts of power, to
shoot down air-to-air missiles in the most realistic test so
far of the laser as a weapon. Air Force Secretary Hans Mark
has described the tests as a "proof of concept" comparable to
General Billy Mitchell's sinking of a battleship with bombs in
1921, a demonstration that was to revolutionize warfare. (96)
The tests will bring so much closer the deadly hunter killer
satellites described earlier.

U.S. research and development on military lasers is in the
order of $200 million a year, making it one of the largest re-
search projects being pursued by the Department of Defense.
The Soviet Union, thought to be lagging behind the U.S. in the
development of laser technology, may be spending as much as
$1 billion a year in an attempt to catch up.

Laser technologies have found a wide range of peaceful applications. The laser gun, for example, can be used in industry for
cutting anything from metals to cloth, and for drilling and

etching. Laser communication systems are now being used in Canada (Waterloo) and the U.S. (Chicago). Lasers are finding an
increasing application in medicine, being used in the areas of
research, diagnosis, treatment and surgery. They are also being
used extensively for basic research throughout the physical and
biological sciences. Laser technologies may advance the development of nuclear fusion power, which may be welcomed by some
but certainly not all, and may have an environmental significance given their capacity to, for example, detect the extent
and type of oil spills. (97)

The properties of laser light - directionality, monochromati-
city, and coherence - are inherent in, and cannot be separated
from, the basic principles and processes of the technology itself. As these properties are improved, the range of applications will be extended. The civilian development of lasers has
so far preceded military applications. If 'death ray' lasers
ever become operational, they may well do so as a result of
purely peaceful applications.

The international machinery for the control and management of
laser technology is non-existent. There is no legal framework
for regulating the military use of lasers and no institutional
arrangements for promoting international cooperation in peaceful applications.

ENVIRONMENTAL MODIFICATION TECHNOLOGIES

We can perhaps be forgiven for believing that the systematic
destruction of the natural environment as a military 'tactic'
is a new phenomenon: the herbicidal crop destruction wrought
by the Portugese on villages in Angola and, more especially,
the massive chemical and mechanical deforestation programs employed by the U.S. in Vietnam (in 1967 alone an area of nearly
4000 sq. km. was sprayed with defoliants) are still fresh in
our minds. (98) Yet virtually every war fought in history has
resulted in environmental damage and the very infliction of such
damage - despoliation of food stocks, the poisoning of wells
and water supplies (often with the bodies of the dead), the
instigation of fires and floods - have all been used to considerable military advantage. (99) Herodotus tells us in vivid
language, for example, how in 512 BC the Scythians, as they
retreated, practised a self-inflicted scorched earth policy so
as to stem the advance of the Persians.

If he were alive today Herodotus would be incredulous of the
potential for waging environmental warfare through the manipulation of geophysical and environmental forces. (100) Military
establishments are currently examining the feasibility of tech-

nologies which would make it possible to generate rain, snow,
fog, hailstones, lightning, tornados, hurricanes, tsunamis and
avalanches, to trigger earthquakes and lava flows, to modify
climate and to disrupt the ionized and ozone layers. (101) The
superpowers also appear locked in a battle, veiled in secrecy,
to develop the technologies which make it possible to use extreme low frequency (ELF) emissions to create powerful magnetic fields which will affect, not only climate, but also human
behavior. Their experiments may have already claimed their first
victims. (102)

Most environmental warfare technologies are still in their ter-
rifying infancy. Yet, as a SIPRI report concludes, their further development appears assured, "hinging only upon the continued discovery and refinement of appropriate technologies".
(103) The same report also gives a chilling indication of the
way in which the military establishment views the prospect of
being able to meddle with natural processes. "We regard the
weather as a weapon" , a U.S. Defense Department spokesman is
quoted as saying "Anything one can use to get his way is a
weapon and the weather is as good a one as any". (104)

Environmental modification technologies have obvious peaceful
applications. Cloud seeding and rain making, for example, may
make it possible to halt the march of deserts and to counter
drought. Fog and cloud generation could be useful in limiting
heat loss from crops subject to frost damage. The suppression
of conditions that could lead to hailstone precipitation could
help to reduce damage to crops. The manipulation of storms
could be used to moderate the intensity of, or to disperse or
redirect, hurricanes. The stimulation of weak earthquakes could
be applied to relieve stress conditions that might otherwise
lead to destructive natural earthquakes. (105)

The incentive to develop such technologies is great. There may
also be a growing demand for them since there are clear trends
that world climate is deteriorating. Climatologists are now
reasonably certain that our planet has passed through a favorable climatic period. (106) Between about 1880 and 1940 global
temperatures increased slightly. As a result, the first half
of this century was the warmest and wettest period for several
centuries. All over the world, agricultural productivity increased. The climate is now cooling, perhaps returning to the
colder and drier conditions of the 1850s. Rainfall belts are
already shifting, usually toward the equator. Growing seasons
in some parts of the world are now measurably shorter. The immediate prospect is for greater unpredictability, reflected in
an increase in droughts and floods. (107) The immediate prospect
is thus one of more crop failures and, inevitably, more hunger,
starvation and perhaps famine. Against this background, the application of environmental modification technologies may be called

for on a large scale to save lives and to maintain peace. (108)

As far as institutional arrangements are concerned, a United
Nations Convention - the so-called ENMOD Convention - has been
drawn up which prohibits the hostile use of environmental modification technologies. (109) The Convention, which is still in
the process of ratification, establishes that each State Party
"undertakes not to engage in military or any other hostile
use of environmental modification techniques having widespread,
long-lasting or severe effects as a means of destruction, damage or injury to any other State Party". (Article I) Environmental modification techniques are defined as those which can
be used "for changing - through the deliberate manipulation
of natural processes - the dynamics, composition or structure
of the earth, including its biota, lithosphere, hydrosphere,
and atmosphere, or of outer space".

The Convention has serious limitations. It does not contain a
ban on all environmental modification technologies for military
or hostile purposes, only those which have "widespread, long-
lasting or severe effects". This important condition is not
explained or defined. The consequence has been that technologies not explicitly prohibited by the Convention have been
taken as implicitly permitted. This effectively legitimizes
the use of some technologies. A partial solution, like so many
other arms control treaties, is the inevitable result. This
gaping hole has prompted Goldblat to classify ENMOD as a
"law of war" rather than a disarmament measure. (110) The answer to the problem of non-use must reside in the prohibition
of *all* environmental modification technologies for military or
other hostile purposes. With such a prohibition, no enumeration
of the activities outlawed would be needed.

Another serious limitation derives from the very dual-purpose
character of environmental modification technologies. The Convention states that its provisions "shall not hinder the use
of environmental modification techniques for peaceful purposes".
Because of their dual-purpose character, however, it is extremely difficult to draw sharp dividing lines between peaceful and
military applications. The Convention thus amounts to a mandate
for the development of military technology. Nowhere does the
Convention prohibit research and development of environmental
modification technologies for warlike purposes. The Convention's
sponsors, the two superpowers, justify this omission by arguing
that the "dual applicability of civilian and military ends of
much research and development in this field" makes verification
very difficult. (111)

Yet another limitation is the traditional one of ineffective
machinery for defining and dealing with acts of violation and
for verification. As contained in the Convention, they are devoid of practical significance.

There is as yet no international instrument which regulates the development of environmental modification technologies for peaceful purposes. Some steps in this direction are, however, being taken. A treaty is presently in preparation in the U.S. (in the Senate Sub-Committee on Arms Control, Oceans, International Operations and Environment) which is primarily concerned with the assessment of unintended harmful effects of peaceful applications of environmental modification technologies. Two bills are also currently before the U.S. Senate which seek to permit weather modification and either to license or control such activity. (112) All these proposals contain provision for international cooperation.

Much more is, however, needed. Some experts are of the opinion that the dangers inherent in large-scale environmental modification (113) are so great that all activity should be prohibited rather than internationalized. A prohibition, however, would meet with insurmountable difficulties; for the science and technology of weather forecasting are inextricably connected with those of weather modification, and peaceful and military uses blur to the point that they become indistinguishable.

The essential task is to continue with the laborious work of building the international machinery required to manage and control the technology. The present international machinery, mainly built around the WMO, and legal framework, provided by the ENMOD Convention, are wholly inadequate. The most urgent requirement in this respect may be a new convention which outlines existing and predicted technologies and specifies concrete steps in the area of international cooperation. Even though couched in broad and inclusive language, the Convention should facilitate cooperation at the global level.

In the longer-term every effort will need to be made to declassify much of the research on meteorological forecasting and environmental modification and to include it in a restructured and strengthened system of international cooperation. Only the appropriation of knowledge for peaceful purposes and the international management of peaceful uses can prevent the deviation of environmental modification technologies for military and war-making purposes.

BUILDING A DUAL-PURPOSE MANAGEMENT SYSTEM

It has been argued that the development of a global planning and resource management capability must include a concerted attempt to come to terms with our technological future. Although there is no way we can predict the emergence and acceptance of all future technologies, we can be sure that the rate and direction

of technological change and innovation are crucial, not only
in determining what kind of future we will have, but also
whether we are to have any future at all. For modern science-
based technology is a double-edged sword: it holds out great
promise for peace and development and it carries the threat of
death and destruction.

Technology is overflowing all the boundaries established by
man to control and manage it and there are at present few
grounds for believing that it can be harnessed to the process
of development, both economic and social, and thus evolved to
the benefit of mankind as a whole. Technology is uniting the
world's rich and poor nations physically, but dividing them
politically, economically and socially.

We have suggested that, in the search for ways out of this
deadly dilemma, a particularly fruitful avenue could be to
seek to design an effective institutional response around the
concept of dual-purpose technologies, technologies which have
an inherent potential for both good and evil, for peaceful and
warlike purposes. We have looked at six such technologies and
been forced to conclude that where international responses
have been formulated - which is certainly not in all of the
cases - they are wholly inadequate. Where they exist, conventions aimed at prohibiting military uses are so full of holes
that they may actually serve to spur warlike applications rather
than to impede them. Institutional arrangements aimed at promoting international cooperation in peaceful uses are often conspicuous through their absence.

There is thus a long way to go before the concept of dual-pur-
poseness receives the attention it deserves in control and management systems. But in the belief that it is sometimes better
to travel hopefully than to arrive, we proffer a few qualifying
observations and suggestions.

In distinguishing between hostile and peaceful uses, we are not
suggesting that it is possible to call a halt to military research. This would obviously be nonsensical. In many areas the
military implications and applications of research activity
cannot be separated from peaceful ones. The only way to put a
stop to the process of military innovation would be, as Hedley
Bull observed some years ago, to engineer "a reversal of the general social trend to innovation". But this, he rightly observes,
"is something against which the most powerful ideological, social, political and industrial forces in modern society are arrayed". (114) As much as we way wish to put clear limits on
scientific inquiry, we are unable to do so. The notion that
military research can be prohibited becomes an empty pipe-dream.

Nor are we suggesting that it is possible to distinguish between
basic research which may have military relevance and that which

does not. This is not because science has changed but because
military requirements have. (115) Much basic research takes
place inside the brains of scientists which, short of brainwash-
ing, makes it impossible to control. Much of it is incremental
which renders it extremely difficult to draw meaningful dividing lines. The whole process of technological research and development, however, is observed through a military microscope.
There is a systematic search for military uses of new innovations and the organized appropriation of knowledge for hostile
purposes. The atom was not split so that a thermonuclear bomb
could be made. Indeed, the man responsible for the atomic surgery, Lord Rutherford, saw no particular significance, military
or otherwise, in his scientific achievement. Similarly, the
laser was not developed so as to make a 'death ray'. Nuclear
bombs and 'death rays' are made because they are wanted, and
technologies are found because they are sought.

Military research and development cannot be stopped but it can
be slowed down, Whether it is or is not is a matter of deliberate choice, a question of policy. Governments are the main
funders of military R & D. In the U.S. and U.K., for example,
more tax revenues are spent on the development of military
technology than on all other government-supported R & D programs combined. In France, about 30 per cent of the governments
R & D budget goes to the military. (116) A shift of government
funding toward the academic and business sector could have a
highly positive impact on the growth of peaceful applications.
The enterprises affected in cutbacks in military budgets would
not be slow in transferring or converting their military hard-
ware to peaceful purposes in order to recoup investments or to
create new markets. Placing financial obstacles in the path of
military research could be expected to stimulate peaceful applications.

Government support for military R & D is motivated not only by
considerations of national security but also by the cherished
belief that the arms race is good for you: it brings you butter
and guns. That notion is a falsehood. It is becoming increasingly obvious that, in an age of sluggish economic growth and chron-
ic unemployment, the arms race is a bane not a boom. Military
activities, rather than being the great provider of much needed
employment, are in fact dead end expenditures and one of the
least efficient kinds of public spending. Studies conducted in
the United States suggest that 60 per cent of U.S. citizens
live in states which actually lose jobs every time military expenditures are increased and that every billion dollars spent
in education, housing, health care, mass transit and other public services generates about 30,000 more jobs than the same
amount spent on defense. (117) Against such a background, the
reorientation of R & D expenditures from military to civilian
sectors may become an economic necessity rather than a matter of

choice.

Military R & D would not cease, but the balance between military
and peaceful applications of the same technology could be progressively shifted. The challenge would be to find the point in
the development path of dual-purpose technologies where the military and civilian paths begin to diverge so that decisions
which favor one direction can be taken at the expense of another.
As noted above, this will be no easy task. But it may not be
impossible and the rewards from getting the sum right could be
very considerable. Consider the case, for example, of the nuclear
fuel cycle. The military and civilian paths diverge at the point
where weapons-suitable material (highly enriched uranium or
chemically separated plutonium, preferably with a low proportion
of Pu240) is produced in the fuel cycle in separated form, available for rapid incorporation into weapons. As long as the fissile
material is locked up in fuel or wastes in low concentrations,
and the would-be weapons manufacturers have to go through an additional stage of chemical or physical separation of the fissile
material, the cycle is relatively safe. With plutonium reproces-
sing and recycling, this distinction becomes blurred, because
weapons-suitable material appears in the *civilian* fuel cycle in
accessible form. (118)

Clearly it is of the utmost importance to identify technologies
with a dual-purpose character as early as possible. The later
they are found, the more difficult it is likely to be to place
obstacles in the way of their further military development. There
are grounds for believing that the scope for obstructing the
emergence of a new weapon or weapons system is in some way in-
versely proportional to the size of the investment in and commitment to it. (119) The investments and vested interests in nuclear
weapons, for example, have given them such momentum that even
such madness as MX systems can be seriously debated. In such
cases there may not, short of a major catastrophe, be any going
back. In the case of some other weapon systems, however, the constituencies are yet to be consolidated and the investments, although perhaps large, are yet to become a budgetary tradition.
These are easier targets. It might be perfectly feasible, for
example, to pull the military R & D rug from under the feet of
laser technologies, certain types of biological and chemical
technologies and environmental modification technologies without
hurting prospects for the peaceful application of these technologies or the career prospects of very many Pentagon and Kremlin
staffers.

Even when the military application of a dual-purpose technology
is discovered 'late', it may prove possible to hinder its further
development at the level of testing. Military commanders are not
generally inclined to resort to weapon systems in conflict without being reasonably sure in advance that they will not blow up

in their face, i.e. that they have been subjected to 'proof
of concept' testing. Testing is more easily monitored than basic R & D. A ban or restrictions on testing might have the effect of rendering judgement on the system so difficult that its
use would be deemed too risky. One can take this argument one
step further and argue that if the military cannot count on
being able to use its untested brainchild, it may foresake it
altogether, being disinclined to invest in its further development.

This is not to suggest that 'test bans' are anything other than
a small part of the answer. These are, as we have seen, at best
imperfect and at worst irrelevant. Moreover, much can be achieved in laboratories in the simulation of systems performance.
What is essential is to take a broad approach to the question
of testing, avoiding the temptation to focus on specific weapon
systems. Restrictions on one type of weapon may simply result
in the development of an even more deadly or exotic weapon
somewhere else: a ban on ICBMs, for example, might be circum-
vented by the development of cruise missiles or orbital bombardment systems. It is worth recalling that it was the provisions
of the Versailles Treaty which pushed Geramny into rocket pro-
pulsion.

These considerations have led Christopher Bertram to recently
suggest that what should be banned is the development of weapon
systems with particular missions, independently of the particular technological means chosen to accomplish the ends. (120) If
agreements can be negotiated at the mission level, they would
help control the rate and change of technological development
and to come to terms with the ever present problem of struggling
to control the many technological inputs which might contribute
to a particular mission. A mission approach rather than a weapons
approach to the development of military capabilities would help
focus attention on the ends of technological development rather
than the means. (121)

We have seen that dual-purpose technologies raise questions which
defy national solution, even in their peaceful applications. We
have seen, too, that with some dual-purpose technologies the
greatest promise for peaceful uses is to be found in their management at the global level; in the development of a collective
system which maximizes benefits and provides for the fair distribution of rights and duties, and opportunities for participation and control. The challenge is thus to build institutional
arrangements which facilitate international cooperation in peaceful uses. The internationalization of issues and the creation of
a global system of shared management would certainly not eliminate or even necessarily diminish the military applications of
dual-purpose technologies. But the promotion of peaceful uses
through the vehicle of international cooperation would most as-
suredly raise consciousness of both promises and dangers. Such

consciousness could prove a major instrument against the appropriation of knowledge for hostile applications.

It is worth recalling that much international institution-building in the post-war period has been guided by a technological
imperative. Indeed, many of the efforts can be fairly characterized as the wrapping of an institutional response around dis-
crete technologies. Before the invention of radio there was no
need to divide up the frequency spectrum. Today, a standing international conference - The World Administrative Radio Conference - exists to do exactly that. Before there were aircraft
there was no need for an International Civil Aviation Organization. Today we need international agreement because the alternative is chaos. Before the discovery of atomic energy there was
no need for a world organization to control its use for peaceful purposes. Today, that is exactly what the International
Atomic Energy Authority tries to do. As Harlan Cleveland observes,
"each new scientific discovery, each technological innovation,
seems to require the invention of new international arrangements
to contain, channel, and control it. A precept of American business", he notes, "is that necessity is the mother of invention.
But in the business of international institution building, the
reverse is true as well: invention is the mother of necessity".
(122)

The shaping of an appropriate institutional response to the
questions posed by dual-purpose technologies must be seen as
the logical continuation of this historical process. The continuation will need to be based upon the recognition that the
only institutional response to a technology system with a dual-
purpose character is a dual-purpose framework for containing,
regulating, managing and developing the technology. More specifically, future activities will need to be guided by:

● The determination to promote the use of dual-purpose technologies for peaceful purposes only;
● The determination to strengthen international cooperation in
their peaceful uses;
● Recognition of the need to ensure that benefits accruing from
peaceful applications are shared among all nations, irrespective
of their economic and scientific status, and with particular
regard to the needs of developing countries;
● Recognition of the need to ensure that peaceful uses are subject to sound environmental practices.

The restriction of the use of dual-purpose technologies to
'peaceful uses only' implies their progressive declassification,
and the building of a combination of national and international
controls and monitoring systems. Roman law proprietary concepts
are inapplicable to technologies which fall in this category.
Such technologies should not be subject to appropriation in the
strict sense in which this includes the right to use and

to misuse (*jus utendi et abutendi*). They can be *managed* in accordance with established standards and rules, but they *cannot*
be *owned*.

The determination to 'strengthen international cooperation in
their peaceful uses' raises institutional implications which
will need to be studied for each case. As we have seen from our
brief review of dual-purpose technologies, however, there is an
obvious need for *institutional innovation*.

The requirement that 'benefits accruing from their peaceful
applications are to be shared among all nations' demands that
all countries *participate in decision-making on and management
of* the dual-purpose technologies. The days when industrialized
countries could hope to themselves manage technologies in the
interest and for the benfit of all countries are over. The Lin-
colnian principle of governance by the people and for the
people must now be translated to the international plane with
the aim of ensuring the equitable participation of developing
countries in the management of the technologies.

The requirement that dual-purpose technologies be 'subject to
sound environmental practices' stems from the fact that, even
in their peaceful uses, they are able to inflict devastating
damage to the environment; a scale of devastation which refuses
to recognize national boundaries. The rational management of
the peaceful uses of dual-purpose technologies thus demands the
application of internationally agreed *environmental standards
and rules of conduct*.

These basic requirements for the international control and management of dual-purpose technologies bear a striking resemblance
to - indeed are virtually identical with - the main attributes
of the common heritage of mankind. (cf. chapter 5) The conclusion
is inescapable. The effective and equitable management of dual-
purpose technologies requires that they ultimately be designated
the common heritage of mankind and thus from the subject of appropriate international regimes.

Here again the concept of the common heritage of mankind appears
to offer us a way out of a major dilemma - the problem of developing a management response to the issues raised by science-based
technology.

NOTES AND REFERENCES

(1) See Alexander King, 'The Use and Abuse of Science and Tech-
    nology for Development', in A.J.Dolman and J.van Ettinger
    (eds.), *Partners in Tomorrow: Strategies for a New Inter-
    national Order*, E.P.Dutton, New York, 1978, pp. 182-192,
    p. 182 ff.

(2) Miriam Camps, *The Management of Interdependence. A Preliminary View*, Council on Foreign Relations, Inc., New York, 1974, p. 8. A similar view is advanced by Eugene B.Skolnikoff in 'Science and Technology: The Implications for International Institutions', *International Organization*, vol. 25, 1971, pp. 759-775.

(3) As Ernst B. Haas observed, "(Technology) breaking upon the world as it did, compounded the feeling of our being developed in a massive 'collective situation' to which there can only be a 'collective response' if anyone is to attain his objectives. In this sense we are really embarked, for the first time in world history, on Spaceship Earth". 'Is there a Hole in the Whole? Knowledge, Technology, Interdependence and the Construction of International Regimes', *International Organization*, vol. 29, 1975, pp. 826-876, at p. 875.

(4) The view of Geoffrey Barraclough. See *Turning Points in World History*, Thames and Hudson, London, 1979, chapter 2.

(5) Immanuel Wallerstein, *The Modern World System*, Academic Press, New York, 1974.

(6) See Silviu Brucan, 'The World Authority: An Exercise in Political Forecasting',in A.J.Dolman (ed.), *Global Planning and Resource Management: Toward International Decision-Making in a Divided World*, Pergamon, New York, pp. 53-71.

(7) Henry Kissinger, 'Central Issues of American Foreign Policy', in Kermit Gordon (ed.), *Agenda for the Nation*, Brookings Institution, Washington, D.C., 1968, pp. 585-614.

(8) On the logic of the global power game see two books by Silviu Brucan: *The Dissolution of Power*, Knopf, New York, 1971, and *The Dialectic of World Politics*, Free Press, New York, 1978.

(9) The view of Francisco Sagasti. See 'Knowledge is Power', *Mazingira*, 2, 1979, p. 28.

(10) Ralph Lapp, *The New Priesthood*, Harper and Row, New York, 1961. The idea of a 'technocracy' is, of course, an old one. The term 'technocracy' was first coined in 1919 by William Henry Smyth for his proposed 'rule by technicians'. Technocracy as a social movement enjoyed a good deal of popularity in the U.S. in the inter-war period. During the 1960s the term gained wider popularity in France where it was identified with the theories of the utopian socialist Saint-Simon who predicted the emergence of a society ruled by scientists. It was also used by such writers as Jean Meynaud who argued, like Lapp, that real power in society has shifted from elected representatives to a technical elite. See Jean Meynaud, *Technocracy*, Free Press, New York, 1969; and W.H.G. Armytage, *The Rise of the Technocrats*, Routledge and Kegan Paul, London, 1965.

(11) See Bert V.A.Röling, 'International Responses to Technological Innovations', in A.J.Dolman, op.cit., pp. 225-246.

(12) This extract from Bacon's *Historia Naturalis* is quoted in Paoli Rossi, *Francis Bacon: From Magic to Science*, University of Chicago Press, Chicago, Ill., 1948, p. 129. Rossi notes (p. 130) that it was Bacon's motive and purpose "to redeem man from original sin and reinstate him in his prelapsarian power over all created things".

(13) J.Robert Oppenheimer, the father of the atomic bomb.

(14) See John U.Nef, *Western Civilization Since the Renaissance: Peace, War, Industry and the Arts*, Harper Torchbooks, New York, 1963, p. 122ff.

(15) For an overview of world military expenditures see SIPRI, *World Armaments and Disarmament, SIPRI Yearbook 1979*, Taylor and Francis, London, 1979; and Ruth Leger Sivard, *World Military and Social Expenditures 1980*, World Priorities, Leesburg, Va., 1980.

(16) See S.P.Dresch, *Disarmament: Economic Consequences and Development Potential*, National Bureau of Economic Research and Yale University, New Haven, Conn., 1972, p. 32, Table 4.

(17) See Ronald H.Huisken, 'The Consumption of Raw Materials for Military Purposes', *Ambio*, vol. IV, no. 5-6, 1975, pp. 229-233, at p. 231.

(18) See Hans W.Singer and J.A.Ansari, *Rich and Poor Countries*, Johns Hopkins Press, Baltimore, 1977, viz. p. 37. It is particularly interesting that Hans Singer should defend this thesis since he was one of the first - along with Myrdal, Lewis and Prebisch - to point to basic inequalities in trading relationships between rich and poor countries.

(19) See UNIDO, *Industry 2000: New Perspectives*, document ID/ 237, October 1979, for various indicators of technological disparities (viz. tables 7(1) - 7(4)).

(20) Ali A.Mazrui, *Africa's International Relations: The Diplomacy of Dependency and Change*, Heinemann, London, 1977, pp. 95-102.

(21) See Denis Goulet, *The Uncertain Promise: Value Conflicts in Technology Transfer*, IDOC/North America, Inc., New York, 1977, pp. 7-12.

(22) On the question of 'technology codes' see two works of Johan Galtung: *Development, Environment and Technology: Towards a Technology for Self-Reliance*, UNCTAD, document TD/B/C.6/23, June 1978; and 'Towards a New International Technological Order', *Alternatives*, vol. IV, 1978-9, pp. 277-300.

(23) This is one of the themes of David Dickson's *Alternative Technology and the Politics of Technical Change*, Fontana/Collins, London, 1974.

(24) For a presentation of their views/criticisms see: Jacques Ellul, *The Technological Society*, Alfred A.Knopf, New York, 1964; Erich Fromm, *The Sane Society*, Fawcett Premier Books, Holt, Rinehart and Winston, Inc., New York, 1955; Jürgen Habermas, *Towards a Rational Society*, Heinemann, London,

1971; Ivan Illich, *Tools for Conviviality*, Harper and Row, New York, 1973; Herbert Marcuse, *One-Dimensional Man*, Routledge and Kegan Paul, London, 1964; Lewis Mumford, *The Myth of the Machine: Techniques and Human Development*, Harcourt Brace Janovich, Inc., New York, 1967; Theodore Rozak, *Person/Planet: The Creative Disintegration of Industrial Society*, Doubleday, Garden City, N.Y., 1978; and E.F.Schumacher, *Small is Beautiful: Economics as if People Mattered*, Harper and Row, New York, 1977.

(25) See Langdon Winner, *Autonomous Technology: Technics-out-of-Control as a Theme in Political Thought*, MIT Press, Cambridge, Mass., 1977.

(26) Barry Commoner, *The Closing Circle: Nature, Man and Technology*, Alfred A.Knopf, New York, 1971, p. 151.

(27) See Sam Cole, 'The Global Futures Debate 1965-1976' in Christopher Freeman and Marie Jahoda (eds.), *World Futures: The Great Debate*, Martin Robertson, Oxford, 1978, pp. 9-48, viz. pp. 43-46.

(28) These and many other wonderous forecasts can be found in Y.Modrzhinskaya and C.Stephanyan, *The Future of Society*, Progress Publishers, Moscow, 1973; and V.Kosolapov, *Mankind and the Year 2000*, Progress Publishers, Moscow, 1976.

(29) As presented in Herman Kahn and Anthony Wiener, *The Year 2000*, Macmillan, London, 1967; and Daniel Bell, *The Coming of Post Industrial Society*, Heinemann, London, 1974.

(30) See, for example, A.C.Sutton, *Western Technology and Soviet Economic Development: 1917-1930*, Hoover Institute on War, Revolution and Peace, Stanford University, Stanford, Ca., 1968.

(31) Technology transfer is of course an East-West process. A report in the Swedish newspaper *Handelsblatt* of 24 December 1979 (p. 8) quotes Polish sources as saying that Comecon countries have been selling some 700 licenses a year to the West for a value of $ 40 million a year (mainly in the chemical industry). This compares with the West's sale of 2400 licences a year to Eastern Europe for $ 300 million a year. That Eastern Europe has more to offer the West than is generally thought is argued in John W.Kiser III, 'Technology is Not a One-Way Street', *Foreign Policy*, no. 23, Summer 1976, pp. 131-148.

(32) For a range of views on the technological dependence of the Third World see Denis Goulet, op.cit.; and Frances Stewart, *Technology and Underdevelopment*, Macmillan, 1977; UNCTAD, *Transfer of Technology, Technological Dependence: Its Nature, Consequences and Policy Implications*, document TD/190, Geneva, December 1975; and the collection of papers in Dieter Ernst (ed.), *The New International Division of Labour, Technology and Underdevelopment*, Campus, Frankfurt on Main and New York, 1980.

(33) On the technological self-reliance of developing countries,

see Francisco Sagasti, *Science and Technology for Development: Main Comparative Report of the STPI Project*, IDRC, Ottawa, 1978; UNIDO, *The Technological Self-Reliance of Developing Countries: Towards Operational Strategies*, document UNIDO/ICIS.133, November 1979; and Dieter Ernst, 'Technology Policy and Transition Towards Self-Reliance - Some Major Issues', *International Social Science Journal*, 1980 (forthcoming).

(34) The following presentations of dual-purpose technologies draw upon the work, completed and ongoing, of the RIO Foundation's project 'Disarmament and Development'. The most important sources are: Dick A.Leurdijk and Elisabeth Mann Borgese, *Disarmament and Development*, RIO Foundation, Rotterdam, June 1979 (viz. chapter 5, 'Science and Technology for Disarmament and Development', pp. 36-54); and the working papers prepared on specific dual-purpose technologies by the specialists who are participating in the project. These working papers include: Frank Barnaby and David Krieger, 'Nuclear Technologies' (1980); Centre for Research of Air and Space Law, McGill University, 'Space and Satellite Technology for Disarmament and Development' (1980); Carl-Göran Hedén and David Krieger, 'Chemical and Biological Technologies' (1980); Irving E. Kaplan, 'Disarmament and Development: A Preliminary Assessment of Environmental Modification Technologies' (1980); R. Morrison and J.O'Manique (The Norman Paterson School of International Affairs, Carleton University), 'Disarmament and Development: A Preliminary Assessment of Laser Technologies' (1980); and Harvey B.Silverstein, 'An Assessment: ASW Deployments as 'Dual-Purpose' Technologies' (1980). The RIO Foundation's first assessment of dual-purpose technologies is contained in David Krieger, *Disarmament and Development: The Challenge of the International Control and Management of Dual-Purpose Technologies*, Rotterdam, February 1981.

(35) Nuclear weapons have almost been used on at least four occasions. General MacArthur sought permission to use nuclear weapons in Manchuria. French generals requested U.S. carriers to launch a nuclear strike at Dien Bien Phu. The world waited to see whether they would be used in 1962 at Cuba. And General Westmoreland sought permission to use tactical nuclear weapons in Vietnam. The possibility of false alerts triggering nuclear attacks is an ever present threat. Equipment failures are reported to cause serious false alarms two or three times a year, although the actual number of false alarms is many times greater. See 'False Alerts of Nuclear Attacks Occur Frequently at U.S. Bases', *International Herald Tribune*, 30 October 1980.

(36) The literature on the risks associated with the development of nuclear energy has grown considerably in recent years. See, for example, Mason Willrich and Theodore B.Taylor,

Nuclear Theft: Risks and Safeguards, Ballinger, Cambridge, Mass., 1974; Union of Concerned Scientists, *The Nuclear Fuel Cycle*, MIT Press, Cambridge, Mass., 1975; Gerald Foley, *The Energy Question*, Penguin, Harmondsworth, 1976; Royal Commission on Environmental Pollution, *Nuclear Power and the Environment*, Her Majesty's Stationary Office, London, 1976; Walter C.Patterson, *Nuclear Power*, Penguin, Harmondsworth, 1976; Denis Hayes, *Nuclear Power: The Fifth Horseman*, Worldwatch Paper 6, Worldwatch Institute, Washington, D.C., 1976; and Nuclear Energy Policy Study Group, *Nuclear Power, Issues and Choices*, Ballinger, Cambridge, Mass., 1977.

(37) It appears that a large-scale accident with nuclear wastes occurred in the Urals as long ago as 1958. Massive amounts of Strontium 90 and other radioactive elements escaped, possibly as a result of an explosion in an underground storage tank. It appears that an area of 1000 sq.km. needed to be evacuated; 30 villages (with a combined population of more than 2000 persons) have disappeared from recent maps of the accident area and a series of dams have been constructed, apparently to deal with pollution effects in the drainage area. The story of this Soviet Harrisburg is told in Zhores Medvedev, *Nuclear Disaster in the Urals*, Angus and Robertsen, London, 1979. Medvedev's thesis has recently been corroborated by a U.S. government study which draws upon CIA reports.

(38) *The Question of Peaceful Explosions for the Benefit of Non-Nuclear Weapon States*, paper circulated at the Non-Nuclear-Weapons States Conference held in September 1968 (document A/Conf. 35/Doc. 2, p. 20).

(39) See *Official Records of the Atomic Energy Commission, First Year, No. 1*, First Meeting, 1946, viz. pp. 5-8.

(40) Statement submitted as U.S. Representative to the Atomic Energy Conference, 5 July 1946.

(41) It is interesting to note that these resources were *not* located in an area 'beyond the limits of national jurisdiction' as stipulated for common heritage resources in the Law of the Sea negotiations. They could be located anywhere. They were to be 'beyond the limits of *functional* national jurisdiction'.

(42) The most important multilateral agreements are: *Antarctic Treaty*, prohibiting any measure of a military nature in the Antarctic, 1961; Treaty banning nuclear-weapon tests in the atmosphere, in outer space and under water (*Partial Test Ban Treaty*), 1963; Treaty on principles governing the activities of states in the exploration and use of outer space, including the moon and other celestial bodies (*Outer Space Treaty*), 1967; Treaty for the prohibition of nuclear weapons in Latin America (*Treaty of Tlatelolco*), 1967; Treaty on the prohibition of nuclear weapons (*Non-Proliferation Treaty*), 1970; and the Treaty on the prohibition of the emplacement

of nuclear weapons and other weapons of mass destruction on the seabed and the ocean floor and in the subsoil thereof (*Seabed Treaty*), 1972.

(43) For a review of arms control agreements, see SIPRI, *Arms Control: A Survey and Appraisal of Multilateral Agreements*, Taylor and Francis, London, 1978.

(44) U.N. Resolution 1884 (XVIII), 17 October 1963.

(45) Elizabeth Young, *A Farewell to Arms Control?*, Penguin, Harmondsworth, 1972, p. 14.

(46) See International Atomic Energy Agency, *International Nuclear Fuel Cycle Evaluation: Summary Volume*, Vienna, 1980.

(47) Ibid, p. 260 (Final Communique of the Organizing Conference of the INFCE).

(48) The library on 'genetic engineering' is extremely voluminous and growing rapidly. Established treatments of the subject include M.Burnet, *Genes, Dreams and Realities*, MIT Press, Cambridge, Mass., 1971; R.Dawkins, *The Selfish Gene*, Oxford U.P., London, 1976; R.F.Beer and E.G.Basset, *Recombinant Molecules: Impact on Science and Society*, Raven Press, New York, 1977; and J.Richards, *Recombinant-DNA: Science, Ethics and Politics*, Academic Press, New York, 1978.

(49) On chemical and biological weapons, see the following SIPRI publications: *Problem of Chemical and Biological Weapon Warfare: The Rise of CB Weapons*, Almqvist and Wiskell, Stockholm, 1971; *Problem of Chemical and Biological Warfare: CB Weapons Today*, Almqvist and Wiskell, 1975; and *Weapons of Mass Destruction and the Environment*, Taylor and Francis, London, 1977, viz. chapter 2.

(50) Convention on the Prohibition of the Development, Production and Stockpiling of Bacteriological (Biological) and Toxin Weapons and on Their Destruction.

(51) See document CCD/400.

(52) See especially 'Compilation of Materials on Chemical Weapons from CCD Working Papers and Statements 1972-1976' of 11 March 1980.

(53) Verification could comprise various types of on-site inspection such as chemical analytical methods of toxidity tests as well as so-called 'non-intrusive methods', such as the phospherous-accounting system, and the remote sensing systems, including the use of satellites. Verification, it is generally agreed, should be performed by a combination of national and international means. See SIPRI, *Chemical Disarmament: Some Problems of Verification*, Almqvist and Wiskell, Stockholm, 1973.

(54) CCD Press Release DC/797.

(55) Ibid.

(56) This convergence has been stressed, for example, by Alva Myrdal. Addressing the CCD in 1973 she observed: "In a similar, although less direct way, the (Stockholm Human Environment) Conference acts as a primer to our task to ban

chemical means of warfare. It has raised to a high pitch -
in the form of self-incrimination no less than accusation -
expressions of concern about the fiendish treatment Man gives
to Nature and to his own condition for survival. Pollution
and poisoning with chemical substances has been placed in
the foreground. It is stated in the solemn Declaration of
Principles agreed upon that "the discharge of toxic substances....in such quantities or concentrations as to exceed the capacity of the environment to render them harmless, must be halted in order to ensure that serious or irreversible damage is not inflicted upon ecosystems". Advocating a system of national laws and regulations, based on
interdisciplinary decision-making, to control civilian production, she commented, "such measures of national self-
discipline, with a fair degree of international prodding....
would anyway probably come to be called for in relation to
environmental protection against damage from chemical agents
as I have ventured to suggest before".

(57) For an overview of early space technology and space programs, see Donald Cox, *The Space Race: From Sputnik to
Apollo and Beyond*, Clitton Books, Philadelphia/New York,
1962; William H.Shauer, *The Politics of Space: A Comparison
of the Soviet and American Space Programs*, Holmes and Meier,
New York, 1976; and Nicolas Mateesco Matte, *Space Policy and
Programmes Today and Tomorrow: The Vanishing Duopole*, Carswell, Toronto, 1980. For a review of the programs of individual countries see *World-wide Space Activities*, Report
prepared for the Sub-Committee on Space Science and Applications of the U.S. House of Representatives' Committee on
Science and Technology, 95th Congress, Government Printing
Office, Washington, D.C., 1978.

(58) On the peaceful uses of outer space, see S.Ramo, *Peacetime
Uses of Outer Space*, McGraw-Hill, New York, 1961; C.S.Shel-
don, 'Peacetime Applications' in L.P.Bloomfield (ed.),
Outer Space, Praeger, New York, 1968, pp. 37-74; *Space Program Benefits*, Hearings before the U.S. Senate's Committee
on Aeronautical and Space Sciences, 91st Congress, 2nd Session, Government Printing Office, Washington, D.C., 1970;
and the United Nations publications *Practical Benefits of
Space Exploration*, sales no. E.69.I.25, New York, 1969, and
The Application of Space Technology to Development, sales
no. E.72.II.A.12, New York, 1973.

(59) The United Nations, *The United Nations and Outer Space*,
sales no. E.77.I.9, 1977, p. 26. As Pierce and Jéquier have
observed: "With small-scale satellite ground stations.....
it is technically feasible and in many cases economically
justifiable to install a telephone exchange in every village,
however remote. From the ground station, inexpensive radio
links can be installed in lieu of the heavier and more costly wires and cables, to cover at minimal cost, large and

relatively under-populated areas. And if no electricity is
available, telephones can be voice-powered, or use alternative sources... Given these technical factors, and considering the indirect benefits of investments in telecommunications, it is likely that telecommunication services
will appear as an increasingly attractive investment opportunity, both socially and economically, for the developing
countries". W.B.Pierce and N.Jéquier, 'Telecommunications
and Development', *Dialogue*, vol. 12, no. 2, p. 27.

(60) Examples of regional systems include ARABSAT (a telecommu-
nications network to provide telephone, telegraph and direct
broadcasting services to member States of the Arab League),
PANAFTEL (ITU's panafrican telecommunication network), EUTEL-
SAT (covering 17 European countries), and the proposed sys-
tem to cover the Nordic countries (Denmark, Finland, Iceland,
Norway and Sweden). Industrialized countries either opera-
ting or proposing to establish national systems include the
U.S., Canada, Soviet Union, France, United Kingdom, and
Japan. Developing countries include India, Indonesia, China,
Brazil, Columbia and Argentina.

(61) In the United States, for example, the monitoring of frosts,
blizzards, ice, ocean currents, and hurricanes is reported
to save at least $ 170 million a year.

(62) Peter Jankowitsch, *International Cooperation in Outer
Space*, Occasional paper 11, The Stanley Foundation, Muscatine, Iowa, 1976. Some 100 major oil, gas and mining companies have formed an association, GEOSAT, to support and
influence the development of ERTS. GEOSAT members have used
LANDSAT to survey a Guatemalian oilfield at a fortieth of
the cost of aerial survey, to find faults associated with
copper minerals, to direct seismic surveys and to plan pipe-
lines. For a short overview of remote sensing applications
see *InterMedia*, vol. 6, no. 2, 1978, viz. pp. 11-12.

(63) On solar power satellites, see 2 studies by the U.S. Depart-
ment of Energy: Carl Q.Christol, *Satellite Power System:
White Paper on International Agreements*, 27 October 1978;
Stephen Gorove, *Solar Power: International Agreements*,
October 1978.

(64) See J.von Puttkamer, 'The Next 25 Years: Industrialization
of Space', *Space World*, vol. N-10-166, October 1977, pp. 4-
13; V.Louvière, 'Space: Industry's New Frontier', *Nation's
Business*, February 1978, pp. 25-41; and Richard van Patten
et al., *The Industrialization of Space*, American Astronautical Society, vo. 36, 1978.

(65) Some 250 examples of space program spin-offs which benefit
the U.S. public are listed in *For the Benefit of All Mankind:
The Practical Returns from Space Investment*, Report of the
U.S. House of Representatives' Committee on Science and
Astronautics, 92nd Congress, 2nd Session, Government Printing
Office, Washington, D.C., 1972.

(66) About 70 per cent of all military messages are today trans-
mitted via satellite circuits.
(67) In the U.S., a distinction is made between peaceful applications, the responsibility of NASA, and military applications, which fall under the Department of Defense. In practice, however, the distinction is far from watertight. Both
institutions participate in each others' activities. The
space shuttle, under development by NASA for peaceful purposes, was financed by the Department of Defense. The shuttle
has a potentially large number of military applications, including its possible use as a killer satellite.
(68) Statement reproduced in *Checkpoint*, newsletter published
by War Control Planners, Inc., Washington, D.C., vol. VI,
no. 1, February 1978.
(69) On military satellites see P.J.Klaas, *Secret Sentries in
Space*, Random House, New York, 1971; Sandra Hochman, *Satellite Spies*, Bobbs-Merrill, Inc., Indianapolis, 1976; and
SIPRI, *Outer Space - Battlefield of the Future?*, Taylor
and Francis, London, 1978.
(70) See SIPRI, *Outer Space - Battlefield of the Future?*, Taylor
and Francis, London, 1978. For a brief overview of future
space weaponry, see Robert C. Toth, 'War in Space: Military
Satellites and Exotic Weaponry Threaten to turn Space into
the Next Battleground', *Science 80*, vol. 1, no. 6, pp. 74-80.
(71) Or to give it its full title, 'Treaty on Principles Governing the Activities of States in the Exploration and Use of
Outer Space, including the Moon and Other Celestial Bodies'.
(72) The problem of finding an adequate definition of outer
space is not yet resolved and is becoming increasingly
urgent. Technical considerations, such as drag effects on
artificial satellites and the presence of atmospheric air,
suggest that the boundary between air space and outer space
could be set at 100 km from earth. Such a boundary would
constitute a natural dividing line not dependent on the
effects of terrestrial gravity which theoretically has no
outer boundary. Technical considerations, however, have
proved a wholly inadequate basis and have become subservient to political considerations.
(73) The Preamble declares that States parties recognize "the
common interest of all mankind in the progress of the exploration and use of outer space for peaceful purposes". The
Preamble is, however, considered to be non-operative and is
not a legally binding part of the Treaty.
(74) The Soviet Union, Eastern European and some Western legal
experts argue that the Treaty provides for the demilitarization of outer space. They argue that under both the Antarctic
Treaty (1959) and the Charter of the IAEA, "peaceful use"
means "non-military" and excludes both offensive or defensive
military activities. They also maintain that since a military
activity cannot be in the interest of all countries (only

single or groups of countries), the requirement of Article I
that space be used "for the benefit and in the interests of
all countries" effectively prohibits all military activities
in and from outer space. On the other hand, the U.S.A. and
some Western legal experts assert that the Treaty does not
prohibit non-aggressive military activities in outer space.
They refer to Article III of the Treaty which maintains that
outer space activities are to be carried out in accordance
with international law and the U.N. Charter. Article 51 of
the Charter, they maintain, gives the right of self-defense
(individual or collective). They also point out that Article
IV of the Outer Space Treaty allows the "use of military
personnel for scientific research and for any other peaceful purposes (and also the) use of any equipment or facility
necessary for peaceful exploration of the moon and other
celestial bodies". These differing interpretations have
given rise to interminable wrangling and much sterile discussion of terminology, for example, on the difference between "peaceful uses", "non-military" and "military non-
aggressive". They also help explain why the Soviet Union
continues to maintain that its activities in space are not
of a military nature and, therefore, not leading to the
militarization of space.

(75) For a presentation of the issues involved in the develop-
ment of an institutional and legal framework see the fol-
lowing works of Nicolas Mateesco Matte: *Aerospace Law*,
Sweet and Maxwell, London, 1969; *Aerospace Law*, Carswell,
Toronto, 1977; and *Space Policy and Programmes Today and
Tomorrow: The Vanishing Duopole*, Carswell, Toronto, 1980.

(76) Next to the Outer Space Treaty the most important treaties
negotiated to date are the Treaty Banning Nuclear Weapon
Tests in the Atmosphere, in Outer Space and Underwater (1963);
the Agreement on the Rescue of Astronauts, Return of Astronauts and the Return of Objects Launched in Outer Space
(1968); a Convention on International Liability for Damages
Caused by Space Objects (1972); and a Convention on Regis-
tration of Objects Launched into Outer Space (1975). The
first of these - the Partial Test Ban Treaty - was the first
step taken by the international community to demilitarize
outer space. It has not proved very effective. The other
treaties are essentially 'acts of convenience' between the
two superpowers.

(77) Document CD/9, 1978.

(78) Document A/S.10/AC.1/7, 1 June 1978.

(79) The French proposal has also been studied by international
non-governmental organizations. On the initative of the
French Pugwash Group, for example, an international sym-
posium on 'An International Agency for the Use of Satellite
Observation Data for Security Purposes' was convened in
Avignon in April 1980. The symposium's 31 participants

from 14 countries considered the setting-up of an International Satellite Monitoring System (ISMOS). The group concluded that an ISMOS should be established for purposes of verification of arms control agreements and implementation of U.N. Security Council decisions and for the management of some military crises. As such ISMOS could contribute to global security through the processes of crisis management and confidence building. ISMOS was considered technologically feasible. The incorporation of ISMOS within the framework of the U.N. - making it a specialized agency with responsibilities and modalities defined by Treaty - was considered the most effective constitutional approach. Recognition of possible superpower resistance to the idea of an ISMOS led the participants, however, to consider two other possible models. In one, the Western European countries would, given their technical capabilities, take the initiative, but a much wider group of nations would be progressively involved. In the other, a group of countries acceptable as 'neutral' by the potential users would establish and operate ISMOS, buying their technology where necessary, and also involving other (including Third World) countries in the implementation and decision-making processes. For a report on the symposium, see *Pugwash Newsletter*, vol. 17, no. 4, April 1980, pp. 86-97.

(80) U.N. document A/34/540, 18 October 1979.
(81) The U.S. has already stated that the ISMA "would be neither feasible nor desirable in the foreseeable future (because) substantial.....political, organizational, technical and financial difficulties would be associated with an international institution charged with collecting and assessing satellite information pertinent to verifying arms control agreements". U.N. document A/34/374, 27 August 2979, p. 27.
(82) For a review of reactions, see ibid.
(83) Whether the exploitation of the resources of the moon and other celestial bodies will ever become feasible let alone economical is of course an open question. It may therefore be relatively painless for States to declare them the Common Heritage of Mankind. It is worth noting, however, that some States - notably those most advanced in space technology - violently oppose the idea and are unlikely, therefore, to ratify the treaty.
(84) The principle of regional presentation, which is becoming increasingly important in the U.N. system, is in obvious need of reformulation. The four 'regions' - Asia, Africa, Latin America and 'Western Europe and others' - are clearly inadequate as a basis for equitable regional representation. The concept of 'region' has many meanings and is nowhere clearly defined. As a basis for equitable representation, the 15 regions defined in the Leontief Report (Wassily Leontief, *The Future of the World Economy*, Oxford University

Press, New York, 1977), might offer a fair, balanced and workable solution. In a Council of 36 members, for example, at least two members would have to be chosen from each of the 15 regions, while six might be chosen at large, to have more flexibility.

(85) For an insight into the nature of the geostationary orbit, see United Nations, *The Physical Nature and Technical Attributes of the Geostationary Orbit*, document A/AC.105/203, New York, 1978.

(86) Satellites in geostationary orbit are almost invisible to ground observers and add to the problem of monitoring the more than 4,500 objects in space. And satellites can 'get lost'. RCA, for example, recently lost a $ 23 million communications satellite. Commanded to slightly shift its orbit, the satellite reportedly "zoomed off on its own". A spokesman for the company was not optimistic about finding it. "So far as we know", he is quoted as saying, "it is 22,000 miles up, and there is only about 35 square feet of it. It is not the most visible object you could think of". Reported in 'Satellite Leave Blank Hole in Space', *The Guardian*, 12 December 1979, p. 6.

(87) Colombia has been forced to take this step by a proposal by the Hughes Corporation to place two communications satellites into the Colombia segment of the geostationary orbit in 1982. The satellites are classified as 'domestic satellites' and are only available to customers in the U.S. Colombia and another nine equatorial states are objecting to this unilateral use of the orbit. The Hughes project is considered to have a specially critical impact on Colombia since it would effectively 'saturate' the country's relatively small segment of the orbit. The Colombian government has accused the U.S. in a protest conveyed to the State Department of "aggression".

(88) For a history of the evolution of ASW technologies and systems, see Jim Bussert, 'Computers Add New Effectiveness to SOSUS/CAESAR', *Defense Electronics*, October 1979, pp. 59-64; and for an overview of military applications see Kostas Tsipis, *Tactical and Strategic Anti-Submarine Warfare*, MIT Press, Cambridge, Mass., 1974.

(89) Milton Leitenberg, 'The Dynamics of Military Technology Today', *International Social Sciences Journal*, vol. XXV, no. 3, 1973.

(90) See 'ASW Market Estimated to Reach $ 46.2 Billion in 1978-1983', *Sea Technology*, September 1979, p. 57.

(91) Resolution S-10/2, 30 June 1978.

(92) There is of course an array of international ocean programs. For a review, see Harvey B.Silverstein, *Superships and Nation-States*, Westview Press, New York, 1978.

(93) The Seabed Treaty is shorthand for the Treaty on the Prohibition of the Emplacement of Nuclear Weapons and Other

Weapons of Mass Destruction on the Seabed and the Ocean
Floor and in the Subsoil Thereof, U.N. resolution 2660 (XXV),
dated 7 December 1970.

(94) For a presentation of the principles of laser technology,
see O.S.Heavens, *Lasers*, Duckworth, London, 1971.

(95) Lasers develop extremely high power. Energy can be stored
gradually over a long period of time and released suddenly.
For instance, if a laser beam pulse contains 1000 Joules
(which is not a large amount of energy), and releases it
over a period of a millionth millionth of a second (a pico-
second), the instantaneous power during this period is about
10^{15} watts. This is about 1000 times greater than the total
power generating capacity of all the electricity generating
stations in the world. If such a laser beam pulse is focused
on a target about one tenth of a millimeter in diameter,
which is quite feasible, the power density is about 10^{19}
watts per square centimetre.

(96) Quoted in Robert C.Toth, 'War in Space', *Science 80*, vol.
no. 6, pp. 74-80, at p. 79.

(97) Oil slicks reflect differently in different parts of the
spectrum. By shining laser light of several different
frequencies at a water surface and measuring the reflection,
it would be possible to detect the presence of oil and perhaps a good deal about its composition.

(98) For a review of the environmental damage inflicted in
Vietnam by the U.S., see SIPRI, *Ecological Consequences of
the Second Indochina War*, Almqvist and Wiksell, Stockholm,
1976; and Bo Bengtsson, *Ecological Effects of Chemical Warfare and Bombing in Vietnam*, Report no. 3, Swedish Agency
for Research Cooperation with Developing Countries (SAREC),
Stockholm, 1976.

(99) For a historical overview of the ecological impact of war,
see SIPRI, *Warfare in a Fragile World: Military Impact on
the Human Environment*, Taylor and Francis, London, 1980.
See also J.P.Robinson, *The Effects of Weapons on Ecosystems*,
Pergamon, London, 1979.

(100) For a discussion of environmental warfare technologies,
see G.F.MacDonald, 'Geophysical Warfare: How to Wreck the
Environment', in Nigel Calder (ed.), *Unless Peace Comes:
A Scientific Forecast of New Weapons*, Viking Press, New
York, 1968, pp. 181-205; R.D.McCarthy, *Ultimate Folly:
War by Pestilence, Asphyxiation and Defoliation*, A.A.Knopf,
New York, 1969; Bhupendra M.Jasani, 'Environmental Modifica-
tions - New Weapons of War?, *Ambio*, vol. IV, no. 5-6, pp.
191-198; and Frank Barnaby, 'Environmental Warfare', *Bulle-
tin of Atomic Scientists*, vol. 32, no. 5, 1976, pp. 36-43.

(101) In 1975, Canada submitted a working paper to the CCD
which groups 19 technologies within three main categories:
atmospheric modification, including the high atmosphere
and ionosphere; modification of the oceans; and modification

of the land masses and water systems associated with them. (Document CCD/463, 1975). Analysis of the list by Sweden led it to conclude that 9 of the technologies listed could be discarded. Of the remaining 10, the following 5 were considered the most feasible: steering of storms, avalanche and landslide generation, modification of permafrost areas, diversion and pollution of rivers and the destruction of dams, and the generation of rain and snow. (Document CCD/465, 1975).

(102) There is reason to believe that the U.S. and Soviet Union are locked in a covert war of electronic countermeasures using increasingly powerful Extremely Low Freqeuncy (ELF), monitored to range between .1 and 34 Hz, magnetic fields. Since October 1976 the Soviet Union has been emitting ELF signals from a number of Telsa-type transmitters. Their frequencies correspond to brain-wave rythms of either the depressed or irritable states of human beings. Scientific- ally tenable tests have shown that the Soviet signals do lock into human brain-wave signals. The U.S. Environmental Protection Agency has assessed the signals as being psycho- active, i.e. liable to produce psychological response and vulnerability in humans. The same agency has noted that Soviet ELF signals can be absorbed and reradiated by 60Hz power transmission lines and even be magnified by water- pipe grids. Since summer 1979 the U.S. has entered the arena of massive ELF emissions. These have been used to override and occasionally blank out the Soviet emissions. To achieve such countermeasure results, magnetic fields of great intensity have been generated. There is evidence that the intensification of magnetic fields is modifying the weather (perhaps unintentionally) in the North American continent. It may also be endangering aviation safety and could have led to the loss of several USAF AS-6 aircraft in the Seattle, Washington area, the Pacific North-West being the scene of much ELF activity. No less sinister is the distinct possibility that ELF emissions have been used to induce earthquakes in different parts of the world. A number of non-governmental organizations have pointed to the dangers of ELF emissions and to the possibility that a potentially catastrophic covert war involving the two superpowers is already taking place. See, for example, the Newsletters of the Planetary Association for Clean Air (100 Bronson/1001, Ottawa K1R 6G8, Canada).

(103) SIPRI, *Weapons of Mass Destruction and the Environment*, Taylor and Francis, London, 1977, p. 60.

(104) Ibid.

(105) See Jozef Goldblat, 'The Prohibition of Environmental Warfare', *Ambio*, vol. IV, no. 5-6, 1975, pp. 186-190.

(106) On the question of changing climate, see Nigel Calder, *The Weather Machine*, Viking, New York, 1979; R.A.Byson and

T.J.Murray, *Climates of Hunger: Mankind and the World's Changing Weather*, University of Wisconsin Press, Madison, 1977; and M.R. and A.K.Biswas (eds.), *Food, Climate and Man*, John Wiley, Chichester, 1979.

(107) The World Climate Conference, held in Geneva in February 1979, was told by Robert Kates that increasing climatic unpredictability has resulted in annual losses of about $ 30 billion in industrialized countries. Some 40 per cent of the losses are due to floods, 20 per cent to cyclones, and 15 per cent to drought. The trend he expected to "continue and perhaps to intensify". Kates estimated the annual losses to developing countries in recent years at about $ 10 billion, or one third that of the industrialized countries. Loss of life due to climatic factors in the Third World is, however, much higher. The casualty figure of nearly 240,000 a year is about 20 times greater than for the industrialized world.

(108) One of the themes in J.Gribbin, *Climate and Mankind*, Earthscan, London, 1979.

(109) The Convention on the Prohibition of Military or Any Other Hostile Use of the Environmental Modification Techniques (1976). The U.S. ratified the Convention in November 1979.

(110) Goldblat, op.cit., p. 188.

(111) See document CCD/PV684, 1975. p. 11.

(112) The competing bills are S.829, introduced by Senator Henry Bellmon, March 29, 1979; and S.1644, introduced by Senator Adlai Stevenson, August 2, 1979; both in the 96th Congress, 1st Session.

(113) Some very large schemes have been proposed, notably by Soviet scientists. Some of their more ambitious suggestions have involved diverting the flow of some major rivers from the Arctic Ocean to the Aral and Caspian seas with the aim of irrigating the arid lands of Central Asia and the Caspian Basin; and the building of a dam across the Bering Straight, to pump warmer Pacific water into the cold Arctic, and to reverse the flow or to 'cancel out' the Greenland, Labrador and other cold ocean currents. Such schemes, which would change wind, rainfall and climatological patterns over enormous areas fit the very worst tradition of attempting to apply technologies without consideration of consequences. They also meet the Soviet penchant for technological determinism as discussed earlier.

(114) Hedley Bull, *The Control of the Arms Race*, Weidenfeld and Nicolson, London, 1961, pp. 197-198.

(115) See Milton Leitenberg, 'The Dynamics of Military Technology Today', *International Social Sciences Journal*, vol. XXV, no. 3, 1973.

(116) See Colin Norman, *Knowledge and Power: The Global Research and Development Budget*, Worldwatch Paper no. 31, Worldwatch

Institute, Washington, D.C., July 1979, p. 17.

(117) See James Avery Joyce, 'Arms Race Cut Job Growth', *Development Forum*, March 1979, p. 14. For a review of the costs of the arms race and their implications for development, see SIPRI, *World Armaments and Disarmament, SIPRI Yearbook 1979*, Taylor and Francis, London, 1979; and Ruth Leger Sivard, *World Military and Social Expenditures 1980*, World Priorities, Leesburg, Va., 1980. On the question of converting arms expenditures to development expenditures, see Ulrich Albrecht, 'Researching Conversion: A Review of the State of the Art', in Peter Wallensteen (ed.), *Experiences in Disarmament*, Report no. 19, Uppsala University, Uppsala, Sweden, June 1978, pp. 11-43. See also the following United Nations publications: *Reduction of Military Budgets of States Permanent Members of the Security Council by 10 Per Cent and Utilization of Part of the Funds Saved to Provide Assistance to Developing Countries*, U.N. sales no. E.75.I.10, New York, 1975; *Economic and Social Consequences of the Arms Race and of Military Expenditures*, U.N. sales no. 78.IX.1, New York, 1978; and *Report of the Ad Hoc Group on the Relationship between Disarmament and Development*, document A/S-10/9, New York, 5 April 1978.

(118) Morrison and O'Manique, op.cit., p. 4.

(119) See on this Deborah Shapley, 'Technological Creep and the Arms Race', three articles in *Science*, 22 September, 29 September, and 20 October, 1978.

(120) Christopher Bertram, *The Future of Arms Control: Part II. Arms Control and Technological Means*, Adelphi Paper no. 146, International Institute for Strategic Studies, London, 1978.

(121) Morrison and O'Manique, op.cit., p. 5.

(122) Harlan Cleveland, 'The Mutation of World Institutions', in Antony J.Dolman (ed.), *Global Planning and Resource Management: Toward International Decision-Making in a Divided World*, Pergamon, New York, 1980, pp. 72-86, at p. 77.

Bibliography

Reference has been made in the volume to the following works. They are listed here as a consolidated bibliography.

Ajami, Fouad: 'The Global Logic of the Neo-Conservatives', *World Politics,* vol. 30, no. 3, April 1978, pp. 450-468.

Albrecht, Ulrich: 'Researching Conversion: A Review of the State of the Art', in Peter Wallensteen (ed.), *Experiences in Disarmament,* Report no. 19, Uppsala University, Uppsala, Sweden, June 1978, pp. 11-43.

Alpert, P.: *Partnership or Confrontation? Poor Lands and Rich,* Free Press, New York, 1973.

Amin, Samir: *Neo-Colonialism in West Africa,* Penguin, Harmondsworth, 1973.

Amin, Samir: *Unequal Development,* Monthly Review Press, New York/London, 1976.

Amin, Samir: *Imperialism and Underdevelopment*, Monthly Review Press, New York/London, 1977.

Amin, Samir: 'Self-Reliance and the New International Economic Order', *Monthly Review*, vol. 29, no. 3, August 1977, pp. 1-21.

Amuzegar, Jahangir: 'A Requiem for the North-South Conference', *Foreign Affairs,* October 1977, pp. 136-157.

Anell, Lars, Birgitta Nygren: *The Developing Countries and the World Economic System,* Frances Pinter, London, 1980.

Arendt, Hannah: *On Revolution,* Winthrop, Englewood Cliffs, N.J., 1971.

Armytage, W.H.G.: *The Rise of the Technocrats,* Routledge and Kegan Paul, London, 1965.

Aspen Institute for Humanistic Studies, *The Planetary Bargain: Proposals for a New International Economic Order to Meet Human Needs*, Princeton, New Jersey, 1975.

Atkinson, Dick: *Orthodox Consensus and the Radical Alternative: A Study in Sociological Theory*, Heinemann, London, 1971.

Bachrach, P., M.S.Baratz: 'Two Faces of Power', *American Political Science Review*, vol. 56, no. 4, 1962, pp. 947-952.

Bachrach, P., M.S.Baratz: *Power and Poverty: Theory and Practice*, Oxford University Press, New York, 1970.

Baran, Paul: *Political Economy of Growth*, Monthly Review Press, New York/London, 1957.

Baran, Paul, Paul M.Sweezy: *Monopoly Capital*, Monthly Review Press, New York/London, 1969.

Barnaby, Frank: 'Environmental Warfare', *Bulletin of Atomic Scientists*, vol. 32, no. 5, 1976, pp. 36-43.

Barnaby, Frank: 'Arms and the Third World', *New Scientist*, April 7, 1977.

Barnaby, Frank, David Krieger: 'Nuclear Technologies', Foundation Reshaping The International Order (RIO), Rotterdam, 1980 (mimeo).

Barnet, Richard J.: *The Roots of War*, Atheneum, New York, 1972.

Barnet, Richard J.: *The Lean Years: Politics in the Age of Scarcity*, Simon and Schuster, New York, 1980.

Barney, Gerald O. (Study Director): *The Global 2000 Report to the President of U.S. Entering the 21st Century* (volume 1: Summary Report), Pergamon, New York, 1980.

Barraclough, Geoffrey: 'The Great World Crisis I', *The New York Review of Books*, January 23, 1975.

Barraclough, Geoffrey: 'Wealth and Power: The Politics of Food and Oil', *The New York Review of Books*, August 7, 1975.

Barraclough, Geoffrey: 'The Haves and the Have Nots', *The New York Review of Books*, May 13, 1977.

Barraclough, Geoffrey: *Turning Points in World History*, Thames and Hudson, London, 1979.

Barrat-Brown, M.: *The Economics of Imperialism*, Penguin, Harmondsworth, 1974.

Bauer, P.T.: *Dissent on Development*, Weidenfeld and Nicolson, London, 1972.

Bauer, P.T., B.S.Yamey: 'Against the New Economic Order', *Commentary*, vol. 63, no. 3, April 1977, pp. 25-31.

Bauer, P.T., J.O'Sullivan: 'Ordering the World About: The NIEO', *Policy Review*, vol. 1, Summer 1977, pp. 55-69.

Bedjaoui, Mohammed: *Towards a New International Economic Order*, Holmes & Meier, New York/London, 1979.

Beer, R.F., E.G.Basset: *Recombinant Molecules: Impact on Science and Society*, Raven Press, New York, 1977.

Bell, Daniel: *The Coming of Post Industrial Society*, Heinemann, London, 1974.

Bell, Daniel: 'The End of American Exceptionalism', *The Public Interest*, vol. 41, Fall 1975, pp. 193-224.

Bell, Daniel: 'The Future of World Disorder', *Foreign Policy*, vol. 27, Summer 1977, pp. 109-136.

Bengtsson, Bo: *Ecological Effects of Chemical Warfare and Bombing in Vietnam*, Report no. 3, Swedish Agency for Research Cooperation with Developing Countries (SAREC), Stockholm, 1976.

Bennigsen, A.: 'Soviet Muslims and the World of Islam', *Problems of Communism*, March/April 1980, pp. 38-51.

Bergsten, C.Fred: 'The Threat from the Third World', *Foreign Policy*, no. 11, Winter 1973, pp. 102-124.

Bergsten, C.Fred: 'The Response to the Third World', *Foreign Policy*, no. 17, Winter 1974-75, pp. 3-34.

Bergsten, C.Fred: 'Interdependence and the Reform of International Institutions', *International Organization*, vol. 30, no. 2, Spring 1976, pp. 361-372.

Bergsten, C.Fred, Georges Berthoin, Kinhide Mushakoji: *The Reform of International Institutions*, A Report of the Trilateral Task Force on International Institutions to the Trilateral Commission, New York, 1976.

Bernstein, H. (ed.): *Underdevelopment and Development: The Third World Today*, Penguin, Harmondsworth, 1973.

Bertram, Christopher: *The Future of Arms Control: Part II. Arms Control and Technological Means*, Adelphi Paper no. 14-6, International Institute for Strategic Studies, London, 1978.

Bettelheim, Charles: 'The Great Leap Backward', *Monthly Review*, vol. 30, no. 3, July-August 1978, pp. 37-130.

Bhagwati, Jagdish N. (ed.): *The New International Economic Order: The North-South Debate*, MIT Press, Cambridge, Mass., 1977.

Bhagwati, Jagdish N.: *The Reverse Transfer of Technology (Brain Drain): International Resource-flow Accounting, Compensation, Taxation and Related Policy Measures*, (doc. TD/B/C.6/AC.4/2), January 1978.

Bhattacharya, Anindya K.: 'The Influence of the International Secretariat: UNCTAD and Generalized Tariff Preferences', *International Organizations*, vol. 30, no. 1, Winter 1976, pp. 75-90.

Biswas, M.R., A.R.Biswas (eds.): *Food, Climate and Man,* John Wiley, Chichester, 1979.

Blake, David H., Ronald H.Wallers: *The Politics of Global Economic Relations,* Prentice-Hall, Englewood Cliffs, N.J., 1976.

Blau, Gerda: *International Commodity Arrangements and Policies,* FAO Community Policy Studies 16, FAO, Rome, 1964.

Bodenheimer, S.: 'Dependency and Imperialism: The Roots of Latin American Underdevelopment', in K.T.Faun, D.C.Hodges (eds.), *Readings in U.S. Imperialism,* Porter Sargent, Boston, 1971.

Boulding, Kenneth: 'Commons and Community: The Idea of a Public' in G.Hardin and J.Baden (eds.), *Managing the Commons,* Freeman, San Francisco, 1977.

Brailsford, N.N.: *The War of Steel and Gold,* G.Bell, London, 1914.

Brandt, Willy: *North-South: A Programme for Survival,* Pan Books, London, 1980.

Brown, Harrison: *The Human Future Revisited: The World Predicament and Possible Solutions,* W.W.Norton, New York, 1978.

Brown, Lester R.: *Population and Affluence: Growing Pressure on World Food Resources,* Population Reference Bureau, Washington, D.C., 1973.

Brown, Lester R.: *Redefining National Security,* Worldwatch Paper 14, Worldwatch Institute, Washington, D.C., 1977.

Brown, Lester R.: *The Global Economic Prospect: New Sources of Economic Stress,* Worldwatch Paper 20, Worldwatch Institute, Washington, D.C. 1978.

Brown, Lester R.: *The Twenty Ninth Day: Accommodating Human Needs and Number to the Earth's Resources,* W.W.Norton, New York, 1978.

Brown, Lester R.: *Resource Trends and Population Policy: A Time for Reassessment,* Worldwatch Paper 29, Worldwatch Institute, Washington, D.C. May 1979.

Brown, Seyom et al: *Regimes for the Ocean, Outer Space and Weather,* The Brookings Institution, Washington, D.C. 1977.

Brucan, Silviu: *The Dissolution of Power,* Knopf, New York, 1971.

Brucan, Silviu: *The Dialectics of World Politics,* Free Press, New York, 1978.

Brucan, Silviu: 'The World Authority: An Exercise in Political Forecasting', in A.J.Dolman, (ed.), *Global Planning and Resource Management: Toward International Decision-Making in a Divided World,* Pergamon, New York, 1980, pp. 53-71.

Brucan, Silviu: 'World Politics in the 1980s', in David Krieger

Disarmament and Development: The Challenge of the International Control and Management of Dual-Purpose Technologies, Foundation Reshaping the International Order (RIO), Rotterdam, February 1981, pp. 111-121.

Bruckmann, Gerhart (ed.): *Latin American World Model: Proceedings of the Second IIASA Symposium on Global Modelling,* (document CP-76-8), Laxenburg, October 1974.

Brzezinski, Zbigniew: 'America in a Hostile World', *Foreign Policy,* no. 23, Summer 1976, pp. 65-96.

Buchan, Alistair: *Change Without War,* Chatto and Windus, London, 1974.

Buchanan, K.: 'The Third World - Its Emergence and Contours', *New Left Review,* vol. 18, 1963, pp. 5-23.

Buckley, Alan D.: 'Foreward', *Journal of International Affairs,* Fall/Winter 1977.

Bukharin, N.J.: *Imperialism and World Economy,* International Publishers, New York, 1929 (first published 1971).

Bukharin, N.J.: *Imperialism and the Accumulation of Capital,* Allen Lane, London, 1970 (first published 1924).

Bull, Hedley: *The Control of the Arms Race,* Weidenfeld and Nicolson , London, 1961.

Bull, Hedley: *The Anarchical Society: A Study of Order in World Politics,* Columbia University Press, New York, 1977.

Bundy, W.P.: 'Elements of Power', *Foreign Affairs,* vol. 23, October 1977, pp. 1-26.

Burnet, M.: *Genes, Dreams and Realities,* MIT Press, Cambridge, Mass., 1971.

Bussert, Jim: 'Computers Add New Effectiveness to SOSUS/CAESAR, *Defense Electronics,* October 1979, pp. 59-64.

Byson, R.A., T.J.Murray: *Climates of Hunger: Mankind and the World's Changing Weather,* University of Wisconsin Press, Madison, 1977.

Calder, Nigel (ed.): *Unless Peace Comes: A Scientific Forecast of New Weapons,* Viking Press, New York, 1968.

Calder, Nigel: *The Weather Machine,* Viking Press, New York, 1979.

Calder, Nigel: *Nuclear Nightmares,* Viking Press, New York, 1980.

Camps, Miriam: *The Management of Interdependence: A Preliminary View,* Council on Foreign Relations, Inc., New York, 1974.

Caporoso, James A.: 'Dependence, Dependency and Power in Global Systems: A Structural and Behavioral Analysis', *International Organization,* vol. 32, no. 1, Winter 1978, pp. 13-43.

Cardoso, F.H.: 'Dependency and Development in Latin America', *New Left Review*, no. 74, 1972.

Carr, E.H.: *The Twenty Years' Crisis: 1919-1939. An Introduction to the Study of International Relations*, Macmillan, London, 1939.

Castaneda, Jorge: *Legal Effects of United Nations Resolutions*, Columbia University Press, New York, 1969.

Castells, Manuel: *The Economic Crisis and American Society*, Princeton University Press, Princeton, N.J., 1980.

Centre for Research of Air and Space Law, McGill University, 'Space and Satellite Technology for Disarmament and Development', Foundation Reshaping the International Order (RIO), Rotterdam, 1980 (mimeo).

Chagula, W.K., B.T.Feld, A.Parthasarathi (eds.): *Pugwash on Self-Reliance*, Ankur Publishing House, New Delhi, 1977.

Chiaromonte, Nicola: *The Paradox of History*, London, 1966.

Chichilnisky, Graciela: 'Development Patterns and the International Order', *Journal of International Affairs*, vol. 31, no. 2 Fall/Winter 1977, pp. 175-204.

Chowdhury, Subranta Roy: 'Legal Status of the Charter of Economic Rights and Duties of States', in K.Hossain (ed.), *Legal Aspects of the New International Economic Order*, Frances Pinter, London, 1980, pp. 79-94.

Claude, Inis L.: *The Changing United Nations*, Random House, New York, 1967.

Clem, R.S.: 'Russians and Others: Ethnic Tensions in the Soviet Union', *Focus*, no. 1, September/October 1980, pp. 1-16.

Cleveland, Harlan: 'Does Everything Belong to Everybody?', *The Christian Science Monitor*, December 19, 1978.

Cleveland, Harlan: 'The Mutation of World Institutions', in Antony J.Dolman (ed.), *Global Planning and Resource Management: Toward International Decision-Making in a Divided World*, Pergamon, New York, 1980, pp. 72-86.

Cline, William R.: 'A Qualitative Assessment of the Policy Alternatives in the NIEO Negotiations' in W.R.Cline (ed.), *Policy Alternatives for a New International Economic Order*, Praeger Publishers, New York, 1979.

Cockcroft, J.D., A.G.Frank, D.L.Johnson: *Dependence and Development: Latin America's Political Economy*, Anchor Books, New York, 1972.

Cohen, Benjamin: *The Question of Imperialism*, Macmillan, London, 1974.

Cole, Sam et al: *Models of Doom*, Universe Books, New York, 1973.

Cole, Sam: 'The Global Futures Debate 1965-1976', in Christopher Freeman and Marie Jahoda (eds.), *World Futures: The Great Debate*, Martin Robertson, Oxford, 1978, pp. 9-49.

Cole, Sam, Ian Miles: 'Assumptions and Methods: Population, Economic Department, Modelling and Technical Change', in C.Freeman and M.Jahoda (eds.), *World Futures: The Great Debate*, Martin Robertson, Oxford, 1978, pp. 51-75.

Commager, Henry Steele: 'In Search of American Statesmanship', *International Herald Tribune*, August 26, 1980.

Commager, Henry Steele: *The Defeat of America*, Simon and Schuster, New York, 1975.

Commoner, Barry: *The Closing Circle: Nature, Man and Technology*, Alfred A.Knopf, New York, 1971.

Cooper, Richard N.: 'A New International Economic Order for Mutual Gain', *Foreign Policy*, no. 26, Spring 1977, pp. 65-120.

Cooper, Richard, Karl Kaiser, Masataka Kosaka: *Towards a Renovated International System*, Trilateral Commission, New York, 1977.

Coplin, William D.: *The Function of International Law*, Rand Mcnally, Chicago, 1966.

Coplin, William D.: 'International Organizations in the Future Bargaining Process: A Theoretical Projection', *Journal of International Affairs*, vol. 25, 1971, pp. 287-301.

Cox, Donald: *The Space Race: From Sputnik to Apollo and Beyond*, Clitton Books, Philadelphia/New York, 1962.

Cox, Robert W.: 'Ideologies and the New International Economic Order: Reflections on Some Recent Literature', *International Organization*, vol. 33, no. 2, Spring 1979, pp. 257-302.

Curry-Lindhal, K.: *Let them Live: A Worldwide Survey of Animals Threatened with Extinction*, Morrow, New York, 1972.

Cutler, Lloyd: 'To Form a Government', *Foreign Affairs*, vol. 59, no. 1, Fall 1980, pp. 126-143.

Dahrendorf, Ralph: *Not the Westminster Model*, Third World Monograph 2, Third World Foundation, London, 1979.

Daly, Herman: *Toward a Steady-State Economy*, Freeman, San Francisco, 1973.

Dam, F. van: 'Noord-Zuid: De Werkelijkheid van 1980-1990', *Economische Statistische Berichten*, November 14, 1979, pp. 1188-1196.

Davidoff, Paul, Thomas A.Reiner: 'A Choice Theory of Planning', *Journal of the American Institute of Planners*, vol. 28, May, 1962, pp. 103-115.

Davies, R.W.: *The Industrialization of Soviet Russia: Vol. 1 - The Socialist Offensive: The Collectivisation of Soviet Agriculture 1929-30,* Macmillan, London, 1979.

Davis, Wayne H.: 'Overpopulated America', in Daniel Callahan (ed.), *The American Population Debate,* Anchor, New York, 1971, pp. 161-167.

Dawkins, R.: *The Selfish Gene,* Oxford University Press, London, 1976.

Declaration of Berne: *The Infiltration of the U.N. System by Multinational Corporations,* Berne, 1978.

Desai, M.: *Marxian Economic Theory,* Gray-Mills, London, 1974.

Deutsch, Karl W.: *Nationalism and Social Communication,* John Wiley, New York, 1953.

Deutsch, Karl W.: 'Some Prospects for the Future', *Journal of International Affairs,* vol. 31, no. 2, Fall/Winter 1977, pp. 315-326.

Deutsch, K.W., J.D.Singer: 'Multipolarity, Power Systems and International Stability', *World Politics,* vol. 16, no. 3, April 1964, pp. 390-406.

Deutscher, I.: *The Prophet Unarmed,* Oxford University Press, New York, 1959.

Diaware, Mohamed T.: 'Une Taxation mondiale de Solidarité', Project TERRE, Club de Dakar, Senegal, July 28, 1977 (mimeo).

Díaz-Alejandro, Carlos F.: 'Delinking North and South: Unshackled or Unhinged', in Albert Fishlow et al, *Rich and Poor Nations in the World Economy,* McGraw-Hill, New York, 1978, pp. 87-162.

Dickson, David: *Alternative Technology and the Politics of Technical Change,* Fontana/Collins, London, 1974.

Djordjevic, Jovan: 'The Social Enterprise of Mankind', in *Proceedings of the First Pacem in Maribus Convocation, Malta, June 28-July 3, 1970,* International Ocean Institute, Misada, Malta, 1971.

Dolman, Antony J.: 'The Like-Minded Countries and the New International Order: Past, Present and Future Prospects', *Cooperation and Conflict: Nordic Journal of International Politics,* vol. XIV, 1979, pp. 57-85.

Dolman, Antony J.: *The Like-Minded Countries and the Industrial and Technological Transformation of the Third World,* Foundation Reshaping the International Order (RIO), Rotterdam, 1979.

Dolman, Antony J.: 'Environment, Development, Disarmament: Three Worlds in One', paper prepared for the United Nations Non-Governmental Liaison Service, Geneva, November 1980. (mimeo)

Dolman, Antony J. (ed.): *Global Planning and Resource Management: Toward International Decision-Making in a Divided World,* Pergamon, New York, 1980.

Dolman, Antony J.: *The Like-Minded Countries and the North-South Conflict,* Foundation Reshaping the International Order (RIO), Rotterdam, February 1981.

Dolman, Antony J., Jan van Ettinger (eds.): *Partners in Tomorrow: Strategies for a New International Order,* E.P.Dutton, New York, 1978.

Donges, Jurgen B.: 'The Third World Demand for a New International Economic Order: Government Surveillance versus Market Decision-Making in Trade and Investment', *Kylos,* vol. 30, 1977, pp. 235-258.

Dormael, Armand van: *Bretton Woods: Birth of a Monetary System,* Macmillan, London, 1978.

Dos Santos, T.: 'The Crisis of Development Theory and the Problem of Dependence in Latin America', in H.Bernstein (ed.), *Underdevelopment and Development: The Third World Today,* Penguin, Harmondsworth, 1973, pp. 57-80.

Downs, Anthony: *Inside Bureaucracy,* Little, Brown, Boston, 1967.

Doxey, Margaret P.: *Economic Sanctions and International Enforcement,* Oxford University Press, London, 1971.

Dresch, S.P.: *Disarmament: Economic Consequences and Development Potential,* National Bureau of Economic Research and Yale University, New Haven, Conn., 1972.

Duchene, François, Kinhide Mushakoji, Henry D.Owen: *The Crisis of International Cooperation, A Report of the Trilateral Political Task Force to the Executive Committee of the Trilateral Commission, Tokyo, October 22-23, 1973,* The Trilateral Commission, New York, 1974, p. 14.

Dumont, René: *Utopia or Else,* Deutsch, London, 1974.

Duvall, Raymond D.: 'Dependence and Dependencia Theory: Notes Toward Precision of Concept and Argument', *International Organization,* vol. 32, no. 1, Winter 1978, pp. 51-78.

Eckholm, Erik: *Disappearing Species: The Social Challenge,* Worldwatch Paper 22, Worldwatch Institute, Washington, D.C., July 1978.

Eddie, G.C.: *Harvesting of Krill,* (pub. GLO/50/77/2), FAO, Rome 1977.

Ehrlich, Paul R.: *The Population Bomb,* Pan, London, 1971.

Ehrlich, Paul R.: *The End of Affluence,* Ballantine Books, New York, 1971.

Ehrlich, Paul R., Anne Ehrlich: *Population, Resources, Environment,* Freeman, San Francisco, 1970.

Ehrlich, Paul R., R.L.Harriman: *How to be a Survivor: A Plan for Spaceship Earth,* Ballantine Books, New York, 1971.

Eisenstadt, S.N. (ed.): *The Protestant Ethic and Modernization,* New York, 1968.

Ellul, Jacques: *The Technological Society,* Alfred A.Knopf, New York, 1964.

Emmanuel, Arghiri: *Unequal Echange: A Study of the Imperialism of Trade,* Monthly Review Press, New York/London, 1972.

Engellau, Patrik, Birgitta Nygren: *Lending Without Limits - On International Lending and Developing Countries,* Secretariat for Futures Studies, Stockholm, 1979.

Erb, G.F., V.Kallab (eds.): *Beyond Dependency: The Developing World Speaks Out,* Overseas Development Council, Washington, D.C., 1975.

Ernst, Dieter (ed.): *The New International Division of Labour, Technology and Underdevelopment,* Campus, Frankfurt on Main and New York, 1980.

Ernst, Dieter: 'Technology Policy and Transition Towards Self-Reliance - Some Major Issues', *International Social Science Journal,* 1981 (forthcoming).

l'Etang, Hugh: *Fit to Lead?,* Heinemann Medical, London, 1980.

Ettinger, Jan van: 'A UN Industrial and Technological Development Fund', Foundation Reshaping the International Order (RIO), Rotterdam, (in preparation).

Everson, I.: *The Living Resources of the Southern Ocean,* (publication GLO/55/77/1) FAO, Rome, 1977.

Eyre, S.R.: *The Real Wealth of Nations,* Edward Arnold, London, 1978.

Falk, Richard A.: 'The Interplay of Westphalia and Charter Conceptions of International Legal Order', in Richard A.Falk, Cyril E.Black, *The Future of the International Legal Order. Volume 1: Trends and Patterns,* Princeton University Press, Princeton, N.J., 1969, pp. 32-70.

Falk, Richard A.: *This Endangered Planet,* Random House, New York, 1971.

Falk, Richard A.: 'Toward a New World Order: Modest Methods and Drastic Visions', in S.Mendlovitz (ed.), *On the Creation of a Just World Order,* Free Press, New York, 1975, pp. 211- 258.

Falk, Richard A.: *A Study of Future Worlds,* Free Press, New York, 1975.

Falk, Richard A.: 'Beyond Internationalism', *Foreign Affairs,*
vol. 23, 1976, pp. 65-113.

Falk, Richard A.: 'Contending Approaches to World Order', *Journal of International Affairs,* vol. 31, no. 2, Fall/Winter 1977,
pp. 171-198.

Falk, Richard A.: 'The Institutional Dimension of a New International Order', in A.J.Dolman (ed.), *Global Planning and Resource Management: Toward International Decision-Making in a
Divided World,* Pergamon, New York, 1980, pp. 87-102.

Falk, Richard A., Saul H.Mendlovitz: *The United Nations,* World
Law Fund, New York, 1966.

Fanon, Franz: *The Wretched of the Earth,* Grove Press, New York,
1966.

Fanon, Franz: *Black Skin, White Masks,* Grove Press, New York,
1968.

Faun, K.T., D.C.Hodges (eds.): *Readings in U.S. Imperialism,*
Porter Sargent, Boston, 1971.

Feis, Herbert: *Churchill, Roosevelt, Stalin,* Princeton University Press, Princeton, N.J., 1967.

Fieldhouse, D.K.: *The Colonial Empires,* Weidenfeld and Nicolson,
London, 1966.

Fieldhouse, D.K.: *The Theory of Capitalist Imperialism,* Longman, London, 1967.

Fieldhouse, D.K.: *Colonialism 1870-1945,* Weidenfeld and Nicolson,
London, 1980.

Finger, Seymour M.: 'United States Policy Toward International
Institutions', *International Organization,* vol. 30, no. 2,
Spring 1976, pp. 347-360.

Fishlow, Albert: 'A New International Economic Order: What Kind?
in Roger D.Hansen (ed.), *Rich and Poor Nations in the World Economy,* McGraw-Hill, New York, 1978, pp. 9-83.

Foley, Gerald: *The Energy Question,* Penguin, Harmondsworth, 1976.

Forrester, Jay W.: *World Dynamics,* Wright-Allen, Cambridge,
Mass., 1971.

Fox, W.T.R. (ed.): *Theoretical Aspects of International Relations,* Notre Dame University Press, West Bend, Ind., 1959.

Frank, André G.: *Latin America: Underdevelopment or Revolution,*
Monthly Review Press, New York/London, 1969.

Frank, André G.: *Capitalism and Underdevelopment in Latin America,*
Monthly Review Press, New York/London, 1969.

Frank, André G.: 'The Development of Underdevelopment', in R.J.

Rhodes (ed.), *Imperialism and Underdevelopment: A Reader,* Monthly
Review Press, New York/London, 1970, pp. 4-17.

Frank, André G.: 'Rhetoric and Reality of the NIEO', May 1978
(mimeo).

Frank, André G.: *World Accumulation 1492-1789,* Macmillan, London,
1978.

Frank, André G.: *Development Accumulation and Underdevelopment,*
Macmillan, 1979.

Fraser, Antonia: *Heroes and Heroines,* Weidenfeld, London, 1980.

Frieden, Jeff: 'The Trilateral Commission: Economics and Politics in the 1970s', *Monthly Review,* vol. 29, no. 7, December 1977,
pp. 1-18.

Friedman, Edward: 'Maoist Conceptualizations of the Capitalist
World System', in T.K.Hopkins and I.Wallerstein (eds.), *Proces-
ses of the World System,* vol. 3, *Political Economy of the World
System Annals,* Sage, Beverly Hills, 1980, pp. 181-223.

Friedman, John: 'The Crisis of Transition: A Critique of Strategies of Crisis Management', *Development and Change,* vol. 10,
1979, pp. 125-153.

Friedmann, Wolfgang: *The Changing Structure of International
Law,* Columbia University Press, New York, 1964.

Fromin, B.S.: 'The New International Economic Order as Viewed
in the CMEA countries', in E.Laszlo, J. Kurtzman (eds.), *Eastern Europe and the New International Economic Order,* Pergamon,
New York, 1980, pp. 1-17.

Fromm, Erich: *The Sane Society,* Fawcett Premier Books, Holt,
Rinehart and Winston, Inc., New York, 1955.

Fromm, Erich: *To Have or to Be?,* Jonathan Cape, London, 1978.

Fulbright, J.William: *The Arrogance of Power,* Random House, New
York, 1966.

Furtado, Celso: *Development and Underdevelopment,* University of
California Press, Los Angeles, 1964.

Furtado, Celso: *The Economic Development of Latin America: A
Survey from Colonial Times to the Cuban Revolution,* Cambridge
University Press, Cambridge, 1970.

Furtado, Celso: *Obstacles to Development in Latin America,*
Anchor Books, Garden City, New York, 1970.

Furtado, Celso: 'Elements of a Theory of Underdevelopment: The
Underdeveloped Structures', in H.Bernstein (ed.), *Underdevelopment and Development: The Third World Today,* Penguin, Harmondsworth, 1973, pp. 33-43.

Furtado, Celso: 'The Concept of External Dependence in the Study
of Underdevelopment', in C.Wilber (ed.), *The Political Economy
of Development and Underdevelopment,* Random House, New York,
1973, pp. 118-123.

Galbraith, John K.: 'The NO-WIN Society', *The New York Review of
Books,* June 12, 1980, pp. 1-3.

Gallagher, J., R.Robinson: 'The Imperialism of Free Trade',
Economic History Review, vol. 6, no. 1, 1953, pp. 1-5.

Galtung, Johan: 'Violence, Peace and Peace Research', *Journal
of Peace Research,* vol. 6, no. 3, 1969, pp. 167-191.

Galtung, Johan: 'A Structural Theory of Imperialism', *Journal
of Peace Research,* vol. 5, 1971, pp. 375-395.

Galtung, Johan: 'The Limits to Growth and Class Politics', *Journal of Peace Research,* vol. 10, 1973, pp. 110-114.

Galtung, Johan: *The European Community: A Superpower in the
Making,* Allen and Unwin, London, 1973.

Galtung, Johan: 'Nonterritorial Actors and the Problem of Peace',
in Saul H.Mendlovitz (ed.), *On the Creation of a Just World Order: Preferred Worlds for the 1990s,* Free Press, New York, 1975,
pp. 151-188.

Galtung, Johan: *Poor Countries vs Rich; Poor People vs Rich.
Whom will the NIEO Benefit?,* Occasional Paper 77/4, Vienna Institute for Development, Vienna, 1977.

Galtung, Johan: 'Self-Reliance and Global Interdependence: Some
Reflections on the 'New International Economic Order'', *Chair
in Conflict and Peace Research,* University of Oslo, Papers, no.
55, 1977.

Galtung, Johan: *Development, Environment and Technology: Towards
a Technology for Self-Reliance,* UNCTAD, (document TD/B/C.6/23),
Geneva, June 1978.

Galtung, Johan: 'Towards a New International Technological Order'
Alternatives, vol. IV, 1978-9, pp. 277-300.

Galtung, Johan: 'On the Effects of International Economic Sanctions', *Essays in Peace Research,* Ejlers, Copenhagen, 1979, vol.
V.

Galtung, Johan: *The True Worlds: A Transnational Perspective,*
Free Press, New York, 1980.

Galtung, Johan: 'Power and Global Planning and Resource Management', in A.J.Dolman (ed.), *Global Planning and Resource Management: Toward International Decision-Making in a Divided World,*
Pergamon, New York, 1980, pp. 119-145.

Galtung, Johan, Peter O'Brien, Roy Preiswerk,(eds.): *Self-Reliance: A Strategy for Development,* Bogle-l'Ouverture Publications,

London, 1980.

Gamble, Andrew, Paul Walton: *Capitalism in Crisis: Inflation and the State,* Macmillan, London, 1976.

Gardner, Lloyd C.: *Architects of Illusion; Men and Ideas in American Foreign Policy,* New Viewpoints, New York, 1972.

Gardner, Richard N.: *Sterling Dollar Diplomacy,* New York, 1969.

Gaskell, Elisabeth: *North and South,* Penguin Books, Harmondsworth, 1970.

Giarini, Orio: *Producing Value for Wealth - The Role of Capital and Capital Needs,* Club of Rome, Rome, October 1979.

Gilpin, Robert: 'Three Models of the Future', in C.Fred Bergsten, Lawrence B.Krause (eds.), *World Politics and International Economics,* The Brookings Institution, Washington, D.C., 1975, pp. 37-60.

Goldblat, Jozef: 'The Prohibition of Environmental Warfare', *Ambio,* vol. IV, no. 5-6, 1975, pp. 186-190.

Goldsborough, J.O.: 'La Politique Etrangère des Etats-Unis', *Politique Etrangère,* vol. 45, no. 3, September 1980, pp. 621-636.

Goodwin, G.L., A.Linklater (eds.): *New Dimensions of World Politics,* Croom Helm, London, 1975.

Gordon, Lincoln (ed.): *International Stability and Progress,* American Assembly, New York, 1957.

Gorove, S.: 'The Concept of the Common Heritage of Mankind: A Political, Moral or Legal Innovation', 9, *San Diego Law Review,* 390, 1970.

Gosovic, Branislav: *UNCTAD: Conflict and Compromise,* Sijthoff, Leiden, 1972.

Gosovic, Branislav, John G.Ruggie: 'On the Creation of a New International Economic Order: Issue Linkage and the Special Session of the U.N. General Assembly', *International Organization,* vol. 30, Spring 1976, pp. 309-345.

Gottmann, Jean (ed.): *Centre and Periphery: Spatial Variation in Politics,* Sage, Beverly Hills, 1980.

Goulet, Denis: *The Cruel Choice,* Atheneum, New York, 1973.

Goulet, Denis: *World Interdependence: Verbal Smokescreen or New Ethic,* Development Paper 21, Overseas Development Council, Washington, D.C., March 1976.

Goulet, Denis: *The Uncertain Promise: Value Conflicts in Technology Transfer,* IDOC/North America, Inc., New York, 1977.

Governments of Algeria and the Netherlands: *Towards a New International Order: An Appraisal of Prospects,* Report on the Joint

Meeting of The Club of Rome and the International Ocean Institute, held in Algiers 25-28 October 1976, Government Printing Office, The Hague, 1977.

Grantham, G.J.: *The Utilization of Krill,* (pub. GLO/50/77/3), FAO, Rome, 1977.

Gribbin, J.: *Climate and Mankind,* Earthscan, London, 1974.

Griffin, Keith: *Underdevelopment in Spanish America,* Allen and Unwin, London, 1969.

Grove, John D.(ed.): *Global Inequality: Political and Socio-Economic Perspectives,* Westview, Boulder, 1979.

Grubel, H.G.: 'The Case Against the New International Economic Order', *Weltwirtschaftliches Archiv,* Band 113, Heft 2, 1977.

Guerrero, Manuel Pérez: 'The New International Economic Order and the International Law', Paper presented to the Third World and International Law, 20th International Seminar for Diplomacy, Salzburg, 1 August 1977 (mimeo).

Gulowsen, J.: 'From Technological to Ecological Dominance', *Acta Sociologica,* no. 4, 1976, pp. 357-74.

Gurr, Ted Robert: *Why Men Rebel,* Princeton University Press, Princeton, N.J., 1970.

Gutkin, Peter C.W., Immanuel Wallerstein (eds.): *The Political Economy of Contemporary Africa,* Sage, Beverly Hills, Ca., 1976.

Gwin, Catherine B.: 'The Seventh Special Session: Toward a New Phase of Relations Between the Developed and Developing States?' in K.P.Sauvant, H.Hasenpflug (eds.), *The New International Economic Order: Confrontation or Cooperation Between North and South,* Wilton House, London, 1977, pp. 20-35.

Haas, Ernst: *The Uniting of Europe,* Stevens, London, 1958.

Haas, Ernst: *Beyond the Nation State,* Stanford University Press, Stanford, Ca., 1964.

Haas, Ernst: 'On Systems and International Regimes', *World Politics,* vol. 27, January 1975, pp. 147-174.

Haas, Ernst: 'Is There a Hole in the Whole? Knowledge, Technology, Interdependence and the Construction of International Regimes', *International Organization,* vol. 29, Summer 1975, pp. 827-876.

Habermas, Jürgen: *Towards a Rational Society,* Heinemann, London, 1971.

Hansen, Roger: 'The Crisis of Interdependence: Where Do We Go from Here?', in Roger Hansen (ed.), *The U.S. and World Development. Agenda for Action 1976,* Praeger, Washington/New York, 1976, pp. 41-66.

Hansen, Roger (ed.): *The U.S. and World Development: Agenda for Action 1976*, Praeger, Washington/New York, 1976.

Hansen, Roger: *Beyond the North-South Stalemate*, McGraw-Hill, New York, 1979.

Haq, Khadija (ed.): *Dialogue for a New Order*, Pergamon, New York, 1980.

Haq, Mahbub ul: 'Crisis in Development Strategies', *World Development*, vol. 1, no. 7, July 1973, pp. 29-31.

Haq, Mahbub ul: *The Poverty Curtain: Choices for the Third World*, Columbia University Press, New York, 1976.

Harrington, Michael: *The Twilight of Capitalism*, Simon and Schuster, New York, 1976.

Harrington, Michael: *The Vast Majority: A Journey to the World's Poor*, Simon and Schuster, New York, 1977.

Harrison, Paul: *Inside the Third World*, Penguin, Harmondsworth, 1979.

Hayes, Denis: *Nuclear Power: The Fifth Horseman*, Worldwatch Paper 6, Worldwatch Institute, Washington, D.C., 1976.

Heavens, O.S.: *Lasers*, Duchworth, London, 1971.

Hedén, Carl-Göran, David Krieger: 'Chemical and Biological Technologies', Foundation Reshaping the International Order (RIO), Rotterdam, 1980 (mimeo).

Heeger, Gerald A.: *The Politics of Underdevelopment*, Macmillan, London, 1974.

Heilbroner, Robert L.: *An Inquiry into the Human Prospect*, W.W. Norton, New York, 1974.

Helleiner, G.K. (ed.): *A World Divided: The Less Developed Countries in the International Economy*, Cambridge University Press, London, 1976.

Helleiner, G.K.: 'An OECD for the Third World', *IDS Bulletin*, vol. 7, no. 4, April 1976.

Helleiner, G.K.: *World Market Imperfections and the Developing Countries*, Occasional Paper no. 11, Overseas Development Council, Washington D.C., May 1978.

Henkin, Louis: *How Nations Behave: Law and Foreign Policy*, Columbia University Press, New York, 1979.

Hermassi, Elbaki: *The Third World Reassessed*, University of California Press, Berkeley, Ca., 1980.

Herrera, Amílcar O. et al.: *Catastrophe or New Society? A Latin American World Model*, International Development Research Centre, Ottawa, 1976.

Higgins, Ronald: *The Seventh Enemy,* Hodder and Stoughton, London, 1978.

Higgins, Rosalyn: *The Development of International Law through the Political Organs of the United Nations,* Oxford University Press, London/New York, 1963.

Hilferding, R.: *Finanzkapital,* Verlag der Wiener Volksbuchhandlung, Vienna, 1923 (first published 1910).

Hill, Martin: *The United Nations System: Coordinating its Economic and Social Work,* Cambridge University Press, London, 1978.

Hinckley, Alden D.: *Renewable Resources in Our Future,* Pergamon Press, Oxford, 1980.

Hindress, B., P.Kirst, A.Hussain, A.Cutler: *Marx's Capital and Capitalism Today,* Routledge and Kegan Paul, London, 1977.

Hinsley, F.H.: *Power and the Pursuit of Peace,* Cambridge University Press, London, 1963.

Hirsch, Fred: 'Is There a New International Economic Order?, *International Organization,* vol. 30, no. 3, Summer 1976, pp. 521-531.

Hirsch, Fred: *The Social Limits to Growth,* Routledge and Kegan Paul, London, 1978.

Hobson, J.A.: *Imperialism: A Study,* Nisbett, London, 1902,

Hochman, Sandra: *Satellite Spies,* Bobbs-Merrill, Inc., Indianapolis, 1976.

Hodgart, A.: *The Economics of European Imperialism,* Edward Arnold, London, 1977.

Hodgkin, T.: 'African and Third World Theories of Imperialism', in R.J.Owen, R.B.Sutcliffe (eds.), *Studies in the Theory of Imperialism,* Longman, London, 1972.

Hoffmann, Stanley: *Primacy or World Order: American Foreign Policy Since the Cold War,* McGraw-Hill, New York, 1978.

Holbrooke, Richard: 'A Sense of Drift, A Time for Calm', *Foreign Policy,* no. 23, Summer 1976, pp. 97-112.

Holdgate, M.W., Jon Tinker: *Oil and Other Minerals in the Antarctic,* The Scientific Committee on Antarctic Research (SCAR), Cambridge, 1979.

Holsti, Kal J.: 'A New International Politics? Diplomacy in Complex Interdependence', *International Organization,* vol. 32, no. 2, Spring 1978, pp. 513-530.

Horowitz, Irving L.: *Three Worlds of Development,* Oxford University Press, London, 1966.

Horowitz, Irving L.: 'The United Nations and the Third World:

East-West Conflict in Focus', in R.Gregg, M.Borkun (eds.), *The United Nations System and its Functions,* Van Nostrand, Princeton, N.J., 1968, pp. 350-357.

Hossain, Kamal (ed.): *Legal Aspects of the New International Economic Order,* Frances Pinter, London, 1980.

Howe, James W.: *The Developing Countries in a Changing International Economic Order: A Survey of Research Needs,* Occasional Paper no. 7, Overseas Development Council, Washington, D.C., 1973.

Hudes, Karen: 'Towards a New International Economic Order', *Yale Studies in World Public Order,* vol. 2, no. 1, 1975.

Hudson, Michael: *Global Fracture: The New International Economic Order,* Harper and Row, New York, 1977.

Huisken, Ronald H.: 'The Consumption of Raw Materials for Military Purposes', *Ambio,* vol. IV, no. 5-6, 1975, pp. 229-233.

Huldt, Bo: 'Institutional Dependence: Sweden and the United Nations - History and Future Perspectives', Paper prepared as part of the project 'Sweden in the World Society', Secretariat for Futures Studies, Stockholm, Sweden, September 1976 (mimeo).

Hveem, Helge: 'The Global Dominance System', *Journal of Peace Research,* vol. 10, 1973, pp. 319-340.

Illich, Ivan: *Tools for Conviviality,* Harper and Row, New York, 1973.

ILO: *Yearbook of Labour Statistics 1979,* Geneva, 1980.

International Atomic Energy Agency: *International Nuclear Fuel Cycle Evaluation: Summary Volume,* Vienna, 1980.

International Foundation for Development Alternatives, *Building Blocks for Alternative Development Strategies,* IFDA Dossier 17, Nyon, Switzerland, May-June 1980.

International Ocean Institute: *Proceedings of the First Pacem in Maribus Convocation,* Malta, June 28-July 3, 1970, volume 3, 'Planning and Development in the Oceans', International Ocean Institute, Msida, Malta, 1970.

Islam, Nurul: *New Mechanisms for the Transfer of Resources to Developing Countries,* United Nations, (doc. E.AC.54/1.83), New York, 13 November 1975.

Jalée, P.: *The Pillage of the Third World,* Monthly Review Press, New York/London, 1967.

Jalée, P.: *The Third World in the World Economy,* Monthly Review Press, New York/London, 1969.

Jankowitsch, Peter: *International Cooperation in Outer Space,* Occasional Paper 11, The Stanley Foundation, Muscatine, Iowa, 1976.

Janssen, R.: 'Afhankelijkheidstheorieën. Het Dependenciamodel:
Een Origineel Latijnsamerikaanse Bijdrage aan de Sociale Wetenschappen', *Intermediair,* October 20, 1978, pp. 17-21.

Jantsch, E.: *Technological Forecasting in Perspective',* OECD,
Paris, 1976.

Jasani, Bhupendra M.: 'Environmental Modifications - New Weapons
of War?, *Ambio,* vol. IV, no. 5-6, 1975, pp. 191-198.

Jazairy, Idriss : 'An Assessment of Prospects in the Light of
Recent Experience', in A.J.Dolman, J.van Ettinger (eds.), *Part-
ners in Tomorrow: Strategies for a New International Order,* E.P.
Dutton, New York, 1978, pp. 46-60.

Jenkins, Robin: *Exploitation: The World Power Structure and the
Inequality of Nations,* MacGibbon and Kee, London, 1970.

Johnson, Brian: *Whose Power to Choose? International Institutions and the Control of Nuclear Energy,* International Institute
for Environment and Development, London, 1977.

Johnson, Harry G.: *Economic Nationalism in Old and New States,*
Allen and Unwin, London, 1968.

Joyce, James A.: 'Arms Race Cuts Job Growth, *Development Forum,*
March 1979, p. 14.

Judge, Anthony: 'International Organization Networks: A Complementary Perspective', in P.Taylor, A.J.R.Groom (eds.), *International Organization: A Conceptual Approach,* Frances Pinter,
London, 1978, pp. 381-413.

Kahn, Herman, Anthony Wiener: *The Year 2000,* Macmillan, London,
1967.

Kahn, H., W.Brown, L.Martel: *The Next 200 Years,* Morrow, New
York, 1976.

Kaplan, Abraham: *The Conduct of Inquiry : Methodology of Behavioral Science,* Chandler, San Francisco, 1964.

Kaplan, Irving E.: 'Disarmament and Development': A Preliminary
Assessment of Environmental Modification Technologies', Foundation Reshaping the International Order (RIO), Rotterdam, 1980,
(mimeo).

Kaufmann, Johan: 'The United Nations as a World Development
Authority', in A.J.Dolman (ed.), *Global Planning and Resource
Management : Toward International Decision-Making in a Divided
World,* Pergamon, New York, 1980, pp. 103-115.

Kay, David A.: 'On the Reform of International Institutions:
A Comment', *International Organization,* vol. 30, no. 3, Summer
1976, pp. 533-538.

Kay, G.: *Development and Underdevelopment: A Marxist Analysis,*
Macmillan, London, 1975.

Kemp, T.: *Theories of Imperialism*, Dobson, London, 1967.

Keohane, Robert O., Joseph S.Nye: *Power and Interdependence: World Politics in Transition*, Little, Brown, Boston, 1977.

Keyfitz, Nathan: 'World Resources and the World Middle Class', *Scientific American*, 235, July 1976.

Khavina, S.A.: *A Critique of Socialist Economic Management*, M'isl, Moscow, 1968.

Kidron, Michael: *Western Capitalism Since the War*, Weidenfeld and Nicolson, London, 1968.

Kiernan, V.G.: *Lords of Human Kind: European Attitudes to the Outside World in the Imperial Age*, Weidenfeld and Nicolson, London, 1969.

Kim, Samuel S.: 'China and World Order', *Alternatives*, vol. 3, no. 4, May 1978, pp. 555-587.

Kim, Samuel S.: *China, the United Nations and World Order*, Princeton University Press, N.J., 1979.

Kindleberger, Charles: 'World Population', *Atlantic Economic Journal*, no. 2, 1975, pp. 1-7.

King, Alexander: 'The Use and Abuse of Science and Technology for Development', in Antony Dolman, Jan van Ettinger (eds.), *Partners in Tomorrow: Strategies for a New International Order*, E.P.Dutton, New York, 1978, pp. 182-192.

Kiser III, John W.: 'Technology is Not a One-Way Street', *Foreign Policy*, no. 23, Summer 1976, pp. 131-148.

Kissinger, Henry: 'Central Issues of American Foreign Policy', in Kermit Gordon (ed.), *Agenda for the Nation*, Brookings Institution, Washington, D.C. 1968, pp. 585-614.

Kissinger, Henry: 'America and the World: Principle and Pragmation', *Time*, December 27, 1976, pp. 43-45.

Klaas, P.J.: *Secret Sentries in Space*, Random House, New York, 1971.

Kolko, Gabriel: *The Politics of War: The World and United States Foreign Policy, 1943-1945*, Random House, New York, 1968.

Kosolapov, V.: *Mankind and the Year 2000*, Progress Publishers, Moscow, 1976.

Kothari, Rajni: *Footsteps into the Future: Diagnosis of the Present World and a Design for an Alternative*, Free Press, New York, 1974.

Krenin, M., J.M.Finger: 'A New International Economic Order: A Critical Survey of Issues', *Journal of World Trade Law*, vol. 10, November-December 1976, pp. 3-22.

Krieger, David: *Disarmament and Development: The Challenge of the International Control and Management of Dual-Purpose Technologies,* Foundation Reshaping the International Order (RIO), Rotterdam, February 1961.

Kuznets, S.: 'The Gap: Concept, Measurement, Trends', in G. Ranis (ed.), *The Gap Between Rich and Poor Nations,* Macmillan, London, 1972.

Laclau, E.: 'Feudalism and Capitalism in Latin America', *New Left Review,* no. 67, May-June 1971.

Lagos, G.: *International Stratification and Underdeveloped Countries,* University of North Carolina Press, Chapel Hill, N.C. 1963.

Lagos, Gustavo, Horacio Godoy: *Revolutions of Being: A Latin American View of the Future,* Free Press, New York, 1977.

Lall, S.: 'Is Dependence a Useful Concept in Analyzing Underdevelopment?', *World Development,* vol. 3, no. 11, 1975.

Lapp, Ralph: *The New Priesthood,* Harper and Row, New York, 1961.

Laqueur, W.: 'Third World Fantasies', *Commentary,* vol. 63, no. 2, February 1977, pp. 43-48.

Laszlo, Ervin: *A Strategy for the Future: The Systems Approach to World Order,* Braziller, New York, 1974.

Laszlo, Ervin et al.: *Goals for Mankind: A Report to The Club of Rome on the New Horizons of Global Community,* E.P.Dutton, New York, 1977.

Latham, A.J.H.: *The International Economy and the Underdeveloped World 1865-1914,* Croom Helm, London, 1978.

Lean, Geoffrey: *Rich World, Poor World,* Allen and Unwin, London, 1979.

Lebedev, N.J.: *A New Stage in International Relations,* Pergamon, Oxford, 1978.

Leff, Nathaniel H.: 'The New Economic Order: Bad Economics, Worse Politics', *Foreign Policy,* vol. 24, Fall 1976, pp. 202-217.

Leger Sivard, Ruth: *World Military and Social Expenditures 1980,* World Priorities, Leesburg, Va., 1980.

Legvold, R.: 'The Nature of Soviet Power', *Foreign Affairs,* vol. 23, October 1977, pp. 49-71.

Leitenberg, Milton: 'The Dynamics of Military Technology Today', *International Social Sciences Journal,* vol. XXV, no. 3, 1973.

Lenin, V.I.: *Imperialism, The Highest Stage of Capitalism,* Foreign Languages Publishing House, Moscow, 1947 (first published 1916).

Leontief, Wassily et al.: *The Future of the World Economy: A United Nations Study,* Oxford University Press, New York, 1977.

Lerner, Daniel: *The Passing of Traditional Society,* Free Press, New York, 1964.

Lessing, Doris: *Briefing for a Descent into Hell,* Knopf, New York, 1971.

Letelier, Orlando, Michael Moffit: *The International Economic Order (Part I),* Transnational Institute, Washington, D.C., 1977.

Leurdijk, Dick A.: *World Order Studies: World Order Studies Policy-Making and the New International Order,* Foundation Reshaping the International Order (RIO), Rotterdam, February 1979.

Leurdijk, Dick A., Elisabeth Mann Borgese: *Disarmament and Development,* Foundation Reshaping the International Order (RIO), Rotterdam, June 1979.

Lewin, M.: *Russian Peasants and Soviet Power,* George Allen and Unwin, London, 1968.

Lewis, Arthur: 'World Production Prices and Trade, 1870-1960', *Manchester School of Economic and Social Studies,* vol. 20, 1950.

Lewis, Arthur: 'Economic Development with Unlimited Supplies of Labour', *Manchester School of Economic and Social Studies,* vol. 24, May 1954.

Lewis, Arthur: *Theory of Economic Growth,* Allen and Unwin, London, 1955.

Lewis John P.: 'A Possible Scenario for the Development Strategy' *OECD Observer,* no. 101, November 1979, pp. 3-11.

Leys, C.: 'Underdevelopment and Dependency: Critical Notes', *Journal of Contemporary Asia,* vol. 7, no. 1, 1977.

Lichtheim, George: *Imperialism,* Allen Lane, London, 1971.

Lindblom, Charles E.: *Politics and Markets: The World's Political Economic Systems,* Basic Books, New York, 1978.

Lipset, S.M., A.Solari (eds.): *Elites in Latin America,* Oxford University Press, London, 1967.

List, F.: *The National System of Political Economy,* Longmans Green, London, 1928 (first published 1841).

Louvière,V.: 'Space: Industry's New Frontier', *Nation's Business,* February 1978, pp. 25-41.

Lozoya, Jorge, Jaime Estevez, Rosario Green: *Alternative Views of the New International Economic Order: A Survey and Analysis of Major Academic Research Reports,* Pergamon Press, New York, 1979.

Luard, E.: *Types of International Society,* Free Press, New York,

1976.

Luxemburg, Rosa: *The Accumulation of Capital*, Routledge and Kegan Paul, London, 1951 (first published 1913).

MacDonald, G.F.: 'Geophysical Warfare: How to Wreck the Environment' in Nigel Calder (ed.), *Unless Peace comes: A Scientific Forecast of New Weapons*, Viking Press, New York, 1968, pp. 181-205.

Magdoff, Harry: *The Age of Imperialism*, Monthly Review Press, New York/London, 1970.

Magdoff, Harry: 'The Limits of International Reform', *Monthly Review*, vol. 30, no. 1, May 1978, pp. 1-11.

Magdoff, Harry, Paul M.Sweezy: 'Emerging Currency and Trade Wars', *Monthly Review*, vol. 29, no. 9, February 1978.

Malley, Gerhard: *Interdependence*, Heath, Lexington, 1976.

Mandel, E.: 'After Imperialism', *New Left Review*, no. 25, May-June 1964.

Mandel, E.: *Marxist Economic Theory*, Monthly Review Press, New York/London, 1968, 2 vols.

Mandeville, Colin: *The Last Days of New York?*, Springwood Books, London, 1980.

Mann Borgese, Elisabeth: *The Ocean Regime*, Center for the Study of Democratic Institutions, Santa Barbara, Ca., October 1968.

Mann Borgese, Elisabeth: *Pacem in Maribus*, Dodd, Mead & Co., New York, 1972.

Mann Borgese, Elisabeth: *The Drama of the Oceans*, Harry N.Abrams, Inc., New York, 1975.

Mann Borgese, Elisabeth: *The Enterprises*, 101 Occasional Paper no. 6, International Ocean Institute, Msida, Malta, 1977.

Mann Borgese, Elisabeth: 'The Age of Aquarius', in A.J.Dolman, J.van Ettinger (eds.), *Partners in Tomorrow: Strategies for a New International Order*, E.P.Dutton, New York, 1978, pp. 193-204.

Mann Borgese, Elisabeth: 'The Impact of Seabed Mining on Developing Countries: Four Models', Paper presented to a Seminar held at the Institut Universitaire des Hautes Etudes Internationales, Geneva, August 1979 (mimeo).

Mann Borgese, Elisabeth: 'Expanding the Common Heritage', in A.J.Dolman (ed.), *Global Planning and Resource Management: Toward International Decision-Making in a Divided World*, Pergamon, New York, 1980, pp. 181-194.

Mann Borgese, Elisabeth, Arvid Pardo: *The New International Economic Order and the Law of the Sea*, International Ocean Institute, Occasional Paper no. 4, Msida, Malta, 1976.

Mann Borgese, Elisabeth, Arvid Pardo: 'The Common Heritage of
Mankind and the Transfer of Technologies', paper prepared for
the IOI Training Course on the Management of Exclusive Economic
Zones, held in Malta in Spring 1980 (mimeo).

Manning, Robert: 'A World Safe for Business', *Far Eastern Economic Review,* March 25, 1977.

Mansour, Fawzy: 'Third World Revolt and Self-Reliance Auto-
Centered Strategy of Development', Document 406, IDEP, Dakar,
1977 (mimeo).

Marcusse, Herbert: *One-Dimensional Man,* Routledge and Kegan Paul,
London, 1964.

Mason, C.M. (ed.): *The Effective Management of Resources,*
Frances Pinter, London, 1979.

Matte, Nicolas Mateesco: *Aerospace Law,* Sweet and Maxwell, London, 1969.

Matte, Nicolas Mateesco: *Aerospace Law,* Carswell, Toronto, 1977.

Matte, Nicolas Mateesco: *Space Policy and Programmes Today and
Tomorrow: The Vanishing Duopole,* Carswell, Toronto, 1980.

Mattick, Paul: *Economics, Politics and the Age of Inflation,*
M.E.Sharpe, Inc., White Plains, N.Y., 1980.

Maynes, Charles W.: 'The Hungry New World and the American Ethic'
Outlook, December 1, 1974.

Maynes, Charles W.: 'A U.N. Policy for the Next Administration',
Foreign Policy, vol. 54, 1975-76, pp. 804-819.

Mazrui, Ali A.: *A World Federation of Cultures: An African
Perspective,* Free Press, New York, 1976.

Mazrui, Ali A.: *Africa's International Relations: The Diplomacy
of Dependency and Change,* Heinemann, London, 1977.

Mazrui, Ali A.: *The Barrel of the Gun and the Barrel of Oil in
the North-South Equation,* Working Paper 5, World Order Models
Project, Institute for World Order, Inc., New York, 1978.

McCarthy, R.D.: *Ultimate Folly: War by Pestilence, Asphyxiation
and Defoliation,* A.A.Knopf, New York, 1969.

McLaren, Robert I.:'The UN System and its Quixotic Quest for Coordination', *International Organization,* vol. 34, no. 1, Winter
1980, pp. 139-148.

McNamara, Robert: *The Essence of Security: Reflection in Office,*
Hodder and Stoughton, London, 1968.

Meadows, Donella H. et al.: *The Limits to Growth,* Signet Books,
New York, 1972.

Medlovitz, Saul H. (ed.): *On the Creation of a Just World Order: Preferred Worlds for the 1990s,* Free Press, New York, 1975.

Medvedev, Zhores: *Nuclear Disaster in the Urals,* Angus and Robertsen, London, 1974.

Memmi, Albert: *Colonizer and Colonized,* Beacon Press, Boston, 1967.

Memmi, Albert: *Dominated Man,* Beacon Press, Boston, 1968.

Mendelson, Maurice: 'The Legal Character of General Assembly Resolutions: Some Considerations of Principles', in K.Hossain (ed.), *Legal Aspects of the New International Economic Order,* Frances Pinter, London, 1980, pp. 95-107.

Mesarovic, Mihaljo, Eduard Pestel: *Mankind at the Turning Point: The Second Report to The Club of Rome,* Signet Books, New York, 1974.

Meynaud, Jean: *Technocracy,* Free Press, New York, 1969.

Michanek, Ernst: *The World Development Plan: Swedish Perspective,* Almqvist and Wiksell, Stockholm, 1971.

Miles, Ian: 'Worldviews and Scenarios', in C.Freeman, M.Jahoda (eds.), *World Futures: The Great Debate,* Martin Robertson, Oxford, 1978.

Miles, R.E.: 'The Pathology of Institutional Breakdown', *Journal of Higher Education,* May 1969.

Miles, Rufus: *Awakening from the American Dream: The Social and Political Limits to Growth.* Universe Books, New York, 1976.

Mishan, Ezra J.: *The Costs of Economic Growth,* Penguin Books, Harmondsworth, 1967.

Mishan, Ezra J.: 'The Post-War Literature on Externalities: An Interpretative Essay', *Journal of Economic Literature,* vol. IX, 1971, pp. 21-24.

Mishan, Ezra J.: *The Economic Growth Debate: An Assessment,* George Allen and Unwin, London, 1968.

Mitchell, Barbara, Lee Kimball: 'Conflict over the Cold Continent', *Foreign Policy,* Summer 1979, pp. 124-141.

Mitchell, Barbara, Jon Tinker: *Antarctica and its Resources,* International Institute for Environment and Development, London, January 1980.

Mitchell, Barbara, Richard Sandbrook: *The Management of the Southern Ocean,* International Institute for Environment and Development, London, 1980.

Modrzhinskaya, Y., C.Stephanyan: *The Future of Society,* Progress Publishers, Moscow, 1973.

Mommsen, Wolfgang J.: *Theories of Imperialism,* Weidenfeld and

Nicolson, London, 1980.

Morishima, M.: *Marx's Economics,* Cambridge University Press, London, 1973.

Morrison, R., J.O'Manique: 'Disarmament and Development: A Preliminary Assessment of Laser Technologies', Foundation Reshaping the International Order (RIO), Rotterdam, 1980 (mimeo).

Morse, Edward L.: 'Managing International Commons', *Journal of International Affairs,* vol. 31, no. 1, Spring/Summer 1977, pp. 1-21.

Moynihan, Daniel P.: 'The United States in Opposition', *Commentary,* March 1975, pp. 31-45.

Moynihan, Daniel P.: 'Party and International Politics', *Commentary,* vol. 63, no. 2, February 1977, pp. 56-59.

Muller, R.E., D.H.Moore: 'A Description and Preliminary Evaluation of Proposals for Global Stimulation', UNIDO, Vienna, March 1979 (mimeo).

Mumford, Lewis: *The Myth of the Machine: Techniques and Human Development,* Harcourt Brace Janovich, Inc., New York, 1967.

Munton, Don: 'Global Models, Politics and the Future', paper presented to the Annual Meeting of the Canadian Political Science Association, London, Ontario, May 1978 (mimeo).

Myers, Norman: *The Sinking Ark,* Pergamon, Oxford/New York, 1979.

Myrdal, Gunnar: *Economic Theory and Underdeveloped Regions,* Duckworth, London, 1954.

Myrdal, Gunnar: *An International Economy,* Harper, New York, 1956.

Myrdal, Gunnar: *The Challenge of World Poverty,* Pantheon, New York, 1970.

Myrdal, Gunnar: 'New Economic Order? Humbug!, *Sweden Now,* no. 4, 1975.

Nabudere, D.Wadada: *Essays on the Theory and Practice of Imperialism,* Onyx Press, London, 1979.

Nef, John U.: *Western Civilization since the Renaissance: Peace War, Industry and the Arts,* Harper Torchbooks, New York, 1963.

Nerfin, Marc (ed.): *What Now. The Dag Hammarskjöld Report on Development and International Cooperation,* Dag Hammarskjöld Foundation, Uppsala, Sweden, 1975.

Nerfin, Marc: 'Is a Democratic United Nations System Possible?' *Development Dialogue,* vol. 2, 1976. pp. 79-94.

Newcombe, Hanna: 'Annual Guaranteed Income Plan for the Nations of the World', *Bulletin of Peace Proposals,* vol.6, 1975,pp.77-84.

Niebuhr, Reinhold: 'Power and Ideology in National and International Affairs', in W.T.R.Fox (ed.), *Theoretical Aspects of International Relations,* Notre Dame University Press, West Bend, Ind., 1959.

Nkrumah, Kwame: *Neo-Colonialism: The Last Stage of Imperialism,* International Publishers, New York, 1965.

Noelke, Michael: *Europe and the Third World: A Study on Interdependence,* European Communities, Brussels, 1979.

Norman, Colin: *Knowledge and Power: The Global Research and Development Budget,* Worldwatch Paper no. 31, Worldwatch Institute, Washington D.C., July 1979.

Nuclear Energy Policy Study Group: *Nuclear Power, Issues and Choices,* Ballinger, Cambridge, Mass., 1977.

Nye Joseph S.: 'Transnational and Transgovernmental Relations' in G.L.Goodwin, A.Linklater (eds.), *New Dimensions of World Politics,* Croom Helm, London, 1975, pp. 36-53.

Nye, Joseph S.: 'Independence and Interdependence', *Foreign Affairs,* vol. 22, 1976, pp. 130-161.

Nyerere, Julius: 'Unity for a New Order', Inaugural Address to the Ministerial Conference of the Group of 77, Arusha, 12 February 1979, reprinted in *IFDA Dossier,* (Lyon), no. 5, March 1979.

O'Brien, P.J.: 'A Critique of Latin American Theories of Dependence', in I.Oxaal, T.Barnet, D.Booth (eds.), *Beyond the Sociology of Development,* Routledge and Kegan Paul, London, 1975.

O'Connor, J.: 'The Meaning of Economic Imperialism', in R.I. Rhodes (ed.), *Imperialism and Underdevelopment: A Reader,* Monthly Review Press, New York/London, 1970.

Odell, Peter: *Oil and World Power,* Penguin, Harmondsworth, 1974.

OECD: *A Comparative Evaluation of World Models,* Chapter 11 of the 'Intermediate Results' of the Interfutures Project', Paris, 7 April 1977 (mimeo).

OECD: *Towards Full Employment and Price Stability: A Report to OECD by a Group of Experts,* Paris, June 1977.

OECD: *Facing the Future: Mastering the Probable and Managing the Unpredictable,* Paris, 1979.

Ostry, Sylvia: 'The World Economy in the 1970s and 1980s', *OECD Observer,* no. 113, March 1980, pp. 13-15.

Oteiza, E., F.Sercovich: 'Collective Self-Reliance: Selected Issues', *International Social Science Journal,* no. 4, 1976, pp. 664-671.

Owen, R.J., R.B.Sutcliffe (eds.): *Studies in the Theory of Imperialism,* Longman, London, 1972.

Paarlberg, Robert L.: 'Domesticating Global Management', *Foreign Affairs*, vol. 54, 1975-76, pp. 563-576.

Palma, Gabriel: 'Dependency: A Formal Theory of Underdevelopment or a Methodology for the Analysis of Concrete Situations of Underdevelopment', *World Development*, vol. 6, 1978, pp. 881-924.

Pardo, Arvid: *The Common Heritage: Selected Papers on Oceans and World Order 1967-1974*, International Ocean Institute Occasional Paper No. 3, Malta University Press, Malta, 1975.

Pardo, Arvid: 'Justice and the Oceans', in John L.Logue (ed.), *Peace, Justice and the Law of the Sea*, World Order Research Institute, Villanova University, Villanova, Pa., 1978, pp. 51-57.

Pardo, Arvid: 'Ocean Management and Development', paper presented to the Pacem in Maribus Convocation, Yaounde, January 1979 (mimeo).

Pardo, Arvid: 'Building the New International Order: The Need for a Framework Treaty', in A.J.Dolman (ed.), *Global Planning and Resource Management: Toward International Decision-Making in a Divided World*, Pergamon, New York, 1980, pp. 195-201.

Pardo, Arvid, Elisabeth Mann Borgese: 'Ocean Management', in Jan Tinbergen (coordinator), *Reshaping the International Order: A Report to The Club of Rome*, E.P.Dutton, New York, 1976, pp. 305-317.

Pardo, Arvid, Elisabeth Mann Borgese: *The New International Economic Order and the Law of the Sea*, IOI Occasional Paper no. 4, International Ocean Institute, Msida, Malta, 1976.

Patten, Richard van et al.: *The Industrialization of Space*, American Astronautical Society, vol. 36, 1978.

Patterson, Walter C.: *Nuclear Power*, Penguin, Harmondsworth, 1976.

Pauker, G.J.: *Military Implications of a Possible World Order Crisis in the 1980s*, The Rand Corporation, Santa Monica, Ca., November 1977.

Pedersen, M.K.: 'The Rise of an Issue: Adjustment Assistance Measures: The Trade Context and its Theoretical Framework', in K.Worm (ed.), *Industrialization, Development and the Demands for a New International Economic Order*, Samfundsvidenskabeligt Forlag, Copenhagen, 1978, pp. 41-63.

Percy, Walter: *Love in the Ruins*, Farrar, Straus, New York, 1971.

Pfaff, William: 'Reflections: Economic Development', *The New Yorker*, December 25, 1978, pp. 44-47.

Pierce, W.B., N.Jéquier: 'Telecommunications and Development', *Dialogue*, vol. 12, no. 2, 1978.

Pinto, Christopher: 'Toward a Regime Governing International
Public Property', in A.J.Dolman (ed.), *Global Planning and Re-
source Management: Toward International Decision-Making in a
Divided World,* Pergamon, New York, 1980, pp. 202-224.

Pirages, Dennis C.: *The Sustainable Society,* Praeger, New York,
1977.

Pisani, E.: 'Here's to Utopia. A Global Tax on Natural Resources'
CERES, January-February 1977.

Poquet, Guy: 'The Limits to Global Modelling', *International
Social Science Journal,* vol. 30, no. 2, 1978.

Portes, R.: 'East Europe's Debt to the West: Interdependence is
a Two-Way Street', *Foreign Affairs,* vol. 23, July 1977, pp. 751-
782.

Pratt, J.W.: *Cordell Hull: 1933-1944,* Cooper Square, Totowa,
New Jersey, 1964.

Prebish, Raul: *The Economic Development of Latin America and its
Principal Problems,* U.N. Commission for Latin America (CEPAL),
Santiago, 1950.

Prebish, Raul: *Towards a New Trade Policy for Development,* UNCTAD
Geneva, 1964.

Puttkamer, J.von: 'The Next 25 Years: Industrialization of Space'
Space World, vol. N-10-166, October 1977, pp. 4-13.

Ramo, S.: *Peacetime Uses of Outer Space,* McGraw-Hill, New York,
1961.

Ramphal, Shridath S.: 'Not by Unity Alone: The Case for a Third
World Organization', *Third World Quarterly,* vol. 1, no. 3, July
1979, pp. 43-52.

Rawls, John: *A Theory of Justice,* Harvard University Press, Cambridge, Mass., 1971.

Rhodes, R.I. (ed.): *Imperialism and Underdevelopment: A Reader,*
Monthly Review Press, New York/London, 1970.

Richards, J.: *Recombinant-DNA: Science, Ethics and Politics,*
Academic Press, New York, 1978.

Richardson, John M.: 'Global Modelling: A Survey and Appraisal',
paper prepared for the Seminar on Natural Resource Policies,
University of Wisconsin, Madison, Wisconsin, December 1977 (mimeo).

Rios Ferrer, Roberto et al.: *Exégesis de la Carta de Derechos
y Deberes Económicos de los Estados,* Editorial Porrúa, Mexico,
D.F., 1976.

Riphagen, W.: 'Some Reflections on "Functional Sovereignty"',
Netherlands Yearbook of International Law, vol. VI, 1975, pp.
121-165.

Robert, Michel: 'Indulgent with the East and Evasive Towards the U.S., Europe is Neither Worthy of it Supposed Destiny, Nor Equal to the Moderating Role it Claims to be Playing', *The Guardian*, May 13, 1980.

Roberts, B.: 'International Cooperation for Antarctic Development, *Polar Record*, vol. 19, no. 119, pp. 107-120.

Robertson, J.M.: *Patriotism and Empire*, Grant Richards, London, 1900.

Robinson, J.: *The New Mercantilism*, Cambridge University Press, London, 1966.

Robinson, J.P.: *The Effects of Weapons on Ecosystems*, Pergamon, Oxford, 1979.

Röling, Bert V.A.: *International Law in an Expanded World*, Djambatan, Amsterdam, 1960.

Röling, Bert V.A.: 'International Law and the Maintenance of Peace', *Netherlands Yearbook of International Law*, vol. IV, 1973, pp. 1-103.

Röling, Bert V.A.: 'The United Nations - A General Evaluation', in A.Cassese (ed.), *UN Law/Fundamental Rights: Two Topics in International Law*, Sijthoff & Noordhoff, Alphen a/d Rijn, The Netherlands, 1979, pp. 23-28.

Röling, Bert V.A.: 'International Responses to Technological Innovations', in A.J.Dolman (ed.), *Global Planning and Resource Management: Toward International Decision-Making in a Divided World*, Pergamon, New York, 1980, pp. 225-246.

Rosecrance, Richard: 'International Interdependence', in G.L. Goodwin, A.Linklater (eds.), *New Dimensions of World Politics*, Croom Helm, London, 1975, pp. 20-35.

Rosecrance, Richard (ed.): *America as an Ordinary Country*, Cornell University Press, Ithaca, N.Y., 1976.

Rosecrance, Richard: 'Wither Interdependence', *International Organization*, no. 3, 1977, pp. 425-475.

Rosecrance, Richard, A.Stein: 'Interdependence: Myth or Reality', *World Politics*, no. 1, 1973.

Rosenstein-Rodan, P.N.: 'The Have's and Have-Not's Around the Year 2000', in Jagdish N.Bhagwati (ed.), *Economics and World Order: From the 1970s to the 1990s*, Free Press, New York, 1972, pp. 29-42.

Rossi, Paoli: *Francis Bacon: From Magic to Science*, University of Chicago Press, Chicago, Ill., 1948.

Rostow, Walt: *The Stages of Economic Growth. A Non-Communist Manifesto*, Cambridge University Press, London, 1960.

Rostow, W.W.: *The World Economy: History and Prospect*, Macmillan, London, 1978.

Rostow, W.W.: *Getting from Here to There: A Policy for the Post-Keynesian Age*, Macmillan, London, 1979.

Rothstein, Robert R.: *Alliances and Small Powers*, Columbia University Press, New York, 1968.

Rothstein, Robert L.: *The Weak in the World of the Strong: The Developing Countries in the International System*, Columbia University Press, New York, 1977.

Rothstein, Robert L.: *Global Bargaining: UNCTAD and the Quest for a New International Economic Order*, Princeton University Press, Princeton, N.J., 1979.

Rodney, Walter: *How Europe Underdeveloped Africa*, Tanzania Publishing House, Dar-es-Salaam, 1976.

Routh, Guy: *The Origins of Economic Ideas*, Vintage Books, New York, 1977.

Royal Commission on Environmental Pollution: *Nuclear Power and the Environment*, Her Majesty's Stationary Office, London, 1976.

Rozak, Theodore: *Person/Planet: The Creative Disintegration of Industrial Society*, Doubleday, Garden City, N.Y., 1978.

Rozenthal, A.: 'The Charter of Economic Rights and Duties of States in the New International Economic Order', *Virginia Journal of International Law*, vol. 16, Winter 1976. pp. 309-322.

Ruggie, John G.: 'Collective Goods and Future International Collaboration', *American Political Science Review*, vol. 66, September 1972, pp. 874-893.

Ruggie, John G.: 'On the Problem of 'The Global Problematique': What Roles for International Organization?', *Alternatives*, vol. V, no. 4, January 1980, pp. 517-550.

Russett, Bruce M.: 'The Rich Fifth and the Poor Half: Some Speculations About International Politics in 2000 A.D.', in Bruce M.Russett (ed.), *Power and Community in World Politics*, Freeman, San Francisco, 1974, pp. 155- 170.

Russett, Bruce M., Henry Brandon: *The Retreat of American Power*, New York, 1975.

Rweyemamu, Justinian: *Underdevelopment and Industrialization in Tanzania*, Oxford University Press, Nairobi, 1973.

Safire, William: 'Sending in the Marines', *International Herald Tribune*, February 15, 1980.

Sagasti, Francisco: *Science and Technology for Development: Main Comparative Report of the STPI Project*, IDRC, Ottawa, 1978.

Sagasti, Francisco: 'Knowledge is Power, *Mazingira*, 2, 1979.

Sakharov, Andrei D.: *Progress, Coexistence and Intellectual Freedom,* W.W.Norton, New York, 1968.

Samuelson, Paul A.: *Economics,* McGraw-Hill Kogakusha, New York/ Tokyo, 1973 (ninth edition).

Santa Cruz, H., J.D.Valdovinos, G.R.Rojas: *Development, the United Nations and the North-South Relationship,* Centre International pour le Développement, Paris, 1977.

Sau, Ranjit: *Unequal Exchange: Imperialism and Underdevelopment,* Oxford University Press, India, 1979.

Schachter, Oscar: 'Toward a Theory of International Obligation', in Stephen Schwebel (ed.), *The Effectiveness of International Decisions,* Sijthoff, Leiden, 1971.

Schachter, Oscar: *Sharing the World's Resources,* Columbia University Press, New York, 1977.

Schrank, Jeffrey: *Snap, Crackle and Popular Taste: The Illusion of Free Choice in America,* Delta, New York, 1977.

Schumacher, E.F.: *Small is Beautiful: Economics as if People Mattered,* Harper and Row, New York, 1977.

Schumpeter, J.A.: *Sociology of Imperialism,* Meridian Books, London, 1955. (first published 1919).

Schurmann, Franz: *The Logic of World Power,* Pantheon, New York, 1974.

Scitovsky, Tibor: *The Joyless Economy,* Oxford University Press, London, 1976.

Scott, Bruce R.: 'The American Scapegoat', *Harvard Business Review,* January-February 1981, pp. 6-30.

Schmid, Gregory: 'Interdependence has its Limits', *Foreign Policy,* vol. 21, Winter 1975-76, pp. 188-197.

Seers, Dudley: 'The Birth, Life and Death of Development Economics', *Development and Change,* vol. 10, no. 4, October 1979, pp. 707-719.

Semmel, B.: *The Rise of Free Trade Imperialism,* Cambridge University Press, London, 1970.

Senghaas, Dieter: 'Conflict Formations in Contemporary International Society', *Journal of Peace Research,* vol. 10, 1973, pp. 163-184.

Sengupta, Arjun: 'Issues in North-South Negotiations on Commodities', *ODI Review,* no. 2, 1979, pp. 72-86.

Sergiyev, A.: 'Bourgeois Theories of 'Interdependence' Serve Neo-Colonialism', *International Affairs,* (Moscow),no. 11, 1976.

Seton-Watson, Hugh: *Nations and States,* Methuen, London, 1979.

Seynes, Philippe de: 'Prospects for a Future Whole World', *International Organization,* vol. 26, Winter 1972, pp. 1-17.

Shapley, Deborah: 'Technological Creep and the Arms Race', three articles in *Science,* 22 September, 29 September and 20 October 1978.

Shauer, William H.: *The Politics of Space: A Comparison of the Soviet and American Space Programs,* Holmes and Meier, New York, 1976.

Shaw, Timothy M.: 'Dependence as an Approach to Understanding Continuing Inequalities in Africa', *Journal of Developing Areas,* vol. 13, no. 3, April 1979, pp. 229-246.

Shaw, Timothy M.: *Towards an International Political Economy for the 1980s: From Dependence to (Inter)Dependence,* Centre for Foreign Policy Studies, Dalhousie University, Halifax, November 1980.

Sheldon, C.S.: 'Peacetime Applications', in L.P.Bloomfield (ed.) *Outer Space,* Praeger, New York, 1968, pp. 37-74.

Shils, Edward: 'On the Comparative Study of the New States', in Clifford Geertz (ed.), *Old Societies and New States,* Free Press, New York, 1963.

Shoad, Marion: *The Theft of the Countryside,* Maurice Temple Smith, London, 1980.

Silverstein, Harvey B.: *Superships and Nation-States,* Westview Press, New York, 1978.

Silverstein, Harvey B.: 'An Assessment: ASW Deployments as 'Dual-Purpose' Technologies', Foundation Reshaping the International Order (RIO), Rotterdam, 1980 (mimeo).

Simoni, Arnold: *Beyond Repair: The Urgent Need for a New World Organization,* Collier-Macmillan, Canada, 1972.

Singer, Hans W.: 'The Distribution of Gains Between Investing and Borrowing Countries', *American Economic Review,* May 1950.

Singer, Hans: *International Development: Growth and Change,* McGraw-Hill, New York, 1964.

Singer, Hans W: 'The New International Economic Order: An Overview', *Journal of Modern African Studies,* vol. 16, no. 4, December 1978, pp. 539-548.

Singer, Hans W., J.Ansari: *Rich and Poor Countries,* George Allen and Unwin, London, 1977.

Singer, J.David, Michael Wallace: 'Intergovernmental Organizations and the Preservation of Peace, 1816-1964: Some Bivariate Relationships', *International Organization,* no.3, 1970,pp.520-548.

Singh, Jyoti S.: *A New International Economic Order: Toward a Fair Redistribution of the World's Resources,* Praeger, New York, 1977.

SIPRI: *Problems of Chemical and Biological Weapon Warfare: The Rise of CB Weapons,* Almqvist and Wiskell, Stockholm, 1971.

SIPRI: *Chemical Disarmament: Some Problems of Verification,* Almqvist and Wiskell, Stockholm, 1973.

SIPRI: *Problems of Chemical and Biological Warfare: CB Weapons Today,* Almqvist and Wiskell, Stockholm, 1973.

SIPRI: *Chemical Disarmament: New Weapons for Old,* Almqvist and Wiskell, Stockholm, 1975.

SIPRI: *Ecological Consequences of the Second IndoChina War,* Almqvist and Wiskell, Stockholm, 1976.

SIPRI: *Weapons of Mass Destruction and the Environment,* Taylor and Francis, London, 1977.

SIPRI: *Arms Control: A Survey and Appraisal of Multilateral Agreements,* Taylor and Francis, London, 1978.

SIPRI: *Outer Space - Battlefield of the Future?,* Taylor and Francis, London, 1978.

SIPRI: *World Armaments and Disarmament, SIPRI Yearbook 1979,* Taylor and Francis, London, 1979.

SIPRI: *Warfare in a Fragile World: Military Impact on the Human Environment,* Taylor and Francis, London, 1980.

Skinner, Reinhard J.: 'Technological Determinism: A Critique of Convergence Theory', *Comparative Studies in Society and History,* vol. 18, no. 1, January 1979, pp. 2-27.

Skolnikoff, Eugene B.: 'Science and Technology: The Implications for International Institutions', *International Organization,* vol. 25, 1971, pp. 759-775.

Slater, D.: 'Underdevelopment and Spatial Inequality', *Progress in Planning,* vol. 4, Pergamon, New York, 1974.

Smith, Tony: 'Changing Configurations of Power in North-South Relations Since 1945', *International Organization,* vol. 31, no. 1, Winter 1977, pp. 1-27.

Smith, Tony: 'The Underdevelopment of Development Literature: The Case of Dependency Theory', *World Politics,* vol. 31, no. 2, January 1979, pp. 247-288.

Solodnikov, V., V.Bogoslovsky: *Non-Capitalist Development,* Progress Publishers, Moscow, 1975.

Solzhenitsyn, Alexander: 'Solzhenitsyn on Communism', *Time,* February 18, 1980, pp. 12-13.

Spengler, Joseph: *Population Change, Modernization and Welfare*, Prentice Hall, Englewood Cliffs, New Jersey, 1974.

Spiro, Herbert J.: *World Politics: The Global System*, Dorsey Press, Homewood, Ill., 1966.

Stavrianos, L.S.: *The Promise of the Coming Dark Age*, Freeman, San Francisco, 1976.

Steenbergen, Bart van: *Orde of Conflict: Tegengestelde Maatschappijvisies Binnen de Futurologie*, Euroboekje, Wolters-Noordhoff, Groningen, 1969.

Steinberg, Eleanor B., Joseph A.Yager: *New Means of Financing International Needs*, Brookings Institution, Washington, D.C. 1978.

Stewart, Frances: *Technology and Underdevelopment*, Macmillan, London, 1977.

Strange, Susan: 'The Study of Transnational Relations', *International Affairs*, vol. 52, July 1976, pp. 333-345.

Strong, Maurice F.: 'Spaceship Earth: A Global Overview', Paper presented at the 47th Annual Conference on 'Growth in a Conserving Society', Geneva Park, Ontario, August 3, 1978 (mimeo).

Sunkel, Osvaldo: 'The Development of Development Thinking', *Liaison Bulletin*, no. 1, OECD Development Centre, Paris, 1977, pp. 9-17.

Suter, K.D.: *Antarctica: World Law and the Last Wilderness*, Friends of the Earth, Sydney, 1980.

Sutton, A.C.: *Western Technology and Soviet Economic Development: 1917-1930*, Hoover Institute on War, Revolution and Peace, Stanford University, Stanford, Ca., 1968.

Sweezy, Paul M.: *The Theory of Capitalist Development*, Monthly Review Press, New York/London, 1968.

Sweezy, Paul M.: 'The Present Stage of the Global Crisis of Capitalism', *Monthly Review*, vol. 29, no. 11, April 1978, pp. 1-12.

Sweezy, Paul M.: 'A Crisis in Marxian Theory', *Monthly Review*, vol. 31, no. 2, June 1979, pp. 20-24.

Sweezy, Paul M.: 'Wither U.S. Capitalism?', *Monthly Review*, vol. 31, no. 7, December 1979, pp. 1-12.

Sweezy, Paul M.: 'The Crisis of American Capitalism', *Monthly Review*, vol. 32. no. 5, October 1980, pp. 1-13.

Swerling, Boris: *Current Issues in Commodity Policies*, Princeton University Press, Princeton, N.J., 1962.

Swerling, Boris: 'Financial Alternatives to International Commodity Stabilization', *Canadian Journal of Economics and Political Science*, vol. 30, November 1964, pp. 526-537.

Szentes, T.: *The Political Economy of Underdevelopment,* Akadémiai Kiadó, Budapest, 1976.

Tammes, A.J.P.: 'Decisions of International Organs as a Source
of International Law', *Receuil des Cours,* vol. 94, no. 11, 1958,
pp. 265-284.

Tévoédjrè, Albert: *Poverty: Wealth of Mankind,* Pergamon, Oxford,
1978.

Third World Forum: *Proposals for a New International Economic
Order,* Report prepard by a Special Task Force of the Third World
Forum, Mexico City, August 21-24, 1975.

Thomas, Clive Y.: *Dependency and Transformation: Economics of
the Transition to Socialism,* Monthly Review Press, New York/Lon-
don, 1974.

Thompson, William Irwin: *Evil and World Order,* Harper and Row,
New York, 1976.

Thompson, William Irwin: *Darkness and Scattered Light,* Anchor
Books, Garden City, N.Y., 1978.

Tinbergen, Jan: *Shaping the World Economy,* McGraw-Hill, New York,
1962.

Tinbergen, Jan: *Lessons from the Past,* Elsevier, Amsterdam, 1963.

Tinbergen, Jan: *Central Planning,* Yale University Press, New
Haven, 1964.

Tinbergen, Jan: *Development Planning,* Weidenfeld and Nicolson,
London, 1967.

Tinbergen, Jan: 'Building a World Order' in Jagdish N.Bhagwati
(ed.), *Economics and World Order. From the 1970s to the 1990s,*
Free Press, New York, 1972, pp. 141-157.

Tinbergen, Jan (coordinator): *Reshaping the International Order:
A Report to The Club of Rome,* E.P.Dutton, New York, 1976.

Tinbergen, Jan: 'The Need for an Ambitious Innovation of the
World Order', *Journal of International Affairs,* vol. 31, no. 2,
Fall/Winter 1977, pp. 305-314.

Tinbergen, Jan: 'Redistributing the World's Wealth', *Development Forum,* April 1978.

Tinker, Jon: 'Antarctica: Towards a New Internationalism', *New
Scientist,* September 13, 1979, pp. 799-801.

Toch, Robert C.: 'War in Space: Military Satellites and Exotic
Weaponry Threaten to Turn Space into the Next Battleground',
Science 80, vol. 1, no. 6, pp. 74-80.

Toynbee, Arnold J.: *A Study of History,* Oxford University Press,
London, 1935-1961 (12 volumes).

Tsipis, Kostas: *Tactical and Strategic Anti-Submarine Warfare*, MIT Press, Cambridge, Mass., 1974.

Tucker, Robert W.: *The Inequality of Nations*, Basic Books, New York, 1977.

Tuomi, Helena: 'Dependency Models in Western Development Research' in Eeva-Liisa Myllymäki, Brett Dellinger (eds.), *Dependency and Latin American Development*, Finnish Peace Research Association, Turku/Tampere, 1977.

Turnbull, Colin M.: *The Mountain People*, Simon and Schuster, New York, 1972.

United Nations: *A Study of the Capacity of the United Nations Development System*, (document DP/5), 2 vols., Geneva, 1969.

United Nations: *Practical Benefits of Space Exploration*, (sales no. E.69.I.25), New York, 1969.

United Nations: *Economic and Social Consequences of the Arms Race and of Military Expenditure*, (sales no. E.72.IX.16), New York, 1972.

United Nations: *The Application of Space Technology to Development* (sales no. E.72.II.A.12), New York, 1973.

United Nations: Symposium on 'Patterns of Resource, Use, Environment and Development Strategies', held at Cocoyoc, near Mexico City on 8-12 October 1974, (document A/C.2/292), UNCTAD/UNEP, 1974.

United Nations: *A New United Nations Structure for Global Economic Cooperation. Report of the Group of Experts on the Structure of the United Nations System*, (document E/AC.62/9), New York, May 1975.

United Nations: *Reduction of Military Budgets of States Permanent Members of the Security Council by 10 Per Cent and Utilization of Part of the Funds Saved to Provide Assistance to Developing Countries*, (sales no. E.75.I.10), New York, 1975.

United Nations: *The United Nations and Outer Space*, (sales no. E.77.I.9), New York, 1977.

United Nations: *Report of the United Nations Conference on Desertification*, (document A/Conf.74/36), New York, 1977.

United Nations: *Economic and Social Consequences of the Armaments Race and its Extremely Harmful Effects on World Peace and Security*, (document A/32/88), New York, August 1977.

United Nations: *The Physical Nature and Technical Attributes of the Geo-stationary Orbit*, (document A/AC.105/203), New York, 1978.

United Nations: *Economic and Social Consequences of the Arms*

Race and of Military Expenditures, (sales no. 78.IX.1), New
York, 1978.

United Nations: *Development and International Economic Cooperation: Preparations for the Special Session of the General Assembly in 1980,* (document A/34/596), New York, October 23, 1979.

United Nations: *Draft Convention on the Law of the Sea,* (document A/CONF.62/WP.10/Rev.3), New York, September 22, 1980.

U.N. Committee for Development Planning: *Towards Accelerated Development: Proposals for the Second U.N. Development Decade,* New
York, 1970.

UNCTAD: *Transfer of Technology, Technological Dependence: Its
Nature, Consequences and Policy Implications,* (document TD/190),
Geneva, December 1975.

UNCTAD: *Report on the Proposal for the Establishment of a Secretariat of the Group of 77,* (document CA/843.GE.76-64251), Geneva
1976.

UNCTAD: *Development Aspects of the Reverse Transfer of Technology*
(document TD/B/C.6/41), Geneva, November 1978.

UNCTAD: *Preparation of a Draft for the Contribution of UNCTAD
to the Formulation of the International Development Strategy
for the Third United Nations Development Decade,* (document TD/
B/AC.31/2), Geneva, January 15, 1980.

UNEP: *Additional Measures and Means of Financing for the Implementation of the Plan of Action to Combat Desertification,*
(document GC.6/9/Add.1), April 1978.

UNIDO: *Industry 2000: New Perspectives,* (doc. ID/237), Vienna,
October 1979.

UNIDO: *The Technological Self-Reliance of Developing Countries:
Towards Operational Strategies,* (document UNIDO/ICIS.133),
Vienna, November 1979.

United Kingdom Royal Commission on Environmental Pollution:
Nuclear Power and the Environment, Her Majesty's Stationary
Office, London, 1976.

United States Government: *Space Program Benefits,* Hearings be-
fore the U.S. Senate's Committee on Aeronautical and Space
Sciences, 91st Congress, 2nd Session, Government Printing Office,
Washington, D.C., 1970.

U.S. Government: *For the Benefit of All Mankind: The Practical
Returns from Space Investment,* Report of the U.S. House of Representatives' Committee on Science and Astronautics, 92nd Congress, 2nd Session, Government Printing Office, Washington, D.C.
1972.

U.S. Government: *World-Wide Space Activities,* Report prepared for the Sub-Committee on Space Science and Applications of the U.S. House of Representatives' Committee on Science and Technology, 95th Congress, Government Printing Office, Washington, D.C., 1978.

U.S. Tariff Commission: *Implications for World Trade and Investment and for U.S. Trade and Labor of Multinational Corporations,* Senate Finance Committee, Washington, D.C. 1973.

Vayrynen, Raimo: 'Interdependence vs Self-Reliance in Economic Relations', *Alternatives,* vol. 3, no. 4, May 1978, pp. 481-514.

Verloren van Themaat, P.: *Rechtsgrondslagen van een Nieuwe Internationale Economische Orde,* Asser Instituut, The Hague, 1979.

Vernay, Alain: 'Grand Designs Eclipsed - But Reality Remains', *Development Forum,* June 1978, pp. 1-2.

Vital, David: *The Inequality of States: A Study of the Small Power in International Relations,* Clarendon Press, Oxford, 1967.

Vital, David: *The Survival of Small States: Studies in Small Power/Great Power Conflict,* Oxford University Press, Oxford, 1971.

Wallensteen, Peter: *Structure and War: On International Relations 1920-1968,* Räben and Sjögren, Stockholm, 1973.

Wallerstein, Immanuel: *The Modern World System,* Academic Press, New York, 1974.

Wallerstein, Immanuel: 'Dependence in an Interdependent World: The Limited Possibilities of Transformation within the Capitalist World Economy', *African Studies Review,* no. 1, 1974, pp.1-26.

Wallerstein, Immanuel (ed.): *World Inequalities,* Bertrand Russell Peace Foundation, London, 1975.

Wallerstein, Immamuel: 'The Three Stages of African Involvement in the World Economy' in P.C.W.Gutkind and I.Wallerstein (eds.), *The Political Economy of Contemporary Africa,* Sage, Beverley Hills, Ca., 1976, pp. 30-57.

Wallerstein, Immanuel: *The Capitalist World Economy,* Cambridge University Press, New York, 1979.

Wallerstein, Immanuel: 'Friends as Foes', *Foreign Policy,* Summer 1980, pp. 119-131.

Ward, B.: *What's Wrong with Economics?* Basic Books, New York, 1972.

Ward, Barbara: *Progress for a Small Planet,* Penguin, Harmondsworth, 1979.

Ward, Barbara, J.D.Runnals, L.d'Anjou (eds.): *The Widening Gap: Development in the 1970s,* Columbia University Press, New York, 1971.

Ward, Barbara, René Dubos: *Only One Earth*, Penguin Books, Harmondsworth, 1972.

Warren, Bill: 'Imperialism and Capitalist Industrialization', *New Left Review*, no. 81, 1974.

Wachtel, H.N., M.Moffit: 'World's Apart', *The Progressive*, February 1978, pp. 24-26.

Weber, Max: *The Protestant Ethic and the Spirit of Capitalism*, Unwin University Books, London, 1965 (first published in 1904).

Weizsäcker, Carl-Friedrich: 'A Sceptical Contribution', in Saul Mendlovitz (ed.), *On the Creation of a Just World Order*, Free Press, New York, 1975, pp. 111-150.

White, John: 'International Agencies: The Case for Proliferation' in G.K.Helleiner (ed.), *A World Divided: The Less Developed Countries in the International Economy*, Cambridge University Press, London, 1976, pp. 275-293.

White John: 'The New International Economic Order: What is It?', *International Affairs*, vol. 54, no. 4, October 1978, pp. 626-634.

White, Lynn, Jr.: *Medieval Technology and Social Change*, Oxford University Press, London/New York, 1962.

Whitman, Marina vN. : 'Leadership Without Hegemony: Our Role in the World Economy', *Foreign Policy*, vol. 20, Summer 1975, pp. 138-160.

Wiesenbach, Horst P.: 'Mobilization of Development Finance: Promises and Problems of Automaticity', paper prepared as part of the IFDA Third System Project, IFDA, Nyon, May 1979 (mimeo).

Wiesenbach, Horst P.: 'Mobilization of International Development Finance: Automaticity and the Incremental Approach, *IFDA Dossier*, no. 9, July 1979.

Willrich, Mason, Theodore B.Taylor: *Nuclear Theft: Risks and Safeguards*, Ballinger, Cambridge, Mass., 1974.

Winner, Langdon: *Autonomous Technology: Technics Out-of-Control as a Theme in Political Thought*, MIT Press, Cambridge, Mass., 1977.

Wionczek, Miguel S.: 'A Diagnosis of Failures and Prospects', in E.Laszlo, J.Kurtzman (eds.), *The Structure of the World Economy and Prospects for a New International Economic Order*, Pergamon, New York, 1980.

World Bank: *World Development Report 1980*, Washington, D.C., August 1980.

Worsley, Peter: *The Third World*, Weidenfeld and Nicolson, London, 1964.

Yeselson, Abraham, Anthony Gaglione: *A Dangerous Place: The United Nations as a Weapon in World Politics,* Grossman, New York, 1974.

Young, Elisabeth: *A Farewell to Arms Control?,* Penguin, Harmondsworth, 1972.

Young, Oran: *Resource Management at the International Level: The Case of the North Pacific,* Frances Pinter, London, 1977.

Ziegler, Jean: *Une Suisse au-dessus de tout Soupçon,* Ed.du Seuil, Paris, 1976.

Zimmermann, Erich W.: *World Resources and Industries,* Harper, New York, 1951.

List of Acronyms

ABM	Anti-Ballistic Missile
ACC	Administrative Committee on Coordination of the U.N. General Assembly
ADWC	Arab Drilling and Workover Company
APSC	Arab Petroleum Services Company
ARABSAT	Arab Corporation for Space Communications
ASAT	Anti-Satellite System
ASEAN	Association of Southeast Asian Nations
ASW	Anti-Submarine Warfare
CCD	Committee of the Conference on Disarmament
CD	Committee on Disarmament
CIA	Central Intelligence Agency
CIEC	Conference on International Economic Cooperation
CMEA	Council for Mutual Economic Assistance (COMECON)
COFI	Commission on Fisheries (of FAO)
COPUOS	Committee on the Peaceful Uses of Outer Space
COSPAR	Committee on Space Research
COW	Committee on the Whole
DAC	Development Assistance Committee (of OECD)
DD	Development Decade
ECA	Economic Commission for Africa
ECE	Economic Commission for Europe

ECLA	Economic Commission for Latin America
ECOSOC	Economic and Social Council of the U.N.
EEC	European Economic Community
EEZ	Exclusive Economic Zone
EFTA	European Free Trade Association
ELF	Extreme Low Frequency
EPTA	Expanded Program of Technical Assistance
ERTS	Earth Resources Technology Satellites
ESA	European Space Agency
EURATOM	European Atomic Energy Community
FAO	Food and Agriculture Organization of the U.N.
FOBS	Fractional Orbital Bombardment System
GATT	General Agreement on Tariffs and Trade
GNP	Gross National Product
IAEA	International Atomic Energy Agency
IAF	International Astronautical Federation
IBRD	International Bank for Reconstruction and Development
ICAO	International Civil Aviation Organization
ICBM	Intercontinental Ballistic Missile
ICJ	International Court of Justice
ICSU	International Council of Scientific Unions
IDA	International Development Association
IDS	International Development Strategy
IFAD	International Fund for Agricultural Development
IFC	International Finance Corporation
IISL	International Institute of Space Law
ILA	International Law Association
ILO	International Labor Office
IMCO	Inter-Governmental Maritime Consultative Organization
IMF	International Monetary Fund
INFCE	International Nuclear Fuel Cycle Evaluation
INMARSAT	International Maritime Satellite Consortium
INTELSAT	International Telecommunications Satellite Consortium

IOC	International Oceanographic Commission (of UNESCO)
ISA	International Seabed Authority
ISMA	International Satellite Monitoring Agency
ISMOS	International Satellite Monitoring System
ITO	International Trade Orgnaization
ITU	International Telecommunications Union
LANDSAT	Land Satellite (Earth Resources) Technology Satellite
MARISAT	Marine Communications Satellite
MIRV	Multiple Independent Reentry Vehicle
MX	Missile Experimental (Mobile intercontinental ballistic missile system proposed for the U.S.)
NASA	National Aeronautics and Space Administration
NATO	North Atlantic Treaty Organization
NGO	Non-governmental Organization
NIEO	New International Economic Order
NPT	Non-Proliferation Treaty
OAPEC	Organization of Arab Petroleum Exporting Countries
OAS	Organization of American States
OAU	Organization of African Unity
ODA	Official Development Assistance
OECD	Organization for Economic Cooperation and Development
OPEC	Organization of Petroleum Exporting Countries
PANAFTEL	Pan African Telecommunication Network
PTBT	Partial Test Ban Treaty
SALT	Strategic Arms Limitation Talks
SDR	Special Drawing Rights
SELA	Latin American Economic System
SIPRI	Stockholm International Peace Research Institute
SSBNS	Strategic Missile Carrying Nuclear Submarines
UNCIO	United Nations Conference on International Organization
UNCLOS III	Third United Nations Conference on the Law of the Sea

UNCSTD	United Nations Conference on Science and Technology for Development
UNCTAD	United Nations Conference on Trade and Development
UNDP	United Nations Development Programme
UNEP	United Nations Environment Programme
UNESCO	United Nations Educational, Scientific and Cultural Organization
UNFPA	United Nations Fund for Population Activities
UNGA	United Nations General Assembly
UNIDO	United Nations Industrial Development Organization
UNITAR	United Nations Institute for Training and Research
UNRRA	United Nations Relief and Rehabilitation Administration
UPU	Universal Postal Union
USAF	United States Air Force
WFC	World Food Council
WFP	World Food Programme (of FAO)
WHO	World Health Organization
WIPO	World Intellectual Property Organization
WMO	World Meteorological Organization
WWW	World Weather Watch

Name Index

Subject Index

About the Author

Antony J.Dolman, a citizen of the United Kingdom, is Senior
Fellow, Foundation Reshaping the International Order (RIO),
Rotterdam. Trained first as a city planner and then as an
environmental planner, he practiced and taught planning in
Europe and developing countries. Growing interest in international relations led him to abandon city planning and to
take up the development problematique. In 1975 he became
associated with the RIO Project and edited the *RIO Report*
(1976) which has now been translated into 11 languages. He
has been involved in various capacities with the programs
of UNIDO, UNESCO and UNEP and has served as a consultant to
a number of international non-governmental organizations.
The author of several volumes on planning, he edited *Partners in Tomorrow: Strategies for a New International Order*
(with Jan van Ettinger, 1978) and *Global Planning and
Resource Management: Toward International Decision-Making
in a Divided World*. The latter is published as a complementary volume to *Resources, Regimes and World Order*.